John Berecz, PhD, ABPP, received a Master's Degree in Counseling Psychology from American University in Washington, D.C. in 1966. He attended Indiana University, Bloomington as a U.S. Public Health Fellow in Clinical Psychology, completing his doctorate in 1970. His dissertation research on smoking cessation won recognition in the yearly American Institute for Research national competition.

In 1971 Dr. Berecz interned at Children's Hospital Medical Center (affiliated with Harvard Medical School). Since 1971, Dr. Berecz has conducted research and taught at Andrews University, where he is professor of psychology.

He maintains a private practice and is a consultant to hospitals and business organizations. He is licensed as a Clinical Psychologist as well as a Marriage and Family Counselor by the State of Michigan. In 1979 the American Board of Professional Psychology awarded him the Diploma in Clinical Psychology. Since 1984 he has served as supervising psychologist at Battle Creek Adventist Hospital, a psychiatric hospital in Battle Creek, Michigan. He also serves the D.C. Cook and Palisades Nuclear facilities as a clinical consultant.

Understanding Tourette Syndrome, Obsessive Compulsive Disorder, and Related Problems

A Developmental and
Catastrophe
Theory Perspective

John M. Berecz, PhD, ABPP

SPRINGER PUBLISHING COMPANY
New York

A Note to the Reader

The ideas, suggestions, and techniques presented in this book are not intended as a substitute for professional consultation. Individuals who manifest persistent symptoms of TS-OCD, or other compulsive behaviors, should consult with a clinical psychologist, psychiatrist, or other qualified professional.

Springer Publishing Company, Inc.
536 Broadway
New York, NY 10012-3955

92 93 94 95 96 97 / 5 4 3 2 1

Library of Congress Cataloging-in-Publication Data

Berecz, John M. (John Michael)
    Understanding Tourette syndrome, obsessive compulsive disorder, &
related problems : a developmental & catastrophe theory perspective
/ John M. Berecz.
        p.   cm.
    Includes bibliographical references and index.
    ISBN 0-8261-7390-X
    1. Tourette syndrome.   2. Obsessive-compulsive disorder.
3. Tourette syndrome—Case studies.   4. Obsessive-compulsive
disorder—Case studies.   I. Title.
    [DNLM: 1. Obsessive-Compulsive Disorder—etiology.   2. Obsessive
-Compulsive Disorder—therapy.   3. Tourette Syndrome—etiology.
4. Tourette Syndrome—therapy.   WM 197 B487u]
RC375.B47   1991
616.8 3—dc20
DNLM/DLC   91-4824
for Library of Congress   CIP

Printed in the United States of America

For Deborah, my lover, friend, and wife;
who is for me as Catherine was for Peter the Great, a woman
whose qualities of mind and heart were such that she was able:

". . . not only to soothe him, play with him, love him, but also
to take part in his inner life. . . ." (Massie, 1980 p. 376)

CONTENTS

PREFACE

Before beginning this text, I'd like to explain how this book came to be written.

My brother Bob and I grew up on a small dairy farm in Wisconsin. I still have vivid images of May mornings when I would try to hurry the cows along the road to their pasture adjacent to my one-room country school. But they were always more interested in the lush grass that grew on the shoulders of our rural "highway" than in my arriving at school on time, so they moved slowly, reluctantly, stealing as many mouthfuls of green turf between steps as I would allow.

The sound of cows grazing in grass still damp with morning dew, is difficult to describe. But that paced, calm, repetitive, squeak-squeak-squeak of grass being pulled and chewed on its way to becoming milk and ice cream used to soothe my soul. Spring days often began with such sounds and often ended with the soporific patter of night rain on the tin roof above my bedroom.

But life was not all sunshine and serenity. The morning sounds of cows grazing, birds chirping, kids laughing on their way to school, were sometimes violently punctuated by piercing shrieks or loud yelps—*my* shrieks and yelps. The cows didn't seem to notice, but sometimes a neighborhood dog barked in answer. In the classroom I didn't shriek, but I jerked my head, rolled my eyes, sniffed, and incessantly cleared my throat. At night I nearly drove my brother mad with my sniffing, hiccupping, and throat clearing. In the darkness of our shared bedroom, I would see if I could get away with just one more throat clearing or sniffle. Inevitably this would push Bobby into an exasperated entreaty, such as:

"Will you *please* shut up and go to sleep!"

To which I'd reply: "OK, well, goodnight."
To which he'd reply: "Goodnight!"
After a few moments of silence I'd repeat: "Well, goodnight."
To which he'd reply: "I *said* goodnight!"
To which I'd reply: "Well, goodnight."
To which he'd shout: "Shut up!"
To which I'd say: "OK! goodnight."

This kind of "ninety-nine-bottles-of-beer-on-the-wall" interaction sometimes continued for several rounds before his anger became intense enough to frighten me into clearing my throat quietly and not saying "good night" yet another time.

Such strange behavior was puzzling to my parents, siblings, teachers, and schoolmates; but it was geometrically more baffling to me, and I was deeply embarrassed by it. When people asked me why I jerked my shoulders or rolled my eyes, I didn't know what to say. I felt ashamed and exposed as if caught with my pants down.

It's a little like trying to explain why you breathe—you *just do*! You don't think about it, you don't feel abnormal, and, unless you've studied physiology and the oxygen transport system, you have a difficult time explaining why you need to keep sucking air into your nostrils. Fortunately, everyone else around you has the same "problem" with oxygen depletion, so no one ever asks you to explain your breathing. Shrieking, shrugging, throat clearing, eye blinking are different. People want explanations.

This book is about finally explaining such behaviors. I suppose it was inevitable that I would someday write such a book after changing my career goal (only once and in the fifth grade) from Greyhound bus driver to "talking-listening" doctor. I didn't know what titles like "psychologist" or "psychiatrist" really meant, but I knew there were doctors who listened to people and tried to figure out why they acted the way they did. I remember thinking that because people teased and made fun of me, I understood what it was like to be "different," and I'd be able to help "different" people. "Anybody can drive a bus," I ruefully rationalized, "but it takes somebody special to understand weird people." And with that my dreams of driving buses to faraway places faded forever.

Today, I'm a clinical psychologist, not a bus driver, but I'd like you to share a journey. with me. I'll take you to a different world—the world of Tourette Syndrome (TS) and Obsessive Compulsive Disorder (OCD). Unknown to most, seldom visited, it appears bizarre from the "outside." People here shake, shriek, curse, appear possessed. It's a bit frightening, but with my "insider's" perspective, you'll begin to understand that what at first appears weird, makes sense after all. It's not Camelot, but neither is it chaos.

In the studios of Iowa City's radio station KCJJ, Saul Lubaroff leans slightly toward the microphone and delivers a polished, articulate report of weekend weather and sports. He puts on a record and, as it starts to spin, he flips off the mike and bursts out a string of earsplitting obscenities. Other workers in the studio hardly seem to notice. He passes Clair, another full time deejay, on his way to get coffee. "You have nice tits," he remarks. "I know," she replies. Clair has learned to expect this, since each time she encounters Saul, he makes a comment about her breasts. Outside the studio, where people don't understand, Saul's outbursts cause problems. In a fancy restaurant he recently yelled "Hey, I masturbate!" Neighbors periodically complain to the landlady about his shouting. When he sees someone in a wheelchair he sometimes shouts "Hi Crip!" or to black persons, "Hiya Niggah!"

The waiter in the Greenwich Village cafe is accustomed to eccentric people and bizarre sights, but tonight the couple seated in the corner captures even his jaded attention. They appear to be ordinary college students, casually yet well-dressed, absorbed in conversation. But talk frequently stops midsentence while the young man shrieks, yelps, kisses the air, sticks his tongue out at his friend, and sometimes spews out street-corner obscenities. The waiter's astonishment would have turned to absolute disbelief if he could have peered into the future and seen that this young premed student named Orrin Palmer would successfully complete medical training and become a physician.

It's an April afternoon at the Metrodome, home of the Minnesota Twins. The fans—23,547 of them—are watching the game, when suddenly, without warning, the Twins' gifted center fielder begins twitching, shaking, and convulsing! Gasping for air, he runs off the field. The same thing happens each of the next two nights. Local fans are concerned but attribute these strange contortions to common causes such as stage fright or "rookie jitters." Fans at Boston's Fenway Park are not so considerate. When the Twins arrive in Boston for a three-game series, the "bleacher bums" are ready—tauntingly shouting "Shake! Shake! Shake!" as Jim Eisenreich takes his place in centerfield. Moments later the distraught center fielder runs off the field into the visitor's clubhouse tearing at his clothes and screaming, "I can't breathe!" Returning to Minnesota after the Boston series, he checks into St. Mary's Hospital in Minneapolis. Baseball for the sensational young rookie Jim Eisenreich is over—at least for this season.

Morris scrubs his hands and arms with Mr. Clean. He scrubs so hard that they become raw and sometimes bleed, but he still doesn't feel they're clean enough. No, Morris isn't a surgeon preparing to enter the operating room, he's an eighteen-year-old driven by washing compulsions.

What do a cursing deejay, shrieking premed student, convulsing center fielder, and scrubbing teenager have in common? Tourette Syndrome (TS) or Obsessive Compulsive Disorder (OCD). This book is about them, and others like them who suffer from compulsive disorders.

Except for this book, virtually all writing about Tourette syndrome begins with the assertion that TS is an organic "disease" whose puzzling nature will be clarified by the study of neurological structures, better mapping of chromosomes, and a clearer understanding of the biochemistry of neurotransmitters, to name but a few of the research foci. Some have called for ". . . an open and more spacious neurology and psychology, excitingly different from the rather rigid and mechanical neurology of the past" (Sacks, 1985, p. 4); but most have looked inward to biology for answers.

In spacious theorizing, nothing serves better as a research tool than carefully listening to persons recounting their own unique experience with a particular affliction. Although the case study has a long and respected history, it has largely been supplanted by more "high-tech" medicine. This is a natural consequence of advances in all branches of science. Biology, chemistry, physics, psychology, among others, have achieved high levels of understanding, and this is reflected in the complex instruments utilized by the professions. The modern physician's "black bag" contains electroencephalographs, electrocardiograms, computerized axial tomography, and positron emission tomography scanners, as well as many other high-tech instruments. Blood pressure cuffs, stethoscopes, and tongue depressors no longer suffice.

Although the precision gained in medical laboratories and research centers has saved many lives in trauma centers and intensive care units across the country, there is a trade-off. Diseases are often studied intensely, but narrowly. The naturalistic, time-consuming telling of one's story has been, for the most part, lost. Patients recount symptoms and physicians diagnose. The family physician who made house calls and lived in the same community for a lifetime has been, for the most part, superceded by a new kind of "technidoc" who often spends more time with lab reports than listening.

Physicians of the past typically lived in the same community with their patients—strolling the same streets. The great English neurologist, Parkinson, was an avid walker, and it was on the streets of London, not in his office, that he delineated the disease that bears his name. Until TS-OCD is studied in the spacious style of "street neurology," we will not understand it. A narrow neurological focus misses the broader patterns.

Writing of Parkinson's street observations, Sacks suggests:

> Parkinsonism, indeed, cannot be fully seen, comprehended, in the clinic; it requires an open, complexly interactional space for the full revelation of its peculiar character, its primitive impulsions, contortions, transfixions, and perversions. Parkinsonism *has* to be seen, to be fully comprehended, in the world, and if this is true of Parkinsonism, how much truer must it be of Tourette's. (Sacks, 1985, p. 116)

Although personal experience forms a base for this book, I hope it will become clear that I don't think subjectivity should replace science. Both are needed. This book is more than a potpourri of personal testimonies. Throughout six years of graduate school, one year of internship, and twenty years of clinical practice and teaching, I have consistently sought clearer insights regarding the puzzles of TS and OCD. I have conducted research on myself and others who have TS, have published numerous articles in professional journals, and have relentlessly searched for a model that "puts it all together," and I believe this book contains such a model.

I have utilized my own experience, listened to the accounts of others, and integrated these subjective insights with findings in the fields of developmental psychology and communications theory. A recently developed mathematical model known as Catastrophe Theory seems especially well suited for integrating these diverse perspectives into a single, coherent whole. As a result, I believe that a new and powerful paradigm for understanding TS and OCD has come into existence.

ACKNOWLEDGMENTS

This book is, in many respects, a distillate of my life. As such, the influences have been myriad, but I'll try not to be obsessive about including everyone.

Mildred Summerton did more than teach high school English and writing classes. She lived intensely and taught us that to write well, one must live well. It was she who took a friend and me to hear a stirring bit of oratory and participate in some handshaking when a young senator named Kennedy was stumping for primary votes in rural Wisconsin.

In college Frank Knittle used to subtract one letter grade for each misspelled word he found in our freshman composition papers. It seemed needlessly harsh at a time when word processors and spell checkers hadn't yet been conceived. But he did more than nitpick; he inspired us to write not only carefully but creatively.

As a psychologist my deepest roots go back to Indiana University where professors like Leon Levy, Richard Young, Alex Buchwald, and Richard Price taught me the importance of academic rigor. At Children's Hospital in Boston, Joseph Lord, Al Trieschman, and Haskel Cohen showed me the heuristic value of psychodynamic thought.

Robert Franklin, my analyst, taught me much about myself and encouraged my earliest attempts to understand Tourette syndrome from the perspective of object relations theory.

Discussions with Harold Jones of Andrews University Mathematics Department, and Ronald Van Valkenberg and Tim Strang of Battle Creek Adventist Hospital have helped to clarify some of the ideas presented.

This book would never have evolved from the mosaic of sometimes-disconnected meanderings into the current gestalt had it not been for the spirited support I received, at pivotal times, from four persons: Jim Hennessey at Springer Publishing Company who was enthusiastic about the application of Catastrophe Theory to compulsive disorders from day one; Kathleen O'Malley, my editor, who guided me through my first book with thoughtfulness and professionalism; and my wife, Deborah, who took time from her law studies to read manuscript "hot off" the word processor, and offered the kind of frank criticisms that only spouses feel free to dispense ("That paragraph is boring." "Who do you expect will understand *that* psychobabble? "That's good stuff!", etc.). Douglas Rogers, an architecture student at Andrews University, transformed my aboriginal sketches into finished figures.

Finally, I would like to acknowledge my debt to those who personally divulged their obsessions and compulsions to me. Their willingness to share these private matters with a wider audience is based on their hope that it will engender greater understanding of these perplexing problems. This book, I hope, will not disappoint them.

Chapter **1**

PEOPLE AND PARADIGMS

This book is about *people*; individuals from all spheres of life—professionals, laborers, skilled technicians, homemakers, students, and more. The people we'll encounter experience a puzzling variety of unusual behaviors over which they seem to exert little control. They often appear behaviorally "possessed," and if demonology were a currently popular paradigm—as it was during the Dark Ages, Middle Ages, and the Salem witch trials—people with compulsive disorders would be prime candidates for dunking stools, trephinations, and a variety of "cures" designed to cajole or drive out the demons within.

This book is also about *paradigms*. After we consider the commonalities that occur throughout the spectrum of compulsive disorders, a new paradigm will be offered which provides a conceptual framework within which these common features can be understood. Kuhn (1962) suggests that a paradigm is a set of basic assumptions that defines both the kinds of concepts that are considered legitimate as well as methods that may be used to collect and interpret data. It is important to understand that evidence supporting the organic paradigm of TS-OCD is based almost entirely on correlational and circumstantial data.

Because human behavior is always a final common pathway—a kind of bottleneck where hundreds of factors coalesce to determine the behavior—it can be studied at many different levels including: distal external influences such as cultural mores; proximal external influences such as family interactions; and internal mechanisms such as biochemical pathways or neurological structures. With so many possibilities, workers sometimes muddle the distinction between correlational and causal variables. In the case of TS-OCD it is important to remember that in order to establish organic etiology, some chemical, neurophysiological, or morphological change must be demonstrated to have preceded the

1

symptoms in question. In the case of vision loss, retinopathy or a severed optic nerve is convincing evidence that organic rather than functional (hysterical) blindness exists. With TS-OCD such organically based cause has *never been demonstrated*. Although the politics for organic etiology began a century ago when Gilles de la Tourette read his paper to the Academie Neurologique in Paris, it has never been supported by anything but circumstantial evidence. Even forceful advocates of the organic paradigm admit as much:

> Tics and Tourette syndrome are caused by primary organic disease of the central nervous system. While the evidence is inconclusive because a specific lesion has not been demonstrated, we believe that *circumstantial evidence* supports an organic etiology for tics. (Shapiro & Shapiro, 1980, p. 79, italics mine)

When a disorder is thought to be organically based, researchers are not likely to investigate family dynamics or child-rearing practices. Consequently the weight of "evidence" will come in on the side of the existing paradigm.

In recent years, the Tourette Syndrome Association (TSA) has been an important player in maintaining the organic paradigm. The growing membership is comprised mostly of parents and the medical professionals who serve the organization in leadership and consulting capacities. It's hardly surprising that TSA strongly supports the organic paradigm of TS, and exhibits an almost phobic aversion to what they disparagingly call the "psychogenic hypothesis." If how you spend your money indicates where your real values lie, the TSA research funding for 1989 clearly illustrates its commitment to the biological paradigm. The following lists the research projects funded by TSA:

Preclinical Studies

Molecular cloning of the D-1 receptor

Motor tics in rodents as a Model of the tics of Tourette syndrome

Serotonin/dopamine interactions in the brain: Potential relevance to Tourette syndrome

Perturbations in early striatal development as a basis for later neurological dysfunction

Clinical Studies

Psychometric standardization of the Tourette Syndrome Unified Rating Scale (TSURS)

PET and Tourette's disorder

Evaluation of the role of a cholinergic agonist in potentiating neuroleptic responses in animals and Tourette's patients

Methylphenidate treatment of attention deficit hyperactivity disorder in boys with Tourette syndrome

Genetics

Random mapping of Tourette syndrome: Inclusion/exclusion of the G-group chromosomes

Linkage studies in Tourette syndrome

Segregation analysis of obsessive compulsive disorder, chronic motor tics, and Tourette syndrome families

Segregation analysis showing autosomal dominant gene transmission in a single large kindred containing multiple affected cases of the Gilles de la Tourette syndrome.

Mapping a Tourette syndrome gene(s) using a new class of informative DNA polymorphisms

Study on heredity factors in Gilles de la Tourette syndrome in the Netherlands

Obviously "Mom-blaming" is not likely to occur if researchers study rodents and DNA instead of parents and children. But studying family chromosomes instead of family communications will not increase our understanding of interactional patterns that place children at risk for compulsive disorders. If we are to understand TS-OCD more clearly, at least as much effort needs to be spent studying interactions in the home as is currently being expended studying interactions in the brain.

Scaring Out the Demons

Like scientists, practitioners also conduct their craft within the framework of a particular paradigm. The choice of paradigm profoundly influences diagnosis and treatment. For example, Benjamin Rush, the father of American psychiatry, believed that many "lunatics" could be cured by frightening them. Hardly a new hypothesis, it was the basis for the original snake pit treatments where insane persons were forced into close encounters with cages of writhing snakes or repeatedly dunked in the hopes that it would literally "scare the devil out of them." A New England doctor of the nineteenth century implemented Rush's paradigm in the following way:

On his premises stood a tank of water, into which a patient, packed into a coffin-like box pierced with holes, was lowered. . . . He was kept under water until the bubbles of air ceased to rise, after which he was taken out, rubbed, and revived—if he had not already passed beyond reviving! (Deutsch, 1949, p. 82)

Current Paradigm

Contemporary psychiatry's prevailing paradigm is not demonology, it's chemistry. Doctors now tranquilize instead of traumatize their patients. Demons are no longer thought to lurk in the shadows, so physicians don't try to scare the devil out of their patients. Dunking stools have been replaced by drugs, and the supply shelves of psychiatric hospitals contain Stelazine instead of strait jackets. Behind nearly every psychiatric disorder from agoraphobia to voyeurism is the ubiquitous "biochemical imbalance." Compulsive disorders—from tics to trichotillomania—could be cured, it is thought, if only the correct chemical concoction could be synthesized. Dupont's marketing motto, "Better Living Through Chemistry," has become society's paradigm; and people in such diverse settings as psychiatric hospitals and crack houses seek the better life through drugs.

But there is a downside to the pharmacologic paradigm. It is that chemistry is *not* the answer to most of the urgent dilemmas of daily life. Although drugs have proven successful in controlling *infectious* disease, they are abysmally inadequate for dealing with interpersonal disease. The problems of unhappy marriages, unruly children, and unpaid bills are only momentarily mollified by drugs—no matter whether the drug is cocaine snorted at a party, alcohol purchased at a package liquor store, or Xanax prescribed by a physician.

Paradigm Shift Needed

Parents and playmates—not physicians or pharmacists—hold the answer to the epidemic of interpersonal disease afflicting our age. "Better Living Through Empathy" might be a better aphorism by which to live. Children who experience *good enough* parenting (not *perfect* parenting) during infancy and childhood won't be as prone to use drugs for mood management during their turbulent adolescent years. A little girl who is appreciated by her father is not likely to engage in promiscuous searches for affirmation later. The baby boy who consistently experiences a soothing caretaker when he's anxious doesn't become agoraphobic as an adult. He internalizes the primary caretaker's capacity to soothe, and doesn't require an external "soother" (another person always with him) in order to feel safe while shopping at a mall or driving to a new city. Children with healthy playground relationships typically have healthy psyches. It is in the early relationships with parents and playmates, not in chemical imbalances that researchers and clinicians will find the missing pieces to the puzzle of compulsive behaviors.

In summary, I'm shifting paradigms from demons and drugs, to parents and peers. The appropriate paradigm for understanding TS and OCD is developmental psychology, broadly defined to include its many related specialty areas such as neonatal attachment and development, infant social and emotional development, parent–child interactions (technically known as object relations theory), socialization and peer relationships, and adolescence. In understanding the data of development we will come to understand compulsive behaviors in their diverse forms.

PARADIGM CLASH: BIOLOGICAL DEFECT OR FUNCTIONAL BEHAVIOR DISORDER?

TS is characterized by multiple tics that usually include facial and body movements (e.g., eye blinking, head shaking, shoulder shrugging) as well as vocalizations (e.g., grunting, elective hiccupping, yelping, hissing, shouting—sometimes obscenities). An almost endless variety of normal muscular behaviors are exaggerated and routinized into "symptoms" by persons with TS.

Such "symptoms" are neurologically normal movements or sounds that are unusual only because of suddenness, intensity, repetitiveness, or social inappropriateness. TS often places people in profoundly trying circumstances; for example, while at a funeral, a person with TS might be compelled to yell, "I'm glad the bastard finally died!" even though such a statement may not (in any way) reflect the speaker's feelings in addition to being socially reprehensible.

Functional Disorders

A central issue in this book is whether TS results from a *biological* defect in some part of the nervous system, or whether it is a *functional* disorder of behavior. If a person receives a severe head injury, suffers a stroke, or otherwise damages portions of the nervous system, significant behavioral problems usually result. Such problems are said to have a *biological* basis. *Functional* problems, are those that result when *learned* behaviors do not operate efficiently. For example, a person who first learns to drive in England, will, in an emergency, automatically swerve *left* to avoid oncoming trouble. Swerving to the left is safe when driving in Britain, but unsafe when driving in the United States. This is a functional disorder of driving, not the result of neurological malfunction—as would be the case if the driver were drunk. The functional disorder results from utilizing a behavior that is helpful in one setting but dangerous in another.

Native language illustrates a functional behavior that is primary, changes little over time, and remains foundational throughout life. During times of stress, for example, everyone swears in their native language. An American mistakenly hammering his thumb instead of a nail is likely to yell, "Shit!" while a Frenchman would shriek, "Merde!" and a Latino would bellow "Cono! Mierda!" These are rudimentary, durable *functional* differences—emanating from intact nervous systems.

This does not mean that functional behaviors operate apart from the body; all behaviors, including speaking, have a biological base. Rather, it means that functional behaviors are not *primarily* driven by bodily processes. Developmentally speaking, the newborn begins life as mostly body and gradually differentiates many higher-level functions. Stress regressively pulls people "back to the body." This is why people hit, shout, or use obscene gestures when extremely provoked. The more provoked the person, the more regressed and somatic their communication. This division of the person into mind and body is, of course, oversimplified, but it is shorthand for talking about two very different spheres of function: the early, somatic world of the body and the more differentiated symbolic world of the mind.

Difficult to Change

It is important to emphasize that just because a behavior is functional does *not* mean it is easy to change. Some may think that because a disorder does not directly result from a biological defect, a person could easily change his or her mind and redirect the behavior. This is not so. Throughout the childhood years there occur "windows" of opportunity that do not remain open indefinitely. Once a child learns to speak in a given language, it will never again be quite so easy to learn another. His original language will always be his mother tongue.

If, during their early years, children learn to use tics as a rhythmically comforting muscular discharge pattern or as body language to communicate, it will not be easy to reverse this behavior. During times of stress they may revert to the original tics to try to retrieve the comfort of earlier times.

Biological Defect Paradigm

Except for this book—which maintains the position that TS is a *functional disorder*—*all* information presented to the public in the form of brochures, magazine articles, news releases, or TV documentaries, emphasizes that a psychological basis for TS does *not* exist. Instead, TS is always described as an *organic* malfunction of the central nervous system that results in involuntary movements and noises. Since such information is provided by neurologists, psychiatrists, pediatricians, endocrinologists, or other members of the medical profession, it isn't surprising that the treatment suggested for this seemingly organic problem is medication.

Drug Treatment

The most commonly used drug has been haloperidol (Haldol®). Although this drug has been somewhat successful in reducing symptoms, it has unfortunate side effects. Sleepiness, lethargy, and a general loss of vitality nearly always occur at moderate doses. At lower doses, symptom relief is seldom adequate. There is little question that tics can be reduced or eliminated with adequate doses of Haldol, but one could also "cure" stuttering in the same way. Given enough Haldol, the average stutterer would likely stop stuttering; of course his conversation would lose any zest or excitement it ever contained, and he would say only a few slurred words, if he talked at all! It's a little like burning down a house in order to get rid of the mice, or plowing up one's lawn to eliminate dandelions.

A case summary by Oliver Sacks illustrates this problem. Writing of his treatment of Ray, a TS patient, he candidly admits using Haldol is, at best, a compromised treatment. When Ray is taking Haldol, he describes himself as "sober, solid, square." His movements are slow, his thinking deliberate. He lacks the impetuosity of his "non-Haldol" self, but also the inspirations and spontaneity. Less sharp, less quick in wit, he doesn't excel in ping-pong or other games at which he used to win. He loses not only his obscenities, but his spunk as well. Most important and disabling, however, he found that on Haldol he lost not only his tics but also his musical energy:

> He found that on Haldol he was musically 'dull,' average, competent, but lacking energy, enthusiasm, extravagance and joy. He no longer had tics or compulsive hitting of the drums—but he no longer had wild and creative surges.
>
> As this pattern became clear to him, and after discussing it with me, Ray made a momentous decision: he would take Haldol "dutifully"

throughout the working week, but would take himself off it, and "let fly," at weekends. This he has done for the past three years. So now, there is the sober citizen, the calm deliberator, from Monday to Friday; and there is "witty ticcy Ray," frivolous, frenetic, inspired at weekends. It is a strange situation, as Ray is the first to admit. . . . Ray does make the best of it, and has a full life, despite Tourette's, despite Haldol, despite the "unfreedom" and the "artifice," despite being deprived of that birthright of natural freedom which most of us enjoy. (1985, pp. 94–96)

This kind of plea bargaining with Haldol—conceding to a lesser evil to escape a possibly greater punishment—is the most widely utilized treatment today. Later in this book I will suggest other treatment alternatives based on a much broader view of compulsive tics than is common today.

Holistic Treatment

Picture a group of London surgeons assembling for their monthly professional luncheon. In 1940 they are animatedly talking shop:

"I say, fellows, why do you think we're doing so much ulcer surgery these days?"

"Haven't the slightest, old boy, what do *you* think?"

"Well, don't laugh me out the door old chaps, but I think it's the air raids!" (laughter)

"The air raids? Surely you're not serious!"

"Exactly, the air raids. Since those Nazi's started bombing London, I've had five times the ulcer patients."

"Now that you mention it, I have too!—just hadn't thought it had much to do with bombs and missiles and all that bloody stuff!"

This is how the field of psychosomatic medicine began. A group of English physicians noticed that a dramatic rise in ulcer cases coincided with German air raids. Ultimately, the best treatment was to stop the air raids, but until that occurred other medicinal procedures (including surgery) had to be utilized. Today, good ulcer treatment is broadly based—holistic—including an expansive range of biopsychosocial factors. Such holistic approaches are utilized in treating many diseases such as diabetes, hypertension, cardiac problems, depression, obesity, to name but a few.

Reductionism Reexamined

This trend toward holistic treatment doesn't come easily for many medical professionals, because the sciences studied in medical schools tend to be *reductionistic*. Biologists, for instance, attempt to be more precise by moving from studying whole animals, to systems, to organs, to cells, to intracellular structures—reducing their focus to ever smaller bits of the body. The same is true of chemists, physicists, and other scientists who provide the research basis for medicine. Consequently it is second nature for physicians, trained in the reductionist tradition, to search for understanding by reducing complex phenomena to more basic (or smaller) units. It should come as no surprise that neurologists and other medical specialists seek to understand TS by focusing their attention on specific regions of the brain, microscopic segments of chromosomes, or the chemical composition of neurotransmitters. For example, Rapoport writes: "I have come to believe that Tourette's disease and Obsessive-Compulsive Disorder are two sides of the same *neurobiological* coin" (1989, p. 93). She suggests that obsessive thoughts are like hiccups of the mind, resulting from electrical firing of *diseased brain circuits* (pp. 78, 95, Italics mine).

In this book I follow a different path. Instead of seeking understanding in ever smaller bits of behavior, I search for patterns in a broader sweep. It's a little like trying to understand the picture on the front page of your morning newspaper—you don't get deeper discernment by using a magnifying glass or a microscope. Nor do you perceive character in Ike's face by studying his left nostril under a high-resolution lens. Magnification enables you to intensely study smaller units of the picture, but the resultant series of dots becomes *less* meaningful as your magnifying power increases (see Figure 1.1A). The *pattern* among the dots—which is the real basis for the picture—becomes lost in the narrowness of high-intensity focus, and the "real" Eisenhower (Figure 1.1D) is lost in the reductionistic concern with his left nostril.

My book includes biography—stories of people living their lives in the real world of home, school, the office; working, playing, laughing, crying. These narratives allow the reader to share the complexity of the person's life, and to examine the intricacy of TS-OCD as it manifests itself across the entire range of the personal life space.

Appearances are Misleading

It is primarily because of the epileptic-like appearance of body-jerking symptoms that TS is seen as a neurological disorder. To most observers,

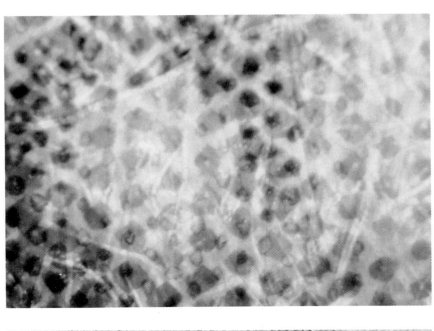

FIGURE 1.1 A portrait of Eisenhower: The reductionistic fallacy of only searching for meaning in small bits.

C

D

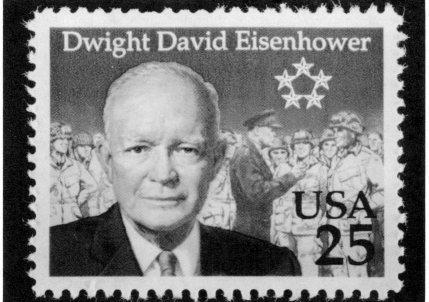

it *does* appear as if a person experiencing TS is suffering from a bona fide physical disease. However, these manifestations are, to borrow an analogy from linguistics, *functional homonyms* of neurological disorders. Just as the words "pool" (to swim in) and "pool" (billiards) look alike and sound alike but are not functionally related so too are the "twitching" of a person experiencing a seizure and the "twitching" of a person experiencing TS—related only in their topographic appearances. Throughout the remainder of this book I will demonstrate that TS is a *functional biopsychosocial* disease.

Although I try to maximize the areas of harmony that exist between my theory of TS-OCD and the excellent work of others, there exists a profound difference between my proposed developmental paradigm and currently popular neurological theories. In my view TS-OCD is not an uncontrollable neurologic spasm of either muscle or mind. It is rather a biopsychosocially generated functional disorder.

Who's in Control—Psyche or Soma?

When determining what controls certain TS-OCD behaviors, the organic paradigm is misleading. Shapiro and Shapiro incorrectly write: "tics are involuntary contractions of functionally related groups of skeletal muscles and involuntary noises and words . . . caused by primary organic disease of the central nervous system" (1980, pp. 78, 79). Popular descriptions in magazine articles or newspapers have the same organic bias, personifying body parts as autonomous agents. Statements like the following occur regularly: "Her foot began twitching, then her knee, finally her entire torso." "First an eye blinked, then a cheek twitched." Such writing erroneously implies that these actions are not initiated by the person. Sounds, movements, body parts are personified as if they had existences all their own. Tics and obsessions are accorded the status of homunculi—little persons within the psyche—instead of manifestations of psychic tension.

Hiccups or Breathing?

The difference between the organic and psychosocial paradigms can be illustrated with an analogy—the difference between breathing and hiccupping. Although TS *looks* like hiccupping it *feels* more like breathing. Hiccups are not under the *immediate* management of the hiccupper. There is no sense of agency, no feeling of steering one's own behavior. It simply happens *to* you, suddenly and uncontrollably. Although a tic *looks* like a muscle hiccupping it is *not* experienced in that way by the ticquer. All persons with TS privately know that they can *temporarily control* their jerking, shouting, or other symptoms, much as they can control their breathing.

This is why even persons with severe cases of TS, who experience *apparently* uncontrollable body spasms, are able to eat without their utensils being "jerked" out of their hands. They operate automobiles without "jerking" into the lane of oncoming traffic. A person with TS could successfully perform brain surgery by sandwiching arm jerks between careful incisions, however most patients would probably opt for a different surgeon. The major problem facing a surgeon with TS would be a marketing or public relations strategy, not one of manual dexterity or control.

But such control is only temporary. The reader can understand this by refraining from breathing for about 45 seconds. The urge to inhale soon becomes overwhelming, obligatory—but there still remains some partial control in deciding at which moment to begin breathing and through which channel (nose or mouth) to inhale. TS is like that—not like hiccups. A person with TS can't eliminate jerking, shouting, or twitching in the long run, but can have some control in the immediate sense.

Although persons with TS experience ever-present internal demands for periodic muscle "bursts," there is some degree of choice—not total—in determining how, when, or where to "burst." Having TS feels like having an internal TV that is always turned on; there is a channel selector and a volume control, but no "off" button. Individuals are unable to turn their TV off but they still retain some control over which channel to play and at what volume. In much the same way that a person can swim by "timing" breathing to occur between strokes, a person with TS can fleetingly function in nonspasmodic ways.

Shame, Self-Control, and Personal Responsibility

This ability of some personal control contributes to the problems of shame and personal blame. If you have no control over your behavior you can hardly be blamed for it. Consequently, the organic paradigm has been welcomed by children as well as by parents because it reduces the sense of personal responsibility. In the same way that it reduces parent-blaming it decreases self-blaming, asserting that various TS-OCD manifestations are—like hiccups—outside the domain of personal control.

However, the child's own self-blame intensifies shame because every ticquing child privately knows that he/she initiates each individual tic. It never becomes quite as automatic as breathing and most children think (albeit briefly) about each individual tic. Since the child experiences tics or obsessions as something he *does* not as something that *happens* to him the sense of shame is increased. Paradoxical instructions such as "Quit it!" are internalized as *reasonable* requests which the "naughty" child has failed to carry out and accusations such as "You're just doing that to irritate me!" are internalized and confirmed. After all it's offensive enough if you *accidentally* drop Mom's favorite milk pitcher, but when you do it *on purpose*, it's appalling!

Because the complexities of TS-OCD are just beginning to be understood, it seems unjust to blame parents for honest mistakes made in the absence of adequate information. Similarly, we should understand that the control children exert over their tics is extremely limited, and we ought to be reluctant to blame them either. When blame and shame are discussed in a later chapter, it will become apparent that blaming is inappropriate and skews our understanding of TS-OCD by reinforcing a "blame-phobic" approach to research and treatment. However in our haste to avoid blame and reduce shame, we have failed to look at important, family-based, developmental issues. Like Esau, we have traded our developmental "birthright" for a neurological "mess of pottage."

Multiple Factors

A heart attack, experts agree, results from the *interaction* of numerous biopsychosocial risk factors including heredity, diet, exercise, personality variables, cigarette smoking, etc. Likewise TS is a final common pathway for multiple influences. It results from a confluence of multiple risk factors dating from the earliest hours of neonatal life and resulting in noticeable tics around kindergarten or first grade. Although there are instances of tics beginning in children as young as two years old or erupting as late as adolescence or adulthood this is not usually the case. This fact is at variance with a "hard-wired" neurological paradigm, as there are no rapidly changing physical phenomenon occurring around the sixth year. If tics occurred soon after birth, at the advent of adolescence, or during menopause, a biological explanation would seem more plausible; but the major "crisis" at age six is not an overabundance of hormones or a reshuffling of physiology, it is the profound psychological event of leaving home for the first time to attend school.

Throughout this book multiple causality is emphasized, to shift focus from neurological lesions to psychological development—in a complementary way. All behavior is *interactively* biological *and* psychological. To ignore either perspective is to constrict understanding. To treat an ulcer *only* with medications and diet is to miss the wisdom of the aphorism "It isn't what you eat, it's what eats you!" that's so important in treatment.

A NEW DEFINITION OF TOURETTE SYNDROME

Before presenting my revised definition of TS it is necessary to briefly review some developmental psychology.

Circular Reactions

The eminent developmental psychologist Jean Piaget first described circular reactions (1952). They occur when the infant stumbles upon a simple behavior and tries to recapture the experience by reenacting the original movements again and again in a rhythmic cycle. Such rhythmic cycles serve to explore and define boundaries, and also have a soothing effect in times of stress. Piaget described three kinds of circular reactions: primary, secondary, and tertiary.

Primary Circular Reactions

(1–4 months) are simple repetitive acts that center on the infant's own body. These are simple behaviors such as thumb sucking or foot grasping normally seen during the first four months of neonatal life. In normal development, they serve to familiarize the newborn with his or her own body and provide comfort in times of tension. In normal development, these simple repetitive behaviors are gradually replaced by higher-order thinking and more complex behaviors. When stress is extreme, either in terms of intensity or chronicity, such mechanisms become *overused* and consequently much more easily revived later (out of phase) as attempts to soothe oneself.

Secondary Circular Reactions

(4–12 months) differ from primary circular reactions in that they no longer center on the neonate's own body; instead, the infant reaches out to manipulate objects discovered in the environment. The baby will shake a rattle, repeatedly grasp a ball, or rhythmically bang "dolly" against the side of the crib. During this era, the infant begins to crawl, manipulate things, and significantly expand horizons.

Tertiary Circular Reactions

(12–18 months), occurring during the first half of the second year, are less involved with rhythmic body movements and constitute a further expansion of the baby's boundaries. During this period, termed the "practicing" period of development, there is an interest in *novelty*. Exploration takes a giant leap in the form of upright locomotion. The enthusiasm and expansiveness of the infant is described by Greenacre (1957) who aptly suggests the infant is having a "love affair with the world." Other observers note that:

> The toddler takes the greatest step in human individuation. He walks freely with upright posture. Thus, the plane of his vision changes; from an entirely new vantage point he finds unexpected and changing perspectives, pleasures, and frustrations. . . . During these precious 6 to 8 months (from the age of 10 or 12 months to 16 or 18 months), the world is the junior toddler's oyster (Mahler, Pine, & Bergman, 1975, pp. 70–71).

A Revised Definition of TS and OCD

Tics are simple, repetitive, behaviors that can be understood as adult residues of circular reactions. They are not weird or crazy, nor are they caused by biological defects; rather they are "closed loops" made up of recursive, self-reflexive behaviors from the earliest months of life. Obsessions are the cognitive "flip side" of somatic tics, often mirroring similar conflicts in a developmentally more advanced manner.

TS is a "mixed bag" of muscular tics, obsessive thoughts, and interpersonal limit testing. It is rooted in the *circular reactions* of infancy, energized by the *autonomy struggles* of toddlerhood, and substantiated by *shame and embarrassment* during childhood. OCD is similar in dynamics, but is primarily composed of "closed loops" of recursive cognitions instead of somatic tics. Traditional diagnostic distinctions between TS and OCD are misleading and have no substantive basis in developmental dynamics. Many adults experience repetition as comforting; consequently tics persist as self-soothing *somatic* repetition, and obsessions continue as self-comforting *cognitive* repetition.

When an infant is excessively stressed, the usual sequence of psychological mastery is slowed or stalled. This "freezes" the coping mechanisms operative at the time. When development continues in other areas of the person's life—as it inevitably must—the tics remain as frozen residues of earlier struggles. Adults with TS are much like the wooly mammoths found beneath the ice with food still frozen in their mouths; except that in this case it is circular reactions—not food—which are "frozen" and remain in the form of tics.

Throughout the remainder of this book, tics—simple, repetitive, body-based behaviors—will be seen as adult preservations of early circular reactions. Tics are not weird or crazy; nor are they caused by biological defects. Rather, they are developmentally frozen bits of behavior from early life. Although "frozen" implies something rigid or motionless, tics are best understood as *circularly reverberating* behaviors—not so much frozen as repetitively recursive. Like a dog chasing its tail, the ticquer expends enormous amounts of energy going in circles.

Extending the metaphor further, a *primary* circular reaction is like a dog chasing its tail and a *secondary* circular reaction is like the dog chasing cars. A higher level of interaction is illustrated by a dog chasing a rabbit. Dogs chasing their own tails are recursively coupled with themselves, completely out of phase with their surroundings. Dogs chasing cars are a little less recursively into themselves but still only loosely coupled with their environments because the dog–car relationship is nonreciprocal. The dog only thinks the car is "fearfully" running away; in actuality the car is not responding to the dog at all (unless, of course, the driver swerves to miss the dog). Only the dog–rabbit relationship is appropriately coupled. Here the rabbit is in fact running in response to the dog's pursuit, making the interaction genuinely reciprocal. Only in such a situation is the dog's behavior appropriately coupled with his *current* situation.

Tics, like dog behaviors, show great diversity. But even with the great variety, there is a commonality in all tics. They are *recursively* out of touch with current realities. Most simple tics are only loosely coupled to the surrounding social situation. Like a dog chasing his own tail, they are driven more from within than by external stimuli. However, there exist complex tics which *are* coupled to the surroundings and which coerce others into participatory roles, much as a rabbit's behavior is coerced by the pursuing dog. Distinctions among simple tics, complex tics, compulsions, or obsessions is more a matter of degree than kind.

Tics are a "Mixed Bag"

The intertwined nature of tics with each other and with obsessive thoughts has been noticed by numerous clinicians. Rapoport noted that a high proportion of the obsessive patients in her study had an assortment of twitches and tics as well.

Adult Tics Reflect Developmental History

This diversity of compulsive manifestations is consistent with my developmental theory of the genesis of TS and OCD. Depending on when stress is first experienced, behaviors may be frozen anywhere in the developmental sequence, and preserved for later use. Consequently one can expect repetitive behaviors and thoughts from anywhere in the behavioral repertoire; and the degree of "primitiveness" of a tic, compulsion, or obsession will reflect the stage of development in which the child was functioning when it was frozen.

Somatic Rituals

These remain as residues from early developmental arrest. Obviously, pre-verbal neonates are unable to use repetitive words or songs to reestablish their sense of mastery, so they naturally turn to their bodies, re-using somatic circular reactions. It's not accidental that Rapoport's (1989) youngest children showed the most primal somatic manifestations of self soothing: "Two of the youngest boys in our study spend three or four hours each day licking their hands" (p. 197).

If severe stresses occur later in development, the person will likely develop complex behavioral or cognitive varieties of repetition instead of— or in addition to—somatic tics. Take the case of Morris, the eighteen-year-old who scrubs his arms raw with Top Job or Mr. Clean. A more detailed study of his case reveals that he began washing when a toddler, but later added more complex routines. When Morris was three, his family moved to a new house. He recalled pulling a chair up to the sink, turning on the faucet, and washing his hands.

> For two years it just made him feel better. He felt he had to do this over and over again, but then the washing need faded out.
> He went without compulsion—miraculously, he now thinks—until junior high school when the compulsions and thoughts came back. (Rapoport, 1989, pp. 75, 76)

Morris' experience illustrates how early self-soothing behavior later seems extremely puzzling—primarily because it occurs in a context so far removed from its beginnings. Understood as self-comforting behavior by a three-year-old who is anxious because of new surroundings, this somatic ritual of washing makes sense. Such behaviors at first may please mothers—aren't they always asking little boys "Did you wash your hands?" The warm, soapy water combined with slow, slippery, self-massaging hand movements is intrinsically comforting.

It is hardly surprising that since Morris used these self-comforting behaviors for two years during his early life he reverted back to them when excessive stress occurred in junior high school. However, by adulthood, the somatically comforting washing behaviors of early life, even when radically intensified into an hour-long effort, were inadequate for coping with the complexities of an eighteen-year-old's existence.

When such "frozen residues" of early life reappear in adulthood, they indeed seem bizarre; however, viewed more broadly, they appear less puzzling. It's worth noting that when these early residues are later revived, they are typically accompanied with other, more complex repetitions as well. In junior high, for example, Morris experienced obsessive *thoughts* of his mother in a wheelchair, his father having an affair with another woman, and various sexual fantasies of his own.

Repetitive Thoughts

Sam, another patient of Rapoport's, is a professional who suffers from a variety of compulsive thoughts and ritualizations. These all involve higher-level processes such as avoiding certain words when reading, avoiding looking at TV, or clocks, etc. However his first compulsions were very somatic. He recalls that when he was about seven, he and his friends often played a game called "Cooties" in which they pretended one person "had cooties" and all the others tried to avoid being tagged and "getting the cooties." During one game Sam became panicky about being touched. "It was more than just a game," he recalled, "it was a matter of desperation for me. I just could not allow myself to be tagged, to have all of the contamination flow into me. I ran very fast to escape" (1989, p. 51).

These vignettes illustrate that when original trauma occurs early in development, the resulting ritualizations are primitive—often somatic. When major trauma occurs later, the repetitive residuals tend to be more cognitive or from a higher level of behavior.

THE RELATIONSHIP BETWEEN TOURETTE SYNDROME AND OBSESSIVE COMPULSIVE DISORDER

The Obsessive-Compulsive Spectrum

To state more precisely the relationship between TS and OCD: *all* cases of TS are *somatic* manifestations of OCD; in other words OCD-TS is always a *dual diagnosis*. To visualize this concept think of a *spectrum* of compulsive disorders with the developmentally early, highly somatic tics of TS at one end and the more developmentally differentiated cognitive manifestations of OCD at the other.

Simply stated, *TS is repetitive flexing of muscle and OCD is repetitive flexing of mind*. This obsessive-compulsive spectrum is best understood in terms of *developmental stages*. Some persons experience OCD *without* TS. Having left the somatic tics of childhood behind, they tend to stabilize at the higher level of cognitive repetitiveness (OCD) instead of the somatic repetitiveness of tics (TS).

Current diagnostic practice is in disarray because it is carried out at a purely descriptive level, with key distinctions existing more in the eye of the beholder than in reality. For example, coprolalia (uttering swear words or obscene sayings at inappropriate times) is considered a core symptom of TS even though it is a complex manifestation more similar to the obsessions of OCD than the tics of TS. Equally bewildering are the DSM-III-R differentiations among Tourette's Disorder, Chronic Motor or Vocal Tic Disorder, and Transient Tic Disorder. Such nosological hairsplitting, based on external behaviors—in the absence of dynamic or developmental considerations—leaves clinicians more bewildered than satisfied. The resulting diagnostic heterogeneity is puzzling, but can be resolved by adopting the developmental paradigm presented in this book.

Before concluding this chapter, two particularly "pure" cases will be briefly presented in order to illustrate the extreme poles of what I call the compulsive spectrum. Rapoport described "George K.," a farmer from Maine who had listened to a fiddle tune playing in his head for thirty-one years. Apparently none of the experts George consulted were able to find other symptoms. Here, then, is a "pure" example of OCD without a trace of accompanying somatizing—his repetitive ritual was wholly "mental."

At the other pole of the spectrum we could place the two young boys referred to earlier who "spend three or four hours each day licking their hands. Each finger gets licked in its turn, the order doesn't change" (Rapoport, p. 197).

Such "pure" cases of somatic versus cognitive rituals are seldom encountered in the real world. The majority of people report "mixed" experience, suffering from both somatic and cognitive repetitions. Rapoport (p. 81) noted that approximately 85% of her OCD patients performed excessive washing at some point in their lives. Still others were reported to exhibit jerking movements of hands and feet as well as complex mannerisms like touching their noses or pulling their hair.

Washing is intrinsically a mixture of both somatic *and* cognitive elements. It may be a simple somatic attempt to comfort oneself as Morris did when he was a toddler. Most washing is carried out absent-mind-edly by ordinary persons as a common cleansing routine after using the bathroom or prior to eating. However, in the case of some teenagers who are ritualistically trying to wash themselves of "evil" (such as mas-turbation), cognitive elements become much more cardinal and the whole procedure more intensely compulsive.

In the next chapter we will consider the developmental paradigm in greater detail, utilizing it to clarify etiological connections between the earliest needs of infancy and rituals of later life.

Chapter 2

THE DEVELOPMENTAL ETIOLOGY OF TS–OCD

I am saying that the proper place to study schizophrenia, and manic depression and melancholia is the nursery, and if this be true then some
modern trends in psychiatry are like barking up the wrong tree. (Winnicott, 1975, p. 171)

AN OBJECT RELATIONS PERSPECTIVE

Agony and Art

Half a century ago some observers viewed hysteria as much more than a
medical disorder. "Hysteria is not a pathological phenomenon," they
suggested, "It is one of the supreme instruments of human expression"
(Horowitz, 1977, p. 145). It would be Pollyannaish to suggest that TS-
OCD styles of coping are behavioral art forms, that someone with multiple tics is a kind of walking Sistine chapel, but the various ways in
which individuals compensatorily fulfill unmet developmental needs
are astounding. There is a lot of agony, but there is also a lot of creativity used in meeting these needs, even when the ways they are met appear peculiar or misdirected to others. It reminds me of an alcoholic patient I once saw, who was unable to purchase beer with food stamps.
Subsequently, he bought cans of pop, dumped the pop, turned in the
cans for a ten-cent-per-can refund, and used the cash to purchase beer!

Flawed Relationships Lead to Compulsions

In this chapter I will show how the constantly changing polymorphous tics of TS are an attempt to compensate for normal developmental needs that were insufficiently satisfied during infancy and early childhood. Central to this discussion is the concept that TS-OCD—in all its myriad forms—is a manifestation of flawed object relations "frozen" during the early months of life. The flaw is primarily unmet developmental needs which are then obsessively—but archaically—recycled in the form of repetitive tics or thoughts. Although later development sometimes has a "thawing" effect, allowing psychological growth to again proceed, this is not the usual course. Typically, tics and other compulsions become firmly routinized around age six and, thereafter, cast a shadow over all ensuing experience. Many compulsions are "public" ones, prime targets for ridicule, further insulating the child from many peer relationships and the ameliorative experiences of normal development. Even "private" obsessions often keep children phobically isolated from the mainstream of their peers for fear of being "found out."

Wooly Mammoths from the Dawn of Life

All tics—transitory or chronic, muscular or vocal—can be seen as somatized reverberations of early life. They echo the earliest needs of infancy and beyond. Needs that are not fulfilled in the neonate, toddler, child, or adolescent remain somatically preserved and are repetitively recycled as out-of-phase need seeking. Like wooly mammoths suddenly frozen with food still in their mouths, tics echo the past. Like dinosaur bones and archeological ruins they do not exactly replicate the past but, when studied, as chronic and continuing efforts to fulfill object-relational needs, TS-OCD manifestations provide insight into the nature of past deprivations and conflicts. In this chapter, various physical and object-relational needs will be discussed, and their relationship to TS-OCD explicated.

Needs From the First Year of Life: The Somatic Months

Need for Rhythmic Discharge

The following discussion will show that TS-OCD develops by piggybacking on the foundation of normal infant responses. We have previously noted the importance of *primary circular reactions* in the life of the 0–4-month-old infant. The neonate fortuitously discovers movements that have value for him or her and tends to repeat them. Such behaviors may well provide the basis for later tics if, as a result of excessive stress, they become inordinately vigorous, rigidly repetitive, or disconnected from the developing behavioral repertoires in which they first occurred.

Piaget's naturalistic observations of the neonate's rhythmic cycles has been confirmed by recent research. Brazelton (1980), using stop-frame photography, was able to observe that the neonate has a pattern of concentrating and withdrawing attention in an alternating rhythm about four times a minute. He observed a total body response pattern of attention followed by a collapse of attention and then further buildup.

Interactional Rhythms—"Dancing with Mamma"

Interestingly, neonatal rhythms are not simply reflexive bodily movements. From the very beginning, they are permeated by people. Newborns only a few days old can differentiate between persons and nonpersonal stimuli in their environments. Lichtenberg (1983) points out that if presented with an object, the infant responds with jerky movements. If, however, a familiar person enters the neonate's perceptual field, the movements *soften*.

Brazelton and Als (1979) found that infants' responses to humans were discriminably different than those to nonhuman objects:

> The contrast of the infant's behavior and attention was striking as early as 4 weeks of age. . . . You could indeed tell from looking at a toe or a finger whether the infant was in an interaction with an object or a parent— and by 4 weeks of age, even which parent it was. (1979, pp. 357–359)

Thus, from the earliest days of neonatal life, newborns respond to both human and nonhuman objects with movements and rhythms. Biological rhythms become intertwined with rattles, pacifiers, parents, and caretakers. It is not surprising that when in certain children these early rhythms hypertrophy into tics and other TS-OCD rituals, they still *coexist* with social interactions as they did in the beginning. The child is not developing new bizarre behaviors, rather the body-movement component has compulsively expanded, dwarfing social relations in the process; but what continues to exist is a complex configuration of biorhythms and social relations.

Failed Soothing

It is impossible to retrospectively track failures in soothing with high degrees of accuracy. Adults cannot recall the earliest months of their lives, and parents are notoriously unreliable as informants. This is why proactive research, of the kind being conducted by neonatal researchers, is so valuable. Nonetheless, in studying the lives of persons with TS-OCD one can find many instances where it is reasonable to infer that the "courting dance" between mother and newborn must have been absent or seriously curtailed. In such cases, we can reasonably speak of increased risk for later hypertrophy of body rhythms.

Especially relevant here is Lichtenberg's observation that the presence of a familiar person in the infant's perceptual space *softens* the naturally occurring rhythms; and the presence of the mother *smoothes* them even more. In the absence of "good-enough" mothering—in situations where consistent parenting is significantly diminished due to absence, alcoholism, depression, or other situations—infants are much more likely to overdevelop their rhythmic movements. This will be exacerbated by high levels of stress or the constriction of bodily movement.

The Needs for Stimulation and Soothing—Response Extraction in Neonates

Recent research has shown the infant to be an active *response elicitor*. Freud believed that the bird egg, with a built-in supply of nourishment and a protective shell against the outside world, was an appropriate analogy to the mother–child dyad. This view has been echoed by some recent theorists (e.g., Mahler, Pine, & Bergman, 1975) who suggest that psychological "hatching" takes place during the fourth month of neonatal life. However, the traditional view of the neonate existing in a kind of quiescent psychological cocoon with mother (e.g., Freud, 1895, 1920) has *not* been confirmed by research. Quite the contrary.

The neonate's need for maternal response is so intense that if a mother is instructed to gaze above the infant's eyes, keeping her face expressionless and immobile, infants will attempt to recapture the mother's attention by trying to meet her eyes, moving their hands and eyes, reaching with arms, legs, and the entire body. If this is unsuccessful, the infants collapse into withdrawal and distress, and a little later the cycle is repeated with increasing evidence of distress (Beebe & Stern, 1977).

Lichtenberg contends that: "Study after study documents the neonate's preadapted potential for direct interaction—human to human—with mother" (1983, p. 6). Neonates respond selectively to sounds in the range of the human voice. Their eyes focus most clearly on objects about eight inches away—the distance to caretaker's eyes when being held for breast- or bottle-feeding (Stern, 1977). By two weeks the newborn gazes at mother's face longer than at a stranger's (Carpenter, 1974). Even the mother's scent seems to have a drawing power for the infant.

MacFarlane (1975) found that when breast pads—one from mother, one from another woman—are placed on either side of eight-day-old neonates, they reliably smell the difference and turn towards mother's pad.

Microkinesic movie analyses reveal that as early as the first postnatal day neonates move in precise synchrony with the rhythms of adult speech (Condon & Sander, 1974). This suggests that mother and newborn are preset for interaction, and they enter into this "dance" almost immediately.

> What emerges is a new twist to our view of object relations—the postnatal baby is a participant and an activator of dialogue, not simply a recipient. . . . The picture that emerges is one of two partners, each prepared to act on and react to the other. (Lichtenberg, 1983, pp. 17, 18)

It is important to note that in the neonate the various needs we are discussing do not occur as *discrete* entities. All are fused in a global, highly somatic sense of self which springs from the maternal–infant dyad. In this respect, the infant's seeking "to dance with Mamma" is related to rhythmic discharge. The jerky movements simultaneously attract Mom's attention and serve to discharge built up tension and excitement as well. Crying is another example of multipurpose behavior. It serves both as rhythmic discharge and to extract responses from the mother. Lichtenberg notes:

> Crying may also be part of a regular compelling pattern of discharge for stimulation. This view seems to be supported by the observation that after periods of crying the level of integration of behavior in other areas may be higher. . . . In each observable pattern of infant behavior, stimulus seeking is so compelling a force that stimulus seeking and discharge must be seen as complementary regulatory governors. (1983, pp. 86, 87)

Vocalizations: An Early Form of Response Extraction

Much as the muscular tics of TS can be seen as piggybacked on early circular reactions, vocalizations can be seen to piggyback on the neonate's earliest cries for attention, nurturing, or soothing. The grunts, yelps, shouts, barks, squeals, shrieks, screams, whistles, clucks, or chirps of TS-OCD can be understood as expanded residuals of early response extraction. The ticquing (vocalizing) toddler is analogous to the crying infant. Both seek attention and nurturance from those significant others upon whom they must depend because of their own helplessness.

The human infant is one of the most helpless creatures at birth, doomed to perish without physical and psychological care. Survival depends on response extraction. As Lichtenberg so aptly observes: "Unlike the hairy primates who remain in tactile contact with their clinging infants, human mothers must be enticed and summoned to attend to their physically distant babies" (1983, p. 22). Other infancy experts have made similar observations:

> The only way available to the infant to alter the situation is to cry. Survival depends upon whether the sound succeeds in summoning a person to administer physical and psychological care, unless there is a caring adult to anticipate that the infant needs tending. (Blanck & Blanck, 1979, pp. 78, 79)

And from Mahler, Pine, and Bergman (1975) ". . . the infant's 'sending power,' his innate ability to evoke the kind of mothering he needs, should be particularly emphasized as an important attribute of his endowment" (p. 202).

The primitive nature of many vocalizations of TS-OCD—grunting, shrieking, clucking, chirping—makes it conceivable that they are piggybacked on early cries for attention. Coprolalia occurs later in development, and is, as we shall see in a later chapter, a very sophisticated kind of response extraction.

In summary, the infant emerges from current research as an *active* force in the dyad—a response extractor. Moss and Robinson (1968) found that *more than half* of the interactions in their study were initiated by the infant. Neonates actively seek stimulation and elicit responses within the mother–infant dyad. Infants are, to use Lichtenberg's words, "skillful seekers of stimulation" (1983, p. 84).

CASE EXAMPLE: THE ENGLISH GENTLEMAN WHO ACTED LIKE A LUNATIC AND ATE LIKE A PIG

Most of the people, whose lives I share with you in this book, I've personally met. We've shared ideas, enjoyed some laughs, and discussed painful experiences. The English gentleman you're about to meet is no stranger to me either. Though I've never had lunch with him, I've read colorful descriptions of his spirited lunches. Though I've never watched him slowly weave down a London street—carefully avoiding cracks or scrupulously touching light poles—others have, and they have left us graphic descriptions of this unique man. With the help of historians, we'll return to London to meet this remarkable person. We'll visit him as he studies in his library, as he eats breakfast in his home, and as he strolls down the street. We'll even see him as a pitiful, half-blind four-year-old, crawling home from school—defiantly refusing assistance. Let's begin by observing him in private.

A few years before His Majesty's redcoats opened fire on some improper Bostonians, a huge man sat reading in a private library in London, a candle near his face and a book held close to his right hand. As he read, he seesawed backward and forward on his chair, letting strange cluckings and whistlings escape from his capacious mouth. His head, which was cocked toward his right shoulder, shook and nodded with the movement of his body and, as he seesawed, the palm of his right hand rubbed his left knee. He was sitting next to the fireplace, and by its blaze and the light from the candle, his face, pitted by smallpox and scarred by scrofula, presented a grotesque sight.

Despite his odd appearance and near-blindness, this man was at home among books. He was Samuel Johnson, author of *London: A Poem, Irene: A tragedy; Rasselas, a novel; Richard Savage, a biography; The Rambler and The Idler, essays, chiefly moral; compiler of the first great dictionary of the English language, and editor of Shakespeare in eight volumes, with notes.* (Norman, 1951, pp. 7, 8)

Hibbert (1971) describes a visit by Ozias Humphry, a young portrait painter, to the "most famous author in England:"

Humphry was astonished by the spectacle. The great author was a huge, scarred man dressed in "a dirty brown coat and waistcoat, with breeches that were brown also (though they had been crimson), and an old black wig. His shirt collar and sleeves were unbuttoned; his stockings were down about his feet which had on them, by way of slippers, an old pair of shoes." He did not speak for some time, concentrating on his tea and his bread and butter, and Humphrey could "hardly help thinking him a madman for some time as he sat waving over his breakfast like a lunatic." But then, at last, he began to talk; and his visitor sat enthralled. (p. 3)

Norman paints a graphic picture of Johnson strolling the streets of London:

He walked slowly, weaving ponderously from side to side, now against the wall, now at the pavement's edge, muttering to himself, whistling and clucking, his hands jerking out in involuntary gestures to startle other pedestrians in the London gloom. He came at length to the west side of Leicester Square, and paused before No. 47 to do a kind of mysterious jig in order to ascend the steps with the proper foot put forward first. Again, at the threshold, he repeated the strange jig, like a man hesitating to enter, drawing back and going forward; but enter at last he did, and found himself in the midst of a celebrated company.

Johnson had appeared; but he remained habitually silent until addressed. "Tom Tyers described me best," he was fond of repeating. "He once said to me, 'Sir, you are like a ghost: you never speak till you are spoken to.'" The awe which a ghost might produce had indeed fallen on the company. It was not only that he never spoke till spoken to—there was a dinner to be dispatched. Looking neither left nor right, head close to his plate, the veins in his forehead distended, and sweat pouring down from under his wig, he dispatched it. Frances Reynolds, the painter's sister, watched with renewed astonishment and disgust. From time to time he left the table, turned his back at a suitable distance and blew his nose. He considered himself a polite man, and did not like to see a handkerchief used at meals. . . . (pp. 9–11)

How can we understand such incongruous behavior? Why would a man eat like a ravenous beast—apparently unaware of his social stimulus value—and yet consider himself too much of a gentleman to blow his nose at the table? What possible sense can be made of a man who discoursed with kings and commoners alike—"probably the greatest talker who ever lived, with the most varied talk and varied audience of any man in history" (Norman, 1951, p. 23)—yet lurched down the streets of London like a drunk and appeared retarded sitting in his library rocking, clucking, whistling, and rubbing his knee with a circular motion of his great awkward hand? To understand this puzzling, paradoxical person we must begin at the beginning.

Born at four o'clock in the afternoon of Wednesday, September 18, 1709, to Michael and Sarah Johnson, Sam's entry into the world was precarious. The prolonged, difficult labor was finally over, but in place of the robust yells typical of healthy infants, the room was filled with somber stillness. Finally, Samuel broke the ominous silence with a few faint whimpers, causing the midwife to mutter "Here is a brave boy." His parents however were not reassured, and fearing that he might not survive the night had him christened immediately. Although he survived the night—indeed the next 75 years—the ensuing weeks were calamitous for the infant.

His father, eager that the frail baby be well nourished, urged that they obtain a wet nurse. The wife of a local bricklayer named Marklew was chosen and Sam was given over to her for the next few weeks. What no one knew was that her milk was tubercular resulting in Sam contracting scrofula—tuberculosis of the lymph glands—and losing much of his eyesight. Writing of this some 50 years later, Samuel portrayed himself as "a poor diseased infant, almost blind."

After 10 weeks at the Marklews, he was returned home. Here was the first major interruption of the normal development of soothing, complementary rhythms between nurturing parent and infant. After two and a half months of becoming accustomed to the rhythms of life with one woman, he was suddenly confronted with the loss of his "mother" who was replaced by a stranger in an entirely new environment. At 10 weeks he could not have known that this "stranger" was his "biomother," only that she was not familiar. This traumatic "abandonment" by his first "mother," was followed by a series of painful surgeries.

Before prodeeding to the next stage of Samuel Johnson's childhood, it is important to note, once more, the importance of the first weeks of life. It is a time during which, under optimal conditions, neonates and their parents integrate the baby's rhythms into the "courting dance" described earlier. This interpersonalizing of one's body rhythms provides a bridge by which caretakers can soothe the infant when it is distressed. Imagine, then, how traumatic it must have been for baby Sam to change mothers at 10 weeks. Just about the time he had become comfortable with his "wet" mother he was suddenly transferred back to be mothered by a woman we know to have been rigid, distant, and depressed.

Michael and Sarah, wanting to do all they could for the ailing infant, took him to a surgeon who made an incision in his left arm in order to drain the infection from his system. It was common practice to keep such a wound open with a thread or horsehair until about age six. One can only imagine the effect such a chronic, obvious somatic blemish would have on a young child's psychological development. Besides the constant experience of pain or irritation, there would be the inevitable questions from other children about "What's that thing on your arm?" We are told, however that this incision was not the last surgery related to his perinatal problems.

> As his condition grew worse and sores appeared, it was realized that he had the tubercular infection of the lymph glands known as scrofula or the "King's Evil." It had spread to both the optic and auditory nerves, leaving him almost blind in the left eye, while also impairing vision in the right, and deaf in the left ear. Some scar tissue remained on his face because of the scrofula. A later operation on the lymph glands left further scars on the lower part of the face and on the neck. Done without anesthetic, it was obviously a traumatic experience for the infant. (Bate, 1975, p. 7)

In Sam's case, the constantly irritating sore on his arm must have been a "burr under the saddle" of his developing psyche. Likewise, his reduced auditory and visual abilities, while not constituting so conscious and obvious a physical handicap as the open wound on his arm, nevertheless profoundly influenced his lifestyle. Further, these chronic conditions were punctuated with painful anesthesia-absent surgeries. Surely this would weaken the psychological resilience of even the most hardy infant.

Sam's father was hardly a healthy counterbalance to his depressed, emotionally distant mother. Taciturn and hardworking, he supplemented his business of selling vellum and parchment by setting up a small parchment factory. Sarah nagged Michael about details regarding his business, and he retaliated by imposing strict economic limitations on certain household items such as tea. When the drizzle of daily tension became too much for him, Michael simply saddled his horse and rode away for orders for his business. For young Sam, however, such escape was impossible, and he grew up in an atmosphere permeated by those uneasy silences which so often characterize unhappy marriages. Johnson describes his unhappy childhood home in the following words:

> My father and mother had not much happiness from each other. They seldom conversed; for my father could not bear to talk of his [business] affairs; and my mother, being unacquainted with books, cared not to talk of anything else. (McAdam & Hyde, 1958, p. 7)

This difficult family situation became even more complex with the birth of Sarah's second child, Nathaniel, when Sam had just turned three. He did not take kindly to this new rival for Sarah's limited affections. Sam often misbehaved, but his mother dealt inconsistently with him; sometimes indulging him, sometimes punishing—even beating—him.

> He could not bring himself to respect her, although he afterwards claimed that he loved her and perhaps, indeed, he really did love her. But as he grew older his outbursts of irritation with her became both more violent and more frequent. "And one day," so he recorded, "when in anger, she called me a puppy, I asked her if she knew what they called a puppy's mother." (Hibbert, 1971, p. 6)

Johnson's life illustrates a number of pivotal issues in the development of TS-OCD. He developed an excessive need for response extraction, and his need for rhythmic discharge hypertrophied, because his highly stressful early years were not mollified by an easily available, soothing mother. Sarah Johnson was chronically unhappy, emotionally distant, and poorly suited for empathic responding. Nor were her deficiencies in this area counterbalanced by an empathic father. On the contrary, the unhappiness existing between his parents likely intensified his own intrapsychic misery which was already overdriven by the numerous physi-

cal problems and the resulting social stigma. Sam overdeveloped his re-
sponse-extracting skills in the effort to meet his needs, but there was not
available for him an empathic, soothing, emotionally available parent
whom he could "internalize." Consequently, he overdeveloped his own
ticquing as a means of providing "object constancy."

DISSOCIATION AND INTEGRATION

Two neonatal processes are particularly important for understanding
TS-OCD: *dissociation* and its developmental reciprocal *integration*. For the
neonate dissociation is the normal condition, and it is only through consistent "good-enough" mothering that the pieces of experience begin to
assume continuity. This is best accomplished when the parents are able
to empathically immerse themselves into their infant's experience and
so meet the infant's needs. These are at first somatic needs, but they
gradually become elaborated and symbolized—or integrated—if their intense somatic demand characteristics are consistently met in the interpersonal context of the parent–infant dyad.

Winnicott (1975) sees the infant as entering the world in an "unintegrated" state. Nurturing interactions, consistently provided by parents,
form the basis for integration:

> The tendency to integrate is helped by two sets of experience: the tech-
> nique of infant care whereby an infant is kept warm, handled and bathed
> and rocked and named, and also the acute instinctual experiences which
> tend to gather the personality together from within. Many infants are well
> on the way toward integration during certain periods of the first twenty-
> four hours of life. (Winnicott, 1975, p. 150)

Movement in the neonate is not goal directed and to that extent is first
experienced as disconnected bits and pieces. Winnicott incisively shows
that what is often termed "aggressive" is really "dissociated" or unintegrated movement:

> Prior to integration of the personality there is aggression. A baby kicks
> in the womb; it cannot be assumed that he is trying to kick his way out. A
> baby of a few weeks thrashes away with his arms; it cannot be assumed
> that he means to hit. A baby chews the nipple with his gums; it cannot be
> assumed that he is meaning to destroy or to hurt. At origin aggressive-
> ness is almost synonymous with activity; it is a matter of part-function.
> (Winnicott, 1975, p. 204)

These developmentally primitive, disconnected "aggressive" movements can lead to personality bifurcation, Winnicott notes. If the parenting ones do not accept and allow a certain amount of aggressiveness toward external objects (i.e., themselves), the infant is at risk for evolving separate lines of development for love and hate, thereby transforming others into good *or* bad, and bifurcating their own experience into good *or* bad—unintegrated—selves.

Integration is facilitated in the infant when the parenting persons achieve an optimal balance between empathic *mirroring* and *optimal frustration* (Kohut, 1977); or between what Winnicott refers to as the mother's *devotion* and *weaning*. Whatever vocabulary one prefers, the notion is that in the beginning the parent provides almost completely for the infant. However, even the most conscientious parent cannot immediately and always gratify each infantile need. Consequently, *if the frustration is not too great*, the infant will "make up the difference," thereby building inner capacities, which would not come into existence if "mini-failures" of parenting didn't occur.

Kohut echoes a similar theme of balance between gratification and frustration when he takes issue with those who might be concerned that maternal empathy can be "excessive," and that "mothering" must have its limits if children are not be become "spoiled": ". . . I do not believe that many cases of harmful maternal spoiling through overempathy and an excess of 'mothering' do in fact exist (p. 78).

Speaking of how a parent ("self-object") provides appropriate soothing when the infant is anxious, frightened, or otherwise disturbed, Kohut writes:

> The self-object then establishes tactile and/or vocal contact with the child (the mother picks up the child, talks to it while holding and carrying it) and thus creates conditions that the child phase-appropriately experiences as a merger with the omnipotent self-object. The child's rudimentary psyche participates in the self-object's highly developed psychic organization; the child experiences the feeling states of the self-object—they are transmitted to the child via touch and tone of voice and perhaps by still other means—as if they were his own. (1977, p. 86)

Such maternally-assisted "weathering" of the myriad daily crises that infants experience is crucial in fostering in the neonate a sense of continuity. However, it need not be perfect:

> These optimal failures may consist in the self-object's briefly delayed empathic response, in mild deviations from the beneficial norm of the self-object's experiences in which the child participates, or in the discrepancy between the experiences provided through the merger with the em-

pathic self-object and the actual satisfaction of needs . . . even serious re-
alistic deprivations (what one might classify as "drive" [or need]
frustrations) are not psychologically harmful if the psychological environment responds to the child with a full range of undistorted empathic responses. Man does not live by bread alone. (Kohut, 1977, p. 87)

Piaget emphasizes biological emergence and intellectual processing,
more than parent–child interactions; yet he also sees development as a
balanced interaction between *assimilation* (incorporation of the external
environment) and *accommodation* (adjustment of psychological structures to meet the pressures of the environment). The parallels to Winnicott's "good-enough" environment and Kohut's "optimal frustration"
seem apparent.

Opposing Forces

Among developmental theorists of differing perspectives there is agreement that optimal development is facilitated by a milieu of consistency
and caring; but caretakers need not be totally accommodating. Of special interest for understanding TS-OCD is Winnicott's further expansion
of this notion suggesting that *opposition* by the environment helps to
clarify boundaries between *Me* and *Not-Me*:

> In health the foetal impulses bring about a discovery of environment,
> this latter being the opposition that is met through movement, and
> sensed during movement. The result here is an early recognition of a *Not-
> Me* world, and an early establishment of the *Me*. (Winnicott, 1975, pp.
> 216, 217)

As we shall see in a later discussion the very essence of tics is muscular "pushing against." When there exists for the infant an overly "impinging" (controlling, stressful, anxiety-arousing) ambiance the normal
defining of self by "pushing against" becomes hypertrophied into the
incessant (pushing-against) muscular ticquing of TS-OCD.

Furthermore, this "pushing against" quality need not be restricted to
muscular movements. We will show how it manifests itself interpersonally in the testiness of tics and the brinkmanship of coprolalia. These
tendencies can be traced to the bifurcation of infantile needs for gratification and aggression (motility). When integration of these two basic
tendencies fails to occur, the infant or young child:

> Perceives a new setting that has some elements of reliability. . . . Stirs
> up the immediate environment in an effort to make it alert to danger, and
> organized to *tolerate nuisance*. If the situation holds, the environment must

be *tested and retested* in its capacity to stand the aggression, to prevent or repair the destruction, to *tolerate the nuisance*. . . . (Winnicott, 1975, pp. xxxii, xxxiii, italics mine)

Tics, Teddy Bears, and Transition

Winnicott is perhaps most widely known for his notion of the *transitional object*. Typically, the transitional object—seen as a concrete representation of the absent mother—is soft, pliable, warm to touch, often saturated with familiar body odors. The blanket, teddy bear, doll, rubber pacifier, even the child's own thumb (recall the primary circular reaction) can facilitate the transition from mother's soothing to self-soothing, and can help define the boundaries between Me and Not-Me. However, Winnicott understood "transition" to include much more than a concrete substitute for mother's breast. For him it began with such neonatal activities as putting the fist in the mouth, etc., and eventually ended with attachment to a teddy bear, a soft toy, or a doll.

The concreteness of the term "transitional *object*" sometimes restricts clinical understanding of the dynamic qualities of transitional phenomena. Winnicott's usage, however, is not restrictive—it includes repetitive words, tunes, etc.:

> By this definition an infant's babbling or the way an older child goes over a repertoire of songs and tunes while preparing for sleep comes within the intermediate area as transitional phenomena. . . .
>
> All these things I am calling *transitional phenomena*. Also, out of all of this (if we study any one infant) there may emerge some thing or phenomenon—perhaps a bundle of wool or the corner of a blanket or eiderdown, or a *word or tune, or a mannerism, which becomes vitally important to the infant for use at the time of going to sleep, and is a defence against anxiety, especially anxiety of the depressive type*. . . .
>
> *Patterns set in infancy may persist into childhood*, so that the original object continues to be absolutely necessary at bed-time or at times of loneliness or when a depressed mood threatens. . . . *A need for a specific object or a behaviour pattern that started at a very early date may reappear at a later age when deprivation threatens*. (Winnicott, 1975, pp. 230, 232, italics mine)

Coping with Mamma's Absence—Tics as Transition Behaviors

From the foregoing it can be seen that in addition to familiar objects, repetitive words, tunes, and behaviors can function to reduce anxiety. Thus tics and obsessive rituals may function as a "behavioral Mamma." Much like teddy bears and other soothing surrogates, they assist the infant in coping with an anxiety-permeated world when development is traumatized, or maternal availability problematic. Instead of utilizing a teddy bear, blanket, doll, or some other transitional object in the task of self-soothing, children with depleted or unresponsive mothers are at significant risk for creating their own "kinesthetic-proprioceptive Mamma" in the form of repetitive muscular movements. Such children are then at greater risk for developing TS-OCD because of the overdevelopment of self-soothing routinized movements—the core component of all tics. Additionally, such children are at risk for using repetitive words, tunes, thoughts, etc., in the same self-soothing way.

Soothing is widely recognized as essential for healthy development. The soothing style of a child's caretakers is crucial in shaping the neonate's regulatory coping mechanisms. When comfortable soothing is part of the ambience around infant and mother, when it occurs naturally, rhythmically, easily, it can be taken over (internalized) by the neonate into a pattern of comfortable self soothing. Mahler and her coworkers have collected observational data corroborating this notion.

> . . . the mother's preferred soothing or stimulating pattern is taken over, that is assimilated, by the infant in his own way and so becomes a transitional pattern, examples of which are the stroking of the face or certain *repetitious movements*. (Mahler, Pine, & Bergman, 1975, p. 55, italics mine)

What is of special interest regarding such mothering patterns is that they are especially likely to be taken over when the pattern signifies some frustration or particular gratification. Carl, for example, was frustrated when his mother warded off his clamoring for her breasts during the weaning process:

> She comforted him by bouncing him up and down in her lap. The little boy later actively took over this bouncing up and down pattern and eventually converted it into a peekaboo game. . . . Carl, even at 16 months of age, would hide behind a chair or bannister, ducking his head or crouching: suddenly he would lift his head and stand up, indicating *with sounds and grunts* that he wanted the adults to exclaim, "Here he is!" (Mahler, Pine, & Bergman, 1975, pp. 50, 51)

Another mother was observed to rock her little girl in a tense, mechanical, unrelated manner; and when it was taken over by the girl, it was not used as part of the mother–child interaction:

> *The rocking was used in this case for self-comforting and for autoerotic self-stimulation, as if the child were playing mother to herself.* . . . she indulged in prolonged rocking, rather than in active distancing or approach behaviors. (Mahler, Pine, & Bergman, 1975, p. 58, italics mine)

We note that transitional patterns (sometimes in the form of tics) may recreate the mother's flawed soothing style, occurring (a) where frustration is too great, overwhelming the ego's capacity for soothing, or (b) when gratification is so constant and excessively available that it prevents sufficient internalization of soothing responses. Either excessive deprivation or excessive gratification can cause problems—the key word is *excessive*.

If mothering is either too scanty or too smothering it prevents internalization or "taking over" of important nurturing behaviors such as feeding and soothing. If a child is to learn to self-feed or self-soothe, he must experience what Kohut (1977) refers to as "optimal frustration." This means that even in cases of "good enough" mothering, there will be times the infant is not immediately nurtured by the parent. If the deprivation is not too great, the infant will eventually learn to take over—to "tie his own shoes." Most TS-OCD children lack good self-soothing abilities and rely on tics and other rhythmic body motions to simultaneously comfort and distract themselves when confronted with anxiety.

Psychological extremes are invariably disruptive to development. I'm reminded of a 10-year-old boy who was physically abused by his father (whom his mother then divorced) from ages two until four. Soon after this, the mother, wanting to "make up" for all the trauma the child had experienced, routinely allowed him to sleep in bed with her until he was 10 years of age. At that time, however, he required inpatient psychiatric treatment for problems due to the sexual overstimulation he felt as a consequence of this inappropriate closeness with his mother and his rage at her recent remarriage. In such instances it is difficult to say which trauma—the abuse or the overgratification—was damaging to the developing child. My experience has been that most children with TS-OCD develop the symptoms in a context of deprivation rather than excessive stimulation.

CASE STUDY: "WHERE HAS MY DADDY GONE?"

Tracy weighed five pounds at birth and her mother reports, "It was a horrible pregnancy—I was sick the entire nine months!" At six weeks, Tracy was hospitalized because she couldn't keep her formula down. She walked at about nine months and talked at one year.

Parents Divorce

When she was two-and-a-half years old, her parents divorced. Tracy's mother graphically described the emotional closeness between father and daughter: "She was like his own arm." After the divorce Tracy saw her father about once a week for 6 months until he relocated to another part of the country, after which she seldom saw him again.

Tics Begin

Shortly thereafter Tracy began blinking her eyes, twitching her face, and making noises. Because one of her tics was incessantly clearing her throat, she was hospitalized for adenoid removal. Tracy recalls being "torn from Mom's arms" at the time of the surgery. Not surprisingly, the noises and tics worsened and, after seeing various nose and throat specialists, she was taken to a large children's hospital where she was diagnosed as having TS. Tracy was six at the time. She was medicated with Haldol® until she was about 10 years old when it was discontinued because of breathing difficulties resulting from excessive weight gain from the drug. She was 15 when I first saw her.

Drugs and "Strait Jackets"

She described her tics as "mostly grunts, 'chirping'—like a 'birdy,' dog barking, and scratching." She also chewed her tongue and inner mouth. Her most noticeable behaviors during the interview were eyeblinking, chirping, and chewing. Her medical chart also revealed some very severe episodes that were worsened by attempts to constrict her.

Tracy was hospitalized on an adolescent psychiatric unit because her behavior at home had degenerated in response to her mother's boyfriend. This man, who lived in the home with Tracy and her mother, was described by Tracy as ". . . a very nervous person, who yells and screams at Mom." Amidst the emotional intensity of domestic strife, Tracy would often shake (tic). Her mother described an episode just prior to hospitalization: "Tracy shook for 6 hours. We finally took her to the emergency room."

The staff were puzzled by the shaking, not certain it was TS, but after confirming the diagnosis with the children's hospital where Tracy had been admitted at 6 years old, they prescribed Haldol and released her. All was not well however, and a few days later she exhibited other regressive behavior. At school it was reported that she was "babbling like an infant—seeming to say anything that came into her mind." This behavior continued on the ride home from school and the bus driver was so concerned that he later called Tracy's mother to report it. Meanwhile Tracy went to a friend's house where the infantile behavior continued until her mom arrived and took her home. The next morning Tracy awoke and began stuttering severely. She attended school the next day in spite of her erratic behaviors. According to her mother, "About three days later her arm started shaking, and I took her to the hospital where they did more CT scans on her, and admitted her to the children's unit."

Constriction and Confusion

Her mother visited the hospital Thursday through Sunday. After her mother left on Sunday, Tracy would behave aggressively and her TS-OCD symptoms would become more severe—so severe that the hospital personnel usually put her in restraints. This served to make things even worse, but the staff felt they had to do this in order to "keep her from hurting herself." Typically these episodes raged on through the weekend, exhausting Tracy as well as the staff.

Putting Tracy in restraints was one of the most iatrogenic treatments that could have been carried out. Most persons with TS-OCD suffer from an "anticlaustrophobic" drive to be free, and restraints only make the attempts to reassure oneself on that account more violent. Putting someone with TS in restraints is like putting an acrophobic atop a swaying radio tower in a strong wind. When I asked Tracy if she was claustrophobic she replied: "Yeah, when I was in the hospital, they put me in restraints a lot, and it was very scary—I was in them a lot."

Tracy's case illustrates the confusion and mishandling that so often occurs with TS patients when medical personnel operate without benefit of a developmental paradigm. In addition to the ridicule and misunderstanding she suffered at school from her peers, the CT scans, surgeries, and restraints she encountered in hospital settings only served to iatrogenically intensify her problems. Coherent treatment can only be provided when the developmental roots and object relational dynamics of tics are clearly understood.

Abandonment—Tracy's Chronic Worry

Abandonment is a principal theme in Tracy's life. Recall that she first started blinking her eyes and making noises when her father left home. Think of how traumatic it might be for a toddler of thirty months to suddenly be without the presence of Daddy—especially when her emotional closeness to him had been intense—"like his arm." Soon afterwards, she again experienced separation trauma when she was "torn from her mother's arms" and whisked off to surgery.

During adolescence, the violent arguments between her mother and the mother's live-in boyfriend raised the specter of "divorce," most likely replicating many of the conditions existing at the time her father left, and causing deterioration in her tenuous adjustment. When she was hospitalized and put in restraints, her anxieties intensified. Just prior to the hospitalization, her mother had announced plans to relocate from their home in the Midwest to California. She and Tracy had taken a plane trip to California, and during the trip, Tracy had become very ill with anxiety and dry heaves. Upon returning home, Tracy became very depressed, withdrawn, and openly expressive of suicidal intentions. Alarmed, her mother insisted she go into the hospital.

It's noteworthy, that even her adolescent responses to stress replicated her earliest problems. Recall that at six weeks she was hospitalized because she couldn't keep formula down; and recently when confronted with the stressful situation of flying to another part of the country prior to moving, she became anxious and had "dry heaves."

If one looks beyond Tracy's adolescent "chirpings" to the origins of her symptoms, there is support for the notion that tics may function as *transitional* behaviors. When, as a two-and-a-half year old, Tracy was abandoned by her father, she did not possess the cognitive or emotional capacity to cope with such massive trauma. The fact that Tracy's separation from her father occurred as a consequence of divorce, means there was probably stress and anxiety between her parents during the months preceding the actual breakup.

Tracy's early existence—even within the uterus—was permeated with stress. Mother described her pregnancy with Tracy as "terrible," and within a month and a half of birth, Tracy was hospitalized for failing to "keep formula down." Clinicians recognize "terrible" pregnancies and digestive problems as clear signals of excessive stress.

From an object-relations perspective, Tracy's early hospitalization must have been extremely traumatic. We've seen that under optimal conditions, maternal–infant bonding begins immediately following birth, with mother and neonate participating in rhythmic cycles of alertness and sleep, eating and elimination, crying and laughter, anxiety and soothing. Although it is unlikely that Tracy experienced many of these comforting cycles, even her stress-permeated home would likely have been more stable than a hospital. A one-week hospitalization—typically traumatic even for adults—constituted one sixth of Tracy's entire life up to that time! Interrupting the tenuous, problematic bonding with her mother at such an early age could only have exacerbated Tracy's abandonment anxieties and intensified her needs for soothing.

Tracy corroborated the centrality of abandonment anxiety in her life. When I asked her what kinds of situations made her tics worse she replied: "Whenever they left." She blinked her eyes more intensely as she told me, "When Mom left [the hospital after Sunday visits] it was really bad."

When I asked her how she felt about her parents' divorce she spoke with despair in her voice: "I feel like he [Dad] didn't want me. Like he was going away because he didn't want me. Nobody wants me—I'm not good enough."

Tics Instead of Nipples and Teddy Bears

Tracy's case tragically illustrates how toddlers turn to tics for comfort. It is difficult to retrospectively assign "weights" to the various object-relational trauma she experienced early in life, but it's reasonable to infer that from the earliest stress-saturated days of her existence, abandonment was a central concern.

When she was hospitalized at 3 years old, it likely resonated with the trauma of her hospitalization at 6 weeks of age. Although it can't be documented, I suspect the usual primary circular reactions (occurring 0–4 months) were likely engaged in the service of self-soothing. It *can* be documented, however, that soon after her father left, Tracy's TS-OCD symptoms erupted with such intensity that even casual observers were alarmed. Not having experienced consistent maternal soothing as an infant, she had no internal resources for self-soothing and now turned to her musculature.

The surgical procedure (adenoid removal) intended to ameliorate the problem iatrogenically intensified the anxieties. There were likely many worries on this little toddler's mind at the time she was "torn from Mom's arms," for hospitalization, but abandonment must have been primary. If during infancy one learns that soothing breasts, nurturing nipples, and comforting cradling will be only sporadically available, it is easy to turn to eyeblinking, tongue chewing, or chirping to comfort oneself. Such behaviors might not be as satisfying, but they are consistently available. You might misplace your blanket or teddy bear, but comfort is "only a tic away."

THE NEED FOR DIFFERENTIATION AND DISCHARGE: EXPLOSION AND ERUPTION DURING THE EARLY MONTHS

It may seem farfetched to speak of a "need" for explosiveness, but the inside-to-out erupting quality of most tics has roots in the earliest months of infancy. The explosive, jerking nature of tics provides instant discharge. And as everyone utilizing such behaviors knows, the amount of "satisfaction" obtained is directly related to how much resistance the discharge "breaks through," that is, how *explosive* the movement. Reverberated in the ticquing of the child or adult is the neonate's *pushing against*, described by Winnicott and referred to in our earlier discussion.

The Somatic Self Normally Shifts Outward

It has already been noted that the neonates's first experiences occur in the context of the mother–infant dyad. The "Mommy-and-I-Are-One" feeling is the quintessence of healthy bonding. Early interpersonal processes are experienced in an undifferentiated way—occur in a context of blurred mother–infant boundaries. They include the circularly comforting processes inhaling and exhaling, drinking and burping, eating and eliminating. Although these are not initially experienced as differentiated behaviors, about the time primary circular reactions give way to secondary circular reactions (fourth month), the infant begins to turn outward. Mahler and coworkers suggest that the infant's sense of self is initially crystallized around a core of inner sensations. As development proceeds, this moves outward: "From the standpoint of the body image, *the shift of predominantly proprioceptive-interoceptive cathexis toward sensoriperceptive cathexis of the periphery* is a major step in development" (1975, p. 46).

Freud referred to such sensoriperceptive awareness as the "peripheral rind of the ego," Winnicott refers to the importance of "pushing against," and we relate this to the origin of motor tics.

Tics as an Explosive Shift Outward

Tics can be understood as hypertrophied normal processes. In ordinary development there is a smooth progression of sensate awareness from the inner, central body sensations to outer, peripheral regions. The sense of "self" begins to "move out" of the body—or at least to the peripheral regions. Motor or vocal tics are an explosive, intensification of normal inside-to-out behaviors. Tics typically explode from within with only slightly more refinement than seen in neonatal belching, flatulence, crying, kicking, etc. Such behaviors in the neonate help to differentiate the nascent self as different from the mother. Furthermore, as sensations move from the center to the periphery—whether they are caused by feces, flatulence, belches, sneezes, or tics—they provide the developing self with boundary differentiation and an anchoring within the skin.

For a person with TS-OCD a tic is satisfying because it pushes through resistance which suddenly gives way, thus allowing an explosive outburst. The satisfaction is directly related to the resistance. A person who violently sneezes after several abortive false starts feels a sense of relief and satisfaction. This is similar to the experience of ticquing. Motor tics involve pushing through tensed antagonistic muscle groups, and thus increasing the richness and intensity of proprioceptive feedback.

Consistent with the developmental need to differentially move from the center to the periphery, most tics have a "bolus of awareness" which moves from some central location to a peripheral expression in some extensor muscle group. Whether tics are in the form of explosive sounds or movements, they typically originate from within and find relief by explosively moving outward—preferably through several layers of resistant muscle groups.

Like the stutterer, who *appears* to be courageously struggling against a "blocked" vocal apparatus, the person with TS-OCD also sets up barriers through which the discharge must pass to finally erupt at a peripheral location. Both stutterers and persons experiencing TS-OCD derive a soothing relief immediately following a breakout in the form of a tic or stutter. This is why persons with TS-OCD or stutterers are *not* usually affected while singing. The act of singing—with the diaphragm pushing air past tensed vocal cords—replicates the subjective experience of ticquing or stuttering; albeit in a smooth, nonexplosive fashion. There is the inside-to-out movement of a "bolus of awareness" as the notes and words move from within the body to the outside in a forceful manner.

CASE ILLUSTRATION: MENNONITES TIC OR SING

It is important to note that it is either tic *or* sing, there is no need for both. Similarly, stutterers stutter *or* sing. Oliver Sacks visited a community of Mennonites where the incidence of TS is extraordinarily high, and made the following observations while attending a family reunion:

> Baking and preparation of food had been going on for days. The village hall had been reserved for the day and was festooned with banners and bunting, and most movingly decorated with photos of Grandma and her ancestors. . . . Inside, the rafters rang with a joyous Tourettic riot. The ex-

uberance of the young was sometimes hard to distinguish from the yelping of the elders. Wandering among them, I could see ripples, waves,
strange concentrations and sometimes whole fields of tics—perhaps a
third, to my estimation had the condition to some degree.

But just as one person's sudden outbursts would set off everybody else
at the table, sometimes there would be a sympathy of calmness, where
the singleness of focus would bring a whole group into a beautiful ticless
calm. One saw then what I have sometimes regarded as the other side of
Tourette's, the exceptional power of attention and concentration that can
allow some Touretters to become watchmakers and craftsmen, to perform
minute and exacting tasks that one would think would be made absolutely impossible by their excited ticcy states.

After they ate, a mood of thanksgiving came over the Janzens and this
was expressed, as always, in religious singing. First English hymns and
songs—"Shall we gather at the river" and "God be with you till we meet
again." Then they went to the old German songbook, the *Gesangbuch*,
which is almost unchanged since the 18th century, to sing the songs that
united them not only with one another and their God, but also with their
four-century-old history. Their favorite song was *"Wo willst du hin weil's
abend ist?"* (Where do you wish to go when evening comes?) *The ticcing
and grimacing that had been so prominent before entirely disappeared as they sang
in unison.* (Sacks, 1988, p. 102, italics mine)

SUMMARY OF THE FIRST YEAR OF LIFE

We have discussed a number of apparently disparate needs, dating to
the earliest hours of neonatal life. We've suggested that although tics
and repetitive thoughts typically appear later at about the sixth year,
closer examination reveals them to be "piggybacked" on the earliest
needs of infancy.

If the effort to developmentally trace the metamorphosis from early
needs to tics seems at times contrived, it is because during the early
days of development nothing is simple or distinct. The various needs
that we've discussed do *not* occur as discrete, discriminable urges,
rather, they *jointly* constitute the developmental matrix out of which all
later maturation flows. Early development occurs along the many dimensions of the somatically permeated maternal–child dyad.

During usual development, when the maternal side of this dyad is
reasonably adequate, early needs are satisfied as a result of "good-
enough" mothering. The intensity of the needs is diminished, and the
infant begins to "internalize" appropriate soothing behaviors as his/her
own. Under usual circumstances the risk of compulsive repetitiveness is

greatly reduced by empathically-attuned, consistently-available maternal responsiveness. While normal residues of such needs remain throughout life (most adults experience pleasure in being hugged, held, stroked, or fondled by a significant other), their intensity is appropriately attenuated, and the behaviors through which these needs are fulfilled become refined and socially appropriate.

In an early environment rich with responsiveness, needs for attention are not likely to become obsessive lifelong pursuits. Concomitantly, the rhythmic buildup and discharge of anxiety or tension becomes integrated into smoothly functioning, comfortably internalized, patterns of behavior. Soothing that is easily and naturally provided by parents soon becomes a taken for granted part of the ambience, neither attenuated in richness nor hypertrophied in intensity.

THE EXPANSIVE, EXHIBITIONISTIC TODDLER: 12 TO 18 MONTHS

As discussed earlier, the way in which an infant's needs are accommodated or frustrated during the first year of life profoundly influences the probabilities of developing—or not developing—TS-OCD. The second year is also critical, because it is during this time that most toddlers begin to turn from the rhythmic movements and somatic preoccupations of the earliest months to symbolic representations and cognitive operations in their rapidly expanding worlds. Although most children make this transition easily, others remain fixated at earlier levels of coping and routinize early repetitive behaviors into enduring tics. In this chapter we will look at some of the reasons behind the failed transitions that result in TS-OCD.

The Need for Expansive Movement

Optimally, developing infants enter the first half of the second year with an eagerness and energy that will likely never be surpassed in their lifetimes. Much of this enthusiasm and expansiveness finds expression in their newly developed skill of walking—quite an accomplishment really. One that quite literally allows them to see the world differently and to make the first great strides toward identity formation:

> The importance of walking for the emotional development of the child cannot be overestimated. Walking gives the toddler an enormous increase

in reality discovery and testing of the world at his own control and magic mastery. . . . We found in boys and girls alike that in the very next month following the attainment of active free locomotion, great strides were made toward asserting their individuality. This seems to be the first great step toward identity formation. (Mahler, Pine, & Bergman, 1975, p. 72)

The toddler's irrepressible expansiveness, newly empowered by loco-motor skills, typically leads to conflict with either Mom or Dad in the latter half of the second year, but during the first half caretakers and infants still enjoy the exhilaration accompanying walking.

The Need for Exhibition

The 12 to 18-month-old toddler is an enthusiastic exhibitionist. It is not enough that he or she can walk, climb, or build a tower of blocks; it is important that either Mommy or Daddy notice and exclaim. Exhibition serves the purpose of extracting responses from Mother which remains almost as important for the toddler as it was for the neonate. It is at this age that the term "emotional refueling" (Furer, 1964) is most apt. Maternal mirroring is actively sought and if it is not easily available leads to what Mahler and co-workers have described as "coercive refueling." This is the *active* response to lack of maternal response. Other children may withdraw and become depressed.

Children with TS-OCD are expert at coercive refueling. Ticquing, touching, making noise, and many other TS-OCD symptoms are coercively attention getting—likely having origins in the second year of life when the toddler develops behaviors to coercively refuel.

CASE ILLUSTRATION: THE TSAR WHO COULDN'T SIT STILL

The lifelong maintenance of the toddler's irrepressible expansiveness, energy, and movement—retained in tics—is well illustrated in the life of Peter the Great, seventeenth-century Tsar of Russia. Few could have guessed what far-reaching effects the birth of this incessantly active child would have on Russia. Named, fittingly, for the impetuous apostle, Peter would have approved of Moscow's celebration of his birth. Cannon thundered and sixteen hundred church bells pealed continuously for three days. An appropriate greeting for one who would retain a lifelong love affair with things explosive and noisy.

Suffocating Luxury

From his first moments of life Peter was surrounded by suffocating luxury accorded only prized children of Muscovite royalty. Cloistered behind walls hung with deep red fabrics, wearing clothing of silk, satin, or velvet, his every wish was immediately met by one of the many servants assigned to care for him.

> The little we know of Peter's earliest years suggests that he enjoyed an intense version of ideal Russian childhood, a world of softness, indulgence at the hands of women and an almost stifling physical and emotional warmth. The baby is watched over by a bevy of adoring ladies whose whole life seems dedicated to its comfort and well-being and the avoidance of anything remotely approximating a draught. . . . Peter's early childhood appears to have been a time of stifling luxury if we are to judge by the objects which then surrounded him. His cradle was a blend of magnificence and softness, the perfect symbol of an overheated royal nursery world. It was covered with Turkish velvet, upholstered in yellow cloth, with straps trimmed in red Venetian velvet. Its eiderdown was edged with gold, as was the pillow, which might have been uncomfortable and indeed would have exposed the newly born Peter to possible suffocation. . . .
>
> In short Peter was born into a soft, indolent and magnificent old Russia, utterly foreign to his temperament. One might even suppose that these childhood surroundings actually aggravated what they were designed to soothe. (de Jonge, 1980, pp. 38–39)

Noisy and active, Peter grew rapidly—walking at seven months. He had everything a child could want. As a two-year-old his retinue included fourteen women, a staff of dwarfs specially trained to act as playmates and servants, and numerous other attendants. During his third year his father ordered several large court carriages, similar to those used by other European monarchs. The chief minister promptly ordered miniature copies of these carriages for Peter. Thereafter a favorite sight at public occasions was the sight of curly headed Peter riding in this carriage drawn by four dwarf ponies with four dwarfs riding at the side and another behind.

Although his toys included elegant creations from all parts of the world—a carved wooden horse with leather saddle, an illuminated picture book, music boxes from Germany—the rambunctious toddler, had little interest in such "quiet" toys, preferring instead to bang on drums and cymbals or to play with pistols and pike. We see in Peter the toddler the same noisy, irrepressible energy that characterized Peter the Tsar.

For example, in his early twenties he visited Frederick III of Brandenberg. Peter discussed ships, guns, and navigation. Thereafter the two rulers went hunting and together watched a fight between two bears. Peter later astonished his hosts by loudly playing drums and a trumpet. In general, his liveliness and curiosity made a favorable impression on them.

Thus we find the explosive, active Peter—whether 24 months old or 24 years old—enthusiastically playing with ships, guns, or drums. Throughout his life he never had the patience to be waited upon, much preferring to expend his irrepressible energy directly.

> His most extraordinary quality, even more remarkable than his height, was his titanic energy. He could not sit still or stay long in the same place. He walked so quickly with his long, loose-limbed stride that those in his company had to trot to keep up with him. When forced to do paperwork, he paced around a stand-up desk. Seated at a banquet, he would eat for a few minutes, then spring up to see what was happening in the next room or to take a walk outdoors. Needing movement, he liked to burn off his energy in dancing. When he had been in one place for a while, he wanted to leave, to move along, to see new people and new scenery, to form new impressions. The most accurate picture of Peter the Great is of a man who throughout his life was perpetually curious, perpetually restless, perpetually in movement. (Massie, 1980, p. 134)

Peter's Tics

In view of Peter's life-threatening encounters with the Strelsty (palace soldiers) during childhood and adolescence, it's not surprising that during his early twenties he manifested symptoms of Tourette Syndrome with enough intensity to attract the comment of historians. Most likely he experienced mild tics before his twenties, but it was during early adulthood that an exacerbation of symptoms occurred. Whenever he was under stress or agitated Peter's face would begin to twitch:

> The disorder, usually troubling only the left side of his face, varied in degree of severity. . . . If the convulsion became more pronounced, his friends or orderlies quickly brought someone to him whose presence he found relaxing. (Massie, 1980, pp. 134–136)

The Nature of Peter's Tics

Although historians have typically described Peter's "convulsions" as epileptic in nature, behavioral descriptions of his condition are more consistent with a diagnosis of Tourette Syndrome. There is no historical evidence that Peter collapsed—totally unconscious—on the floor, foamed at the mouth, or lost control of his bodily functions. Historically based retroactive diagnosis may seem tenuous, but there is a basis upon which seizure disorder can be ruled out—duration.

Epileptic seizures—of whatever variety—are characteristically short in duration. Grand mal seizures typically last 2 to 5 minutes, petit mal attacks 1 to 30 seconds, psychomotor attacks 1 to 2 minutes, and infantile spasms last only a few seconds. Furthermore, epileptic seizures have a clearly definable onset and offset. Typical Grand mal seizures are characterized by a cry, loss of consciousness, falling, tonic, and clonic contractions of the muscles of the extremities, trunk, and head. Urinary and fecal incontinence may occur. The less severe conditions do not usually result in loss of consciousness or bladder or bowel control but there is always an altered state of consciousness. In the case of petit mal attacks, for example, there is a clouding of consciousness with or without loss of muscle tone. The person usually suddenly stops any activity being carried out, and then resumes it when the attack is over. This kind of attack may occur several or many times a day. A person experiencing a psychomotor attack usually does not fall, but may stagger while performing automatic, purposeless movements and making unintelligible sounds. In all instances of genuine seizure, the attack is brief—lasting a few seconds or a few minutes—with a precise onset and clearly deviant behaviors during the attack. None of these conditions are met by Peter's "attacks," which were more omnipresent and integrated with his normal activities.

Various theories circulated as to what caused his "convulsions," one of the most popular being that Sophia, his half sister, had tried to poison him in order to secure the throne for herself. Cardinal Kollonitz, the Primate of Hungary, embraced such a theory in his description of Peter's tics:

> His left eye, his left arm and left leg were injured by the poison given him during the life of his brother; but there remains of this now only a fixed look in his eye and a *constant movement of his arm and leg*. To hide this, he accompanies this involuntary motion with *continual movements of his entire body*. . . . (Massie, p. 224, italics mine)

On the occasion of a visit with Sophia, Electress of Brandenburg, and her daughter, Sophia Charlotte, Peter was unprepared to meet such aristocratic Western ladies, and when ushered into their presence, he faltered, was unable to speak, and blushed. He covered his face and muttered in German, "I don't know what to say." However, these poised and elegant ladies soon charmed Peter out of his debilitating shyness and the evening was a grand success.

"He has a natural, unconstrained air which pleased me," wrote Sophia Charlotte. His grimaces and facial contortions were not as bad as they had expected and, Sophia Charlotte added sympathetically, "Some are not in his power to correct." (Massie, 1980 pp. 176, 177)

The Restless Tourist

At the age of forty-five Peter saw Paris for the first time. As was typical, he flung himself headlong into the visit—determined to get the most out of it. He began sightseeing by rising at 4:00 A.M. and walking by the light of dawn down the Rue St. Antoine to visit the Palace Royale. His entire visit was conducted at such a frenetic pace that Marshal de Tessé and the eight body guards assigned him experienced little success in their efforts to keep up with him. His every action seemed to them impetuous and his disdain for ceremony astonished the French. The ever-impatient Peter, wanting to be free to come and go on his own terms, often took a rented carriage or even a hackney cab instead of waiting for the royal carriage assigned him.

What is common in these accounts is the fact that Peter's tics were a part of his daily life—embedded in his incessant activity—hardly noticed by his daily companions, but more in evidence when he was with strangers or meeting foreign dignitaries. We can learn much about the malady by studying the cure:

> Better than anyone else, Catherine could deal with Peter's convulsive fits. When the first symptoms of these attacks appeared, the Tsar's attendants would run for Catherine, who would come at once and firmly lay him down, take his head in her lap and gently stroke his hair and temples; until the convulsions abated and he fell asleep. While he slept, she would sit silently for hours, cradling his head, soothingly stroking it when he stirred. Peter always awakened refreshed. But his need for her went far deeper than mere nursing. Her qualities of mind and heart were such that she was able not only to soothe him, play with him, love him, but also to take part in his inner life, to talk to him about serious things, to discuss his views and projects, to encourage his hopes and aspirations. Not only did her presence comfort him, but her conversation cheered him and gave him balance. (Massie, p. 376)

Clearly, these tics—so much a part of Peter's life—seemed to observers both pervasive and mild, otherwise they wouldn't have suggested that they occurred "especially when he did not take care to control it," or regarding his facial grimaces, "they are not in his power to correct." Tics were a part of his life to the end: "His previous disorder still afflicted him, the tremors still shook his giant but weakening frame, and only Catherine, taking his head in her lap, could bring him peace" (Massie, p. 841).

In summary, Peter's adult life retained, almost unchanged, the expansive energy of the twelve-to-eighteen-month-old. Whether toddler or tsar, Peter was irrepressible.

THE AMBITENDENT TODDLER: 18 TO 24 MONTHS

Ambitendency Defined

Mahler and coworkers define ambitendency as:

> The simultaneous presence of two contrasting, behaviorally manifest tendencies; for example, a child may cry and smile virtually at the same time, approach mother and at the last minute veer away, or kiss mother and then suddenly bite her. Ambitendency is behaviorally biphasic. (1975, p. 289)

Another way of saying this is that ambitendency is the behavioral side of ambivalence. It is observable back-and-forth behavior. Mahler et al. suggest that it is replaced in later development by an internal, conflicted mental state—a kind of approach-avoidance conflict:

> Conflict is first acted out, that is to say, indicated by coercive behavior directed toward the mother, designed to force her to function as the child's omnipotent extension; these alternate with signs of desperate clinging. . . . These alternating behaviors are the ingredients of the phenomena we designate as "ambitendency"—that is, as long as the contrasting tendencies are not yet fully internalized. (Mahler et al., 1975, pp. 107–110)

In the present discussion ambitendency will figure importantly in our understanding of TS-OCD. Tics are prime examples of ambitendency. Tics are *behavioral* manifestations of behaviors that are simultaneously attention seeking and repelling. In higher level TS-OCD manifestations (e.g., coprolalia, touching, echolalia, etc.), there is an additional interpersonal component present. In summary, persons with TS-OCD *ambivalently* think and *ambitendently* act in ways that both attract and repulse others.

"Fart-and-Apologize"

Brian was a ten-year-old boy with TS-OCD whom I'd seen in therapy for several months. As therapy progressed he became quite friendly and enthusiastically participated in the sessions. Frequently, however, as we talked and engaged in some play therapy activities together, Brian would pass flatus, look quickly at me, and immediately say, "Sorry John!"

This sort of "fart-and-apologize" ambitendency is at the core of most TS-OCD experiences. When severe stresses occur early in infancy, the developmental "freezing" is likely to result in ambitendent *motor* tics. Trauma experienced later in development is likely to be experienced as *cognitive* ambivalence (obsessiveness). Individuals chronically exposed to extreme stress sometimes develop *both* somatic and cognitive coping mechanisms. Samuel Johnson (see pp. 000–000) is one such person whose tics and obsessions included a wide variety of somatic and cognitive components. In later chapters we will discuss other persons who utilize multiple tics and obsessions, and (not surprisingly) discover that these persons had particularly chronic and torturous infancies and childhoods.

Eighteen Months: An Important Watershed

The middle of the second year is like a developmental continental divide. Numerous developmental experts have seen this as a difficult and important crossroads in development. It is a time when the toddler begins to seriously deal with autonomy and control issues. For the first time he/she recognizes that the ability to control the parent is not automatic. As Mahler, Pine, and Bergman write:

> He must gradually and painfully give up the delusion of his own grandeur often by way of dramatic fights with mother—less so, it seemed to us, with father. This is the crossroads that we term the "rapprochement crisis." (Mahler et al., p. 79)

With a slightly different perspective, Lichtenberg sees 18 months of age as a crucial developmental time:

> *The firm foundation of the toddler's self-as-a-whole—potent enough to emerge more fully from restrictive aspects of the interactional matrix, and powerful enough to restructure a sustaining relationship with the caretaker—derives, I believe, from the impetus of a series of maturational and developmental advances that enrich the toddler's life at about 18 months. (1983, p. 120)*

Blanck and Blanck see 18 months as so crucial that they refer to this time period as a "fulcrum" around which development pivots and develop a diagnostic framework they call "The Fulcrum of Development" (1979, p. 72).

This is a decisive time in the development of TS-OCD. Almost imperceptibly the very accomplishments that were a joy both to mother and toddler (walking, talking, curiously "grabbing" things) become arenas for autonomy struggles. Usually this upsurge of autonomy allows the toddler to escape what Lichtenberg calls the "restrictive aspects of the interactional matrix." However, for infants and children who develop TS-OCD, such autonomy sometimes recycles as endless struggles with their mothers.

Parens (1979) describes an interaction between Mary, one of the children in his study, and her mother:

> When Mrs. W. brought Mary back from the hall, the first few times Mary smiled and permitted herself to be passively returned to the Infant Area. But then progressively she complained more vigorously, vocally, bodily contorting to extricate herself, and eventually she cried angrily, waved her left arm in a striking movement against her mother several times and kicked her, at first from a distance but twice actually struck her mother with her arm. Once she also struck herself. (Parens, 1979, p. 403)
>
> In a subsequent conflictual interaction: Mary is crying angrily in mother's arms, she seems to want to get out of those arms; mother puts her down gently, without observable rejection, and Mary cries even more loudly and angrily. Mother cannot hold her and cannot put her down.
>
> We assumed that the conflict between child and mother, an *interpersonal* conflict, led to the emergence of an *intrapsychic* conflict in the child. When Mary's strivings for autonomy were thwarted by her mother, she experienced progressively mounting hostile feelings toward her frustrating mother. This state of unpleasure, however, led the child to need comforting from the gratifying good mother, and Mary, crying and angry, turned for comforting to this same mother toward whom her hostile feelings were directed. (Parens, 1979. p. 403)

Tics are Ambitendent Behavior

At about 18 months autonomy is pronounced and interpersonal conflict high—even in optimally developing toddlers. In some toddlers interpersonal conflict becomes somatically routinized in the form of tics or cognitively routinized as obsessions. A tic is a behavioral vehicle for interpersonal conflict, while an obsession is a mental vehicle for conflict.

Parens unwittingly but *precisely* describes the dynamics of TS-OCD when he writes:

> *The pressure from within often seems to propel the child in exactly the direction prohibited by mother.* There the child usually encounters persisting opposi-

tion from mother, which in turn engenders further hostile feelings toward her. (1979, p. 406, italics mine)

This observation, coming from a careful observer of maternal–child interactions, is quite remarkable—especially since he was not writing about TS-OCD. Nonetheless he precisely describes the core experience of TS: *precisely what is proscribed becomes obligatory.* Understood in this way it can be seen that tics and obsessions somatize and preserve these early interpersonal conflicts.

"Tape My Mouth!"

The mother of a teenaged boy with TS-OCD confided to me that her son had recently begged her to tape his mouth shut. He was traveling to the Washington, D.C. area for clinical studies at NIMH and was certain that once on the plane he would yell "Hijack!" This is the adult version of the toddler's thrust in "exactly the direction prohibited by mother," because "Hijack!" is the very worst thing you can yell on a plane. This same individual would not yell "Hijack!" in church because it's not the most highly prohibited outburst. In church he would likely to yell something blasphemous or antireligious. More will be said about this when we discuss brinkmanship in the chapter on coprolalia, but for the present it's noteworthy that TS-OCD always pushes the person in precisely the direction proscribed—with such incredible exactness that individuals feel compelled to yell "Hijack!" in an airplane, and "Fuck!" in church, but not vice versa.

TS-OCD: The Manifestation of Chronic Ambitendency and Ambivalence

From an object-relations perspective, the tics of TS and obsessions of OCD are expressions of ambitendency and ambivalence. Whether this ambitendency turns out to be temporary (transient tic) or chronic (TS) depends primarily on where in the developmental sequence stress became overwhelming enough to delay further development.

Persons with TS-OCD ambitendently (behaviorally) or ambivalently (cognitively) reverberate earlier conflicts. They have never adequately resolved the conflicts surrounding the fulfillment of early needs. When a parent chides an adolescent to, "Quit acting like a two-year-old!" there is more etiological wisdom contained in that statement than either realizes. This is especially true of the shift from the self of action to the self of contemplation. When the maternal–infant dyad is permeated with conflict, or when there is excessive stress in the general environment, the transition from ambitendent motoric behavior to contemplative cognitions may be seriously disrupted.

The ambitendent person remains somatically entrapped. He functions more in body than in mind; more in the intensity of the maternal orbit than in the socially larger context. This developmentally flawed pattern is broad, extending over a variety of TS-OCD patterns, although, as we've pointed out earlier, TS tends to be the motoric end of the spectrum, coprolalia in the middle, and the obsessions of OCD at the more developmentally mature cognitive pole.

Developing Self

At about 18 months of age, Lichtenberg sees the sense of self becoming more refined and less somatic:

> The emergent property of self that appears in the middle of the second year is that of the self-as-a-whole as mental "director." Another way of expressing what I mean by "mental self" is to say that a shift occurs from the self as doer in an *action* sense, to the self being and doing *subjectively*. If we look at the picture with the caregiver, there is a beginning shift from *interaction* to *intersubjectivity*.
>
> The self as the source of contemplation, in comparison to the self in an action response, places a conceptual distance that further differentiates the sense of self. (1983, pp. 116, 117)

Although motoric and contemplative selves coexist for most persons throughout their life spans, as the infant begins to mature, there is rapid development and differentiation, with the contemplative self playing an increasingly significant role in shaping a person's experience.

FROM "JE BOUGE" TO "JE PENSE"—BIFURCATED DEVELOPMENT OF THE SELF IN TS-OCD

In discussing the notion of self-as-director, Lichtenburg uses an interesting illustration:

> A patient who has been in insulin coma treatment gradually arouses. At first he blinks and rolls his eyes and makes rhythmical movements with his mouth. Then he is able to respond, robotlike, to seeing the glass of sugared juice and to instructions to drink. After a bit, often in baby

talk, he indicates a "Me want"—taking increasing control of the coming-to process. (p. 117)

Most persons have a similar experience upon awakening in the morning. There is a gradual awareness that another day is about to begin, stretching, yawning, and other body-awareness maneuvers follow in unhurried succession.

Persons with TS-OCD have the opposite experience. As sleep quickly fades, there is a brief period of feeling calm, relaxed. Very soon however, the body "takes possession" of the mind. By a cruel irony he/she is awakening *to* instead of *from* a nightmare—the nightmare of living a life punctuated by intense muscular movements, high-pitched sounds, unwanted thoughts, ridicule, and shame. Unlike Descartes who said "*Je pense, donc je suis*" (I think, therefore I am), the person with TS says "*Je bouge, donc je suis*" (I move, therefore I am).

A number of theorists (e.g., Nicolich, 1977; Holt, 1967; Noy, 1979) have noted two developmental paths for the symbolic representation of experience—parallel tracks whose functions are interrelated. One track is primarily sensory (sounds, sights, tactile sensations, etc.); the other is built around rules of syntax, word order, symbolic representations, etc. When a toddler begins to speak of a "hammer" instead of a "boom-boom" or a "dog" instead of a "bow-wow" the shift from sensational to symbolic has occurred. Developmentally, this is a giant leap from the experiential self to the conceptual self. Healthy growth depends on balance between these two tracks.

As normal development takes the neonate from infancy and toddlerhood to teenage and adult years, there develops a comfortable collaterality—a balanced integration of body and mind. However when stress occurs with overwhelming intensity or frequency, or when maternal mirroring is distant, depleted, or otherwise nonsupportive, the integrative capacities are unlikely to develop fully, leaving the child with a bifurcated sense of self.

Lichtenberg and Slap (1972, 1973) suggest that if intense affective states (e.g., anger, humiliation, etc.) are chronically present the unity of the self becomes endangered, giving rise to split organizations of experience. Subsequently, persistent dichotomous suborganizations may form which seriously limit the flexibility of the self.

Personality Bifurcation

Personality develops gradually so bifurcation often evolves imperceptibly. However there are some critical points where splitting is especially likely to begin or further deepen. The first of these critical points is at about *18 months*. As we've already discussed, the middle of the second year is a crossroads for the developing toddler. If because of stress, physical illness, lack of maternal mirroring, or other reasons development lags or is arrested, the toddler doesn't make the transition to symbolic representation. The shift from soma to psyche is stymied, and bifurcation of development begins. Instead of an integrated soma–psyche experience, such children tend to regressively remain in the soma.

Subsequently, when the toddler moves into the tasks of autonomy with a global, somatically invested sense of self he is likely to encounter conflict on many levels. In response to such conflict the toddler begins to develop a *compliant* self and an *autonomous* self.

The roots of the compliant self are found in being fed, bathed, diapered, and held by the primary caretaker. These and other interactions of physical closeness with the primary caretaker coalesce to form a rudimentary self structure. This self is likely to be compliant in order to maintain maternal closeness. As the toddler moves into the second year however, experiences of being physically restrained (for diaper changes, etc.) or physically forced to comply (e.g., being deposited in one's bed at a given time whether sleepy or not) begin to increase and another rudimentary self-structure—the autonomous self—begins to develop.

During optimal development the compliant and autonomous selves become integrated into a single superordinate self, or at least the boundaries separating them remain highly permeable, with a sense of agency passing easily back and forth. In the case of TS-OCD-prone toddlers, struggles for autonomy, physical trauma, or other stresses deepen the bifurcation. In such cases differentiation slows, and the self functions primarily in the world of the body. Motoric activity hypertrophies while psycholinguistic complexity is attenuated. Words have not become a bridge to contemplation or introspection and the child utilizes body language more than linguistic structures or symbolic representation.

"Motoric" Peter

One such example was Peter the Great. His highly energetic and active nature has already been described, so the focus now is on his lack of linguistic development. During his adolescent years Peter spent much time pursuing his earliest love—war games. In the fields and woods near Moscow he organized elaborate "battles." Unlike most other boys his age, he was able to order supplies from the government arsenal; and records show that he ordered uniforms, banners, cannon, and horses. On his 11th birthday he was allowed to fire salutes. He enjoyed this so much that he sent messengers almost daily to request gunpowder. When Peter was not yet 13, he ordered 16 pairs of pistols, 16 muskets, and 39 carbines. When not occupied by war games, Peter was curious about almost everything, especially things physical. He loved the feel of tools in his large, muscular hands, and savored the explosive action of chisels biting into wood or chipping into stone. He loved the clang of hammers on glowing red iron in the blacksmith's shop.

Peter's was not the typical tsar's education. He "escaped" to the out-of-doors, to interact with people and with tools in a practical way. Muskets and cannon were more important to him than paper and pens and he roamed about his open-air classroom with insatiable curiosity and boundless energy. Although his spelling and grammar never advanced beyond that of a beginning elementary school student, he was by no means uneducated. He just pursued a "nontraditional" curriculum. For example, he read few books, preferring instead to learn how type was set and books were bound.

One cannot say that Peter's lack of linguistic development *caused* his tics, but one can see that his early anchoring in the motoric sphere and his neglect of the contemplative domain combined to increase the likelihood that, as an adult, he would deal with his own mental turmoil by motoric activity rather than introspective mentation. The lack of a contemplative side or self in Peter is so drastic, that "bifurcated" hardly seems the appropriate word for describing his personality. He possessed a "motoric self," a pervasive "physicality" which was never really modified by contemplative thought. Consequently his behavior often appeared impulsive and capricious, but if his asymmetrically developed personality is understood, his impetuosity can be seen as the obligatory consequence of his development.

Comparing Peter and Sam

It is interesting to compare Peter the Great with Samuel Johnson, whose linguistic abilities were highly developed—albeit probably not of his own motivation. Sam had early somatic problems: poor eyesight, hearing loss, and the incision on his arm. Although his linguistic skills were highly developed, Samuel Johnson also had a "motoric self" much like Peter's. He was, like Peter, very energetic throughout his long life. His autonomous forcefulness—especially in things physical—was omnipresent. Ever ready to reassure himself about his physical prowess, he relished opportunities to "show off" his athletic competence.

This seems obviously compensatory for his early physical limitations. When Sam was young, his uncle—apparently a boxer of some repute—taught Sam to fight, and despite his nearsightedness, he became so adept that he could walk the most dangerous streets of London at night without fear. Once, according to Bate (1975, p. 11), when four men attacked him he kept them all at bay until arresting officers came to his aid. And such demonstrations of physical one-upmanship were not limited—as is more typically the case—to adolescence.

Throughout life Johnson happily demonstrated his robustness of constitution. When in his fifties, though he had swam but little in over thirty years, he impressed a lifeguard at Brighton to comment "You must have been a stout-hearted gentleman forty years ago." On another occasion—driven by his autonomy, athletic abilities, and ever-present brinkmanship—"he went into the river at Oxford, and swam away to a part of it that he had been told of as a dangerous place, and where some one had been drowned" (Hill, 1897, p. 224).

Sam Climbs the Gate

Arriving at an elegant dinner party being held in his honor, Sam's propensity for physical activity easily outweighed social considerations:

> Johnson appeared at the great gate; he stood for some time in deep contemplation, and at length began to climb it, and, having succeeded in clearing it, advanced with hasty strides towards the house. On his arrival Mrs. Gastrel asked him "if he had forgotten that there was a small gate for foot passengers by the side of the carriage entrance." "No, my dear lady, by no means," replied the Doctor; "but I had a mind to try whether I could climb a gate now as I used to when I was a lad." (Hill, 1897, Vol. I, p. 49)

Sam Wins a Race!

At another dinner party, when Johnson was in his mid-fifties, a young woman boasted that she could outrun anyone there. Johnson immediately replied:

> Madam, you cannot outrun me. . . . The lady at first had the advantage; but Dr. Johnson happening to have slippers on much too small for his feet, kick'd them off up into the air, and ran . . . leaving the lady far behind him, and . . . returned, leading her by the hand, with looks of high exultation and delight. (Hill, 1897, Vol. II, p. 278)

Bifurcated Personality—Literary Giant "On a Roll"

An anecdote, told some years after his death illustrates Samuel's ever-ready "physicality."

The elderly Mr. Langton and a friend were out walking when they came to the top of a very steep hill. Back in 1764 Johnson and Langton had also walked to the top of this hill, and the elderly Langton recalled that "Johnson, delighted by its steepness, said he wanted to 'take a roll down.' They tried to stop him. But he said he 'had not had a roll for a long time,' and taking out of his pockets his keys, a pencil, a purse, and other objects, lay down parallel at the edge of the hill, and rolled down its full length, turning himself over and over till he came to the bottom." (Hill, 1897, Vol. 2, pp. 390, 391)

The English Gentleman Who Hopped Like a Kangaroo

As Johnson entered his sixties, the same bifurcation of somatic and intellectual sides of his personality existed—as indeed they did his entire 75 years. On the one hand he could be eloquent—almost refined, then easily and quickly give himself over to physical activities seemingly incongruous with the intellectual side of his being.

Once when traveling abroad, Johnson was discussing Sir Joseph Bank's discovery of the kangaroo. The 63-year-old Johnson volunteered an imitation of the animal.

The company stared . . . nothing could be more ludicrous than the appearance of a tall, heavy, grave-looking man, like Dr. Johnson, standing up to mimic the shape and motions of a kangaroo. He stood erect, put out his hands like feelers, and gathering up the tails of his huge brown coat so as to resemble the pouch of the animal, made two or three vigorous bounds across the room! (Pottle & Bennett, 1936, p. 98)

Johnson's neonatal problems with poor eyesight, impaired hearing, and an open incision undoubtedly affected his early development profoundly. However his "physicality" was modified by a highly developed linguistically sophisticated self. Sam was truly a *bifurcated personality*. Peter was much more "mono-motoric" in development. This is also evident in the extent to which they experienced problems on the compulsive spectrum. Peter—"mono-motoric"—only showed simple motor tics. Sam, complexly bifurcated, experienced compulsions and obsessions along the *entire* spectrum. From simple cluckings and whistlings, to complex obsessions about how to enter a doorway, Samuel Johnson was a man for all seasons. He personified TS-OCD in all it's complexity.

SUMMARY

We've looked at some of the basic needs of the first two years of life and seen that the manner in which they are accommodated or frustrated has a profound impact on the developing child. We've seen that the motor tics of TS and the obsessions of OCD are out-of-phase attempts to meet some of the earliest needs of infancy and childhood. It's been further suggested that tics "piggyback" on early rhythms and behavior patterns, which Piaget (1952) described as circular reactions. We've also noted that repetitive tunes and thoughts, and other behaviors can function as *transitional* patterns; easing the anxiety associated with moving away from mother. Frustration of early needs leads to obsessive and often routinized overconcern with such issues. For example, themes of abandonment may resonate from the earliest years of life throughout the teens, causing children to use tics as self-comforting behaviors as we saw in Tracy's life. Somatic integrity and freedom of movement were prominent themes in the lives of Peter the Great and Samuel Johnson.

As the toddler moves through the second year, we've examined some of the profound changes that occur when the "center of operations" shifts from the soma to the psyche. It's been noted, and illustrated in the life of Peter the Great, that children with TS-OCD become "stuck" in the body, never quite accomplishing a smooth transition from motoric to mental. The experience of Samuel Johnson illustrated the use of compensatory tics across a broad range of unmet early needs; and although he certainly developed his linguistic and symbolic mental operations much more extensively than did Peter, there is ample evidence he was somatically "stuck."

Having considered some of the primary needs of the first two years of life, we're ready to consider the toddler, preschool, and elementary school experiences of the TS-OCD-prone individual. It will become apparent that ridicule and shame deepen the bifurcation of personality as development proceeds. Instead of becoming comfortably integrated, the compliant and autonomous selves—the "nice" and the enraged—become split even further. How this occurs, and how shame play a central role in the metamorphosis from transitory tics to lifelong TS-OCD, are topics for our next chapter.

However, before proceeding further, we will briefly consider the development of the self, as this topic spans the developmental eras covered in the current chapter as well as the next. Indeed, it is germane for the remainder of the book, having important implications for etiology, prevention, and treatment.

MULTIPLE PERSONALITIES, MULTIPLE SELVES, AND PART-SELVES: UNDERSTANDING TS-OCD AS A DISSOCIATIVE DISORDER

We've seen from the previous discussion how a nascent sense of self gradually forms as a result of consistent parenting (caring) experienced in a milieu of reasonable predictability. Although we often speak of *the* self, it is probably more reasonable to speak of a *family of selves* or of *several selves*. Although a lot of media attention has been focused on the dramatic and sensational aspects of Multiple Personality Disorder (MPD), the normal development processes involve multiple personalities.

In the usual course of maturation most of us develop several "selves." On a typical day, we frequently switch among our multiple selves in a comfortable, flexible manner, wearing "several different hats" with ease. The switching occurs easily, automatically, and frequently throughout the day—sometimes from moment to moment. The ego states associated with such roles as teacher, spouse, aerobics instructor, parent, "life of the party," devout churchgoer, differ widely yet form a complementary "family of selves." But in a normally cohesive self system, all the "family members" talk to each other. There are no "feuding cousins" or "angry in-laws" who refuse to attend "family picnics." The disorder seen in MPD is not that such individuals have multiple selves—we all do—it is that these selves function independently and without knowledge of one another—they don't "talk" to each other. Often developed in response to severe trauma early in childhood, the various *alternates* function in isolated complementarity—each tending to a specific aspect of the business of living without awareness or communication with other "family" members.

For example, many MPD patients develop alternates that deal only with hostile affects. This is quite commonly seen in females who were severely punished whenever they became angry, often being told they would go to hell. Still others develop alternate personalities to deal with physical or sexual abuse. A few examples will suffice to illustrate how dissociation represents an attempt to cope with overwhelming trauma. For example, a nine-year-old boy who developed MPD had been buried in the ground by his stepfather:

> The stepfather put a stove pipe over his face so he could breathe. Of course, the boy became frantic. He screamed and cried. As he became still more upset, the stepfather threatened to leave him and tell everyone he had run away. The boy's screams became louder. His stepfather told him

to "Shut up." When the boy, out of control with terror, continued to scream, the stepfather voided into the stove pipe over the boy's face. The boy was not physically injured, but this demeaning and terrifying ordeal inflicted massive psychological abuse. (Wilbur, 1985, p. 26)

Alternates may develop as a way of coping with sexual abuse. Wilbur reports on a female MPD patient who had first been raped by her father when she was four and a half years of age. She subsequently was abused not only by her father but also by some of his friends:

At the time of the rape she developed a very passive alternate who allowed this type of abuse to continue. She learned that if she dared to resist, she suffered severe physical abuse, as well as sexual violation. (1985, p. 29)

Alternates may also function to preserve a talent or protect a biological function:

One little girl was very musical and loved to play the piano. She refused to play anymore after her mother threatened to break her fingers if she made any more mistakes. She never played in the presence of another person again; but an alternate, created to preserve the love of music, would hurry to the piano and play for hours when the girl was entirely alone in the house. No other human being ever heard her play. (1985, p. 29)

Such tragic experiences, occurring early in life, disrupt the cohesiveness of the self system in semipermanent ways, and *dissociation* is utilized as a way of coping with intolerable anxiety. This cursory survey of MPD will suffice for our purposes. Many excellent references exist for the interested reader (e.g., Braun, 1986; Kluft, 1985).

Tics—Scattered "Pieces" of Self

TS-OCD is a dissociative disorder similar to MPD except that instead of *multiple personalities*, there exist *multiple pieces* of self (see Figure 2.1). In order to understand tics as pieces of the self, we will briefly look at optimal development, integrating our previous observations with self theory.

Clinicians sometimes "adultopomorphize" children, attributing to them adult characteristics that have not yet developed. For example antisocial (psychopathic) personalities have sometimes been characterized as suffering from "lacunae" of the superego, or as having a "swiss cheese" conscience. A more developmentally accurate view is that little

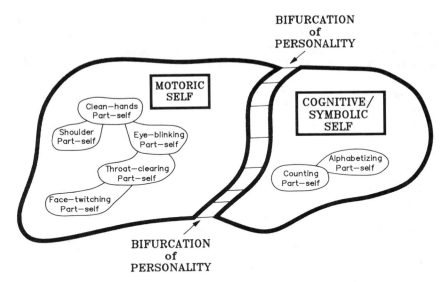

FIGURE 2.1 The structure of the self in TS-OCD is deeply bifurcated and is comprised of an assortment of loosely associated part selves. Such lack of cohesion in the self is more likely to result from chronic developmental stressors, spanning months or years, rather than from single traumatic incidents. Failing to make a smooth transition from the somatically permeated world of infancy to the adult world of symbolic representation and cognitive activity, the tic-prone person remains somatically "hooked." Such individuals reverse the usual "mind-over-matter" hierarchy, tending to remain enmeshed in the body.

moral development ever took place. One might say the sociopath had a "cottage cheese" conscience or a "curdled milk" conscience instead of one like "swiss cheese." The metaphor of swiss cheese implies a well formed structure with holes or gaps in the formation, but one can hardly picture "lacunae" in nonexistent "structures," or imagine an eight-week embryo with a broken leg.

In the present context the term *dissociation* may be similarly misleading, because it implies a splitting off—a severing of association. Braun (1986) correctly observes that

> . . . what we see as MPD, especially in children, may well be a disorder of lack of association, since a significant association may never have been achieved from which to be dissociated. (1986, pp. 7–8)

Various writers have referred to the embryonic beginnings of self in terms such as "ego nuclei" (Glover, 1932, 1943), or "disparate nuclei of the self" (Gedo & Goldberg, 1973). Kohut (1977) emphasized the importance of attaining a *cohesive self*, suggesting this occurs when objects (parents) supply the neonate with functions not yet available to the developing psyche. The newborn subsequently experiences these functions as his own, and the nurturing parent becomes a "self-object"—experienced as part of the indistinctly developing self. Even after the infant begins to clearly distinguish between self and others, there remains a long period of dependency upon parents. It is during this time that Winnicott's *transitional* object becomes most salient—the beloved teddy or blanket becoming absolutely necessary for a peaceful transition to sleep.

It is also during this time that ticquing and other *transitional behaviors* are most likely to originate and persist. In the next chapter it will be shown how, as a result of humiliation and shame, personality development in the person with TS-OCD becomes deeply bifurcated. In this split system, multiple selves function primarily in one of two major domains—soma *or* psyche. More will be said about bifurcation later, but here the somatic domain—where pieces of selves disconnectedly orbit in unassociated spheres—will be further examined.

Tics as "Somatic Anchors"

TS-OCD is a "multiple-pieces-of-self" disorder in which tics function as "somatic anchors" for disparate self experiences. Repetitive behaviors function as "anchors" around which other experiences coalesce forming "part-selves." Such clusters of experience become autonomous at a very early age—never quite forming into a superordinate self system. Like a corporation with numerous vice presidents and no CEO, or a political coalition with numerous candidates but no strong leader, persons with TS-OCD experience a fractured sense of identity.

Winnicottian Nightmare

The psychological life of the person with TS-OCD is subjectively one of fragmentation—paradoxically held together by a series of repeated movements (tics) or thoughts (obsessions). In terms of our previous discussion, TS-OCD can be seen as a disorder involving *multiple transitional behaviors*—a kind of "Winnicottian nightmare" where several blankets, or pieces of blankets, are required to calm the child before sleep. The child with TS-OCD often utilizes several tics to remain calm, reminding one of a child for whom a single teddy bear does not suffice, but instead pieces of teddy—an arm, a leg, perhaps an ear—are utilized in an incessant effort to calm oneself enough to go to sleep.

A Family of Part-Selves

For the ticquer, each particular tic has a "personality" of its own and each draws consistent, predictable interpersonal responses from the environment. Each tic provides the *somatic anchor* for a *part-self* and the accompanying experiences that gradually coalesce around this "psychic node" during development. Repetitive throat clearing, for example, is experienced as a reaffirmation of the *"throat part-self,"* which resides in the neck just behind the Adam's apple. This "part-self" reliably draws angry responses of "Quit it!" or "Get a drink!" or "Do you need a cough drop?" The *shoulder part-self* is activated by shoulder jerking, which reliably reduces somatic tension in the upper torso, but consistently recruits laughter, ridicule, and comments such as "What's wrong?" "Why are shaking?" "Are you cold?" from the social milieu. The *behind-the-eyes part-self* is engaged by repetitive, intense squint-blinking that provides a disco-like visual experience to the soma, and invariably elicits comments such as "Have you been to see an eye doctor?" "Why do you keep making faces with your eyes?" and other humiliating interpersonal comments. The *clean hands part-self* is activated by repetitive washing and returns to the soma (literally) the warm experience of cleanliness, germ-free safety, and massage-like soothing. Like other part-selves, however, it also enlists social stigma in the form of ridicule, teasing, or nicknames ("washer boy"), and curiosity that turns to despair in family members.

Many more examples could be given, but the point should be clear. Each tic, compulsion, or obsession acts as an anchor for an accompanying part-self around which certain emotional states reliably occur. The notion of experiences "agglutinating" around a core and forming a sub-personality is not new. Jung's theory of personality utilized the notion of "complex" with experiences being "drawn" towards it. More recently, mathematicians in the area of catastrophe theory (e.g., Zeeman, 1977) have written about *attractors*—stable limit cycles—in the nervous system that might be comprised of millions of neurons, but which nevertheless oscillate in predictable cycles. This analysis has been applied to understanding the dynamics of the brain, heartbeat, neural impulses, and so on.

Tics are *attractors*, providing stable somatic anchors around which other experiences coalesce. Likewise obsessions provide cognitive anchors, and some behaviors, like compulsive hand washing, provide hy-

brids of somatic and cognitive experiences. To some extent tics and obsessions *produce* predictable emotional experiences. Consequently these
part-selves become autonomous quite early in development, resisting
integration under a broader self system.

In summary, it has been shown that TS-OCD exists along a spectrum
of dissociative disorders of the developing self. Although co-consciousness occurs among the various part-selves, there exists little real integration among them. This has important implications for treatment that
will be discussed later. The somatic side of the bifurcation "houses" a
wide array of part-selves each of which is highly autonomous, yet undifferentiated and disconnected from the larger self system. With this
understanding of the somatic self, it is possible to look broadly at problems of bifurcation between the somatic and psychological sides of personality.

Behaviorism and Developmental Theory

In this chapter the language of psychodynamic developmental theory
has been primarily utilized. These terms are especially well suited to
discuss the intense, personal experiences that first occur in the context
of the caretaker–infant dyad. However they are by no means the only
ones that prove useful. The apparent omission in this chapter of behavioristic terminology reflects an attempt to keep theoretical "multilinguis-
tics" within manageable boundaries. I am, however, in agreement with
Wachtel (1977) when he suggests:

> There is more than one way to skin a cat . . . accounts of personality
> development from learning theory and psychodynamic perspectives need
> not be incompatible. Both approaches can be used as vessels for smug-
> gling contraband metaphysical freight or as legitimate tools for discerning
> previously unseen connections between events. (1977, p. 75)

Terms such as "reinforcement," "shaping," and "successive approxi-
mation" have their parallels in psychodynamic theory as well. For example, when Kohut speaks of "optimal frustration" as the cornerstone
upon which self structure is built, it seems similar to "successive ap-
proximation" as used by behaviorists in other contexts; both terms refer
to the gradual development of new behaviors necessitated by the absence of externally provided "nurturance" or "reinforcement." Clearly,
there is a difference of perspective, with behaviorists looking "outside–
in" and experiential developmentalists seeking to understand the infant
"inside–out." Nonetheless, these perspectives are complementary and
each can sensitize us to differing but important considerations. As

Wachtel puts it: "Neither analyses starting from motives and thoughts and seeking overt expressions, nor analyses starting from observable events and treating motives and thoughts as a function of them are God-given" (1977, p. 75).

Although ticquing can be understood as "soothing" by developmentally oriented clinicians, it is also accurate to characterize ticquing as highly "reinforcing." Indeed object-relations theory can be seen as a careful study of "conditioning and learning" as it occurs in the caretaker–infant dyad. Ticquing, obsessing, and other compulsive problems can be legitimately analyzed from experiential, behavioristic, or social psychology perspectives. Truth is not at issue here, the goal is to utilize whichever theoretical perspective promises to be most *useful*. Wachtel's excellent book (1977) addresses many of the principal issues.

Transitional Objects

In closing the chapter, a case taken from a behavior modification textbook will be briefly analyzed. This case purports to illustrate principles of aversion therapy, but it will be shown how it can also be developmentally understood as providing a retarded person with a "Winnicottian" transitional object:

> Scotty was a seven-year-old institutionalized severely retarded boy, diagnosed as having Down's syndrome, who habitually beat his head with his hands. This self-destructiveness was so severe that Scotty spent 24 hours a day in a crib with his hands tied to his waist and a modified football helmet on his head. Because of the severity of the problem, the staff psychologist designed a behavioral procedure involving electric-shock punishment. This quickly eliminated Scotty's head beating in the training situation. But what about other situations?
>
> The psychologist realized that it would not be safe to let the boy run freely on the ward until some desirable alternative behavior to head beating was developed. (Martin & Pear, 1988, p. 201)

Utilizing a conditioning procedure known as escape conditioning, staff conditioned Scotty to grasp a metal toy truck in order to escape a mild electric shock. After he learned that response, the metal truck was replaced with a toy tiger. As with the truck, Scotty could escape being shocked by grasping the toy at all times. During the time his hands were occupied with holding the truck or toy he didn't destructively beat his own head. Consequently, the program was considered to be successful.

Although procedures utilizing (mild) electric shock may seem abhorrent, this procedure was first cleared by an ethics committee, and continually monitored throughout implementation. Obviously such drastic means would not have been used if less intense programming would have been successful. What is of particular interest in the present discussion are not the pros and cons of aversion therapy, but rather how clearly this outcome—unbeknownst to the behaviorists who conducted the study—illustrates Winnicott's notion of the transitional object. Few behaviorists read Winnicott and few analysts spend much time studying Skinner.

> Some readers might think it cruel to make a child dependent on a toy through electric shock. Actually, the child was much better off with this dependency than without it. No longer did he have to be restrained in bed 24 hours a day. He could run, play, and learn social interaction and other vital skills. *At first, he was extremely dependent on this toy; in fact, once when accidentally deprived of it he beat his head frantically. But over the span of about a year, he gradually became less and less dependent on his toy, and eventually, did not beat his head even when without it.* (Martin & Pear, pp. 202, 203, italics mine)

SYMPTOM SUBSTITUTION

Finally, a word is in order about the divisive issue of symptom substitution. Traditionally, behaviorists have contended that the symptom *is* the problem, while psychodynamic clinicians have argued that removing symptoms is like picking leaves off a tree, but never getting to the "root" of the problem. If one "cures" an enuretic of bedwetting without addressing issues of dependency, passive aggression, and the like, the core problem will simply become manifest in another system in the form of rashes, headaches, or the like. Wachtel has suggested that from the analyst's perspective, symptoms are communication, and taking away symptoms would be like "asking the patient to shut up" (1977, p. 290).

The behaviors of TS-OCD always communicate a message if one is sensitively attuned. Such communications may be developmentally out of phase, since they originate in earlier times. However it would be superficial to *only* concern oneself with the *removal* or *containment* of tics or obsessions without "listening" to the nonverbal messages carried by the symptoms. Tics are "body language" par excellence and ought to be studied as such. But there is nothing incompatible about *simultaneously* fostering the development of alternatives—alternatives that can replace TS-OCD symptoms as ways of expressing oneself, soothing oneself, gaining attention, and so on without increasing shame, anger, and other negative emotions that fuel the recursive rituals.

Chapter 3

SHAME: CEMENTING TS-OCD INTO PERMANENCE

We've seen that excessive stress in such forms as autonomy struggles with parents, trauma in the environment, physical problems, and parental abandonment, among others, can anchor a developing toddler so firmly in the somatic orbit that further growth of the self towards symbolic and contemplative thought becomes stifled. The self may develop a split identity in such situations, with too much emphasis on the "somatic me." Bifurcation of personality begins during the second year of life, and it is during this time that the origins of TS-OCD can be seen. When the child leaves home to enter school TS-OCD typically erupts in fully recognizable forms.

Leaving Home

In families with working parents, leaving home may occur earlier—in smaller increments—as children are left with baby-sitters or preschool teachers. As children increasingly leave home earlier, the average age of initial TS symptoms will probably drop as well. Most literature to date reports six or seven as the median age TS symptoms are first observed—corresponding to entering first grade.

From Soma to Society

Entering school at five or six years of age is a giant step away from the somatically soaked maternal orbit. Compared to home, the complexities of school are immense, and the somatically anchored ambitendent child attempts to deal with these complexities using an earlier primitive "body language" which is now developmentally out of phase. Further, most of the crises now relate to social anxieties not somatic discomfort. Tension no longer occurs in rhythms of eating, elimination, and diapering; what matters most now is how many friends one has, if one reads easily, and whether the teacher treats one well. The crucial concerns are social, not somatic.

Leaving one's primary caregiver is an enormous transition for a child, and even though he or she may become dyadically attached to the teacher, the intensity of the relationship will be diluted by the sheer number of other "siblings" competing for the teacher's attention. The anxieties around entering school can be enormous; and if early development has been problematic, the early needs—for attention, discharge, soothing, and so on—may become obsessively revitalized in the form of tics or other self-soothing rituals.

Ridicule by Peers

Any unusual behaviors will subject the child to ridicule by peers. Six-year-olds have not yet attained the grace of "looking the other way" when someone with a handicap is present; quite the contrary, it arouses their unabashed interest. This is the age at which children ask "Mommy, why does that man keep shaking his head?" or "Mommy why is that lady so fat?" or "Mommy, how come that bald man has red spots on his head?"

In his insightful book about shame, Kaufman notes:

> Derisive laughter and ridicule are nowhere more prominent than among the child's own peer group. One's emerging alliances with the outer world are fragile though significant. To be mocked, ridiculed, or laughed at is to be held in such contempt that one is not fit to belong. (1985, p. 21)

Internalizing Shame

Although shame originates as an *interpersonal* phenomenon, it easily becomes internalized and thereafter experienced as part of the self:

> Shame originates interpersonally, primarily in significant relationships, but later can become internalized so that the self is able to activate shame without an inducing interpersonal event. Interpersonally induced shame develops into internally induced shame. Through this internalizing process, shame can spread throughout the self, ultimately shaping our emerging identity. Prior to internalization, shame remains a feeling which is generated and then passes on, whereas following internalization, shame can be prolonged indefinitely. (Kaufman, 1985, p. 7)

TS—A SHAME-BASED SYNDROME

Tics *inevitably* arouse curiosity, usually leading to teasing by peers and feelings of shame on the part of the child. This deepens bifurcation of the personality because the somatic self begins to feel shame, humiliation, and rage. The distance between this enraged self and the publically pleasant, compliant, self increases; with the compliant self becoming more split off, less integrated, and more obsessively "nice." The social self appears friendly but just beneath the surface lurks the enraged, hostile self. The public self is permeated with reaction formation niceness in the attempt to balance the rage behind the scenes.

Shame Shrivels the Self

Shame is singularly powerful among negative emotions in its power to shrivel the self. The shamed self shrinks, constricts, compresses, and attempts to absorb itself into nothingness. "I could have crawled into a hole and died!" is how this experience is typically described. Shame overpowers with suddenness. Experienced as a surge of awfulness that quickly rises from the abdomen to heat the back of the neck and further humiliate the self by blushing the face, there seems to be no escape and no way to hide one's humiliation from the observing eyes of others. This kind of inescapable intensity accounts for the tenacity with which shame and self become fused as the *shameful self*. Once shame is experienced, even infrequently, it cannot easily be shaken off, acted out, or displaced. It pulls awareness inward, engulfing and permeating the developing sense of self.

Often ridicule and the resultant shame involves some part of the body evaluated as undesirably different (e.g., a clubfoot, large nose, small genitals, etc.). The nascent integration of body and mind is thus threatened. Comments such as "I hate my body!" which clinicians typically hear from the obese, occur ubiquitously among the general population as well, often in more subtle forms, targeting specific bodily zones: "I hate my ears . . . crooked nose . . . chubby hands . . . complexion . . . eyebrows, etc. The average person is plagued by numerous "imperfections" of which they—more than others—are aware. Most suffer with a diminished sense of self because few of these "blemishes" are repairable at reasonable cost. While orthodontia can revamp crooked teeth, and contact lenses can remove "coke bottle" glasses, few people have access to more elaborate interventions such as face-lifts, breast implants, tummy tucks, and the like. Most suffer silently, their misery being continually exacerbated by comparison with caricatures of perfection created by Hollywood, *People* Magazine, *GQ*, and TV.

Anger Defends the Self

Whereas shame pulls awareness inward, engulfing the self, anger tends toward explosive eruption. The angry self seeks to destroy the tormenter or at least to act out vengeance upon him or her. Even when anger is suppressed and experienced as bitterness, resentment, or hostility; it nevertheless is directed outward. The inner lives of resentful people are rich with revenge. Vivid fantasies of harm and destruction acted out upon others is the norm. Anger thus serves a self protective function. It allows the shamed or humiliated self to fight back. Instead of withdrawing into nothingness, it allows one to act powerfully—at least in fantasy—against one's persecutors.

BIFURCATION OF THE SELF

The powerful emotions of shame and anger form the power behind the splitting of the self system. The introspective, psychological selves coalesce around experiences of shame, while anger tends to activate the somatic self. A deep bifurcation develops between the shame-based "nice" me and the enraged me, with little in the way of subtle shadings or nuances connecting the two. Persons with TS-OCD tend to be somewhat "all-or-none" in their emotional experience. The deeply split personality allows for niceness or anger but in a mutually exclusive manner. This personality splitting has also been facilitated by the organic paradigm of TS, which has reduced shame by disavowing personal responsibility for symptoms; but at the price of increasing distance between the "nice" me and the "bad" (organically damaged) me.

Bifurcation of the self is difficult to mend. The two selves do not mollify one another; instead they exacerbate the split. Like the obese person who feels compelled to be "jolly," the person with TS is obligatorily "nice." In the long run, however, this increases the likelihood that he will be taken advantage of by others who, sensing his sycophantish insecurity, cannot resist exploiting it. In the broad scheme of social relations, acquiescent, conciliatory behavior—especially in response to attack—invites further exploitation. This increases the chronic internal rage and the bifurcation widens. On the other hand, rageful responding to teasing also increases the likelihood that it will be repeated. In either instance, once peers begin to ridicule, it is difficult for a child to cope.

Although most TS-OCD persons are charmingly adept at compliance, anger suppression, flattery, and a host of other "nice" behaviors, this is a caricature because another part of the self is primitively rageful. With increasing maturity, most of the psychological business of life is carried on by the "nice" self and the rageful self, like a naughty child sent out to play while polite company is visiting, is kept well under cover—except when such "neurological" symptoms as head shaking, shrieking, shouting, swearing, or obscene gestures erupt in spite of high doses of Haldol®.

Shame and Personal Responsibility: A Synergism that Splits

It's estimated that from 12% to 28% of children under the age of 13 experience tics at some time in their development. Thus, nearly a third of all children at times utilize body language to extract responses, discharge impulses, sooth themselves, assert autonomy, or in some way modify their biopsychosocial milieu. However a much smaller percentage go on to maintain lifelong ambitendence (TS) or ambivalence (OCD). One of the most decisive factors in determining how permanent such behaviors become is how much shame and humiliation are experienced by the child as a result of his or her tics. Without ridicule, shame, and the consequent bifurcation of personality transitory tics would not persist as TS.

It is when the ambitendent child is teased about a tic that it is likely to become chronic. This is why most TS symptoms are reported to "begin" at about 6 or 7 years of age. As we have shown, that is not the real point of origin, but the stresses involved with entering school, and the exposure to a much wider world of teasers multiplies the occurrences of humiliation and significantly increases the likelihood that transitory tics of childhood will become the more enduring ambitendent tics of adult life.

Additionally, the TS-OCD person's sense of personal responsibility synergistically reacts with shame in the process of making bifurcation permanent. As we've said earlier, all persons with TS-OCD privately know that they initiate the jerking, shouting, or other manifestations, and maintain some limited control over these behaviors. In most cases, they blame themselves for not following the advice of their elders ("Quit it!" "Stop that!"). This heightened sense of personal responsibility translates external ridicule into excruciating inner shame.

Bifurcated Personality Development with Other Handicaps

Although most persons with stigmatizing handicaps develop bimodal personalities, the severity of the bifurcation and degree of reparative integration possible in later life depend heavily on the intensity of shame experienced in the early years. Humiliation and shame harden bimodal development driving the somatically entrapped angry self into ever-deepening humiliation, anger, and somatic soothing; while simultaneously increasing the compliant self's efforts to please others and win approval. Most persons with "shameful" handicaps oscillate between rage and "niceness." Children with seizure disorders, speech problems, clubfeet, or other publicly ridiculed features all tend to be publicly "nice" and intellectually angry. The situation is even worse for children with TS.

What Makes You Ashamed?

Most persons are ashamed of numerous personal characteristics. Shape or size of nose, color of eyes, thickness of eyebrows, distance between front teeth, angle at which ears are attached to the head, size of breasts or penis, presence of acne or birthmarks—these are items people include on the list of "Things I don't like about myself." Although the list seems to change with maturity, it remains essentially similar; worries about acne are simply replaced by worries about wrinkles with neither adolescents nor middle-aged adults particularly enthralled with their epidermis. Adolescents often can't stand the color of their hair, middle-agers abhor the absence of it. Nails are never right; one or all are either dirty, ragged, broken or chewed—but *never* right.

Even nonphysical characteristics are singled out for shame rumination if they're perceived as part of the persona. The thick lenses required for clear vision, the hearing aid that's impossible to completely conceal, the size 46 trousers, the ugly shoes one has to wear in order to accommodate arch supports—all such accessories are experienced as liabilities and devalue the person in the eyes of others and self.

If all this is true for "normal" persons, imagine the psychological experience of the handicapped. Is it any wonder that they are always trying to be "nice?" They can't afford further humiliation. They are psychologically bankrupt—walking "chapter elevens." If once a month you experience a grand mal seizure and regain consciousness to find yourself lying flat on the ground—possibly in your own urine or feces—with a circle of frightened faces looking down at you it requires a lot of "niceness" the other 29 days of the month to "make up" for such a "shameful" episode. And when that ring of pale faces and frightened eyes is comprised of the other third graders in your class—people you have to see each day—the humiliation can be almost unbearable.

Tics are "Shame Generators"

The child with TS-OCD faces more humiliation than children with some other handicaps because TS-OCD is a more "active" handicap. Just as turbines at the bottom of a waterfall constantly generate electric power, tics constantly generate shame. Most physical or behavioral differences have a much more passive public face. After an initial period of "getting used to," others tend to forget about angular features, big ears, or unsightly birth marks (when is the last time you really thought about Gorbachev's?). Not so with tics. This is because tics are *constant and chronic* "shame generators." Unlike the child who experiences a seizure once a month, or perhaps even several times a week, the child with TS experiences shame-generating tics *several times a minute*! And there is enough variety to maintain the interest and curiosity of observers. The only other behavior (which will be discussed thoroughly in a later chapter) that comes even close to such moment-by-moment shame generation is stuttering. But even stuttering can be avoided if a child doesn't talk. For children with TS only sleep offers shelter and even that is compromised by dreams of being the center of ridicule.

Kaufman's delineation of the experience of shame is insightful:

> To feel shame is to feel *seen* in a painfully diminished sense. The self feels exposed both to itself and anyone else present. It is this sudden, unexpected feeling of exposure and accompanying self-consciousness that characterize the essential nature of the affect of shame. Contained in the experience of shame is the piercing awareness of ourselves as fundamentally deficient in some vital way as a human being. To live with shame is to experience the very essence or heart of the self as wanting.
>
> Shame is an impotence-making experience because it *feels as though* there is no way to relieve the matter, no way to restore the balance of things. One has simply failed as a human being. No single action is seen as wrong and, hence reparable. So, "*there is nothing I can do to make up for it.*" This is impotence. (1985, p. 8)

Ridicule Leads to Shame

Shame is fortified by personality bifurcation (noted earlier) and by the internalization process necessary for its formation. Shame is not ridicule. Shame is the product of ridicule. It is the chronic internal experience of the damaged, lessened self which continues to reverberate long after the actual teasing or ridicule has ceased.

The natural tendency is to hide the embarrassed *part-self*—to disown it as "not me." This is why personality bifurcation occurs, splitting off a shameful part-self. This is similar to, but less intense than classic cases of multiple personality disorder (MPD). All persons have multiple selves, but there is co-consciousness among the selves—the primary differing characteristic between normal personalities and MPD.

Negative Nicknames

Name-calling and other forms of teasing keep shame alive. One of the enigmas of children is the glibness with which they engage in verbal cruelty. Possibly—like adult gossip—it serves to reduce personal anxiety about self, by focusing on others. Among children anything that is unique may become a target for ridicule. Often this is perpetuated by that insidious and feared playground weapon, the nickname. Sometimes nicknames are racially based (e.g., spick, chink, nigger, jap, etc.), but more typically they target specific characteristics. Like heat-seeking missiles, children sense vulnerabilities in one another and attack at that point. The obese child is called "Fatso," the intellectually slow is disparagingly referred to as "Retard" and the flat-chested adolescent girl is called "Ironing Board." Few children escape unscathed because almost everyone has "defects"—none of us is perfect. Furthermore, nicknames are not restricted to physical characteristics; they are often based on behavioral reactions, as seen in the following example:

"Bud-Susie." I recall one of my fourth-grade classmates giving us the "scoop" on his little brother Patrick who was entering school for the first time: "If you call him 'Bud'," Johnny informed us one day on the playground, "he'll get mad, and if you call him 'Susie', he'll cry." Thereafter Johnny's little brother became known throughout the school as "Bud-Susie," because of course we did tease him and he did get mad and cry.

"Peabody." A college-aged client once told me, with anguish, of his childhood struggles with nocturnal enuresis (nighttime bed-wetting). The most distressing part of the experience was not the bed-wetting, but the fact that somehow the kids at school found out and nicknamed him "Peabody."

Abuse Often Begins at Home

Tragic as such occurrences seem among childhood peers, it is even more deplorable when parents or siblings are the source of such verbal abuse. Family therapists are all too well acquainted with the many cases where a child is called "Shorty," "Chunky," "Beefy," "Dumbo," "Meathead," and so on by other family members in "fun" ("fun" being a euphemism for ridicule). Even in the rare cases where such names are genuinely affectionate "pet" names, they often do not carry similar connotations outside the family.

In summary, shame is perpetuated by its internal nature, by fragmentation in the not-yet-cohesive self system, and by ridicule or teasing— often in the form of negative nicknames.

CASE STUDY: THE LAWYER WHO TWITCHED AND BLINKED AND NEVER PRACTICED LAW

The Best of Times, The Worst of Times

To every person life dispenses indelible experiences; never-forgotten events that reverberate memory circuits for a lifetime. These intense experiences usually include what Dickens called "The best of times and the worst of times." For TS children, the elementary school years are "the worst of times." Each new day is pregnant with pernicious possibilities. Laughter—that joyous, tumble-down-a-mountain-stream emotional outburst—is the most feared enemy, because it can so instantly transform the best of times into the worst of times. Indelibly.

Whereas ordinary people sometimes begin the day by waking up *from* a nightmare, people with TS-OCD begin the day by waking up *to* a nightmare. The nightmare consists of facing each new day with a body that feels helplessly out of control and a mind overburdened with shame and despair. Paradoxically, such persons *actively generate* the very social stigma they wish to avoid. Children often cope by either withdrawing or (like the number two car rental company), "trying harder." This veneer of compensatory "niceness" barely masks the anger seething just below the surface.

Gerry was good at managing this balancing routine. In spite of his twitching and jumping, he was one of the most popular kids in his fifth grade class. Although at home he was constantly barraged with "You're a mess today!" or, "Can't you control yourself?", he was popular with his peers at school. For the most part he was able to overlook their ridicule and teasing, and to transcend it all by trying harder to be well liked. But he wasn't always successful, as you can see from these pain-filled recollections:

Home and School—Memories That Hurt

"There were five or six of us sitting around a table. We were all having a pretty good time; our assignment was to learn to work in a committee. Then it happened—I remember it like it was this morning—some of the kids started laughing, so I turned to one side to see what was funny, and I realized that someone was mimicking *me* and all the kids were laughing at *me!* I can't tell you what that felt like. There aren't words for it. I was *totally* defenseless. I felt naked! I'd been in situations where one kid was teasing me or making fun of me, and that I could handle, but here everyone was laughing. I had no idea what to do when everybody around me was making fun of me. When you're surrounded by a group, there's nowhere to go. So I just buried my head in my book and started sobbing. I can't remember anything else."

"It sounds like school was pretty horrible that day. Could you go home and talk with your parents about something like that?"

"Not really. They were always bugging me about my tics, telling me to quit it. I guess partly that was because when they took me to doctors, the message was always the same: 'Your son's normal. There's nothing physically wrong with him. It's a mental problem—an emotional problem.' So I guess they figured since nothing was wrong with me, I was doing it on purpose and it was OK to yell at me about it.

"But I still managed to live a pretty normal life, in spite of my parents bugging me, and the occasional ridicule at school. See, I chose to focus on the first part of the doctors' message about there being nothing wrong with me. I denied the fact that I had TS (in those days they didn't diagnose it anyway) and went ahead and did everything everyone else did. I was with them every step of the way. I totally ignored the part of me that was out of control."

A Body Out of Control:

"Which part was out of control?"

"My body. I guess I felt since I couldn't control my body, I needed to control everything else. And as I've looked back over the 40-some years I've lived, I notice that I always gravitate towards positions of power. If you put me into an organization, I quickly become an officer or leader. But I never want the top spot, because I don't like to be in the spotlight, so I usually try to become treasurer. That gives me a lot of control, because I learned years ago whoever controls the purse strings has the power. When I was in college, I became vice president and house director for my fraternity. That meant that it was my responsibility to maintain control in the frat house. I had to stop water fights, food fights, whatever was going on that was inappropriate. So, you might say that what I was unable to do with my body—control it—I was doing with this organization. And I did a good job. Our house was always in good condition when I was director."

"What about your high school years? How were things during that time?"

"Those were bad years. My father died my freshman year and that set me back a lot. I've probably still not fully recovered. We had a lot of unresolved conflict. He was a man who fathered a son of whom he was never proud. I sensed that; he was always on my case about something. I didn't feel he liked me. And when he died, that was all left hanging. So all during high school, I never achieved my potential. I was getting B− grades when I should have been getting A's. Also, because I was under a lot of stress, tics were a lot worse. I was a horror to look at. So my mother, who was always afraid I was going to 'break,' would say 'Don't overexert yourself! If it's causing you too much trouble, it's not worth it—let it go!' I'm sure she was just trying to help, but I got the message that I didn't *have* to do well in school—that a B was just as good as an A, and that wasn't helpful to my career.

"When I was accepted to law school, as an adult, my mother's first response was: 'Are you sure you can handle this—are you sure it won't make you sick?' So now one of the messages I try to communicate to parents of kids with TS is: 'Yes, the stress of school will make the tics worse and that's too bad, but it is the price the child may have to pay for success.' "

"So how do drug therapies factor into this attempt to be successful? Have you ever utilized medication to help reduce tics?"

"I tried Haldol for six months. It was a disaster! For me as an adult, Haldol was not worth the price. I'd lived for 36 years with the symptoms—without medication and as an adult the price was too high. I just couldn't function with the effects of the drug—the dulling of the mind, lack of energy, not getting up in the morning, just totally not being myself. So after six months, I said 'No more! Not for me!' Although I'm personally unable to use medication, I can't say what others should do. I realize that for a young child growing up, if the symptoms are *really* interfering with development, drugs might have a place. It's got to be a decision between child, parent, and physician."

Law School and Later

"I graduated from college planning to teach at the junior high school level. But when I took the New York City Board of Education license exam, it took them a year to notify me of the results, by which time I thought I'd failed the exam. In the meantime I started working as an electrician's apprentice. Both my father and grandfather were electricians, so it came naturally. Then I went back to school evenings and got a Master's in labor relations. After I finished the

Master's I continued on for a law degree. I wanted to practice labor relations law. Unfortunately, in 1980 many companies were trimming back by eliminating labor relations departments, so it was *very* difficult to find a job in that area. Although I graduated near the top of my class, I could never get a job."

"And you think your tics had something to do with your not getting hired as an attorney?"

"Definitely. I would get called back for second or even third interviews, and then when I would meet with the firm, I would never get called back. This happened at least a dozen times. Finally, I got hired by a labor relations consulting firm and two days later I was fired."

"And this was TS related?"

"I'm sure of it. During the job interviews, they made it very clear: 'We like you very much. You're articulate, intelligent, make a good appearance, we're proud to have you represent the company.' During the interviews, I could contain the tics. But after I got hired, I spent an entire day with one of the partners working with a client in New Jersey. It's impossible to contain the tics for a whole day. The next morning, they called me into the office and said 'You're not going to work out.' "

"So after a dozen job interviews you *finally* get the kind of job you want, and two days later you're fired. That must have been pretty tough."

"It was a very low point in my life. My father-in-law, who had never even mentioned my tics, came and talked to me and said he'd wondered if that was the reason I never got a job. I agreed and decided it was time to get some help. I called my friend Barry, whose brother is a psychiatrist. The next night Barry called back and asked me a series of questions—all of which I answered 'Yes,' and he said 'My brother thinks you have Tourette Syndrome.' My first question was 'What is Tourette Syndrome?' I'd never heard of it. I'd never in my life seen anyone else with TS.

Not a One-of-a-Kind Oddity

"Someone put me in touch with Tourette Syndrome Association (TSA) and the next day my wife and I and our one-year-old daughter were sitting in this tiny little office in Bayside, New York. I met some truly incredible people there. My first contact was with a woman named Rhoda and her caring and concern were just wonderful.

"Even though I'd been to TSA and met some of the officers, I never saw any other people with TS. Then two years ago, I went to TSA National in Cincinnati and it was like all of a sudden coming to a place where TS was almost normal— like a different planet—so many other adults with TS. A place where it's acceptable to have tics and vocalizations—nothing's prohibited. You could sit and do whatever nonsense you wanted to and if anyone's laughing, we're laughing with each other. We'd sit around in the back part of the auditorium laughing at each other when we'd do different things.

"Steve was the ringleader, because he's the most vocal. He's also a comedian. Steve's somehow incorporated his tics into a comedy routine. He has a genuinely fast mind; he's a very funny man, so while the physicians are up there making their presentations, Steve is back there basically heckling. You can call it coprolalia or whatever you want to, but basically, the speaker is being heckled. Some of the speakers actually enjoy it because it's genuinely funny. But now, all of a sudden, this behavior is acceptable. Steve, who out in the real world may be an oddball, comes here and he's a star—he's a Tourette celebrity. Now I ask you, 'How the hell can you be a Tourette celebrity?' The rest of the world thinks you're nuts, but when you come here (TSA convention), you're acceptable, and you can shine for a few moments. This doesn't exist in the real world. It's a totally different experience, and it gives people a great sense of belonging."

"So where does that leave you today?"

"The most important thing to me now is my family—my wife and my children. Whereas before I very much wanted to be an attorney and excel professionally, I now realize that it would not have brought me the satisfaction that having a secure family life has brought."

Commentary

Gerry's *bifurcated personality development* seems quite clear. He described his childhood years as a time when his body was "out of control" and perceptively described much of his later concerns with power as an attempt to be in control with his mind since he couldn't control his body. He was articulate about how he dealt with ridicule by working very hard at being "popular." In all of this the bifurcation is prominent: the humiliated, angry, shamed Gerry facing hardship both at school and at home, transcending this by becoming popular, well liked, and a leader. It is very difficult to integrate such disparate selves. As Gerry put it: "I totally ignored the part of me that was out of control."

Again, we see the tragic consequences of a physician stating "There's nothing *physically* wrong with him." Gerry's parents utilized this as permission to *paradoxically* instruct him to "Quit it!" and punished him when he didn't comply with that impossible directive. Parents of children with TS are often *overattentive*, regardless, but any propensity to pester receives immense reinforcement when medical professionals suggest the child is ticquing on purpose. This often reads as a "Sic 'em!" message to parents, with devastating consequences for the child.

Parents, children, teachers, and doctors unwittingly create a "Scylla-Charybdis" sandwich, leaving children suspended between shame and despair. The little girl who believes the pediatrician's pronouncement

"There's nothing wrong with her" is likely to view herself as a shame-fully naughty child who misbehaves (tics) for "attention" or simply to be obnoxious. If, on the other hand, a little boy believes the doctor's statement: "It's an organic disease—he can't help it" it's a relief to be released from responsibility for ticquing but depressing to be diagnosed as permanently damaged.

Ashamed of Shame?

Before concluding this chapter I would like to comment on the lack of attention that shame—a pervasive correlate of "growing up"—has received in psychological writings. Only recently have clinicians begun to seriously address the etiological implications of shame, and speak of shame-based syndromes. Discussions of shame, like talk about death, are often considered taboo. Shame is acknowledged, but the dearth of discussion belies a discomfort with its presence. For example, Erik Erikson's writings (1950, 1968) are customarily referred to in developmental or personality texts; but this is usually done to emphasize his "psychosocial" expansion of Freud's "psychosexual" stages, and little careful study of the stages follows. If his writings are discussed further, it is usually trust versus mistrust, or identity versus role confusion that receive attention, and his second stage—*autonomy versus shame*—is often overlooked. As we've seen however, the autonomy–shame tensions of the second year of life constitute the dynamic core of TS-OCD, and further understanding will necessitate keeping shame and autonomy at the *center* of discussions about etiology, prevention, and treatment. This will be taken up in more detail later.

Chapter 4

COPROLALIA: UPPING THE ANTE DURING ADOLESCENCE

THE AMBITENDENT ADOLESCENT

Earlier chapters have shown that the earliest roots of TS-OCD date to the second year of life. However, when stresses remain high, intrapsychic structure undifferentiated, and development dichotomous, the ambitendent child is at high risk for becoming an ambitendent adolescent, and ultimately a chronically ambitendent (TS-OCD) adult. Blanck and Blanck describe one of their patients—an artistically talented woman in her mid-thirties—who brought a sketch to one of the sessions that depicted a teenaged girl punching a larger woman. The woman cried throughout the session leading the Blancks to conclude that ". . . Even as late as adolescence there was still ambitendency (Mahler) in the simultaneous rage and attempt at tactile contact. This was in operation in relation to her husband as well" (p. 29). This kind of fused (simultaneous) need seeking—often of widely disparate needs—is common among persons with TS-OCD.

From Autonomy to Appreciation

As the person moves from toddlerhood and the early years of childhood toward adolescence and adult maturity, basic needs change. For toddlers and young children *autonomy* is primary; but this changes to need for appreciation which is seen so dramatically in the typical adolescent's obsession with peer approval. Being liked becomes *the* primary need. The earlier "Ha! Gotcha last!" gives way to the much more complicated and frightening "Would you like to go to a movie with me?"

In the case of persons with TS-OCD, the needs for autonomy and appreciation remain global, fused, and permeated with ambitendence. As the somatically anchored TS-OCD person attempts to deal with the complexities of adolescence using earlier "body language," the situation worsens. The individual becomes entrapped in a web of fused, simultaneous need seeking where any behavior *partially* fulfills one need, but *simultaneously* makes it impossible to fulfill others. Some brief clinical examples illustrate this point.

The Boy Who Farted and Apologized—Over and Over Again!

Recall the case of Brian discussed earlier. He illustrates that as children move toward adolescence, the primitive urge for explosive discharge remains fused with the need for appreciation. Experiencing Brian's glib but immediate apologies following flatulence left little doubt regarding the premium he placed on appreciation.

The Young Man Who Stuck Out His Tongue at His Friends

In the preface Orrin Palmer was introduced, sitting in a Greenwich Village cafe with his girlfriend. Orrin's behavior is an example of the fusion of autonomy and appreciation needs. Recall that as he and his girlfriend sat at the table:

> Every few minutes his conversation stopped mid-sentence while he yelped, grunted, shrieked, kissed the air, *stuck out his tongue at his friend* and occasionally spewed street-corner obscenities. *The girl did not seem to notice.* (Hochman, 1980, p. 88, italics mine)

Here we see the fusion of autonomy and appreciation needs. Orrin is ambitendently asking his date "Will you still go out with me if I yelp, grunt, shriek and continue to carry on in this potentially embarrassing way?" "Let's test it even further, will you still like me if I stick my tongue out at you?"

Writing of Orrin's social life, the author relates: "He has many understanding friends, a pretty girlfriend, and has not been overwhelmingly hampered socially, because *he is friendly and tries to make others feel comfortable about his condition*" (italics mine). Orrin is quoted as saying:

> People understand . . . even in a movie or play I explain to people sitting near me that I have this illness and make noises, that I can't help it.

They are great, they always say, "Don't worry about it." (Hochman, 1980, p. 116).

Like Brian, who passed gas and apologized, Orrin would solicitously "explain," be granted "permission" by surrounding people, and then carry out disruptive behaviors. This is not to suggest that Orrin or others with TS-OCD can easily control such somatized, overlearned behaviors during a specific concert; but it illustrates that during some earlier phase of development the needs for autonomy and appreciation became fused.

Would You Still Like Me If I Poked You in the Ribs?

Another ambitendent person described his experience in these words:

> As the years passed, the tics became worse. Not only did the twitches increase in intensity, other forms of tics appeared. At times I would suddenly jerk my arm violently, kick out with my leg, twist my torso, and throw my head to the right, left, or backwards. At the age of 15 or 16, I began to make vocal noises which gradually increased in severity and intensity. It often sounded like a sudden explosion, and anybody within hearing distance would suddenly jump from fright. . . . The severity and intensity of the tics has never been constant. When sitting alone and reading, or just daydreaming, there was no more than mild twitching. But as soon as another person entered the room, a feeling of tension would suddenly engulf me and the tics would start acting up. . . . If a person other than my wife or children enter the room, my voice will usually act up and if someone sits right next to me, I often begin twitching my arm and poking him in the ribs. (Werner, 1976, p. 2)

Persons with TS-OCD balance such intrusive assertions of autonomy with needs for attention and appreciation. Here the "nice" self "apologizes" for the flatulence, or poking, or other disturbing behavior carried out by the autonomous and angry self.

> I have generally found that no matter how abnormal and undesirable a condition appears at first, most intelligent people are extremely patient and understanding once the condition becomes familiar to them. I do not require sympathy from others, but I have resigned myself to the fact that I am dependent upon their patience and understanding. All I had to do was to prove that I could function despite my apparent disability and, thank God, I have succeeded in proving this many times over. (Werner, 1976, p. 4)

Tics: Somatized Routines for Meeting Object-Relational Needs

It has been shown that tics attempt to *simultaneously* meet object relational needs of infancy (stimulation, discharge, differentiation, soothing), toddlerhood (expansiveness, exhibition), early childhood (autonomy), and adolescence (appreciation, self-esteem). What is fascinating to note is how nearly *all* TS symptoms retain elements of earlier needs while attempting to simultaneously meet more contemporary needs.

Herein lies the entrapping, circular nature of TS-OCD. Instead of meeting object relational needs in a more normal sequential way, TS-OCD persons never completely satisfy single needs because such needs are not developmentally differentiated. Consequently, attempts to meet such needs tend to be primitive and global—undifferentiated. It is difficult to meet your needs for autonomy and appreciation in the same relationship simultaneously. Most people find it difficult to like a person when that person is telling them off. A mother finds it difficult to cuddle or soothe a baby who's trying to hit her in the face or wriggle free.

COPROLALIA: FROM ONE-UPMANSHIP TO BRINKMANSHIP

The study of coprolalia is fascinating because this shouting of forbidden words embodies the defiance and rage of the autonomous child and at the same time, the need for attention and appreciation so vital to adults. It is *not* coincidental that coprolalia typically makes its initial appearance during adolescence. Summarizing a number of studies, Shapiro, Shapiro, Bruun, and Sweet (1978, p. 149) report that coprolalia occurs in about 55% of TS patients and that the average age of onset is about 13.5 years, with an average of 6.4 years between onset of TS and coprolalia. This is consistent with the current understanding of TS-OCD as needs-fulfillment behavior. Coprolalia is also interesting because it is midway between TS and OCD—bridging the gap, as it were, between primitive somatic behaviors, and higher-level social behaviors.

What will become apparent, as I share with you my experiences at the 1989 National Convention of the Tourette Syndrome Association, is that coprolalia is not a crude neurological reflex; quite the opposite. It is fine-tuned *brinkmanship* at its best: a social chess game that pushes opponents to the very edge, yet never quite over. Brinkmanship refers to a highly sophisticated interaction that retains core elements of the

"Gotcha" (one-upmanship) of earlier years, but does it in a much more socially sensitive manner. This "will-you-still-like-me-if-I-insult-you" sandwich is flavored with a lot of humor in order to make it palatable.

Coprolalia, more than any other TS symptom, challenges the organic paradigm. This is no epileptiform convulsion–no knee jerk reflex arc. It requires an exquisitely tuned sense of social parameters in order to successfully pull it off, yet it contains primary process expressions of the "crudest" sorts. This is not the kind of behavior carried out by the reptile brain or the deeper parts of the premammalian brainstem. On the contrary, coprolalia integrates the most basic behavioral needs with the highest social realities and this requires high-level cortical functioning of the kind we've suggested is learned in the developmental journey from infancy to adulthood—much like one learns language, music, art, and social manners.

A Most Unusual Convention

"This convention," I thought, "is like vaudeville theater—and it's tax deductible!" Unlike the tedious, sleep-inducing atmosphere one finds at many professional meetings, the mood at the 1989 convention of the Tourette Syndrome Association (TSA) was more festive than scholarly. Not that the academics didn't give it their best shot, but any might-be-pompous presenters were easily undone by creative hecklers (psychiatrists label them "coprolalic") sprinkled throughout the audience.

Candlelight and Silver

The occasion is the evening keynote presentation. Seated around tables with china, silver, and cloth napkins picturesquely folded into crystal goblets, is an amazingly diverse group of people. Parents, children, teachers, social workers, psychologists, physicians, coalesce in what feels like a large family reunion. The food is excellent—from hors d'oeuvres through baked Alaska—conversation is lively, and a variety of behavioral oddities are noticed with about the same passing interest one gives pedestrians while eating at a sidewalk cafe. Sudden shrieks and yells lose their intensity when mixed with sounds of silver and dishes, laughter and conversation. A young man stands up and begins to beat his knife and fork against his dinner plate in the style and intensity of a jazz drummer, it attracts only momentary notice. There is almost a surreal quality. Here shakers and shouters, twitchers and tremblers, cursers and cursed at, all gather around the supper table and experience a level of acceptance and harmony difficult to find elsewhere on the planet. It's like living in another place or time—a curious-but-kindly Camelot.

As waiters hurriedly clear dishes from tables and well-dined conventioneers turn their chairs in the direction of the speaker's platform, I sense a subtle change in the auditory ambience. The seemingly random yells and shrieks now change to a chorus of "boo!" The speaker is making his way to the podium, and I'm about to learn that coprolalia is *not* a neurologically driven, reflexive shouting of random obscenities. On the contrary—like humor—it is exquisitely tuned to situational parameters, balancing brinkmanship and autonomy with the finesse of a high-wire acrobatic act. It always involves speaking or shouting precisely what is forbidden in specific situations. During the meal, sudden shrieks or shouts had tested the tolerance of nearby diners, but this was not "testy" enough for a speaker some distance away. Hence, the startling yelps, shrieks, and shouts that had been randomly punctuating the air only seconds before, gave way—as the speaker approached the lectern— to a steadily rising chorus of "Boo!" It reminded me of what an auditorium sounds like when the concertmaster sounds a note and the orchestra tunes up for the performance. Indeed, the coprolalics in the audience were "tuning" for the "performance."

Keynote Address with Audience Participation

Now the speaker is introduced; we are told of his many notable achievements in the field of child psychiatry, his research accomplishments through the years, and his consistent interest in TS, including his service to the Association through committee memberships and elected office. The psychiatrist from the Yale Child Study Center makes his way toward the microphone. His scalp glistens under the synergistic effect of perspiration and bright overhead lighting. I scrutinize the speaker: "Is this going to be a 'sleeper' or a great speech?" I wonder. "Looks like an impressive guy . . . sharp suit . . . poised . . . sure is bald." He begins speaking in a paced, serious, methodical manner. Suddenly, about three sentences into his presentation, someone in the audience shouts: "Get hair!" (followed by audience laughter)

Tonight the audience participation is lively:

"Boring!" shouts someone a few sentences further into the speech (more laughter).

"Hey listen! I'm a virgin!" a voice cries out.

"Bullshit!" replies another.

I wonder to myself, "Was that last sequence just coincidence, or do they 'converse' with each other?" The answer was soon obvious because during the remainder of the presentation various audience members coprolalically communicated with one another or with the speaker. These "conversations" occurred in brief sequences, erupting unpredictably, yet following a pattern of one-upmanship-communication among various coprolalic "leaders" in the audience:

"Cheap sex here!"

"Cheaper sex here!"

"Psychoslut!"

Or (in the tone and cadence of a hen clucking over having just laid an egg):

"Fuck, fuck, fuck chick-e-e-n! Fuck, fuck, fuck chick-e-e-n!"

"I fuck chickens!"

"I fuck chickens but what do you fuck?"

There is here a sequence of one-upmanship among various audience members with each playing off the other:

"I wonder, I wonder, I wonder, I wonder *what* I wonder!"

"You don't wonder—you don't even think!"

Some remarks seem less "conversational"—less directed to other coprolalics and designed more for the general audience. Yet even in these sequences there is a one-up quality of outdoing the other.

"Fire!"

"I've got a gun!"

(Confronting someone with a weapon is more immediately serious than a fire.)

Numerous remarks continue to be directed to the speaker:

"Oh, shut up!"

"Boring!"

"Louder!"

And finally, as the speaker is about to "wind up" his presentation, he remarks: "Before I close, I want to give one more case study illustrating . . . " Someone quickly shouts: "Quit now!"

I leave the meeting, a few minutes early, pondering what I've just experienced. Astonished at the social sensitivity of the shouting, I'm reminded of a comment by the surrealists: "Hysteria," they wrote, "is not a disease, it is art." Could the same be written about coprolalia? Doubtless, there are times when such shoutings seem reflexive, uncontrollable, but tonight I'm aware of humor, of conversational fine-tuning, and of an exquisite sense of social boundaries that underlies all successful humor. Puzzled, preoccupied, I absentmindedly meander down the hall searching for the men's room.

Encounter in the Hall

"Look out!" someone shouts, "She bites!" Had I not been so deep in thought—ruminating—I might have heard the barking and growling behind me, but now it's too late. I feel teeth against the calf of my right leg. I wince—waiting for the pain. "Why don't people keep their dogs on leashes?" I angrily wonder. Whirling around, I tense my other leg, ready to kick. "Maybe the dog is getting some teeth into my leg, but it's going to have a sore mouth out of this!" I'm about to give it my best kick when suddenly—midair—I freeze. The jaw I'm about to dislocate belongs not to a dog but *to a lady*!

THE LADY WHO BARKS AND BITES

Just "Grazing"

As it turns out, she doesn't bite deeply into my leg, preferring instead just to "graze." As she later explained it:

"Biting is something I just *need* to do at times. It's just a nagging feeling. Like when I bit you, I really wanted to bite your shoulder. You have a very nice shoulder, but since I was on the floor, I went for your legs. My parents have black and blue marks all over their shoulders. But they don't have as many as they used to, because a lot of the time now, I just graze."

"You just graze?" I'm puzzled.

"Yeah, I just graze—I just sort of nibble, run my teeth across lightly. I bite a lot less than I used to. When I need to bite, I bite this finger [indicating one of her own fingers], and it doesn't have any nerves left in it. My folks are really good, they let me graze, and if sometimes I just *have* to bite they'll let me bite for a certain amount of time, and then if I can't let go, they'll just pop [release] my jaw. Sometimes when I'm biting them, I get very irrational and yell 'That doesn't hurt!' But they understand, and after they've let me bite for awhile they just pop my jaw, and we all go on our way. That's just the way it is."

"How long have you been biting or grazing?" I ask.

"I've done it ever since I've had Tourette—since I was 18. It's just a need, and it releases energy. I used to have a need to really chomp down and hurt people—I didn't graze then, I just started biting and then I'd say 'Oh, that doesn't hurt!"

"But you really knew it hurt?"

"Oh yeah, I knew it hurt, but when I get into a Tourette mode, I'm always right! I say weird phrases that I mean—when I'm in that mode—but that I would say normally. Like I say 'It doesn't hurt!—It doesn't!' I get very irrational. I'm always right and everyone else is always wrong; I sometimes even sound like a baby."

"When we first met—when you bit my leg—you were crawling around on the floor and people were saying 'Watch out! She bites!' how did that make you feel?"

"It doesn't bother me when people say, 'Watch out! She bites!,' but I would rather they said 'Go ahead and graze . . . I'll let you graze, but don't bite me.' Then I could go ahead and release enough energy so I could go on and be normal."

A Tic is Like a Ball of Energy

"What do you mean about 'releasing energy'?" I continue.

"I have this big ball of energy building up mostly in here (indicates abdomen and pelvic regions), but I can feel it all over. It's like a *ball* of energy. Sometimes it's very big and dense, sometimes big and diffuse. Other times it's small, but very dense.

"What was it like when you were biting my leg?"

"Well, I had calmed down quite a bit by then. When I started, it was quite large and dense; but when I was biting you, it was smaller and less diffuse—I wasn't calmed down completely, but it was much less."

"How often does this energy build up?"

"All the time. It builds up constantly, but when it gets to a certain point I have to let it out. I usually try to let it out mainly at home, or around my friends. I never let it out at school. I'd rather be with people when I tic, so I don't hurt my head by banging it against things. But I can tic by myself if I have to. Usually I do it in bed. I've broken four beds with violent tics, so now my mattress is on the floor. It's not very far to the floor if I roll off, and I can't break anything."

Feeling Like the Animals

"When you were letting off energy by biting my leg, did you *feel* like a dog?

"Yeah, sometimes when I'm barking or crawling around on the floor, I think of myself as a dog. But other times, I just think of myself as a *person* crawling around on the floor barking, growling, biting, or whatever. It depends—I get into these different modes. Sometimes I get into my animal mode, and other times I get into my normal Tourette mode. The animal mode is a special part of my Tourette mode.

"Sometimes when I'm in the animal mode, I lift my leg and I'll sniff, I've even wet my pants—wetting your pants is a marvelous tic!—embarrassing, but pleasant."

"Have you ever felt like any other animals besides a dog?"

"A water buffalo and a cow. Moo-o-o-o-o-o! Moo-o-o-o-o-o! Moo-o-o-o-o-o! (She loudly demonstrates). Basically I make the same sounds for a cow and water buffalo, but when I'm a water buffalo, I stretch my neck out like this (demonstrates). When I'm a cow, it sounds the same, but I *feel* like a cow and I don't stretch my neck out.

"Baa-a-a-a-a! baa-a-a-a-a! baa-a-a-a-a! Sometimes I feel like a sheep. I will go up to you and nuzzle you and nibble you a little when I'm a sheep, 'cause sheep do that."

(Suddenly, and loudly) "Suck my cock! (pause) Oh, shut up! Oh, shut up, Paul!"

"And who is Paul?" I ask.

"Nobody I know, I just got the name off a name tag at the banquet tonight."

Coprolalia—A Foul-Mouthed Version of One-upmanship

"Speaking of the banquet, could you explain the meaning of all this talk about "fucking chickens?" I heard someone tonight sounding like a chicken cackling about having just laid an egg—'fuck, fuck, fuck chicke-e-e-n! fuck, fuck, fuck chick-e-e-n!' What's that about?"

"Steve does that. Then Elaine came up with: 'I fuck chickens!' And I came up with: 'I fuck chickens, what do you fuck?'

"We each have our own little version. I always have to get in the last word. Like if someone says: 'Cheap sex here!' I say: 'Cheaper sex here!' and then I'd get all the business (laughter). Sometimes I even rhyme things. Like Elaine started saying 'I have AIDS!' so I came up with: 'I have AIDS, I really do, gonorrhea and syphilis too!'

"I also like alliteration—starting everything with the same letter. Like take your name—John, I could say something like 'John jumps jelly beans in January.'"

Tics and Obsessions are Intertwined

"Isn't that a little obsessive trying to get all J's together?"

"Un huh, but it's a tic and my obsessiveness and tics go hand in hand. I've had compulsions all my life. I've counted—all my life I've counted. My homework has never been right. And when I used to do chores, I used to take people with me to check on me, because I was sure I would forget something. I *knew* I would do things wrong or leave a rabbit's cage open so that all the rabbits would get out. I did that once. I *did* leave the rabbit cages open and the rabbits *did* get out—one time. After that, I had this compulsion to keep checking the rabbit cages and I would check them for a half hour. We only have twenty rabbits, so it really wasn't necessary to check them for a half hour.

Up Your Nose!

(She begins barking) "Ruff-ruff! ruff-ruff! r-r-r-r-r-ruff! ruff! Baa-a-a-a-a-a-a-a! Do you have a good-sized nose? Let me see, yeah, you have a moderately good-sized nose. My father can get a half dollar up his nostrils—*that* is a good-sized nose. You couldn't do that—I would say you have a penny- or dime-nose. Not a nickel. A lot of people have weird noses where their nostrils don't go all the way to the end of their nose. I have this fetish for noses. I've stuck everything up my nose. Everything goes up my nose—vinegar—vinegar is one of the best highs you can ever have—I got chemical pneumonia from it."

Curious, I ask: "What other kinds of things have you put up our nose?"

"Hot peppers, rabbit droppings, rabbit food, dog droppings, horse droppings—I like droppings. Anything—everything—leaves, paper, dirt, stones, everything goes up my nose."

"What do you think of just before you put things up your nose?"

"I just think: 'It's gotta go up there!' 'It *has* to go up there!' "

"My guess is that sometime when you were a child someone must have told you not to put things up your nose. Maybe no one exactly said 'Don't stick droppings up your nose,' but somewhere along the way your Mom must have told you not to put things there."

"Oh, shut up! . . . Shut up! . . . Oh, shut up! . . . Shut your mouth! . . . Suck my cock! . . . Oh, shut up! . . . Oh, shut up! . . . Oh, shut up!"

Earliest Compulsions

"How old were you when your symptoms began?"

"When I was younger, I cleared my throat. For as long as I can remember, I cleared my throat. That was the only symptom I had until junior high. Then, in the seventh grade, I started barking."

"Did kids in school make fun of you for clearing your throat?"

"No, they didn't for clearing my throat, but they did when I started barking in the seventh grade. I have things written in my year book like 'Ruff, ruff—have a good year!' And I would be called names. I can't remember now what they were but I know kids called me cruel names. But I had some kids who barked back at me; which was really neat, 'cause I could bark to them, and we would bark back and forth."

(She begins to stare at my knee and leans over—we were both sitting in the hallway—and begins nibbling my knee.) "I'll graze—you have very nice legs—so thin. I'll just graze, I won't bite, you don't have to worry."

Early Physical Focus

"What is your fascination with legs?" I asked.

"One of my legs is larger than the other. I guess it's because I'm self-conscious about my legs that I notice other people's legs. I had several operations on my leg to lengthen the tendon. The first one was when I was 18 months old—very young. I had three or four more after that, right on into the fifth grade. They tried all different kinds of things, like stretching it with a cast, or stretching it physically, but none of it worked very well and one of my legs is still shorter than the other.

"I started walking late and always walked funny. Kids teased me about the way I walked. I've been teased from kindergarten up. When I walk, because of my shorter leg, my bottom wiggles so kids teased me about it. They called me 'Wiggle butt' or 'Boom Butt.'"

"Kids can be pretty cruel can't they?"

"Oh yeah, awful! It really bothered me, because I knew I wasn't doing this on purpose—it wasn't something I *wanted* to do. It wasn't something I could help. They were bugging me about things over which I had no control."

"Did you ever tell them: 'Oh, shut up!'"

"No, I never did, but I wish I could have. My family helped a lot to lessen my anger. They told me that there will always be jerks in society and to just do the best that I could and to forget about it. And that's what I tried to do with my Tourette. I've tried to ignore what people say about it."

"I wonder if you're yelling 'Oh shut up!' now is a kind of delayed response to the ridicule you had to tolerate as a young child?"

"Maybe."

At this point it is very late in the evening, so I thank her for the information she shared with me and we go our separate ways. I only saw her from a distance the next day. On the last day of the convention—I was sitting near the rear of the main auditorium listening to a lecture, when she approached me and asked me if I would go out in the hall and be with her while she "released some energy." I agreed, and on the way out, she explained that she would be returning home in the evening by plane and didn't want to have it occur on the flight. It was about three o'clock in the afternoon and her flight didn't leave until nine-thirty in the evening, but she felt she needed to do her tics now.

Letting It All Hang Out

She lay down on the floor and began pounding her heels and legs into the carpet in a rhythmic manner. I encouraged her to describe the experience to me:

"I'm feeling quite relaxed. Oh, s-h-h-h-h shut up! Shut your mouth! I hope that doctor is gone. I don't want him to come near me. Yesterday, when I was letting out energy—before I bit you—one of the doctors was trying to make me stop ticquing. And what I needed to have was exactly what Cheryl (a nurse who assisted her) was doing. She just held my head to make sure it was safe and she let me tic. That is all I need. Then there was another doctor—downstairs a little later—who kept wanting me to get up and shake hands with him. He was trying to distract me, but distracting doesn't work with me. If they distract me, I will hold it in, but I've got to get it out sooner or later, so it's really silly to have anyone try to stop me from doing it.

"Kind of like putting a lid on a teakettle—just builds up more pressure?"

"Yeah, that's what it's like."

(She continues kicking in rhythmic, convulsive, whole-body fashion. It has the appearance of a grand mal seizure in slow motion. During the entire episode, however, she is fully conscious and converses with me, much as someone can converse while riding an exercise bike. Still apparently upset by the comments of some of the convention physicians, she continues.)

"Then this doctor told me that I needed to have someone look after me—babysit me for awhile because I might tic again. But there are people around here I know, so all I have to do is ask them 'Will you go out in the hall with me?' I don't need a babysitter. I'm an adult and I don't like being told I need a babysitter. My doctor at home—he isn't one of the one's who tries to stop me. He just lets me go totally out. He understands this is what I have to do."

Resisting Primary Process Urges

She sits up now and lets out a long strange noise that sounds like a cross between her sheep "ba-a-a-a" and a football cheer: "Ra-a-a-a-a-ah! I'm going to grab your genitals, and I'm trying very hard not to."

"What can I do to make it easier for you?" I ask (while slowly pushing her body away from me).

"Just don't let me do it."

"I won't—I know we'll both be more comfortable if you don't."

(Laughing) "Yes! I think we probably would!"

(By now her movements are much less intense. We continue talking.)

Energy-Releasing Behaviors

"Do you have ways of releasing energy at home that are socially acceptable?" I ask.

"Yes, I swim and I walk." They both help me quite a bit when I feel the energy building up. The hardest thing is my dance class. It's folk dance—very loose and very moving—I've had the kind of tics in class that I'm having here now. The dance class seems to make it worse—but swimming and walking help."

"I would guess that those activities help let off *physical* energy. Do you have any ways of letting off *social* steam?"

"Well since I've been talking to you, I've figured out that it is important for me to have the last word. Like even when I agree I find myself saying 'Yup!' or 'Yeah!' "

"That's good, it allows you to get in the last word in a way that is socially positive."

Even Dictaphones Are Fun to Chew

(By now she seems to have gotten most of the major tics out of her system and is just patting her hands on the floor. Now she shows a sudden interest in the dictaphone that I've been using (with her permission, of course) to record our conversations. She begins running her teeth along the edges of it and starts exclaiming.)

"Tic, tic, tic, tictaphone! Tic, tic, tic, tictaphone! Hi! Anybody in there? Hey! anybody in there? Hi-i-i-i-i-i-i!" (kisses the dictaphone several times in succession). "There, now I think I'm socially comfortable, I'll be OK on the plane now. Thanks. I like you. You really know what I'm going through."

Later in the day, after checking out, I notice her as I walk through the lobby on my way to the parking garage. She is sitting in one of the overstuffed chairs, suitcase by her side—asleep.

Commentary

She described her *excessive energy* as an "energy ball." Sometimes dense, sometimes not so heavy, but always there—building up.

Early physical trauma was one of the primary risk factors present in her early life. The series of surgeries on her leg, beginning at about 18 months old and continuing until fifth grade, certainly had impact on her psychological development, anchoring her sense of self more firmly in the body than is optimal. This was then intensified when her playmates ridiculed her about the way she walked, calling her "Wiggle Butt" and other derogatory names.

All this activity, centered around her leg, undoubtedly caused her parents to inadvertently become *hyperattentive*. They may not have constantly told her to "Quit it!" about her tics, but they were likely coerced by her physical condition and her tics into devoting inordinate amounts of time to her.

Paradoxical instructions probably came from playmates and teachers. Recall that she said she had cleared her throat for as long as she could remember, but that it was only when she started "barking" in the seventh grade that peers started making fun of her. At that point, it is likely that she was told to "Stop!"

It is also during the school years that she experienced high *stress*. Few experiences create more stress than being ridiculed by one's peers, and her nickname of "Wiggle Butt" indicates a chronic, early stressor, that didn't seem to let up. When she began "barking" it is likely that other nicknames followed.

Primary process remains a significant part of her current life as it was during her childhood. Stuffing all types of things up her nose, including various kinds of animal droppings, is an indicator of her "earthiness." How much this was repressed in her childhood is difficult to know, but her continuing difficulties suggest problems were present.

Her *bifurcated personality* is something one experiences in her presence. Even while she carries on an intellectual conversation, this is punctuated with animal sounds and urges to grab genitals. The poised and the primitive coexist.

In summary, this woman presents a dynamic and lucid illustration of the labile nature of obsessive and compulsive disorders. In her presence—when she's letting the "energy" out—one has a feeling of "What's next?" Her tics are dramatic and change rapidly. However she *does* have the ability to control her tics for several hours at a time; so although she exhibits a broad spectrum of compulsions and obsessions, the driving force behind them is not so intense as to require outlet on a moment-by-moment basis, as is the case for many. In this respect, she seems more like Peter the Great than Samuel Johnson. As long as she can get periodic relief by letting go, she is able to function somewhat normally when in public. Even her crawling on the floor, barking, and grazing my leg, must be understood in the social context of the national convention of the Tourette Syndrome Association—a generally compassionate group of persons who are accustomed to such unusual behaviors.

THE BILINGUAL COPROLALIC: SWEARS IN THE LANGUAGE OF HIS LISTENER

Interview on the Run

Milton is a tall, handsome young man. During the TSA convention, he perpetually paced around during meetings. Sitting near the rear of the auditorium, he regularly exited and reentered the room, yelped and shouted frequently. Seldom sitting for more than a few seconds, he seemed constantly in motion. It was obvious that sitting down to visit with him would not fit his style, so I walked alongside him while he was pacing the halls and asked if I could interview him. The swarthy young Puerto Rican agreed, smiling easily and conversing rapidly. I paced alongside him up and down the hall, gathering the following information.

"When did your TS begin?"

"I was around five. I don't remember much about my childhood. Because I was very shy, people were making fun of me all the time. It was worse in kindergarten and first grade. I went to the same school kindergarten through 12th grade, so by the time I got to high school, the kids didn't make fun of me any more."

"What were things like at home for you?"

"Well, a lot of people with TS say their parents don't understand them, but that wasn't true of my folks. We got along fine. My father is a pediatrician and my mother had some kind of TS when she was younger. I remember she used to jerk her head, and when she read the paper she sometimes tore it in two by pulling on the sides. I remember seeing her do that stuff. If it weren't for the support of my parents, I wouldn't have gone as far as I have.

"I have a college degree in management. I went to a regular Catholic high school—not too many problems. I took five and a half years to graduate, but I made it! It's been tough finding a job because of my TS. Even though I have a degree in management, I work at a Seven Eleven convenience store—it's the only place I could get a job. I like computers, but I can't deal with them—my fingers hit the wrong keys."

"What are your most common tics?"

"Yelping and coprolalia. I say bad words—anything from 'pussy' to 'I don't give a shit!' "

"Do you say them in English or Spanish?"

"Either way. If I'm with people who speak English, I tend to say things in English; around Spanish people I say it in Spanish"

"Bilingual coprolalia?"

(Laughing) "Yeah, 'bicopral!' " I think if I was around some French guy, I'd invent some bad French words to say."

"I also touch myself a lot, I hit myself on the wall, I hit other people—but I say 'Sorry, I didn't mean to.' I bit my tongue, *it was severe.* I nearly destroyed my mouth once chewing on it. I grind my teeth at night. I chew my lips. You can tell, I'm pretty severe.

"My tics are always changing, I go through different periods with different combinations. Also, I often *blend* my tics. Like I'll start moving my arm (demonstrates socking the air) and then say 'Y-o-o-o-o-o-shit!'

"Somebody told me that people with TS tend to do it less when they're around strangers and then "burst out" or "let go" when they get home. With me it's just the opposite. When I'm around people I don't know, I get real noisy, then when I get back to my room, I relax. I can go 12 to 14 hours without doing a noise if I'm by myself watching TV or reading a book or whatever."

"How about if you're in a room and you know you're *supposed* to be quiet?"

"Yeah, then I have to make noise."

Just then Milton spotted a friend with whom he wanted to have lunch, quickly asked me if I had any more questions, and was gone almost before I could spurt out "No, this has been very helpful—Thank you!"

Commentary

My interview with Milton was succinct and intense—much like the young man himself. His *excessive energy* was bursting out all modalities. He walked, talked, yelped, shouted, cursed with machine-gun pace. The entire interview took less than five minutes.

He did not specifically mention his parents as being *overattentive*, but the fact that his mother jerked her head and pulled newspapers apart, would de facto mean she would be sensitive to her son's developing tics, and likely, inadvertently, try to control in her infant what she couldn't control in herself.

Although Milton didn't report any early or chronic physical problems, the intensity of his *somatizing* is remarkable. His tics involve very primitive (developmentally early) behaviors such as chewing on his tongue, biting his lips, touching and hitting himself. Even his "higher-level" coprolalia is often *blended* with body movements like socking the air with his arm.

Like Peter the Great, this young man is firmly anchored in his soma. His self is a "body" self. What is most salient about him is not so much the *bifurcation* of personality but the *somatization* of it. It isn't so much that there were parallel lines of development (somatic and cognitive), rather it is that he lives so much of his life in his body.

Again we see the crucial role of shame: "People were making fun of me all the time," he recalled. In addition to this ridicule—most likely originating from peers—teachers and other adults would likely have asked him (paradoxically) to "Stop doing that!"

Milton's swearing in the language of his listeners provides a fascinating example of the high level of social awareness present in persons with coprolalia, even when it exists alongside physically intensive symptoms. If the primary forces driving obscene outbursts were neurological in nature, it would make sense to curse in Spanish when around English-speaking listeners, and vice versa. Quite the opposite occurs, however, as the coprolalic interacts with his listeners in a game of social brinkmanship. This is strikingly illustrated in a case discussed by Catrou (1890) and more recently by Shapiro, Shapiro, Bruun, and Sweet (1978). A nine-year-old boy lost his coprolalia when he was told the words were not swear words.

Chapter 5

DANGEROUS BRINKMANSHIP

Robb is a boyishly handsome man who looks more like 30 than his chronological age of nearly fifty. When you're with Robb, you don't feel put off by his behavior; his tics are not obtrusive. The flamboyance and exhibitionism in many of the coprolalic cases discussed thus far, is replaced by a more gentle "quiet" humor. One doesn't feel edgy—worrying about "What will come next?" He's a pleasant man, immediately likeable. Yet all is not well. Robb is driven to a "Russian-roulette" kind of brinkmanship that endangers his very life. But that's getting ahead of the story.

THE ELECTRICIAN WHO HAD TO TOUCH BARE WIRES

Life with Grandma

"Grandma! Oh, *please,* Grandma! Please take it off, I promise I'll be good—*Please! I promise* I won't do it again!"

"Twitchy"—that's what the other kids called him—had again been reduced to begging. The tear tracks, weaving their way among the freckles of his six-year-old cheeks, were hardly noticeable. What was arresting was the naked desperation in his eyes—when you could see his eyes. It was no small accomplishment to actually look—fleetingly—into this young boy's eyes. His face, pale and contorted with fear, twitched constantly. He shook his head rhythmically—sandwiching eye blinks and grimaces between shakes.

But grandmother, with a confidence born of ignorance, remained resolute. Her composure was disquieting. She'd witnessed this sequel to her "habit breaker" many times. First the fighting, then the screaming, and finally—it always came to this—the hoarse pleading and the promises. Slowly, reluctantly, she would give in. "You can't keep a child's arms tied behind his back with bicycle inner tubes forever!" she thought. She moved towards him—glacially, coldly. "Now I don't want to see you *ever* punch yourself in the sides with your elbows again! Is that clear?"

"I promise Grandma, I promise!"

But even as she slowly loosened her bicycle-inner-tube strait jacket, Grandmother knew the promises wouldn't be kept. "Twitchy" would promise again and again not to do all those strange things—blink his eyes, shake his head, grimace—and worst of all—punch his ribs; but he would not (or was it *could* not?) stop. No, she was convinced, he *could* stop if only he tried harder. And if it took tying his elbows behind his back with bicycle inner tubes to help him remember . . . well, then that's how it would have to be!

Then it came to her. She had been struggling for too long by herself. The child's grandfather was no help. He never took such things seriously. "Leave the kid alone," he would say, "he'll outgrow all that jumpin around, he's just got ants in his pants. Shucks, I was kind of a live wire myself when I was a kid." But she knew better. A stop had to put to all this nonsense before it got out of hand. "As the twig is bent . . ." wasn't there some proverb like that? It was time to get additional help and she knew precisely who would help her.

School Days—Reading, Writing, and Ridicule

Grandma and Miss Standish were on the same wavelength. They had spoken many times through the years when Chester ("Twitchy's" father) had been in school, and she was still teaching the first four grades. Over 35 years in the same classroom! There was some talk about her retiring, but fortunately (*calamitously* for "Twitchy"), she decided to stay on another couple of years. Miss Standish was of the "old school." She was stern, Grandmother maintained, because she cared about the kids. But being on the receiving end of this "caring" was not an experience children recalled with fondness. I could still hear the hurt and humiliation in Robb's voice when he told me of his elementary school experiences some 40 years later:

"People were always telling me to 'Stop it!' And in that little Nebraska farm town folks weren't very sophisticated in those days. I hated school. Kids were always teasing me and nobody ever called me Robb. It was always "Shakey," "Twitchy," or "Blinkey," depending on who you were talking with. And teachers would slap you. My grandmother went to school and told the teachers it was just a habit, so they all tried to break me of it. When slapping didn't work, they figured they could embarrass me into quitting. So they sat me in front of the class facing the other kids—knowing the other kids would imitate and ridicule me. Of course you know what happens—it just makes it worse. It wasn't a fun time!"

As Robb relives some of these experiences, I notice his tics increase a bit, and there is tension in his face. But there is also something cathartic going on—he seems eager to talk, so we continue.

"What were your primary tics during those early school years?"

"I first started out sniffing and blinking my eyes—real bad. I still have those. The arm jabbing lasted about two or three years—my Grandmother finally gave up on the bicycle inner tubes—then it went into my hands and I beat the sides of my legs. Then I did lip curling where my mouth was sore all the time. You curl your lip up, almost touch your nose with it. That lasted for years. I remember I used to put things on it that tasted bad, so I wouldn't lick my lips all the time. I think the lip curling started because I tended to hide my face—because of my eye blinking—in my hands. I had my hand over my face so much of the time that I started playing with my lip and my finger."

State Mental Hospital

"A lot of my childhood is blurry—you block a lot of it out." (Robb was pensive for about 60 seconds—it seemed more like 10 minutes. His body shifted subtly—bracing as if to walk into a cold wind.) "They put me in the state mental hospital." (He continued haltingly. There was pain in his blinking eyes—the tic increasing as if to "blink back" the psychic tears that still fought for expression four decades after the experience.) "Nebraska Psychiatric Institute it was called. After my grandmother and teachers couldn't get me to quit—after they felt they couldn't control me, they finally just put me in the state mental hospital."

"Well, as you might guess, that was *not* a fun time either. It was just a giant holding pen where they put children they couldn't handle. They used to have a man sit outside your door at night so you couldn't go anywhere. They did a lot of threatening in those days. There was no treatment—just custodial. I think I saw a psychiatrist only once the entire time I was there! They wouldn't let my Dad come and visit me."

"How old were you when you were hospitalized?"

"Gosh! I'm not sure, but I think I was about 12. Yeah, I was there for two or three years, and I got out when I was 15."

"And what happened when you got out?"

Marriage and a Son

"After I got out, I finally got away from my grandmother. I moved to Hastings where my mother lived and I stayed with her for awhile. My parents divorced when I was about a year old and one of them was incapable of taking care of me (my Mom) and the other didn't want to. But by the time I got out of the mental hospital, my Mom had steady work and I was able to work as well, so I lived with her for about a year, and then I got married. I was 16. That lasted about two years. I had a son by her."

"What went wrong in the marriage?"

"She drank a lot, and when she did, she would run around on me with guys she met at bars. I caught her with a guy once, and I left because I was afraid for her safety—afraid of what I might do to her. I got custody of our son, but again my grandmother stepped in and took over. She ended up getting my son."

"How'd she manage that?"

"Well, after the divorce, I tried to take care of my son for a year or two, but in those days if a man got custody of a child, the different agencies hassled you all the time—you know, social service people. They were always checking up on me, trying to find things wrong, so I moved in with my grandmother—it was the only place I had to go. Then I joined the navy, and when I went in, my grandmother and I made an agreement that once I got permanent assignment, they would all come with my son and we'd live together. Well, I was in boot camp only a couple of weeks when I got a court summons charging me with desertion. I couldn't show up for the hearing—I was in boot camp!—and so my grandmother automatically got him. I didn't have anything to do with her for a lot of years after that."

Navy

"What was it like for you in the navy?"

"Not too good. I got through boot camp OK, but got into trouble almost as soon as it was over. At my first duty station, I was attending gunner's mate school. I wink (tic) a lot and the navy chief who was teaching the class didn't like me winking at him. He warned me one day: 'If you wink at me anymore, I'm gonna send you over for a psych evaluation!' Well, as you can guess, I did and he did!

"He sent me over to the hospital and they put me on the psychiatric ward—in isolation. It was one of those places that has mattresses on the walls, ceiling, floor—so you can't hurt yourself. They kept me there a couple of weeks. We had like 60 guys in there and only two or three orderlies watching, so the only way they could manage all of us was with Thorazine® (chlorpromazine). Every morning they'd line you up and zap you with Thorazine and then you'd stand around like a zombie all day. That's what they did the whole time I was in there."

"Do you recall how long you were there?"

"I was there two or three months. They wanted me to sign my veteran's rights away, but I refused. Finally, they got tired of trying to talk me into it and gave me a medical discharge—said I was a paranoid schizophrenic. They gave me a quart bottle of Thorazine—500 mg. to take with me when I left. Naturally, I couldn't function on that stuff—couldn't work or anything. I decided I *had* to get off it and that's when I was introduced to Valium® (diazepam). I ended up taking Valium for 20 years. I started out taking not too much, but with Valium you get addicted. I was taking 50 to 70 pills a day. It never helped my Tourette, but with that much Valium, you don't care if you twitch or not.

Married Again

"I started drinking in 1964, got remarried, and discovered alcohol. Then I basically did the same thing with alcohol that my first wife had done. I spent most of my time in bars and running around. I had two sons with this woman and—surprisingly—it lasted 12 years. But finally, my alcoholism got so bad she divorced me. Two months later, I got married again—to one of the gals I'd been running around with. We both used alcohol all the time and lived a pretty wild life. When she got pregnant—since I'd had a vasectomy—I knew it wasn't mine, so I divorced her. I was 36 at the time.

And Married Once More

"I decided to go back to college. I worked as a security guard and got free classes. While I was there, I met this real nice girl; we decided to get married. We got along fine, but her parents were real wealthy. She was used to Nieman-Marcus and I'm a Sears kind of guy. Her dad kept sending money—I would get mad about it and send it back. It just felt like he was trying to buy me. We both were into alcohol and that didn't help the fighting either. She decided to go into treatment and she quit smoking and drinking—everything! She wanted me to do the same, but I wouldn't. Between the alcohol and Valium, I was out of it most of the time. It was so bad, I kept passing out. One night it got so bad that I went home and tore up the house—destroyed furniture and everything. Then she was finally able to talk me into going into treatment. They put me in for 28 days and I stayed sober for six months. But she didn't like me sober. That happens a lot, I've heard. Once you're sober you're a totally different person, and your partner doesn't like it. Well, after six months, I retreated back into drinking and things just got worse. We split up in January of 1984 and divorced in 1987."

"How's your social life now?'

"I have a girlfriend—we've been living together for five years—no marriage though! I figure if you marry four times there's something wrong with you. I guess I'm just not the marrying type."

Living at the Edge—Touching Hot Wires

"What are things like today with your TS?"

"I really have no trouble with it. I like my work; my coworkers are great guys. After my third divorce, I got a job with the county doing electrical work, plumbing, and other maintenance jobs. Everything's been going great. I just run into trouble sometimes when I'm working with high-voltage wires.

I've got a lot of compulsions to touch things, and when you're working with high-voltage wires, that can get you knocked on your ass! I *do* touch 110. I've been knocked down several times, but I just feel like I've *got* to touch it, so I do! I know it's gonna get me, but I also know that 110 won't kill you—most of the time. Sometimes it can, but most of the time it won't. See, your heart is in tune with that kind of voltage and it can stop your heart—that kind of voltage can stop your heart if you touch it—60 Hz—can stop your heart, but normally it doesn't. It would be a rare thing. So there's a chance it could and that's what intrigues me so much. I think I can probably get away with it, but there's that one chance that maybe I won't."

"A Tourette version of Russian roulette?"

"Yeah, it's kinda neat! I don't think Tourette people have a death wish, but at the same time, if you go, so what?—as long as you're enjoying yourself doing it. 'Cause when you're growing up, you don't have very many good times; so if you're having a good time—even if it shortens your life—so what? It's worth it. It's worth it to have fun—worth it to enjoy yourself."

"Are you saying that the risk and excitement enhances your life?"

"Yeah, it's great! After I do it, I'm up for the rest of the day—I just have a ball! I always talk to myself later and I say 'Robb you idiot—one of these times it's gonna get you!' I chastise myself for doing it—for doing it *just one more time*. Later at night, sitting at home thinking about it, I think 'Gee, that was stupid.!' But I continue doing it anyway."

"How often do you get this irresistible urge to touch bare 110 wires?"

"It only hits me once in awhile—it's hard to say exactly—several times a year. Sometimes it can be twice in a week and other times I can go for months without it bothering me."

"Can you tell ahead of time when it's coming on—do you ever get up in the morning and think 'Today I'll have to touch 110.'?"

"Well, not exactly first thing in the morning, but yeah, I know that I'm going to do it ahead of time. I can feel that I'm getting in a compulsive mode. Like I'll be working with some cable, and usually they have wire nuts on them to protect the wires. When I begin taking the nuts off and start lining them up in exact rows, I know I'm there."

"You take off the wire nuts and line them up?"

"Yeah, I'll take off the nuts and line them up on the floor against the wall.

And they have to be *perfectly* spaced. And once I'm sitting there doing this, I know I'm going to touch the wires. I'm in a compulsive mode. First I touch the white one, which is neutral. You won't get zapped too bad from the white one— sometimes not at all—it depends on what's hooked up behind it. You can touch one and not get zapped, you can touch the other and not get zapped; but if you touch them together you know you're going to get it!

The Magic Number Six

"Sometimes I'll do that six times—I have a fetish about six. I count everything in sixes. If I'm sitting in a bar, I count ceiling tiles—always in sixes. I'll count: 'One, two, three, four, five, five. One two, three, four, five, five.' I never say the word 'six' when I'm counting. I'll skip it and go right to seven. If I'm counting steps when I'm walking, it's the same thing, I never say 'six.'"

"So you count 'One, two, three, four, five, five, seven'?"

"That's right, One, two, three, four, five, five, seven. I think the way it started was because I count only on one hand—I never use my left hand—I always count on my right hand, and there's only one thumb, so I use it twice like this 'One, two, three, four, five, five (demonstrates).'"

"Okay, so you've got these two wires lined up—"

"You line up the white wire and count 'one' as you touch it. Then you count 'two' on the hot wire. Then "three" . . . "four" . . . "five" . . . and then you've got to touch it real quick—both of them together—and that's when it will get you."

"The 'six' will get you?"

"Yeah, but you *have* to do this—you can't stop in the middle of one of these— you've *got* to finish it."

"And you've gotten some pretty good 'kicks' out of this sort of thing?"

"Yeah, but I do it so fast, sometimes it just tingles. It's 60 CPS so it can jerk your whole arm. Sometimes it lasts awhile—especially if you hold on to it a little longer—it can really get you pretty good. I guess it's kind of lucky I can feel it coming on, because if I started lining up wire nuts and it's high voltage—like 220 or 480—I'll just get up and leave. I know I *have* to leave, because if I touch 220 it'll blow my shoes off—it's going to burn me real bad—it could even kill me. A lot of our new equipment is 480, but I haven't really had a problem with it. I know what it is, and I guess fear overtakes the compulsion. I'm not gonna kill myself. I can stop it—I want to survive. Right now is the best time of my life. I'm financially better off than I've ever been, I'm happier than I've ever been, my children are grown, I have grandchildren, I don't want to die!

"Do you have any other compulsions?"

"All my other compulsions are counting compulsions—I touch the same doorknob everyday when I go to work. I count the bricks on the wall—it always has to end in six. I'll walk down to the boiler room where I work. As I'm going down the hall I count my steps—one, two, three, four, five, five steps and then I rap one of the bricks with my knuckle. Then I count six more sequences of one, two, three, four, five, five. The hallway is pretty long, but if I didn't shorten my steps I'd run out before I got to the end, so about halfway down, I start taking smaller steps so I won't run out of wall before I get to the end."

"Does anything special occur when you get to that 'grand finale' six times six?"

"There's a corner right there and I put my shoulder against it and roll around the corner so that my right shoulder hits one wall and I roll around and it hits the other wall. Then it's about eight feet to the next left turn I have to make and I roll around that one with my left shoulder. So I guess you'd say that I finish up the six times six by rolling around with both shoulders. Then I can go up to the shop and be OK for awhile."

"How long will you be OK?"

"Until I walk by that wall again. That's the one place that's real repetitive to me. Most places I do just randomly—sometimes I do, sometimes I don't—but once I get down that hallway I *always* do that. When I'm down there, most people can't see me. Once I hit the doorknob at the beginning, and start walking down the hall most people can't see me. Nobody asks me what I'm doing. All my buddies know—I've explained it to them, but I don't let management know."

"You mention that when you get in a 'compulsive mode' you *have* to do certain things. Is there any way you've been able to limit any of these compulsions?"

"Only when it comes to counting—sometimes I'll set a limit for myself—cause when you're driving down the highway counting telephone poles, and you're going from Nebraska to Louisiana you're gonna count a lot of poles! So I'll set a limit—like a mile marker where I'm going to quit. So I'll just count poles for the first five miles or whatever limit I decide ahead of time. Or if I tried to count every one of those little lights in the ceiling (pointing to a multi-bulbed light array in the lobby), there's no way I could do it, so I'd take one row—set a limit."

"And what if it didn't end up in six?"

"Then I'd have to do the next row; or I might even have to leave a couple out to make it come out on six. You know—sometimes you have to 'cheat' to make it come out, because it gets to the point where you say to yourself 'I can't keep doing this—I'm tired of it.' I'll sometimes get to where I'll 'split one' with my eyes. I'll close my right eye and look over my nose and cut one of those little lights in half to make it come out right—you know, little tricks like that to make it come out right—little games you have to play with yourself when you get tired of doin' this stuff. There's a lot of things to count! But I was always real good in math—I was a whiz! I could add things, subtract, divide—in my head—real fast. That was the only thing that saved me in school. I never passed an English course in my life, but my math kept me in school."

"So at this point in your life there's sniffing, blinking, shaking, and 'magic-six' kinds of counting—is that it?"

"Yeah, and straightening things—things have to be in order with the rest of the room. Like I went to a meeting a while ago and they had a very orderly desk up there where people were giving a talk, except there were two name badges lying up there a little cockeyed and it just didn't look right to me. Everything else was so straight. If everything had been in a mess, I don't think it would have bothered me nearly as much, but having those two items out of line really got to me. I finally got up out of my seat and went up to the platform and straightened the two badges, then I felt OK again and I could listen to the rest of the lecture. Before that I couldn't pay much attention to what they were saying. My focus was just on those badges."

"You apparently felt comfortable enough here at the TSA meetings to do that. Would you have done that elsewhere—like at other meetings?"

"No, probably not, I would have just left the meeting."

Commentary

Somatic focus amplified by *constriction* was a pivotal part of Robb's early life. Although his memory of those early years is mercifully murky, we know enough about his grandmother to surmise that she was psychologically toxic to his early development. It isn't simply in the dramatic events—such as tying his arms behind his back with inner tubes—that we see her noxious qualities; it is evident in the way she set up the school environment to be hurtful, and in the deceptive way she obtained custody of his child. Think of what it must have been like to grow up around such a woman during the many moments of each day. It is certain that she continually tried to control him—often through such noxious means as ridicule and physical constriction. This increased his autonomy strivings, and permanently anchored his sense of self and awareness in his body.

Robb's grandmother was the quintessential *overattentive* parent, constantly attempting to contain his behavior. In her futile attempts at constricting his movements she enlisted the aid of psychologically insensitive teachers. Consequently both at school and at home Robb remembers that "People were always telling me to 'Stop it!'"

One can assume that when teachers display insensitivity or ridicule, the peer group will strongly replicate similar behaviors. It comes as no surprise that Robb's recalls "I hated school!" The cumulative effect of these influences was to produce an early environment of stress and humiliation. This continued when he was placed in the state mental facility and persisted throughout his troubled navy career.

This case clearly illustrates the quality of *brinkmanship*, present in *all* persons with TS. The testing of limits is measured, careful, but none-theless compulsive. The touching of bare electric wires is not random or accidental. It is carefully calibrated to produce just the right mix of danger and defiance—it is "at the edge." As Robb put it, "I've been knocked down several times, but I just feel like I've *got* to touch it so I do. I know it's gonna get me, but I also know 110 won't kill you—most of the time."

It is of interest to compare Robb's *private* brinkmanship—it was himself he was "pushing to the edge"—with the *social* brinkmanship we've just seen in coprolalia. I've suggested previously that coprolalia is a socially sophisticated form of ambitendence, somewhere in the middle of the TS-OCD spectrum. Developmentally, it appears more sophisticated than tics or private compulsive rituals because it involves interacting with other persons and that increases its complexity—just as intercourse is more complex than masturbation.

However, being with Robb feels more "adult"—less chaotic—than interacting with many coprolalics I've met. I think this is because Robb's private "game" is quite refined and cognitively complex. It's more an obsession than a tic; and although it incorporates a somatic component—one that could be lethal!—the real dynamic is more cognitive than somatic. Further, he is companionable and polite; confining his brinkmanship to a quiet, careful game of solitaire. Coprolalics, as will be seen, continually live at the "edge;" but this is not the edge of electrocution or self harm, it is the edge of social acceptability. Their brinkmanship is interpersonal and sometimes offensive.

In concluding this chapter, we will meet a woman whose primitively aggressive brinkmanship contrasts with Robb's careful walking of the obsessional tightrope.

THE LADY WHO SHATTERED MIRRORS
WITH HER FIST

Punching the Wall

I was some distance from the lobby when it happened—the punch at the wall—the sound of tinkling like a wind chime in a breeze—the ensuing hubbub.

"Get a doctor her hand is bleeding!"

"Somebody clean up this glass!"

"I don't need a doctor, I'll take care of it!"

"But your hand is bleeding badly!"

"I *said*, I don't need a doctor, now butt out! I'll take care of the glass too, just everybody butt out!" Her voice was a plaintive potpourri of anguish, insistence, and shame. Slowly—it seemed like eternity to her—the lobby emptied.

Denise's hand was abundantly bandaged when I interviewed her later, but I knew from the frayed edges of gauze and uneven pieces of tape that she had meant it when she had insisted: "I'll take care of it!" This wasn't, after all, the first time she had smashed a wall, or mirror, or picture. She spoke quickly, intensely; her accent was unmistakably East Coast.

"It was stupid! Makes me disgusted when I hurt myself like this."

"Do you usually try to calibrate how hard you hit things?"

"Yeah, if it's not hard enough, I don't get any satisfaction out of it, but if it's too hard—like this—I hurt my hand, and that upsets me. It's so stupid!"

"When did hitting things start?"

Punching the Dog

"My tics started around age seven. I started blinking and twitching my head. Then that would disappear for a while and I would start something new. Like after I quit blinking and twitching for two or three months, I started shrugging my shoulders. Then it stopped, but a little while later all three came back. Then, when I was about nine years old, I started making noises and cursing. I would just say the word 'Hell!' for no reason, and it was about this same time that I started hitting my dog.

"You started hitting your dog?"

"Yeah, it was really strange, I didn't *want* to hit him, and I didn't know *why* I hit him, but I just started hitting my dog."

"And your parents, how did they respond to all this?"

Paradoxical Instructions and Punishments

"They would yell 'Stop it!' and ask me 'Why are you so nervous?' But the tics weren't so bad that they made a big deal of it. They never made a big deal of anything! But when the teachers sent a letter home saying they'd noticed the eye blinking, my parents took me to a doctor. He said it was fairly common—that I would outgrow it. Said it was a nervous habit and that it would go away.

"It *never* went away! I started having even more tics—sucking on things, kicking different things. The tics got worse. So my parents took me back to the doctor, and this time he told them that I was just doing it for attention. After that, they figured I was doing it on purpose so they started punishing me. I'd get hit. If they saw me doing something like blinking my eyes or sucking on something, or kicking something, they'd smack me or yell at me to stop it."

"Did you have any problems besides the tics and cursing?"

"I had some obsessive compulsive stuff when I was younger, but I never told anybody about it. It was weird. For some reason I had to peel the wall paper in my bedroom . . . just a little . . . like a little rat, ya know? I suppose my parents noticed it because I'd peel all the paper off in a small area, but they never said anything about it. Whether they noticed it or not, I still don't know for sure."

"What happened next?"

"When I was 14, my tics all left. I didn't have any for three years."

"Nothing at all?"

"Nothing. No problems at all."

Sister Marries, Grandmother Dies

"But then when I was 17 my sister got married and my grandmother died within a couple of months, and my tics started again. I was very close to my sister Karen—she was my best friend. It really blew my mind when she got married. We were really close. She was my best friend."

"What about your grandmother, what was it like with her?"

"My grandmother *hated* me! I still can't deal with it. She never liked me so when she died, I had that whole thing just hanging there. I could never deal with it—still can't."

"So during your 17th year you had a reawakening of the earlier tics?"

"*Everything*" from before—*plus*! I had all the old tics plus I started making noises."

"Hadn't you made noises before?"

"I had cursed before, but I had only minor vocalizations—just minor. Now I had nonstop tics and constant noises. I was screaming and doing all this crazy stuff, and we knew it wasn't just a 'nervous habit.' Before that, every doctor I went to see would just say: 'It's a nervous habit, she'll outgrow it. Ignore it and it'll go away.' But it didn't go away, it got worse. The doctor still couldn't find anything wrong, so out of frustration, he gave me Elavil."

Drugs Didn't Help

Elavil

Immediately after I took the Elavil, I had an outburst of Tourette—I mean full-blown tics! Screaming, kicking, hitting, all this crazy stuff. This went on for a couple of years. Then when I was about 19, my mother read this article in the *Reader's Digest* and it explained the symptoms of a girl who sounded like me. So she sent away to TSA and according to the materials she got back, she figured I had Tourette. She didn't say anything about it, but about six months later— things kept getting worse—she finally told me she thought I had TS and that maybe I could see a doctor about it.

Haldol®

"So I approached the pediatrician and right away he put me on 3 mg of Haldol/day. It totally blew me away. I slept 18 hours a day. I gained 40 pounds. I got fired from my job because I couldn't drive anymore. I figured that was the end of me anyway, so I tried to commit suicide."

"How old were you at this time, and how lethal was your attempt?"

"I was 20. I pulled my car into the garage and turned on the engine and sat there for awhile. They found me and took me to the hospital. I was hospitalized for three weeks."

"That's serious."

"While I was in the hospital, they took me off Haldol. That's when they were trying clonidine for TS, so I took clonidine—pill after pill. My tics would get better, then they'd get worse. Then they'd get better, then worse. I don't know if the clonidine helped or if it was just natural waxing and waning."

Percodan®

When I had surgery on my jaw—I kept hitting myself in the jaw and knocked it all out of whack—they gave me Percodan. That helped my TS, but it's a narcotic so they couldn't keep me on it. Then they gave me something else, they switched me to something different. Finally, I said "Forget it!" and I went to another doctor. She's got me down to three per day now.

"What's been happening the last 10 years?"

"Not much. I went to college, but I didn't graduate. Dropped out. I work for TSA in the office. That's about it. Not much going on."

Commentary

Denise's excessive energy was evident during my interview with her. She fidgeted, spoke with pressured speech, and generally seemed to be "bubbling over." Historically, it seems obvious that she must have been a very energetic and angry little girl. By nine years of age she was not only twitching, jerking, and shrugging, she was hitting her dog. She also began cursing—at a relatively young age compared to most coprolalics.

She didn't offer much information about her parents, but initially they weren't overconcerned about her unusual behaviors. For example, they didn't confront her about her compulsive "picking at the wall paper" in her room. It's possible, or course, that they simply didn't notice, but her memory seems to indicate a casual attitude at first. However once the teachers in school became concerned about her eye blinking and sent a letter home, the overattention began in earnest. Subsequently she was besieged with paradoxical instructions which were backed up with punishment. Once the physician engaged in victim blaming by suggesting Denise was ticquing for "attention," this implicitly gave the family permission to punish her further. After that time, she reports ". . . if they saw me doing something, they'd smack me or yell at me to "Stop it!"

Such professional insensitivity is deplorable but unfortunately prevalent. One of the reasons the biomedical theory has such appeal to parents and patients alike is that it makes such victim blaming less likely. If TS is a biological disease, it hardly makes sense to suggest that someone is performing tics for "attention." Physicians don't blame patients for genuine organic problems, such as hyperthyroidism, metabolic problems, or blood or lymph diseases.

Victim Blaming

In emphasizing multiple factors of causality in this book, I do not want to foster even the slightest notion that persons with TS or OCD can "help" themselves by using more "willpower," or that they are behaving this way for "attention." There are numerous behaviors, begun early in life, that cannot be "turned around on a dime." More will be said about this during the discussion of treatment, but it needs to be clearly stated at the outset, *learned* behaviors are often very difficult to change. Professionals should never blame patients by suggesting they are ticquing or obsessing by choice—for attention. If professionals do this, the blame lies with them for their lack of understanding.

COMPARING ROBB AND DENISE

In Denise we see vividly portrayed the kind of brinkmanship observed in the electrician. Again, it is a measured brinkmanship. Like Robb, who touched 110 volts but walked away from 220, Denise tried to punch walls hard enough to get satisfaction but not so hard as to damage her hand. She was quite articulate about this: "If it's not hard enough I don't get any satisfaction out of it, but if it's too hard—like this—I hurt my hand, and that upsets me."

Denise, however, is developmentally more "primitive" than Robb. It's a little like comparing Peter the Great and Samuel Johnson. Denise is highly energetic, brutally somatic. Like the "motoric" Peter she deals with conflict by acting out. Although one suspects it is people she would like to hit, she limits punching to walls, mirrors, windows, and other such inanimate objects. The closest she comes to striking others is hitting her pet dog—and herself. Robb, like Samuel Johnson is developmentally more complex and his tics have a much more "nuanced" quality about them. There is planning, ritual, and social savvy. However even Robb *must* test the limits. And Denise, though much more brutal and primitive about her expressions, still "calibrates" her compulsions. Just as Robb touches 110 but not 220, she attempts to hit walls "hard enough" but not "too hard." Robb and Denise's commonalities are more extensive than their differences; which seem more in degrees than kind. In fact, as we've seen whenever we look closely at anyone with TS-OCD, there is much in common. Differences are typically seen in the intensities, varieties, and modalities of behavioral expression more than in real psychological experience.

Interesting in this regard is Brian's "self-brinkmanship." He's the 11-year-old who would fart and apologize. In the course of his treatment, I sometimes fixed a snack for him in my office kitchen. He was fascinated with the garbage disposal, often turning it on and off while asking "Hey John, what would happen if a person stuck his hand in it while it was going?" Of course he knew the answer to his rhetorical question as his musings would reveal: "Boy! I'll bet it would really mess ya up!"

Brinkmanship—even when dangerous to self—is a pervasive phenomenon among persons with TS-OCD. Even when not manifested as an obvious tic or obsession, it is nonetheless usually present. Although many tics are *socially* "testy," Shapiro and colleagues (1978) list instances where the tic involves testing the limits with oneself such as "touch eyes with fork" or "bite drinking glass." I've known clients whose repertoire included "staring at the sun;" and we've already seen how the woman who bit my leg stuffed all sorts of "forbidden" things up her nose.

It seems clear that behind such TS-OCD behaviors is a "proscribing" parent from the past. What child hasn't heard a parental voice saying: "Don't stare at the sun!" Don't chew on the edge of your glass like that!" "Keep your fork away from your eyes!—You want to be blind or what!" The adult tic echoes the parental proscription.

Particularly illustrative of this point is one of the complex tics listed by

Shapiro and colleagues (1978, p. 139): "Thrust hand into toilet, wash face to ear, rub whole arm on cheek." With but a modicum of imagination, one can hear Mommy's voice saying: *"Don't put your hand in the toilet!"* "Well, now that you have, *please* don't put your hand on your face afterwards!" "Wash yourself before you touch your face again!" The tic—creatively ambitendent—*simultaneously* defies and obeys. The child defiantly plunges his or her hand into the toilet, but compliantly obeys by "washing." Hardly a neurological reflex!

What remains puzzling is why some children deal with stress by using TS-OCD styles of coping while others do not. This has been studied on a case-by-case basis, but in a subsequent chapter a closer look will be taken at risk factors that "load the dice" in the direction of TS-OCD. Before considering prevention and treatment, a model of Catastrophe Theory will be discussed in the next chapter. This theory will help the reader understand how various factors increase the risk of transforming temporary tics or transient thoughts into the more enduring rituals of TS-OCD.

Chapter 6

CATASTROPHE THEORY: A MATHEMATICAL MODEL FOR UNDERSTANDING TOURETTE SYNDROME AND OBSESSIVE COMPULSIVE DISORDER

The awe-inspiring *smooth* movement of planets around the sun is described well by classical physics, but many phenomena are not because they "jump" when they reach a certain critical point. Ocean waves smoothly build up to a certain critical point and then abruptly "break." There is a gradual increase of weight as one steadily stacks straws on a camel's back, but under a load of $N + 1$ the overloaded back *suddenly* buckles. Such abrupt changes are far more awkward for mathematical analysis than stars in their courses. And although planets move unvaryingly, asparagus grows steadily, and water flows smoothly, many other things occur by "fits and starts." Bridges collapse suddenly, earthquakes and tidal waves strike without warning, unexpected forest fires are ignited by lightning or arsonists, drivers "run" stop signs causing unforeseen collisions, and cells become unexpectedly cancerous multiplying excessively. These are known as *catastrophes*, because of their sudden and often devastating onset.

Woodcock and Davis observe:

> Many processes yield graphs with obstinately ill-behaved curves: there are spikes, breaks, and regions where one value of x corresponds to any of several values of y, or vice versa. The planets travel in stately Newtonian

paths, but meanwhile winds wrap themselves into hurricanes, chickens alternate with eggs, and we change our minds. Discontinuity is as much the rule as the exception. To take a relatively simple example, the physical properties of water are discontinuous at the freezing and boiling points. A graph of its temperature versus the flow of heat energy shows large, abrupt thresholds at those points, and no simple equation can relate the two quantities. (1978, p. 6)

In the remainder of this book the term *catastrophe* will be used in a technically precise sense to designate *discontinuous* (abrupt) phenomena. The key here is *suddenness*, not disaster. In our analysis we would call a surprise birthday party—even when it turns out well—a catastrophe. The hours of planning, inviting of guests, shopping, decorating, arranging a caterer all gradually build up to a chorus of happy voices *suddenly* shouting "Surprise!" as the friend walks through the door. In our current discussion, that *moment* of surprise—the sudden "jump" from "coming home tired" to "Wow! it's a party!" is a catastrophe.

An Elegant Mathematical Model

Catastrophe Theory (CT) was invented by the French mathematician Rene Thom and provides a mathematical rationale for analyzing a wide variety of discontinuous phenomena. Zeeman, for example, has applied CT to a diverse array of happenings including aggression in dogs, phase transitions between liquid and gaseous states, buckling elastic beams, behavior of the stock market, and anorexia nervosa. He has used the model to derive equations for analyzing nerve impulses and the heartbeat. Poston and Stewart (1978) have analyzed problems ranging from the stability of ships and oil rigs, to the size of bee societies. In the current discussion CT will be used to integrate the various developmental, motivational, and behavioral components of TS-OCD under one, manageable theoretical framework.

What kind of mathematics does CT offer? The answer is topology, a sophisticated descendent of geometry. Topology differs significantly from Greek geometry, however, because it is not restricted to straight lines, restricted curves, or regular solids. It deals with *all* conceivable forms; including multidimensional forms that cannot easily be drawn or imagined. Just as geometry treats the properties of a square or a triangle without regard to its size, topology deals with *dimensionless* properties. For example, the property of a point being either inside or outside a closed curve is what topologists call an *invariant*. It doesn't change when the curve is distorted. Topology gains its power to classify and manipulate many varieties of form by giving up concepts such as size, distance, and rate.

Although Thom, a French topologist, is the acknowledged "father" of CT, it has received much impetus from E. Christopher Zeeman, who received his doctorate from Cambridge in 1954. He specializes in a branch of topology called "knot theory," a topic that can become quite "entangled" with problems such as how to "untie" a 10-dimensional knot by manipulating it in 16-dimensional space. The mathematical proof of Thom's theorem is difficult, but the results are easier to understand, and can be applied to problems in the sciences without reference to the proof.

Zeeman describes CT as follows:

> The theory is derived from topology, the branch of mathematics concerned with the properties of surfaces in many dimensions. Topology is involved because the underlying forces in nature can be described by smooth surfaces of equilibrium; it is when the equilibrium breaks down that catastrophes occur. The problem for catastrophe theory is therefore to describe the shapes of all possible equilibrium surfaces. (1976, p. 65).

Dealing with Everyday Problems

CT is attractive because of its broad scope and suitability for analyzing nonquantitative data. No small part of its appeal comes from its proposed relevance to the nitty-gritty problems of life. Zeeman and his colleagues have extrapolated it very broadly. CT has been employed to analyze prison riots, trends in the stock market, embryology, delinquency, the meaning of proverbs, censorship in a permissive society, the cost of waging war, and—yes—the rise and fall of the Roman Empire. This of course has led some critics to suggest that CT is no theory at all but rather a metaphor that can be broadly applied to almost anything.

In reading their writings, however, one does not come away feeling that they are possessed with grandiose delusions about CT as a panacea. Instead, the suggested applications are offered heuristically, and when experimental findings consistent with the model are available, they are presented. I don't find CT very convincing when applied to the stock market or the rise and fall of the Roman Empire. However, scientists study at various levels of analysis and the issue is not one of truth but, rather, usefulness. As Thom put it:

> The choice of what is considered scientifically interesting is certainly to a large extent arbitrary. Physics today uses enormous machines to investigate situations that exist for less than 10^{-23} seconds, and we surely are en-

titled to employ all possible techniques. . . . But we can at least ask one question: many phenomena of common interest, in themselves trivial (often to the point that they escape attention altogether!)—for example, the cracks in an old wall, the shape of a cloud, the path of a falling leaf, or the froth on a pint of beer—are very difficult to formalize, but is it not possible that a mathematical theory launched for such homely phenomena might, in the end, be more profitable for science? (Woodcock & Davis, pp. 8–9)

Zeeman and Thom have utilized CT in differing ways. Thom has referred to CT as "a way of generating and classifying analogies both within and across disciplines." Writing for a student magazine at The Mathematics Institute in 1973, he asserted:

The catastrophe model is at the same time much less and much more than a scientific theory; one should consider it as a *language*, a method, which permits classification and systematization of given empirical data. (Woodcock & Davis, p. 29)

For Thom CT provides an interdisciplinary language for the physical, biological, and psychological sciences.

Zeeman seeks a much closer relationship between qualitative and quantitative modeling, attempting to quantitatively test predictions made by the model. Although this has been accomplished in a few cases, most applications of the model have not generated "hard data."

Goodness of Fit

As we've noted previously, CT is relevant when gradual changes in motivation or situational forces lead to *sudden* changes in behavior or events. CT, like other models, is an attempt to summarize data in a more precise way, enabling the investigator to "see" new relationships that might otherwise be passed over. The "bottom line" is goodness of fit. Does the data coincide with the model without distortion? Are new relationships more apparent when data is "mapped" in terms of the model? As Mark Kac wrote: "The main role of models is not so much to explain and to predict—though ultimately these are the main functions of science—as to polarize thinking and *pose sharp questions*" (Woodcock & Davis, p. 73, italics mine).

In the present context CT will assist us as we attempt to "pose sharp questions," refine diagnostic boundaries, evolve better therapeutic techniques, and delineate domains for empirical research. CT provides a way of organizing ideas from a variety of disciplines under "one roof."

Tics are Catastrophes

In a subsequent chapter on treatment, it will be shown that tics involve a sudden destabilization of normal muscle balance. The relevance of catastrophe theory for understanding TS-OCD becomes apparent. Utilizing CT enables us to understand tics as "micro-catastrophes" that incessantly erupt as explosive reversals of muscle-innervation equilibrium. At a higher level of analysis, tics *suddenly* destablize social interactions as well.

Having already discussed the developmental origins and communicational meanings of tics and other TS-OCD manifestations, it now remains to integrate these perspectives with the help of mathematics. In the past, mathematical models have often described behavioral phenomena post hoc, without addressing the etiological and motivational issues so important to clinicians. Most mathematical models have worked best when applied to narrowly defined behaviors of the kind studied in reaction-time experiments, or serial-learning studies using nonsense syllables. Such studies usually generated smooth learning curves and were amenable to traditional analyses using differential equations.

Fits and Starts

Things that change suddenly—by fits and starts—are far more common in psychology than orderly, well-behaved occurrences. Panic attacks, temper tantrums, eating or drinking binges, physical or sexual abuse, kleptomania, exhibitionism, stuttering, are but a few of the *discontinuous* problems routinely faced by clinicians. It's probably the case that *most* clinical problems are "sudden-change" events. Tics are a fits-and-starts catastrophe par excellence. Consequently, CT is particularly suited for mapping tics and other TS-OCD behaviors into a mathematically consistent model. In some respects the model is like multidimensional cybernetics. The cusps, folds, and bifurcation of the CT behavior surface have much in common with the kinematic graphs, basins, and feedback loops of cybernetics. In summary, the mathematics are elegant and the models versatile; providing the best paradigm to date for understanding TS-OCD.

UTILIZING CT TO ANALYZE TS-OCD

Seven Elementary Catastrophes

Thom mathematically demonstrated that when phenomena are controlled by no more than four factors, it is possible to describe all possible discontinuities ("jumps") with seven elementary catastrophes. In the simpler cases—where two or three controlling factors drive a single behavior—these catastrophes can be plotted as topological surfaces, providing visible representation of the likelihood that certain behaviors will occur and others will not. In more complex cases, such as four control factors driving two behaviors, it becomes impossible to plot the behavioral probabilities in two- or three-dimensional space.

For purposes of clarity, we assume that tics, mapped as probabilities on the behavior surface are controlled by two major moods—anger and shame—on the control surface. This allows us to utilize the *cusp* catastrophe model. When we discuss treatment, we will use a slightly more complex catastrophe known as the *butterfly*. More will be said about that later.

Behavior Surface

In utilizing CT we first ascertain whether tics and other compulsions/obsessions commonly found in TS-OCD exhibit any or all of the five properties characterizing cusp catastrophes. Each of them will be considered in turn as illustrated in Figure 6.1, which is the behavior surface of the cusp model. This surface is really a collection of all possible probabilities that a behavior will occur or not occur. The height of the surface indicates the relative likelihood that a behavior will occur, that is, the higher the surface the more likely the behavior occurring and, conversely, the lower the surface the lower the probability of a particular behavior occurring at that point. According to Zeeman, if the behavior under consideration exhibits at least two or three of the following five properties, it is a good candidate for analysis as a cusp catastrophe:

1. The behavior is always *bimodal* in some part of its range. It can be seen that the back edge of the sheet is smooth, sloping gently upward as one moves from left to right. At the back edge behavioral probabilities shift smoothly. At the front edge however, the situation is quite different with behavior probabilities being distinctly bimodal.

2. *Sudden jumps* are observed between one mode of behavior and the other at the front edge of the surface. Imagine a fearful cowering dog

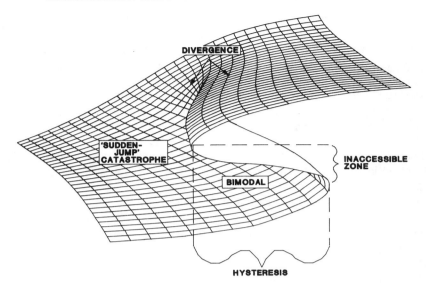

FIGURE 6.1 Five characteristics of the cusp catastrophe are: (1) bimodal behavior, indicated by (2) sudden jumps or rapid transitions; (3) hysteresis, the
jump from the top sheet down to the bottom sheet occurring at a different
point of the range than the jump from the bottom sheet back up to the top
sheet; (4) an inaccessible zone existing between the top and bottom sheets; and
(5) divergent behavior occurring when even slight differences in driving forces
exert significant influence near the back edge of the behavior surface.

(front left corner). If provoked with increasing intensity, the dog will
gradually become more aggressive. This steadily increasing aggressiveness translates into an increased probability of attack which is represented by a gradual upward slope on the front edge of the surface.
However, after moving some distance to the right, the probabilities suddenly and dramatically *jump* up to the top of the fold which represents
attack. It is this sudden switch from fearful withdrawal to attack which
is termed a *catastrophe*.

3. If the attacking dog can be successfully intimidated, aggression
will cease and the dog will *suddenly* run away. Notice however, that the
jump from the top sheet of the behavior surface to the bottom sheet
does not take place at the same position as the jump from the bottom
sheet to the top one, an effect called *hysteresis*. The oscillatory jumping
back and forth that is sometimes seen is referred to as a *hysteresis cycle*.

4. Between the top and bottom sheets there is an *inaccessible zone* on
the behavior axis. This is the clinically familiar phenomenon of "all-or-

none" extremism so often seen in a variety of emotional disorders. That inaccessible range of *moderation* necessitates oscillation between extremes. The "starve-or-stuff" cycles of persons with eating disorders, the manic-depressive cycles of persons with mood disorders, and the sober-drunk cycles of alcoholics illustrate the phenomenon.

5. The cusp catastrophe implies the possibility of *divergent behavior*. Think of this as a sort of continental divide where a small difference in slope near the beginning of a stream has the end result that the stream flows either into the Atlantic or the Pacific oceans. The phenomenon of a small initial change of path causing a major change of later behavior is known as *divergence*. This is not a common occurrence in physics, which is generally nondivergent—a small initial change usually results in only small changes in subsequent effects. In biology and the social sciences however, it is very common. It had long been mathematical "folklore" that divergent phenomena are impossible to model. However, it's now realized that divergence is a characteristic property of stable systems. CT is a "natural" for modeling such systems.

In summary, Zeeman observes that:

> In fact the cusp-catastrophe shows that the five qualitative features of *bimodality, inaccessibility, sudden jumps, hysteresis and divergence,* are all interrelated (see figure 6.1). . . . Whenever we observe one of these five qualities in nature, then we should look for the other four, and if we find them then we should check whether or not the process can be modelled by the cusp-catastrophe. Indeed our verbal usage in ordinary language of pairs of opposites frequently indicates a bimodality that has grown smoothly out of some unimodality, and which may be modelled by the upper and lower sheets of a cusp-catastrophe surface. (1977, p. 18)

THE CUSP-CATASTROPHE MODEL OF TICQUING

Figure 6.2 maps ticquing on the cusp-catastrophe surface. The two major moods underlying tics—shame and anger—are plotted on the *control surface* (the horizontal plane on the "floor" of the model). Note that anger increases as one moves diagonally forward to the right from the neutral zone centered at the back edge, and shame increases as one moves diagonally forward toward the left.

The probability of a behavior occurring as a joint function of two moods is indicated by height on the vertical axis. This means that the behavior surface is really a likelihood distribution with each probability

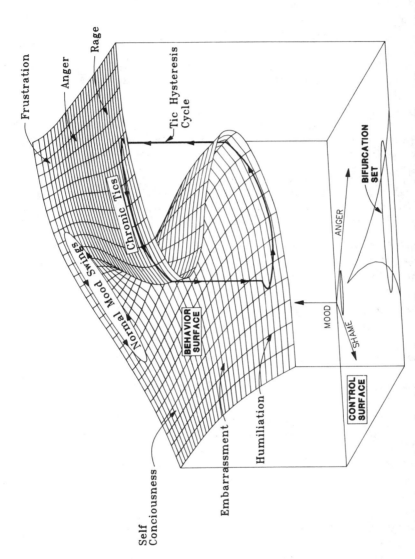

FIGURE 6.2 Most tics are driven by shame and anger. On one axis shame ranges from self consciousness to intense humiliation pulling the self inward. Anger on the other axis ranges from mild frustration to rage, pushing the self outward in explosive bursts. Tics momentarily relieve the chronic buildup of shame and anger with sudden muscular outbursts, but almost immediately the buildup of shame and anger recurs, necessitating further ticquing.

plotted as a point on the vertical axis; the height of the point corresponding to the probability of a behavior occurring as a joint function of the emotional mix at that particular point on the control surface. The sum total of all these points plotted next to one another constitutes the top sheet of the model. One might think of it as a sheet of sandpaper with each particle of sand representing a probability.

However think of it as "rubber" sand paper, since topological surfaces can be understood as rubber sheets that can be stretched—but not torn—without seriously changing the relationships contained thereon. As was pointed out earlier, topology is essentially dimensionless. Consequently you could "stretch" a rubber sheet on which was mapped a dot within a circle, and no matter how much or how little or in what directions the sheet was stretched (so long as it didn't tear) the dot-within-a-circle relationship would be preserved.

The *S* curve on the surface where the upper and lower sheets fold over into the middle sheet is called the *fold-curve*. The projection of this curve down onto the "floor" (control surface) is called the *bifurcation set*. This maps the area where divergence occurs and the line specifies at precisely what point on the control surface the emotions will reverse, causing a "jump" on the behavioral surface above. Notice that this bifurcation has a sharp point—a *cusp*—at the very beginning of the "continental divide." Hence the name *cusp-catastrophe*. Notice also that the bifurcation set is not symmetrical—with a shorter concave curve on the left and a long, approximately straight border on the right. It is this asymmetry that produces hysteresis on the behavior surface.

Measuring Moods on the Control Surface

In our analysis, shame and anger are the two primary mood factors (on the control surface) influencing ticquing (on the behavior surface). Technically known as *Likert* scales, these mood axes are *ordinal* scales, which means that they measure in terms of "greater than" or "less than." Unlike measuring with a yardstick in which each inch is comparable (i.e., the distance between 4 and 5 inches is precisely the same as the distance between 34 and 35 inches), an ordinal scale *ranks* the mood states on an emotional ladder but does not allow us to assume equal intervals between the ranks—the rungs on the ladder are not equally spaced.

This is consistent both with the "dimensionless" aspects of topology and with the experience of feeling emotions. Most people judge mood intensity as "greater than" or "less than" another mood to which it is being compared. However when you report that something made you "twice as angry" you don't have in mind the same kind of relationship as when you relate that you were able to sell something for "twice as much" as you paid for it. In the case of emotions, you're probably recalling becoming "much more angry," with the intensity of your mood rising significantly higher than a short while before. In the latter instance you could mean that having purchased an old piece of furniture at a garage sale for $35 you were able to refinish and sell it for $70. If you were to confide to me "I lost twice as much on my diet this week as I did the week before," and I knew you had lost a pound and a half in the previous week, I could accurately calculate that you lost three pounds this week. Money, inches, pounds, and other kinds of *equal-interval* measurements allow us to compare quantities. Emotional experiences are difficult to compare precisely and are usually *rank ordered*.

Ranking Emotional Experience

Most persons rank anger moods in approximately the following way: *mild anger* translates into feeling bothered, pestered, or slightly irritated; *moderate anger* is experienced as aggravation, annoyance, or frustration; and *intense anger* is felt as explosive rage or fury. Analogously, *mild shame* is experienced as brief or mild embarrassment, or awkwardness; *moderate shame* feels more intensely embarrassing, more exposed and vulnerable; while *intense shame* is experienced as feeling totally "naked," humiliated, or mortified with the accompanying urge to "crawl in a hole and die." These experiences are very real and truly a substantive part of our lives; they simply can't be measured with precise instruments such as yardsticks, speedometers, or stopwatches.

Permit me a caveat. Probably nothing in psychological experience is so simple as to be determined by only two factors—certainly not tics. In all likelihood, *complex amalgams* of moods on the control surface subtly propel the multiform manifestations of TS-OCD on the behavior surface. However, adding factors geometrically increases the complexity of the model, quickly defeating the purpose for which it was invented: clarification. This is especially true because understanding of both CT and TS-OCD is still evolving.

Nonetheless, the basic theoretical issues remain valid, even in simplified form; and future research by mathematicians in topology, and clinicians in TS-OCD will likely allow us to expand our knowledge base. Meanwhile, it's probably a good strategy to study the "gross anatomy" of TS-OCD rather than the "intracellular structures."

Shame Combinations

Tics actively *generate* shame, except possibly in neonates or infants, consequently shame is nearly always present in people with TS-OCD—most often in combination with anger. However, anger is not the only emotion that co-occurs with shame. Kaufman, for example, (1989, pp. 113–155) has reformulated various syndromes allocating to shame a more primary etiological role. He achieves this by coupling shame with a variety of emotions such as anger, fear, distress, dissmell, and disgust. Later we will examine a number of shame–affect couplings and discuss how such combinations produce the potpourri of manifestations seen in TS-OCD. In the interest of clarity, and because of the ubiquitousness of the shame–anger combination, most of our applications of CT to TS-OCD will use this couple; however we will briefly look at other combinations later.

Before proceeding with a detailed study of CT and its extenseive application to TS-OCD, a number of related clinical issues will be discussed as well as some case studies. A discussion of how the sense of self interacts with shame and anger follows.

Shame Constricts the Self

The text has shown that the effect of ridicule is to shrivel the self—often expressed as "I could have crawled into a hole and died!" The picture of self burrowing into a hole and pulling the dirt and turf over itself in "shameful inconspicuousness" is *not* an exaggerated metaphor. Shame is seldom mild. It occurs with sudden all-or-none intensity. Experienced as a surge of awfulness that suddenly soars from the pit of one's abdomen to the blushed skin of one's face, it takes one by surprise and seems impossible to control.

Shame adheres to the self with "super-glue" tenacity. It is not something that can easily be thrown off, acted out, displaced, or forgotten. Shame pulls awareness inward while engulfing and permeating the self. There is no escaping.

Anger Explodes

By contrast, the natural expressive pathway for anger is outward—explosively, if the intensity is high. Instead of withdrawing into oneself, the urge is to destroy the other. Even when anger is passively or chronically experienced as resentment, bitterness, or hostility, it nonetheless inclines outward. When not acted upon, the fantasy life is rich with rageful fantasies of destruction to others. For the child with tics, anger thus serves a protective function. It allows one to "fight back" against teasing. Instead of shrinking into an inconspicuous speck, one can act out—at least in fantasy—against the tormenters. Anger enlivens and empowers even if sometimes negatively.

In CT terms, the explosive–implosive equilibrium between anger and shame on the control surface translates into ticquing on the behavior surface. All tics are not "created equal," however, and the idiosyncratic dynamics of precisely how an individual's emotional conflicts map onto the behavior surface of the cusp model to form various tics will occupy much of the remainder of this chapter.

Development of Bimodality

Figure 6.3 illustrates tics as the behavioral expression of soothing and anxiety. As will be presently seen, tic catastrophes result from various combinations of moods besides shame and anger, much depending on where in the developmental sequence coping mechanisms were "frozen." The bimodality of specific behaviors seen at the top surface of the cusp model has already been noted. As shown in previous chapters, persons with TS-OCD have a much broader bimodality based on developmental circumstances facilitating *ambitendency*. In CT terms, ambitendency is the hysteresis cycle; a chronic tendency to suddenly flip-flop between contradictory approach–avoidance behaviors.

When development is reasonably adequate, bifurcation of personality is not likely. Moods and behavior hover comfortably along the *back edges* of the control and behavior surfaces—out of reach of the bifurcation set. Although there are times—even in the course of optimal development—when a child experiences embarrassment or anger, these do not lead to chronically bifurcated expressions of emotions. The child may explosively "throw a fit" on occasion, but this is not chronic. Instead, the sense of self hovers in the area of conflicting moods until a smooth behavioral expression is assembled. Once the resolving behavior has occurred, mood returns to a centered quiescence. This is reminiscent of the neonatal rhythms of arousal and quiescence.

Living at the Edge—The Front Edge

Chronically high levels of arousal—especially shame, anger, fear, and other "galvanizing" moods—push development toward the *front edges* of the control and behavior surfaces. It is in this zone that bifurcated ex-

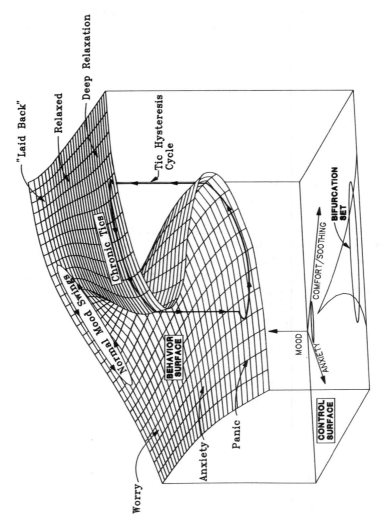

FIGURE 6.3 Tics are a behavioral attempt to diminish anxiety and simultaneously to soothe oneself. Anxiety on one axis ranges from worry to panic. Comfort on the other axis ranges from "laid back" to deep relaxation. Tics are a disruptive catastrophe occuring at the front edge of the behavior surface, replacing the normally smooth mood swings that exist near the back edge.

pression occurs. Gradual, modulated expressions of embarrassment or anger are replaced with bimodal catastrophes—tics. The smooth *circular reactions* of neonatal life move forward into the zone of bifurcation, becoming behaviorally jerky, repetitive, and discontinuous with the rest of emotional development.

Herein is the foundation for bifurcation of personality. Instead of integrated emotions spanning the entire personality the child begins to experience clusters of shameful emotions, which coalesce into a shameful self, and clusters of angry emotions which form the angry self. The conflict is no longer between two moods or two expressional pathways for behavior, it is between two *selves*. At this point the child experiences chronic discontinuity of behaviors and the broader bifurcation of personality is well underway.

Tics: The Jump from Compliance to Defiance

The tic is an "I don't give a damn!" catastrophe that moves the self from "nice" compliance to angry defiance. Almost immediately, however, and with a lot less conflict—the person slides back down to the embarrassment surface. This, in turn, leads to a buildup of anger that bursts out as ticquing which, in turn, induces shame, and thus, the hysteresis cycle is adequately fueled to oscillate incessantly during waking hours. By the time a circular reaction reaches the front of the behavior surface, it has lost most of its original comforting qualities; the smooth transitions having been replaced by the fits and starts of the hysteresis cycle.

Hysteresis Increases

A relatively permanent hysteresis cycle occurs in which overinhibition of anger leads to a buildup of resentment and rage that increases ticquing and pushes the person farther to the left, into the shame zone. Recall that hysteresis refers to the fact that the jump between the control surface and the behavior surface doesn't occur symmetrically. When the TS-OCD person moves from left to right along the control surface—from shame-based "niceness" to eruptive anger—it takes a high level of anger to break through the shame-based "niceness." However, once the breakthrough has occurred, the movement back to the left—in the direction of shame-induced withdrawal—occurs more readily (Figure 6.2).

Inaccessible Zone

The area inside the cusp, where the behavior becomes bimodal, is inaccessible. This is where the jump between surfaces occurs. A good analogy is the transition between liquid and gaseous phases of matter; they can be analyzed as a cusp catastrophe with temperature and pressure mapped on the control surface and density on the behavior axis. The top sheet then represents the liquid phase and the bottom sheet the gaseous phase. The two catastrophes are boiling and condensation. And as anyone who has heated a pan of water knows, heat may be applied steadily, warming the water gradually, but the boiling begins suddenly—discontinuously with the previous gradual heating process.

Herein lies the challenge of treating tics. Although many individuals become angry slowly or steadily—somewhat like warming water, the individual with TS-OCD tics (boils) suddenly, without warning. The *middle sheet* connecting control with behavior and allowing the person a smooth transition from mood to behavior is missing in the bifurcated personality.

Most persons have a number of in-between compromise behaviors that allow them to deal with shame or anger in a modulated way. This is not the case for the ticquer. Like a performer on stage, the ticquer experiences a constant sense of being under scrutiny. Like the paranoid person who is always vigilant, the person with TS-OCD is constantly mobilized. There is no zone in which genuine relaxation can occur during the waking state. This all-or-none quality of the ambitendent person results from the missing middle sheet. Therapy is the attempt to increase such connections allowing for smoother emotional transitions and for relaxation during waking hours.

Divergent Behavior

As noted earlier, a small perturbation in the initial state of the system may result in a large difference in the final state. Developmentally speaking, divergence is characteristic of TS-OCD. The tics or counting games of childhood—initially so close to normality—become the compulsion catastrophes of adult life. Although childhood tics often have a tentative "let's-try-this-out" quality about them, a few years of the shame-rage cycle transforms them into the all-or-none intense tics seen in adolescents or adults.

Therapeutically, there is a positive side—even with the chronic tics of adult TS-OCD. Small cognitive changes on the control surface affect vast behavioral repertoires. This is cause for optimism, because if triggering moods/thoughts on the control surface could be modified, entire sets of bifurcated behaviors might be changed as well.

CASE STUDIES IN CATASTROPHE: FROM TICS TO TRICHOTILLOMANIA

Tic Catastrophes—Strobe Lights of Emotion

Many behaviors are bimodal—jumping from one surface to the other of the CT model. This occurs because of the missing middle sheet (inaccessible zone) between the top and bottom sheets of the behavior surface. In experiential terms, bimodal behavior feels all-or-nothing, on-or-off. Instead of experiencing a smooth transition from the "faintly felt" to "extremely intense" poles of emotional experience, the bifurcated personality experiences sudden jumps from the minima to the maxima of numerous emotions. Intensifications of emotion are immediately followed by a burst—short circuiting the middle moderate zone—that catapults the person to extremely intense, but extremely brief eruptions of emotion. Like strobe lights, tics are tolerated by self and others because the intensity is moderated by the brevity.

Binge-and-Purge Catastrophes

Similar dynamics can be studied in slow motion—drawn out over longer periods of time—by examining eating disorders such as bulimia. Shame is an intrinsic part of the cycle. Originally experienced primarily while bingeing on food, it gradually becomes internalized, until deep personal shame engulfs the self, persisting long after the binge has stopped. During the bulimic gorging, shame gradually intensifies until (*abruptly*) the purge cycle flips on.

Kaufman (1989, p. 134) suggests that the purge cycle intensifies shame to the point of *disgust*, in a process known as *affect magnification*. Bingeing *gradually* accelerates the shame, but purging (vomiting) *explosively* brings shame to peak intensity. When shame peaks there is a "bursting effect" leaving the person feeling cleansed, purged, and temporarily purified. Magnifying shame in intensity and duration allows it to burn itself out. Tomkins defines this strategy as "a species of masochistic behavior the aim of which is to increase negative affect to such a point that it produces an explosive overt eruption of affect which ultimately thereby reduces itself" (1963, p. 283).

Touching Catastrophes

The electrician who touches bare wires is an example of intensification-to-burst dynamics extending over a longer period of time than typical bulimic cycles. Recall Robb's description:

> It only hits me once in awhile—it's hard to say exactly—several times a year. Sometimes it can be twice in a week and other times I can go for months without it bothering me.

Robb's experience illustrates how persons with TS-OCD "short-circuit" emotions through rapid *affect magnification*. Chronic emotions or compulsions are exchanged for high-intensity bursts. The experience typically begins with a gradual awareness of the driving emotions and the resultant compulsion:

> I know that I'm going to do it ahead of time. I can feel that I'm getting in a compulsive mode. Like I'll be working with some cable, and usually they have wire nuts on them to protect the wires. When I begin taking the nuts off and start lining them up in exact rows, I know I'm there. And once I'm sitting there doing this, I know I'm going to touch the wires.

He went on to describe how he amplifies this to the bursting point:

> When you're working with high-voltage wires, that [touching bare wires] can get you knocked on your ass! I *do* touch 110. I've been knocked down several times, but I just feel like I've *got* to touch it, so I do! I know it's gonna get me, but I also know that 110 won't kill you—most of the time. Sometimes it can, but most of the time it won't.

Like the bulimic who feels cleansed after vomiting, Robb feels high after touching the bare wires:

> It's great! After I do it, I'm up for the rest of the day—I just have a ball! I always talk to myself later and I say "Robb you idiot—one of these times it's gonna get you!" I chastise myself for doing it—for doing it *just one more time*. Later at night, sitting at home thinking about it, I think "Gee, that was stupid.!" But I continue doing it anyway.

Ticquey Tit Talk—Coprolalic Catastrophes

Recall Saul, the Iowa City deejay, who routinely "compliments" Clair, his coworker, saying "You've got nice tits!" This thought has likely occurred to other office workers as well, but only Saul bursts the thought into words. For him the middle sheet, allowing one to *think* forbidden thoughts without bursting into words, is missing. This characteristic of "getting it over with and letting it all hang out" instead of containing negative and forbidden thoughts, words, or feelings is pervasive over a wide range of TS-OCD manifestations. The bursting quality is particularly evident with coprolalia, where following brief periods of inhibition, individuals let go with a "string" of obscenities—not a single word, not an isolated utterance, but a volley of words suddenly erupting. As we've noted in earlier chapters, coprolalia involves a well-developed awareness of social parameters. Saul's "compliment" is a clear example of bursting within boundaries. Pushing the limits right to the edge, but not quite going over. There are, after all, cruder things he could say.

Trichotillomanic Catastrophes

"Hairpullers," as trichotillomanics are commonly known, are typically women, and the behavior usually begins during the teen years. Hair-pulling is another case of the *intensification and bursting* of emotional turmoil.

Jackie wore a wide-brimmed straw hat and mirrored sunglasses. Her eyebrows were heavily penciled and her eyelashes long and jet black. There was something incongruous about her glamorous look and her sad eyes.

In the examining room, when questioned about why she had come to the clinic, she said it would be easier to show the problem than to talk about it. With that, she began wiping off her eyebrow pencil with a tissue. Next she peeled of her eyelashes, and finally her wig. The startling result was that she looked like an undressed mannequin.

> "This is really embarrassing," she said, "but you wouldn't understand if I didn't show you. Only my husband and parents have ever seen me like this. Even the kids don't know." She rubbed her hands over her face. "I was like anyone else until I was 13." People admired my green eyes and long lashes. My grandma said I started to pull out my eyelashes to get Mom's attention; the house was always so full of Mom's friends. I didn't like it; I don't know. The next thing I remember is how I started to pull out my hair and eat the roots." (Rapoport, pp. 149–150)

Proposed formulations to explain trichotillomania have ranged from the absurd to the esoteric, but again, it can be mapped onto the CT model moving us in the direction of coherent understanding. The core dynamic involves jumping from chronic, low grade discomfort to intense but brief bursts of pain. Tolerance for chronic, dull discomfort is either absent or greatly attenuated. What exists is a proclivity for action and a fearlessness with respect to acute, intense discomfort. *Chronicity is replaced with outburst*—the dull headache exchanged for a blow to the head. Compulsive head banging, or face slapping is a graphic illustration of such a hysteresis cycle.

The strobe light phenomenon seen in tics is also present in trichotillomania. For reasons she didn't fully understand, Jackie preferred the intense, focused, qualities of the burst over the vaguely experienced, chronic discomfort of losing her mother's attention, or perhaps feeling vaguely guilty about sexual desires (or some other guilt). Without personally interviewing Jackie, it is difficult to be certain about what moods actually drove the bursting (pulling); but even without knowing the etiological details, it is clear that trichotillomania provides brief, intense bursts. More information might allow us to understand what kinds of moods or thoughts such bursts alleviated through amplification, but even without such knowledge, it is clear that the dynamics are similar to other catastrophes analyzed in this chapter.

Differing Catastrophes, Similar Dynamics

These seemingly disparate behaviors (ticquing, vomiting, touching bare electric wires, talking about "tits," plucking one's hair) share much in common. All seek to resolve discomfort, shame, or other taboo thoughts or emotions by rapidly intensifying them to bursting proportions. In the short run, the bursting is fleetingly successful by diverting awareness. In the long run, however, such behaviors produce additional shame, which refuels the *hysteresis cycle*. It has been previously noted that tics function as "shame generators," and the same is true of most of the catastrophes discussed in this chapter. Pulling out all of one's hair, for example, produces a "shameful" appearance that outweighs the temporary relief gained from the burst of painful distraction while the hair is being pulled.

Omnipresent Shame

As always, we find shame to be an important part of the picture. Jackie felt intense shame when exposing herself to Dr. Rapoport. This was obvious from her teary eyes and apologies. However, the deeper, self-engulfing shame painfully permeated each day of her life—especially during adolescence:

> "The worst part," Jackie added, "is that I couldn't do any of the fun things like swimming, riding in a roller coaster, being in the wind. I was

always afraid my wig would blow the wrong way and someone would see I was bald, or my eyelashes would come off. It was a crazy, awful adolescence." (Rapoport, 1989, p. 150)

"PERFECT" COMPULSIONS—AN ATTEMPT TO REPAIR THE SHAMEFUL SELF

When it is understood that perfectionistic striving is a defense against shame, many puzzling relationships fall into place. Most of the rituals traditionally subsumed under the category OCD, have underlying perfectionistic strivings associated with them. In Jackie's case for example she had to pluck her hairs "perfectly." This meant that if she plucked one left eyebrow, she had to balance this by plucking one right eyebrow. If she pulled out three hairs above her right ear, she had to pull out three from above her left ear.

Recall also how "perfectly" Robb (Chapter 5) lined up wire nuts just before shocking himself: "When I begin taking the nuts off and start lining them up in *exact rows*, I know I'm there." Not only were the wire nuts lined up perfectly, he felt compelled to touch the wires six times, because as he put it: "I have a fetish about six. I count everything in sixes." Recall how *precisely* he followed this procedure:

> You line up the white wire and count "one" as you touch it. Then you count "two" on the hot wire. Then "three" . . . "four" . . . "five" . . . and then you've got to touch it real quick—both of them together—and that's when it will get you . . . You *have* to do this—you can't stop in the middle of one of these—you've *got* to finish it.

We can see in Jackie's "perfect" hair pulling and in Robb's "perfect" shocking of himself the fusing of perfection and compulsion into a defense against chronic anxiety. Tragically, the defense itself generates more shame, refueling the cycle.

It should be noted that from a CT viewpoint tics, trichotillomania, and shocking oneself are essentially similar; the common denominators being *bimodal*, "*sudden-jump*" handling of shame and anxiety. These occur as *hysteresis cycles* on the behavior surface of the CT model (see Figure 6.2). In the case of tics, shame is attenuated by a sudden, intense burst directed outward—usually against someone else. In the case of trichotillomania the sudden burst is directed inward—toward the self—with the sudden, concentrated pain providing a focal displacement for chronically experienced discomfort and briefly distracting attention from self-focused shame to somatically focused pain. The same occurs when Robb shocks himself with electricity. This activity focuses and distills a much broader array of negative emotions (shame, anger, anxiety) into a single concrete event that provides relief by the cycle of *affect magnification/focus, bursting, and brief relief.*

TS-OCD—A Closed Loop Hysteresis Cycle

This is how seemingly disparate behaviors become assembled into tightly-coupled closed loops. First comes the anxiety and the helplessness, then the compulsions, twitches, or rituals in an effort to distract and/or comfort oneself, and finally the resultant shame and the ensuing effort to rid onself of shame by the obsessive, never-satisfying, relentless pursuit of perfection.

This is why I've chosen to hyphenate TS with OCD. I believe it *is* a unitary phenomenon—TS-OCD. The "TS" has traditionally designated somatic tics, shouting, and a wide variety of behaviors of the kind infants and children utilize to comfort themselves or to assert their autonomy. "OCD" has typically been used to tag rituals when they involve higher mental processes, such as counting, checking, and so on. Interestingly, however, ritualistic *washing* is a hybrid partaking both of somatic and cognitive elements, and I believe that most "washers"—like Morris (Chapter 1)—have a complex loop containing early anxiety, repetitive behaviors, shame, and shame-driven striving for perfection.

More broadly, it is not serendipitous that shame and perfectionism coexist in highly conservative subcultures such as the Shakers and Mennonites. As previously shown the two are complementary, and in the current discussion it is apparent that shame and perfectionism play off each other. Possibly it makes little difference which component of this egg–chicken duo comes first. Although I would guess that shame is usually the precursor, in response to which perfectionistic strivings come into existence, it is also possible that in a perfectionistic family, a child's continual "coming up short" would engender excessive shame.

Internalizing and Externalizing Moods on the Control Surface

During each developmental epoch, we assume two kinds of driving moods at the control surface dynamically straining toward equilibrium and expression at the behavior surface. The internalizing moods (such as shame) draw the self awareness inward, while anger inclines the self toward outward expression. It is this introversive–extraversive balance that, under conditions of equilibrium, comfortably locates the sense of self behind the face approximately two or three inches "deep." Shame pulls the self deeper, anger projects it externally, and other moods move awareness elsewhere, taking at least parts of the self along. During sexual orgasm, for example, awareness is genitally located, hunger produces abdominal awareness, and the need to urinate results in bladder awareness.

Self Awareness

The sense of self gradually grows out of the multitude of bodily experiences that occur during early development. This remains throughout life the "skeletal frame" upon which personality is built. Sometimes one experiences only partial self-involvement as when an eye or ear itches mildly and is relieved by brief rubbing. Under such circumstances the person is aware of "rubbing my *eye*," not "rubbing *myself*." When a person says "I have a throbbing headache" one can assume more of the self is involved in that situation than the one expressed by the statement "These shoes pinch my toes." Circumstances modify self-involvement. "Pinched toes" would be much more serious—and thereby more self-involving—five miles into a marathon than while trying on shoes for size at a shoe store.

Under most conditions, the system of selves is *subconscious*, as are the multiple part-selves that comprise it. For example, before reading this sentence, you probably weren't thinking about how you constantly swallow saliva. It happens automatically and isn't distasteful. However, if you were to collect a "sample" of saliva—your own!—in a cup, it would be distasteful to drink it. One can become even more "grossed out" by thinking of the same sequence with mucus and nasal drip. In a similar way part-selves are taken for granted unless problems increase awareness. Thus the foot part-self hardly enters awareness until someone steps on your toe. For the person with a club foot, however, it is a significant part-self. The chronically self-conscious child is typically not a happy child.

In TS-OCD negative self-consciousness reaches pinnacle proportions. Introversive moods dominate and the shameful self feels constantly "on display" and perpetually in danger of "contamination" or criticism. And, as if carrying out the orders of sadistic gods of destiny, tics and other "odd" behaviors keep shame in fresh supply. In the most basic sense, TS-OCD is a disorder of the self system. As we've previously seen, it involves a kaleidoscopic array of part-selves. Inevitably these tic-based part-selves always involve shame and hypertrophy of self-consciousness. Most TS-OCD symptoms involve cognitively or somatically "picking" on oneself. We've seen this vividly in Jackie, who literally plucked her hair; but it occurs ubiquitously in TS-OCD as the incessant ticquing keeps both the part-self awareness at a high level and the concomitant shame in the foreground.

Zach: Saving Saliva

In the previous discussion it was stated that swallowing saliva is usually a *subconscious*, automatic process. Not so with TS-OCD! It—or almost any other body or mental process—may become a focal concern, as it did for nine-year-old Zach.

When Zach was six years old he started picking up things with his elbows in order to avoid getting his hands dirty. By the time he was seven, he was washing his hands 35 times a day in the classic OCD attempt to be "perfectly" clean. About this time he also started engaging in rituals that he linked to swallowing saliva:

> When I swallowed saliva I had to crouch down and touch the ground. I didn't want to lose saliva . . . I tried to tell my ma. I told her I had to do it. She says, "You're doing some strange things, why do you do it?" I said, "Cause I don't want to lose any saliva." (Rapoport, 1989, pp. 43–44)

Recall the earlier discussion on the development of tics. It was suggested that tics are created by amplifying *normal* muscle movements. Everyone *occasionally* blinks their eyes, clears their throat, or sniffles their nose, but for the ticquer this becomes *incessant*. Likewise, in the above example the obsession is created by amplifying *normal* thoughts. It's not weird to be aware of your saliva under appropriate conditions. We speak of desserts as being "mouth watering." But except when we smell such foods, this awareness is *subconscious*, not *hyper*conscious as it became in Zach's life. Once something becomes a focal point of consciousness it is a small step to couple other behaviors to it, as Zach did with swallowing saliva and crouching down to touch the ground.

Mosquitoes of the Mind

Stanley, another OCD patient, described it well: "These obsessions were like 'mosquitoes of the mind.' I couldn't make them go away. They wouldn't stop: always there, insistent, itching, a force" (Rapoport, 1989, p. 130).

For Stanley, the "mosquitoes" started "bugging" him in the sixth grade when suddenly he became obsessed with placing his shoes down on the floor perfectly:

> "Perfectly" is the key word for the beginning of my illness. I had to put my shoes down perfectly. I had to write using perfect penmanship, talk perfectly, without any slips of tongue, variations in speech tone or rate. My steps had to be in perfect cadence with arms as they moved machine-like alongside my body. (Rapoport, 1989, p. 130)

In the eighth grade he was afraid that an "unclean" air conditioner in his eighth-grade social studies classroom would contaminate him. By high school he was always counting numbers, which interfered with his performance as a member of the marching band. He would get confused trying to count his numbers and keep step at the same time. He tried out for the golf team, but his cleanliness obsessions got in his way:

> Hitting the balls would spread the dirt and make things, including me, "unclean." I knew that to hit the ball in a clean iron stroke you had to dig into the ground and create a divot. But I couldn't make myself do it. I missed the ball a few times and didn't make the team. (Rapoport, pp. 129–131)

Typically, trying to be "perfect" is elusively masked in commonplace behaviors such as washing, checking, counting, and so on, behaviors that don't seem moral in nature. Sometimes, however, the perfectionistic striving does express itself in a moral way, such as in the traditional religious ritual of prayer. *Marion* at age 12 used to pray *briefly* before getting into bed to "fool" her grandmother who slept in the next room and who would then hear Marion climb into bed. However, after her grandmother began to snore, Marion would creep out of bed and quietly pray for *three more hours* (Rapoport, p. 89).

Many more examples could be given, but in virtually all cases of TS-OCD we find hysteresis cycles: hyperattentiveness to certain details of the self (mental or somatic) that most people scarcely think about; repetitive, ritualistic coping strategies; and *shame* which serves to refuel the cycle. The content varies from person to person, but the basic components of the cycle remain strikingly similar. It is this essential similarity that allows us to utilize the topologically derived CT for analysis.

TICS AND OBSESSIONS—TOPOLOGICAL EQUIVALENTS

It's been shown that topology deals with *invariant*, dimensionless relationships. A dot contained within a closed curve is topologically equivalent to all other closed curves with dots within. It makes no difference how large or small the figures or how misshapen. Consequently it makes little difference from a topological perspective whether the dot is contained within a circle, an ellipse, or even a cube or triangle. These are all topological equivalents, since the "dot-enclosed-within-the-figure" relationship is maintained. In much the same way, all tics are topologically equivalent to one another. Even more astounding, they are not only equivalent to one another, they are equivalent to obsessions. Let us look more closely at this idea.

Whitney's Singularity Theory

An American mathematician, Hassler Whitney, published an article in 1955 in which he proved that every *singularity* of a smooth mapping of a surface onto a plane, after an appropriate small perturbation, splits into *folds* and *cusps*. What this means in nonmathematical terms is that certain topological relationships remain stable even when other variables are changed. Think of a globe of the world, for example. As you spin the globe, the various countries mapped on the surface become a blur. Yet, the outline of the globe—the edges—remain stable. The singularity arising at equatorial points when such a sphere is projected onto a plane is known as a Whitney *fold*. The second kind of Whitney singularity is the *cusp*, which occurs when a surface like Figure 6.4 is projected onto a plane.

A World of Cusps and Folds

Putting aside the complicated mathematics underlying these findings, it is important to note that mappings of smooth surfaces onto planes are all around us. Since these smooth mappings are found everywhere, CT uses this information to study many different phenomena and processes in all areas of science. The majority of objects surrounding us are bordered by smooth surfaces which are then projected onto the retinal plane of the eye. Consequently, the *persisting singularities* on the surface of the retina are folds and cusps.

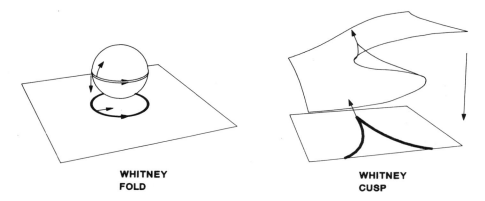

**WHITNEY
FOLD**

**WHITNEY
CUSP**

FIGURE 6.4 The American mathematician Hassler Whitney proved that every singularity of a smooth mapping of a surface onto a plane splits into folds and cusps after an appropriate small perturbation. Mappings of smooth surfaces onto planes are all around us and are projected onto the surface of the retina of the eye. Whitney's singularity theory suggests that only the cusp and fold are stable and persist after small deformations of the mapping.

The Proprioceptive "Retina"

It is remarkable that the limitless number of objects in our environment can all be mapped into fold and cusp configurations on the surface of the retina, which then relays this information back to the visual projection areas of the cortex. It seems plausible to suggest that there exists a *proprioceptive* "retina" where various states of muscle tone and movement are mapped much as visual stimuli are mapped on the visual retina. Clearly this "retina" doesn't exist as a specific organic planar surface, but it is well known that the human organism exists as an interdependent system of feedback networks made possible by (literally) billions of potential interneuronal connections. In this intricately balanced system, there is moment-by-moment monitoring of the state of the organism in many dimensions. Body temperature is maintained within a narrow band, typically hovering between 98 and 99 degrees Fahrenheit. The chemical constituents of the blood are carefully monitored as is oxygen content; and the body makes provision to correct any deficits.

The visual retina maps and feeds back to the brain the visual surroundings and computes the location of the organism with respect to proximal objects. In much the same way, the "proprioceptive retina" feeds such information as muscle tone, movement, and intensity of movement to higher centers in the brain. It seems consistent with CT and with the biological sciences to suggest that *tics exist in the mind as proprioceptive singularities*. Just as the folds and cusps on the eye's retina provide important visual information, tics provide discreet, recurrent muscle-based information. Like familiar visual objects that allow the organism to "feel at home" in "familiar surroundings" tics are muscular "objects" providing feedback that is familiar and feels safe. Tics even have the added advantage of a "carry-with-you" mobility which allows them to be used in any new situation to create a sense of familiarity and comfort.

It is in this sense that *tics are topologically equivalent to each other*. Each tic involves certain fundamental elements that remain consistent across situational variables and across combinations of muscles. Thus, all tics involve *recurrent sudden movements*, of familiar *body parts*, in *normal-but-exaggerated* ways that have *shame-generating consequences* in most social environments. Topologically speaking, it makes little difference whether the tic is head jerking, eye blinking, elbow flapping, throat clearing, and so on. These and all other tics are topologically equivalent when mapped onto the CT behavior surface. Just as the sizes or shape of the figure is irrelevant in the dot-within-a-figure relationship, so the tic frequency, intensity, muscle tone, and size of the observing audience are irrelevant when considering tics. Understanding such specifics may be useful when designing treatment programs or for other purposes, but has little relevance to topological equivalence.

Going a step further, just as it's been shown that the specific characteristics of tics are not of primary importance, so the differences between tics and obsessions have been overrated by clinicians. Topologically speaking, the shared similarities between tics and obsessions are greater than their differences. Tics and obsessions involve *recurrent, sudden bursts* of familiar *cognitions or movements* that are *normal-but-exaggerated* and that result in *shame* to the self.

A Cognitive "Retina"

It has been shown that virtually all visual stimuli capable of being sensed by the eye are mapped onto the retina in the form of folds and cusps. Likewise, it's been suggested that tics, regardless of their variety, are mapped into the brain in the "form" of familiar movements. Although this area of the brain can't be delineated at a specific organic location such as the retina, it likely exists as a projection area on the cortex. A kind of "proprioceptive retina" exists where moment-by-moment muscular activity is mapped. Following the same line of rea-soning, it can be suggested there is also a "cognitive retina" where fa-miliar thought rituals (obsessions) exist as familiar foci of contempla-tion. Like visual objects constantly impinging upon the retina, or repetitive muscle movements, recurrent cognitive sequences (such as counting, alphabetizing, or other forms of ordering) are likely mapped into the same portion of the cortex time after time and subsequently provide "instant familiarity" in times of stress or in novel situations.

Topological Thinking About Behavioral Problems

In summary, I'm suggesting that a concern with *functional* rather than *metric* relationships allows for a more integrative understanding of TS-OCD. Because all visual inputs can be reduced to two basic mappings on the retina—cusps and folds—it doesn't seem unreasonable to assume that muscular and cognitive inputs also can be summarized in terms of a relatively few generic "forms." In this sense the visual retina and the proprioceptive and cognitive "retinas" are topological equivalents. This underlying unity of sensory phenomena lies at the core of CT and is the reason we find it such a useful "map" for a variety of TS-OCD mani-festations.

THE DISEMBODIED LADY—A MIRROR IMAGE OF TS

Sometimes phenomena can be explained best by considering what oc-curs when they are absent. This is especially true of unconscious bodily processes. For example, oxygen is taken for granted unless one suffers from lack of it, as with emphysema, or if nearly drowning or the like. Similarly, the "sixth sense" of proprioception—the subconscious sen-sory stream of impulses from the movable parts of the body (muscles, joints, tendons) that continually monitors and adjusts position, tone, and motion—is usually taken for granted. Oliver Sacks (1985, pp. 42–52) reports a case where this vital sensory ground of existence was lost.

Christina is described as a "strapping young woman of about 27, given to hockey and riding, self-assured, robust, in body and mind" (Sacks, 1985, p. 43). A mother of two young children, she worked as a computer programmer at home, and cultivated a taste for ballet, poetry, and the finer things of life. Prior to her hospitalization for gallbladder surgery she seemed the quintessential well-rounded person. However, while in the hospital, Christina suffered a rare polyneuropathy which left her without a sense of proprioception: "'Something awful's happened,' she mouthed, in a ghostly flat voice, 'I can't feel my body. I feel weird—disembodied'" (p. 44).

Described as "floppy as a ragdoll, unable to even sit up," at the beginning of her illness, she eventually recovered some of her ability to function by *consciously* attending to what had heretofore been automatic. She learned to walk, talk, and generally get about, but only with great effort and concentration, and her posture, speech, and movements had a stiff, artificial quality about them. Nor was her subjective experience ever normal again. Months later she reported: "I feel my body is blind and deaf to itself. . . it has no sense of itself."

Sacks elaborates on the difficulties faced by her in daily life—difficulties that are also met by those with TS:

> She has no words, no direct words, to describe this bereftness, this sensory darkness (or silence) akin to blindness or deafness. She has no words, and we lack words too. And society lacks words, and sympathy, for such states. The blind, at least, are treated with solicitude—we can imagine their state and treat them accordingly. But when Christina, painfully, clumsily, mounts a bus, she receives nothing but uncomprehending and angry snarls: "What's wrong with you, lady? Are you blind—or blind-drunk?" What can she answer—"I have no proprioception"? The lack of social support and sympathy is an additional trial—disabled, but with the nature of her disability not clear—she is not, after all, manifestly blind or paralysed, manifestly anything—she tends to be treated as a phoney or a fool. This is what happens to those with disorders of the hidden senses. (p. 50)

TS-OCD—"Overembodied" Persons

Whereas Christina suffers a *disembodied* existence, persons with motor tics live an *overembodied* life. Christina suffers *de-afferentiation*, while persons with tics experience *hyper-afferentiation*. In an ironic sense, persons with tics live a "fuller, richer" life than ordinary persons as a result of the more highly developed sense of proprioception. However since this manifests itself in "sudden jumps" and other phenomena puzzling to onlookers, society shames such expressions. Like Christina clumsily ascending the steps of a bus without an apparent reason for her awkwardness, the ticquer suffers from a silently driven need that manifests itself in a public way. As Sacks aptly put it when discussing Christina's social difficulties: "The lack of social support and sympathy is an additional trial—disabled, but with the nature of her disability not clear. . . . This is what happens to those with disorders of the hidden senses."

We've seen in *disembodied* Christina the precise *virtual image* (flip side or mirror image) of ticquing. In exploring yet another facet of the complex package of behaviors known as TS-OCD, we can now understand tics as *functional hyper-afferentiation* of normal bodily experiences. Earlier we traced the developmental shift from motoric to cognitive functioning taking place about the middle of the second year, and suggested that when this was delayed because of stress the likelihood of the child transcending the "motoric" body ego was reduced and the probability of ticquing was increased.

Unlike Christina's disembodiment which was organically based, the *hyper-embodiment* seen in TS-OCD seems more functional. The young child in distress is unwilling to "move out of the body" not because of organic lesions but because it's more "comfortable" to stay with the familiar. The "body-ego" described by Freud is not a neurological anomaly, but a primal ego experience. To remain within it is a developmental dilemma not a neurological disorder.

Topology of Tics

Having argued for the "topological equivalence" of the seemingly disparate behaviors subsumed under the diagnosis of TS-OCD, we now turn to a more detailed delineation of various tics and obsessions. It is the shared "topological" characteristics which allow us to analyze all of them with the CT model, but this in no way reduces the necessity for careful, individualized analyses of the myriad manifestations. The discussion will follow the developmental sequence from the earliest hours of neonatal life to adulthood. Such an arrangement implies that it is possible—though not yet proven—to trace tics and obsessions seen in adults back to their developmental origins by carefully studying their characteristics and correlating these with the developmental epochs where such behaviors first occurred.

Chapter 7

ADVANCED THEORETICAL CONSIDERATIONS: A DEVELOPMENTAL TAXONOMY OF TICS AND OBSESSIONS

For illustrative purposes, tics will be utilized as the model behavior in applying CT, but a similar analysis holds for the more subtle "mental tics" seen in what has heretofore been labeled OCD. Tics come in countless varieties, driven by many different moods—shame and anger being the most common pair. This is not surprising, because tics *generate* curiosity and ridicule, which in turn refuel the cycle with shame and anger. Occasionally, however, anger is not one of the primary driving moods; and even more rarely, shame may be absent from the constellation. Accordingly, we will look at a variety of mood "partnerships" on the control surface that codeterminately drive tics on the behavior surface.

DEVELOPMENTAL CATASTROPHES

The taxonomy that follows is tentative, but consistent with both CT and developmental research. This can be thought of as a call for research more than a definitive theory. It seems important to understand tics and other TS-OCD manifestations as *communicational* phenomena, not spastic neurological symptoms. Consistent with CT, this taxonomy is based on the notion that tics are codetermined by two primary mood states. Additionally, an attempt will be made to suggest which moods are likely to be dominant during a particular developmental epoch. The extent to which adult tics arise out of specific developmental eras or experiences is an empirical question which has yet to be investigated. Hopefully this discussion will provide the heuristic impetus and theoretical parameters for conducting such research.

Neonatal Emotions: The Odyssey from Soothing to Shame

Emotions of neonatal life are nebulous and labile, fluctuating easily and creating a constantly changing mosaic of felt experience. Such moods are difficult to label because the neonate doesn't clearly differentiate boundaries and "thinks" totally in presymbolic ways. The experience of shame—induced by the scornful scrutiny of significant others—is not yet present. Under conditions of stress the infant may retreat "inward" and attempt to comfort him or herself through rhythmic self soothing or rhythmic rituals which distract the self from proximal aversive stimuli; but shame is not yet part of the repertoire. An infant has to be taught that he or she is shameful.

As seen earlier, infants regularly engage in rhythmic behavior loops Piaget called *circular reactions*, and it has been proposed in this text that such patterns can comfort in times of distress. Additionally these patterns serve to keep the infant's focus inward, thereby reducing the salience of external aversive stimuli in subjective experience. It is these kinds of *sedative* behaviors that form the core of the infant's coping equipment for dealing with stress.

Infancy Can Be Startling

Having established that shame is not a strong driving force in the early months of life, let us briefly examine what kinds of experiences comprise stress for the infant. If infants haven't yet learned to be ashamed what do they "worry" about? Neonates face many "startling" experiences in what William James called the "blooming, buzzing, confusion." Doors slam, horns honk, people sneeze, tableware recurringly clatters to the floor. In addition to such auditory "startles" there is no lack of "proprioceptive catastrophes." When you're little people throw you high into the air—it surely *feels* high—above their heads, and rapidly move you in and out of automobiles. Adults take you along on bicycle rides, hurtling you through space, binding your destiny to theirs with a backpack-like capsule known as an "infant carrier."

Another form of distress experienced by infants that is less intense but even more frightening than overstimulation is *abandonment*—referring here to emotional unavailability not necessarily physical absence. From the earliest neonatal hours, babies seek emotional contact with the mothering one. As early as the first postnatal day, microkinesic movie analysis discloses that the baby moves in precise synchrony with the rhythms of articulated adult speech (Condon & Sander, 1974). Infants begin to *expect* regularities in their interactions with parents, and when such expectations are violated, it is emotionally distressing. Call (1980) carried out a series of experiments in which he instructed mothers to keep their faces expressionless when they approached their babies. Lichtenberg reports on these studies:

> If a mother approaches a six-week-old who is lying quietly and places her face in the child's visual field, the infant responds with mounting excitement all over his body. If the mother, following instructions, holds her face expressionless, the infant at first increases his part of their previous routine of synchronous gestures. When the mother fails to respond, the infant's efforts become more hectic and disorganized, until finally he lapses into a pained immobility. This reaction is explainable only by taking into account the repetitious interactional exchanges that have preceded it. The specificity of matching the pattern that begins with the mother's face entering the infant's visual field and the cooing, clucking, smiling exchanges that follow must be seen against the background of a structured interaction, built out of repetition and expectancy. (Lichtenberg, 1983, p. 159)

When maternal attention is chronically diverted through depression, alcoholism, drug use or other circumstances that interfere with the smooth reciprocity between mother and developing infant, the void may become filled with overuse of repetitive self focused behaviors.

CLUSTER I—THE MATERNALLY IMMEDIATE MONTHS (0–8)

The primary needs during these first months involve soothing and discharge. Tics from this time, like the *primary* circular reactions upon which they are based, focus on the self. "Piggybacked" onto the earliest life-sustaining behaviors of sucking, breathing, and elimination, such tics provide avenues of somatic discharge, differentiation, and soothing. For the optimally developing infant, body differentiating behaviors such as touching oneself, stretching, wriggling, and looking at moving objects and faces that appear above one's crib, provide opportunities to differentiate body boundaries. Additionally, internal behaviors such as belching, sneezing, crying, or laughing, or passing urine, flatus, or feces provide deep kinesthetic feedback to the developing infant.

When behaviors from these earliest weeks of life become routinized into tics they sometimes become socially obnoxious, but, more often, their major focus is tension reduction through discharge and self soothing *not* interpersonal brinkmanship. Such tics might include sucking one's tongue; smacking the lips; sniffing; touching or smelling oneself (especially forbidden areas) inserting fingers or objects into one's mouth, nose, ears, rectum, vagina; grinding teeth, biting nails, chewing pencils, chewing tongue, slapping self, tugging or plucking hair or brows, and so on.

Recall the woman who barked and bit my leg (see Chapter 4); she was fond of stuffing droppings and other contraband up her nose when she was a child: "Hot peppers, rabbit droppings, rabbit food, dog droppings, horse droppings—I like droppings. Anything—everything—leaves, paper, dirt, stones, everything goes up my nose."

Recall the two young boys in Rapoport's study who spent several hours each day methodically licking their fingers, one at a time. Such primitive tics seem not far removed from the primal behaviors of neonatal life. The crucial issue for later development is how "shamegenic" they are. If one chews the inside of one's mouth or grinds one's teeth only your dentist may know. If, however, you suck your fingers or put rabbit droppings up your nose, shame and ridicule are sure to follow in the later months of life as parents and peers become privy to such strange behavior.

In summary, tics founded on the earliest needs of the neonate, are not driven by shame and anger but by distress emotions resulting from the various forms of emotional unavailability. In response to such distress the infant turns inward with a variety of self-stimulating, self defining, and self-discharging behaviors. Not yet having developed shame and anger, the baby focuses inward in repetitive but angerless and shameless "catastrophes." Having considered the self-soothing, self-differentiating era, the next stage to explore is the self-discharging (or exploding) months.

CLUSTER II—MATERNALLY PROXIMAL MONTHS (8–18)

These tics, like the *secondary* circular reactions upon which they are based, remain strongly focused on the self, but do have a slightly expanded circle of awareness. Tics of this cluster have their roots in the preverbal wish to be noticed by mother and in the innate drive to master one's nonpersonal surroundings by manipulation. They communicate a nonverbal message of the genre: "Look at me, hold me, soothe me, Mommy!" Tics here are likely driven by distress related to broken bonding with the mother or traumatically changing or threatening physical surroundings. There is distress, but not in the form of self-consciousness or shame. Tics originating in this period are often designed to engage the attention of others or reestablish close physical contact; they are not very explosive and are "connecting" in quality. Examples include making faces, raising eyebrows, rotating the head, hand over the face peekaboo style, oral or tactile contact with other persons such as touching, smelling, sucking, licking, or kissing and echolalia and echopraxia.

Another group of tics from this era are more explosive than those mentioned, yet self-focused. These are perhaps the most puzzling in adults—why would someone hit themselves in the face or literally bang their head against the wall? The answer to this comes from the earliest developmental weeks when, lacking a good interpersonal bonding object, the infant begins to turn discharge back on self. From this era come the various "catastrophes," such as grunting, shrieking, plucking hair or eyebrows, and pinching or tugging on body parts (Have you noticed how Carol Burnette has made a trademark out of her ear tugging tic?)

Figure 7.1 maps tics from the first months of life. Driven by disengagement distress and engagement hope as the two primary moods on the control surface, they are manifest on the behavior surface in a variety of tics mostly self-focused and mostly concerned with tranquilizing. These are the tics that are the least "angry" of all. Many of these primitive behaviors do not exhibit the spasmodic qualities seen in most tics. Licking one's fingers, for example is not a sudden or jerky movement; rolling one's head from side to side (as Samuel Johnson was fond of doing) appears different from head jerking. Consequently, some of these earliest tics appear on the lower left of the behavior sheet never really "jumping" to the top sheet and developing a hysteresis cycle. Yet, they are importantly related to other behaviors that definitely function as "catastrophes."

In short, many of these early foundational repetitive behaviors appear not to be tics at all. They are often mild in intensity, retaining much of the smoothness of normal behavior; and just as it is difficult to distinguish a developing sniffing tic from the sniffles of a head cold, differential diagnoses among these early repetitive behaviors is difficult when undertaken on the basis of appearance alone. Nonetheless they can be understood within the broader context of CT as belonging to the family of tic behaviors, especially when their occurrence corresponds with times of maternal deprivation or emotional unavailability. In such cases, early preventative measures that succeed in reducing stress in the environment and/or increasing maternal availability may have significant effects.

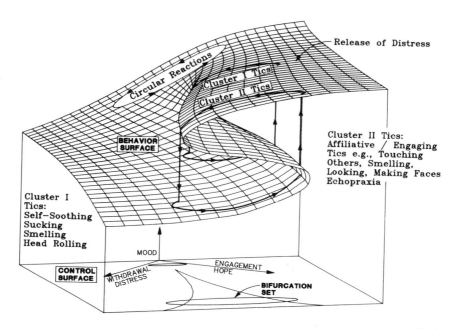

FIGURE 7.1 Tics in clusters I and II are rooted in the first year and a half of life. The two driving moods on the control surface are distress and hope. The infant experiencing distress about being left alone or finding the environment traumatic or unpredictable may withdraw inward to the comfort of soothing behaviors such as sucking or chewing the mouth, licking lips, or smelling oneself. Often these do not appear as jerky or spasmatic tics, but instead echo the primary circular reactions out of which they have arisen. Cluster II tics involve a mood of hope which is present on the behavior surface as seeking engagement. Like secondary circular reactions, such behaviors involve objects or people outside oneself, and attempt to engage the caretaker. These tics often originate in the distress of broken bonding or traumatic surroundings, and function to re-engage others.

CLUSTER III—THE AMBITENDENT MONTHS (18–36)

These are the autonomous months, when optimally developing toddlers may sometimes be found alternately yelling "No!"—to a mother who wonders what's gone wrong with her sweet baby—and demanding "Me sit on Mommy's lap!" Soothing is no longer sought primarily within oneself; rather, if emotional availability is not adequate, the toddler *actively* seeks interaction, a process Furer (1964) termed "refueling."

This is an anger-energized version of the earlier "engagement-hope" mood. The toddler now *demands* attention, becoming more insistent when it is not forthcoming. There remains an intense need for emotional contact, but the behavior of the toddler may be so obnoxious or the parent so depleted that coercive operations such as whining, bed-wetting, hurting oneself, or spilling things may occur with higher than usual frequency.

Push–Pull Patterns

Ambitendent (tic-prone) toddlers have difficulty with "pure" autonomy and tend to oscillate between "No!" and "Please don't leave me." Normal autonomy needs become fused with concern about losing the love object resulting in oscillatory patterns of clinging/pushing away, hugging/hitting, approaching/retreating. Numerous approach/avoidance behaviors permeate the relationship between toddler and parents. Verbally translated such behaviors communicate: "Let me go!—Hug me!"

In family systems where physical punishment or aggression is prevalent, ambitendence is amplified with verbal translation taking the form: "Hold me!"/"Hit me!" Sometimes when previously compliant toddlers become autonomous, "ticquogenic" parents overuse punishment or physical restraint in the vain attempt to "contain" unwanted behaviors.

Figure 7.2 illustrates that tics with roots in this epoch are driven by the *conflict* between engagement and disengagement needs, but this is now *actively* pursued and is typically energized by anger. Normal toddlers defiantly *shake the head* or *stomp a foot* while simultaneously shouting "No!" to one of her parent's commands. *Shrugging* or *twisting* away from the pursuing parent is another common autonomy maneuver often utilized by toddlers.

Push–Pull Tics

Tics rooted in this era, creatively routinize the "No!" of autonomy while simultaneously engaging the attention of others. The "push-away" tics include pushing, nudging, hitting, or kicking others. The "pullling" tics try to get attention by shrieking and various other vocalizations. Finally, there are a number of tics that are intrinsically push-pull. Kissing, touching, and smelling others are some that include both elements.

Compared to the more passive, self-soothing tics arising out of earlier developmental eras, the tics of this era tend to be interpersonal with an angry edge to them. These are tics from the "terrible twos" where the war between the generations is waged in it's most primal patterns. The toddler who is entwined in a family system permeated with negative

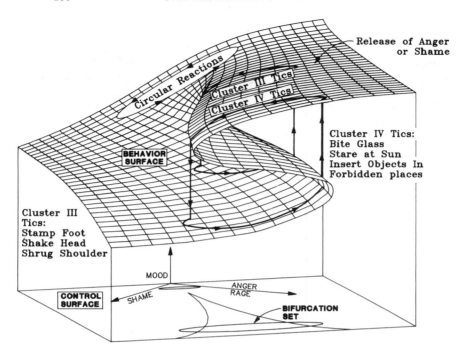

FIGURE 7.2 Cluster II tics are permeated with the conflict of engagement and autonomy. Fueled by shame (at failing to achieve autonomy) or anger (at caretakers who challenge the toddler's omnipotence), they have a "push-pull" quality. Tics such as head shaking ("No! No!") or shoulder shrugging creatively assert autonomy while engaging others. Cluster IV tics grow out of the pre-school years when prohibitions and boundary setting are at a zenith. Such tics, rooted primarily in prohibitions, involve autonomy conflicts, but are less somatic in nature than cluster III tics; involving instead more interpersonal and cognitive elements.

emotions or who seeks mothering from a parent who is emotionally unavailable will either "coercively" seek to extract emotional responses, or withdraw into self-stimulating patterns of repetitive behavior, which are self-focused but socially obnoxious as well.

Proprioceptive Mommy

This also is the time of transitional objects. Soothing is still needed and the beloved teddy bear, dolly, or blanket provides the toddler insurance against abandonment. For the somatically overinvested toddler, proprioceptive feedback can provide comfort. The deep-muscle soothing provided by torso twisting, shoulder shrugging, and the like provide a "proprioceptive Mommy" for some toddlers functioning as a powerful transition object. It has advantages over the blanket or teddy bear, being always present, easily engaged, and deeply soothing.

CLUSTER IV—THREE TO SIX YEARS

Autonomy continues to be a central concern during these years, culminating with the child's giant step away from home into the larger social world of school. Tics having roots in the preschool years become less somatic. Although it sometimes appears as if the individual is doing harmful somatic things to her or himself (such as staring at the sun, biting the edge of a glass, inserting objects into the nose, ear, rectum, vagina, etc.)—closer analysis reveals that such seemingly bizarre behaviors are really autonomy conflicts between the self and internalized parental voices saying: "Don't stare at the sun—you'll go blind!" "Don't splash the wall when you pee pee." "Don't make faces at your sister." "Don't touch the fan!" "Don't stare at people on the bus!"

This cluster includes an almost infinite variety of behaviors from which children have been forbidden: touching taboo areas of another person's body; inserting objects into one's body orifices; poking oneself—especially the eyes—with pens, pencils, or other sharp objects; touching operating equipment such as fans, saws, or garbage disposals; biting the edge of a drinking glass or the oral thermometer being used to assess one's temperature; removing bottle caps with one's teeth; chewing the erase end of a pencil and continuing to chew on the metal part; squeezing a thin wine goblet or an uncooked egg; inserting sharp or occluding objects into ears or nostrils; inserting fingers into a contaminated environment (e.g., rectum) and immediately into a more sterile environment (mouth). More examples could be given, but in general these tics *catastrophically* resolve the conflict between the angry surge for autonomy and the subsequent shameful "niceness" of the control surface with an almost infinite variety of tics on the behavior surface.

Some of these behaviors (e.g., removing bottle caps with one's teeth) do not occur repetitively with high frequency, and consequently don't seem as "neurologically spasmodic" as most tic behaviors; however they are dynamically similar to the high frequency tics like teeth grinding or pencil chewing.

Interesting in this regard is Sack's description of the photographer who accompanied him to study the Mennonites:

> His playful and compulsive tendencies even extend to his camera—he will sometimes toss it up in the air and catch it with a snap or bang it suddenly on the table. But now in his excitement [to get a picture of the sunset] things went violently, Tourettishly wrong. He slammed his favorite lens onto the camera body—and smashed it with the force of impact. Lowell turned very pale and remained quite silent for the rest of the evening. "I was shocked," he said later. "I just couldn't believe that I did it. I've broken glasses, radios, things like that, but never anything so important to me. I felt terrible. I had lost control." The image of Lowell standing there in the reddening sunset with the ruins of a $500 lens clutched in his hands brought home to me . . . the danger of Tourette's. (1988, p. 98, author's brackets)

Sacks continues:

> Some Tourettic obsessions have a whimsical quality—sudden impulses, for example, to bite the soap, to tap the teeth, to throw one's glasses out the window, to count the number of books on a shelf, to divide a square mentally into quarters. But other mental tics can sometimes become destructive. Kurlan told us of Janzen family members who had lost fingers by suddenly thrusting them into flames or machines. (p. 100)

You Can't Make Me!

As we have seen throughout this book, what appears "whimsical" or random becomes understandable and even "logical" if one views the behavior developmentally. Biting soap, tapping one's teeth, or throwing glasses out the window are all behaviors that have been forbidden by mother, father, teacher, God, Mother Nature or some other authority. These teachings are then internalized and provide the basis for the following private but pervasive "mental" dialogues between mother and child—early voices that continue to echo throughout a lifetime.

MOM: "When you wash, be sure to get behind your ears but be careful not to get soap in your eyes."

TERRY TOURETTE: "You can't make me, I'm grown up now and I can even *bite* soap if I want to."

MOM: "Don't tap your teeth with that pencil, you're going to damage them—those are your permanent teeth you know. Why do you think we take you to the dentist? Stop it right now!"

TERRY: "You can't make me now. See, I'm tapping my teeth even though I know it might hurt them. It's dangerous—but not really very seriously, so I just have to test the limits."

MOM: (Exasperatedly, upon discovering Terry's broken glasses on a chair after they had been accidentally sat upon) "How many times have I told you not to put your glasses just *anywhere* you happen to be when you take them off. Glasses are expensive, do you think we have money to throw away?"

TERRY: "So who cares? I hate those glasses. The kids at school call me 'Four Eyes' and I can see pretty well without them anyway. Besides, I'm grown up now and *you can't make me* wear them. See, I can even thrown them out the window!"

What is at the core of Cluster IV tics? Autonomy. The "Why-should-I?" response to a few of the myriad instructions the child receives in the process of growing up.

CASE ILLUSTRATION

The *London Daily Telegraph* (April 17, 1990, p. 13) recently published an article entitled "One Man's Lonely Fight Against His Own Nature:"

> Because its origin is unknown, Tourette's Syndrome—named after a French doctor who first defined it—cannot be cured, only controlled in varying degrees by powerful tranquillisers, or by a leukotomy, an operation which involves incision in the brain's frontal lobe.
> So far only two people in the country have been given the operation and one, Michael Brooks, is the subject of a Channel 4 film, *Against my Nature*, which is to be shown on Monday.
> As a child he became seized with the urge to tear his clothes, and break his fountain pen and glasses, something he could at least do in private, merely earning the reputation of being accident-prone. . . . For him pain acts as a deterrent, but touretters for whom the compulsion is stronger lose fingers by sticking them in machinery, and eyes by poking them.

Comparing his "urges" to the alcoholic's "thirst" for liquor, Michael likens his behavior to an addiction "that does not give, and did not originate in, pleasure." He observes that his compulsions require enormous self-vigilance, yet, paradoxically, the more he concentrates on himself the worse the urges become—this is especially true if he has nothing else to occupy his mind. For example, his employing agency recently reorganized to reduce costs and he lost his job after having worked as an engineer for a number of years. After that, reports the article:

> He no longer had anything to distract him, and his destructive urges became intolerable.
> He kept smashing up his flat, finally not bothering to mend, replace, or even tidy away the broken windows and torn blankets. Even in the street urges to tear his clothes overwhelmed him, and he could see his girlfriend Irene only in one or other of their flats, where, if he tore her clothes or hurt her, it would at least be in private.

In the television film one of his surgeons, admitting that the operation is not a "magic cure," remarked that in the all-important first few months after the operation, Michael must "Fight like hell for his freedom." The newspaper article relates that "He is fighting, but is terrified that he has regressed from his initial improvement." Surgery for TS-OCD seems a little like trying to control stuttering by removing the tongue. Such drastic interventions are, however, consistent with organic etiology.

CLUSTER V—SELF-ESTEEM CONCERNS (6–12 YEARS)

As the child momentously moves from home to school—from playroom to schoolroom—awareness shifts from a focus on autonomy to one of increasing concern with *self*-evaluation. This happens most poignantly on the playground, although comparison with peers occurs in the classroom as well. Tics rooted in these later developmental epochs are more socially embedded, often involving keen social discernment (see Figure 7.3). One must understand social parameters well in order to function successfully "at the edge."

Frequently Cluster V tics don't appear to be tics at all. They might not have a convulsive, jerking "neurological" appearance and are seldom repetitive in the several-times-per-minute way that eye blinking or throat clearing usually are. These tics can best be described as interpersonally *testy*. Although such "testiness" doesn't appear tic like or spasmatic, it still has all the repetitive and compulsive characteristics of more common tics or obsessions. Thus saying "Goodnight" until others become exasperated enough to say "shut up and go to sleep" may seem very different from persistent throat clearing, but it is topologically equivalent.

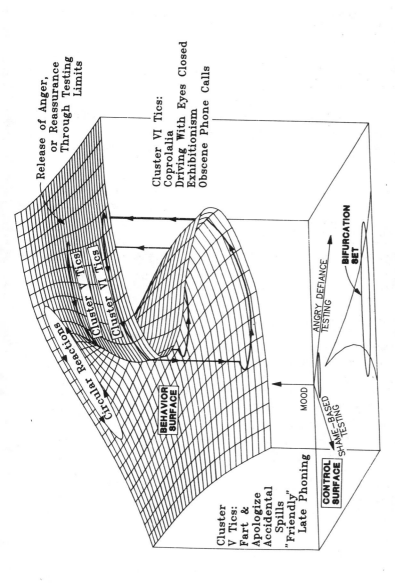

FIGURE 7.3 The two driving moods on the control surface are shame and anger. On one axis shame-based insecurity leads to constant testing of social relationships with obnoxious behaviors retracted by apologies. The "I'm-sorry-I-spilled-grape-juice-on-your-carpet" blend of obnoxious and obsequious behaviors dominates cluster V. With increasing anger, testing takes the form of coprolalia, exhibitionism, and various other "at-the-edge" behaviors typical of cluster VI. Notice, however, that each of these catastrophes *blends* shame and anger in differing proportions. The coprolalic utterance "I masturbate!" is more shameful and less angry, while "Hiya niggah!" is more provocative and less shameful.

How Do You Drive Your Car?—Ticquing with the Pedal to the Metal

It is of interest to briefly compare a few "auto-assisted" tics. "Auto" tics are obviously not possible in young children, but they amply demonstrate issues that were activated long before the obtaining of a driver's license.

For some persons with TS-OCD driving never becomes an area of autonomous defiance or "testiness." In Sack's *Life Magazine* article, for example, there is a picture of David Janzen driving his automobile with one hand on the steering wheel, the other arm twisted midair with fist in a clenched position, while his daughter unconcernedly rides in the back seat playing with a toy. The caption beneath the picture reads:

> David, driving daughter Barbara on an errand, suffers a sudden convulsion. One hand shoots up, but the other keeps control of the wheel. Such moments don't affect David's ability to drive safely, and regular passengers hardly notice. (1988, p. 102)

For others, however driving becomes another behavior in the repertoire of self-focusing, self-injuring behaviors. For example, we're told that Michael, the leucotomized London man:

> Still suffers from compulsions to tear his clothes, smash windows, shout obscenities and bark, though to a less intense degree than before the operation. He no longer gets compulsions to slash himself and poke his eyes, but still dares not drive a car for fear of deliberately crashing it.

For Michael driving is a Cluster IV tic—one of a number of behaviors driven by the need to autonomously defy early parental orders—even when they were right.

There are also examples of "testy" driving tics. Comings (1990) reports three cases of people closing their eyes while driving. Few details are given, so it's difficult to derive the correct dynamics. Some of these could be a case of defying the instruction to "Watch the road when you drive." But in at least one case there was a more testy interpersonal aspect:

> One young man said it only came on when he was driving the most dangerous roads such as mountain curves. This so frightened his wife that she refused to let him drive when she was in the car. (1990, pp. 13–14)

Finally, there is the case of the man whose wife bugged him about not driving more smoothly. As their marriage relationship worsened (for numerous reasons unrelated to his driving), his driving became more jerky. His "auto" tic incited her to insist he equip the car with cruise control, which of course he did not do. After they split up he related that he was driving along by himself one day when he suddenly realized he was no longer jerking the car. The reasons for the car tics had ceased to exist!

More Testy Tics

Persons who telephone late at night or early in the morning "just to say hi" "forgetting" you live in a time zone that's three hours different exhibit the kind of ambitendent "friendliness" that *tests* the relationship. Although a telephone call is not generally thought of as a tic, the dynamics are similar to those of more obvious tic behaviors such as repetitively saying "goodnight." Behaviors in Cluster V test how far one can deviate from social expectancy without being totally ostracized. Such "testiness" serves to reassure the ambitendent person that others must *really* like him. After all, if a person still likes you after you fart in their face, they must think you're OK. Included in this cluster are teasing and all the related "I was just kidding" kinds of obnoxious behaviors. These verbally translate into: "Would you still like me if I touch, bump, or nudge you?" "What if I say bad words?" "What if I belch?" "I didn't mean to spill grape juice on your new tablecloth . . . I'm really sorry!"

Other testy tics might include turning around and staring at someone until they become uncomfortable, then giving a friendly smile; bumping into someone and apologizing; sticking out one's tongue directly at someone but then quickly looking away—as if to "withdraw" it; quiet flatulence with apology.

CLUSTER VI—UPPING THE ANTE DURING ADOLESCENCE (12–21 YEARS)

From testiness to defiance

The difference between "testiness" and defiance is not easily defined, but as adolescence progresses and shame deepens, tics become more anger permeated. As we've observed earlier, this is the age when coprolalia makes its appearance, providing a good example of the shift from testiness to defiance. Thus, instead of an inarticulate or muffled shouting of a single word such as "fuck," the more defiant behavior would be to yell "Hiya Niggah!" to a large muscular black man in a cafe. A little less dangerous, but still defiant would be to say "Hi Cripp!" to a person in a wheel chair. Such anger-permeated tics quickly generate reactionary rage in others, subsequently refueling the shame–anger loop.

Also included in this cluster would be the traditional forms of male sexual exhibitionism—the bus stop "flasher" (a kind of visual rape), and other less direct forms such as obscene phone calls (a kind of auditory rape).

Sometimes the defiance is directed toward a general audience such as when an adolescent with TS-OCD begged his parents to tape his mouth shut prior to his boarding an airplane in order to prevent him from yelling "Hijack!" once the plane was airborne. At other times it is very specifically directed toward a target person as illustrated above.

It is in this cluster that the importance of the social context to TS-OCD becomes most apparent. Ambitendent persons typically have an exquisite sense of interpersonal parameters. They typically know—often as a result of years of experience—exactly how far to push the testiness without being socially ostracized. Like expert handball players who have a good "court sense" (automatically knowing where and how the ball will bounce off the walls), persons with TS-OCD know precisely how much they can get away with in every social situation. This is not a conscious thought pattern, but it is nonetheless present. There exists a sort of "social symbiosis" in which the ticquer and observer unwittingly participate. Society carefully defines how one may observe an "unusual" person. You don't directly stare at an obese person's stomach or at an amputee's prosthesis. These are social manners that must be taught, as many embarrassed parents can readily recall. Children unabashedly ask "Mommy, why does that man in front of us have a hook on his arm instead of a hand?" or "Wow! look at that lady! I'll bet she weighs a thousand pounds!" Children have to be taught to whisper, to cast sideways glances, and ask questions later. Such rules apply to a wide variety of potentially embarrassing situations. One doesn't gawk at a woman adjusting a bra strap or a person changing the volume on a "squealing" hearing aid.

Ambitendent Etiquette: How to Remain Friends at the Edge

TS-OCD persons have behavioral repertoires ranging from the obsequious to obnoxious. The type of behavior usually falls somewhere within this range—testing the limits without incurring social ostracism. This is why the changing symptoms of TS-OCD are so puzzling to neurologists. Tics are *situationally fine-tuned* by the ambitendent person. The degree to which the person can switch "channels" or reduce the "volume" varies considerably from person to person, but even the most obligatory tics often remain within a situationally defined range of acceptability.

Take, for example, the case of a man with TS-OCD who routinely engaged in moderately loud vocalizations when in familiar surroundings. When, however, he attended a concert by opera star Luciano Pavarotti he was able to remain quiet during crucial "soft" passages of the songs. To have made loud noises during the low parts of such a program would have invited expulsion from the auditorium or arrest, with accompanying embarrassment and social ostracism.

Developmental Shifts of Bifurcation

Figure 7.4 illustrates a shift of the bifurcation set to the rear and to the right. This models the typical developmental course of tics and obsessions. Less and less behavior and thoughts remain "out of reach" of the bifurcating cusp. In adults with TS-OCD very little waking time is free from tics or obsessions. Some individuals are able to inhibit their tics while in public, but for most individuals this is not the case.

The cusp also moves to the right, which means that as children grow up tics are more likely to be driven by shame. Although anger is always present, its influence becomes less and less pervasive as the person moves away from the "terrible twos" and other early childhood epochs. As the child matures, the peer group—especially during adolescence—does not tolerate anger very well because it disrupts the harmony of the "herd" which, in turn, dilutes the cohesiveness that is so important in establishing the generation gap.

The power of the peer group reaches pinnacle proportions during the adolescent years, squelching anger and amplifying shame. Since the anguish of shame is borne by target individuals—not by the group—the "deck is stacked" in the direction of repression of anger and exacerbation of shame. Indeed, most adolescents are ashamed of numerous "defects" which are in most cases simply deviations from the group norm. Under the best of circumstances adolescence is a time of high vulnerability and few pass through without picking up some "shame scars." Just as hypochondriasis is a "normal" adolescent response to the rapidly changing body, shame is an almost certain consequence of the peer group's pervasive demand for conformity and uniformity.

Having acquired a substantial grounding in developmental issues and CT, prevention and treatment of TS-OCD will be considered.

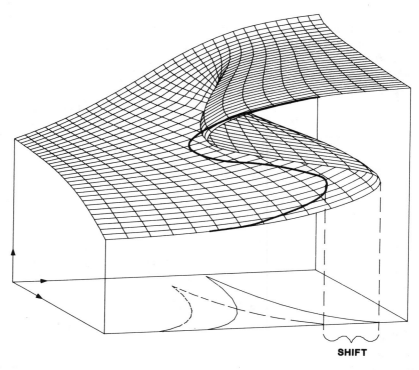

SHIFT

FIGURE 7.4 As tics or obsessions develop, the bifurcation cusp shifts to the rear and right of the control surface, splitting more and more behavior into catastrophic divergences.

Chapter 8

PREVENTION OF TS-OCD: UNDERSTANDING AND MINIMIZING RISK FACTORS

In this chapter eight risk factors frequently present in cases of TS-OCD will be considered. Earlier in the text, it was suggested that a broadly developmental paradigm with a strong emphasis on *multiple* causality should be used when studying TS-OCD. Within such a paradigm, *prevention* makes sense because many of the risk factors can be modified or reduced in intensity. Even supposing there is a chromosomal basis for TS-OCD, a person's genetic endowment is only one of several factors that must be present for transitory tics or obsessions to become chronic TS-OCD. And although changing chromosomes isn't likely to become a viable way to change behavior patterns, there are many risk factors that *can* be modified. In a way analogous to how factors like genes, a high-fat diet, lack of exercise, stress, smoking, and alcohol use all combine to induce coronary heart disease, so multiple risk factors may additively increase the likelihood of transitory tics or passing obsessions becoming chronic TS-OCD.

This chapter is one of the most tentative yet most important in the book. I am keenly aware that the risk factors being discussed are based on clinical observation; but they occur so regularly in persons with TS-OCD that I believe future research will delineate how they coalesce to cause compulsiveness. Careful prospective studies could clarify relationships among the risk factors and the development of TS-OCD, but in the meantime I believe that many cases of TS-OCD can be *prevented*— which is the best cure—or treated early in development, even while further research is being carried out. The risk factors to be discussed—factors such as stress, repression, or shame—are the kinds of influences that ought to be minimized in the lives of all children. In the case of the child with a propensity to TS-OCD, this minimization becomes vital.

The risk factors are not necessarily discussed in order of importance: more research is needed before it can be decided which factors are crucial (always present) for the development of TS-OCD, and which function like catalysts (necessary but not sufficient). Nonetheless, I will share my clinical intuitions as I discuss each risk factor. For example, I'm personally convinced that ridicule and shame are *always* present; whereas I believe early physical constriction or somatic focus function as amplifiers—occurring in many but not all cases.

Developmental theory would lead us to expect that the greater the number and intensity of risk factors present in early development, the higher the likelihood of lifelong compulsiveness. The earlier trauma is experienced, the more serious the consequences, since the infant has few coping mechanisms. Usually chronic or repeated trauma is more damaging than a single incident even if the latter is quite severe.

Some of the risk factors to be discussed have been mentioned by previous authors. Mahler and Gross (1945), for example, referred to multiple factors and suggested that a history of too much or too little freedom of movement was basic for the development of tics. As we have seen in a number of case studies physical restraint seems to be an essential risk factor. Such constriction can be physically induced by others such as being tied in one place with a rope or may be intermittent and due to circumstance such as illnesses or when limbs are broken. Psychological constriction or suffocation sometimes results from overprotective parenting or from infantalization. But whether constriction is psychological or physical it causes intense conflict—especially in "motoric" children who seem predisposed to high levels of activity. Such conflict becomes internalized as a struggle between the active and passive elements of the psyche, and may be expressed in ticquing.

INTERACTION OF MULTIPLE RISK FACTORS

A persistent question haunts us: Why does *this* particular child develop TS-OCD while another in apparently similar circumstances escapes it? Why, for example did three-year-old Morris' handwashing *persist* into adult life? Or, why was Sam's playing "cootie" the beginning of a life dominated by ritualization? Surely, countless other children have played such games without making them lifelong patterns. Currently there are no definitive answers to these important questions, but I believe clues can be found in the *configuration* of risk factors. Future developmentally based research may provide clearer answers. Presently, however, it still seems prudent to minimize such risks whenever and wherever they occur.

Excessive Stress

Here the word *stress* includes environmental stressors such as noise, overcrowding, and hunger, and interpersonal stressors such as ridicule, arguments, and shouting. Of these, it is the interpersonal stressors that damage a child most and increase the risk of developing compensatory repetitive behaviors such as tics or other comforting routines.

Chronicity amplifies risk. Samuel Johnson, for example, described the chronic interpersonal stress between his parents in the following words: "My father and mother had not much happiness from each other. They seldom conversed."

In such a home, silence is *not* golden, and the chronicity of family interactions amplifies their etiological importance. One can assume that this ambience of unhappiness was everpresent and that it impacted Johnson's development on a daily basis over long periods of his childhood.

Chronic tension often occurs in the school setting. One patient reported:

> My kindergarten teacher was warm, nurturant. I was teacher's pet. Even now, at age 20, I still feel like there's a bond with her. But my first grade teacher was a witch—very demanding, authoritarian—very strict in all classroom activities. She had a quick temper. She tried being nice, but you knew she would always go back to being a witch, so you couldn't really trust her niceness.

Such uneasiness on a daily basis during an entire year of elementary school can be significant.

Stress is sometimes specific, but somtimes broad, often permeating entire situations (school, home, playground) and making it difficult to quantify. Some might argue that discussing such a broad factor adds little to our understanding of TS-OCD, however, I think it's necessary to mention generalized stress at the outset. Although our understanding of risk factors is still embryonic, it seems clear that stress may halt or severely slow development which can result in fixation at the physical level or at least attenuated problem solving at the symbolic, cognitive level.

Stress in the Life of Peter the Great

Peter was three and a half when his serene luxurious existence was shattered by the death of his father, Tsar Alexis. When Peter was about 10, he observed the savage murder of Matveev—a family friend who had been like a grandfather to Peter. An account of what transpired follows; such savagery and violence must have been traumatic even for a rambunctious lad like himself.

In an attempt to quiet some rebelling Strelsty soldiers (shaggy, bearded musketeers and pikemen who guarded the Kremlin), Peter's mother had been advised to appear at the top of the palace stairs with her two children. Holding Peter with one trembling hand and Ivan with the other, she courageously appeared before the angry soldiers in order to dispel rumors that Ivan had been murdered. The calm that followed was only temporary, however, and when their commander Prince Dolgoruky tried to bring order to the mutinous troops with "tough talk," it had the opposite effect.

The frenzied soldiers rushed up the Red Staircase toward their commander, and seizing him by his robe threw him over the balcony onto the sharpened pikes of the soldiers in the street below. The crowd roared its approval, and within seconds the commander's body had been butchered, spattering everyone around it with blood. Rather than quenching their fury, however this violence seemed to heighten their thirst for blood. Storming the stairway, they seized Matveev and hurled him down onto the upraised blades of steel in the street below. Seconds later, the man who had been the closest family friend of Peter's parents was hacked to pieces.

Nor was this to be Peter's last brush with the dreaded Kremlin guards. When he was 17, his sleep was interrupted one night when messengers burst into his room to inform him that the Strelsty were on the march, coming to get him. Peter leaped from his bed and, still in his nightgown, mounted a horse and started riding to the Troitsky Monastery, some 45 miles northeast of Moscow. The trip took the rest of the night, and when he arrived, he was so weary, he had to be lifted from his horse. Exhausted, he burst into tears, sobbing convulsively while he lamented to the abbot that his sister was planning to kill him and all his family.

The violence of the Strelsty revolt marked Peter for life. The security and tranquillity of his boyhood was shattered, never again to be as stable. Few children are exposed to such violence and butchery during childhood and adolescent years. However, a violent alcoholic parent who periodically drinks and breaks furniture or abuses his spouse and children may be creating stress not totally unlike that which Peter experienced.

Excessive Energy

I have never seen a child with TS-OCD who was not "wired." As children develop and there is some movement from motoric to cognitive repetitiveness—from TS to OCD—the "raw energy" is not always as obvious, but it is nonetheless present. It could be argued that there is an "egg-chicken" problem in trying to understand whether the high activity causes the TS or is merely a response to the ridicule and social ostracism that routinely result from the curious symptoms of TS. My own sense is that persons with TS are bundles of energy who, like boiling teapots, cannot be contained. Trying to "put a lid on it" is not a real possibility for either children or their parents. There's simply too much energy to contain and it *must* erupt—volcanolike—in the form of periodic ticquing. Like little Peter, "intelligent, active, and noisy," people with TS find themselves blessed (or is it cursed?) with the same "titanic energy" that characterized the czar of Russia; who was described by his biographer as "perpetually curious, perpetually restless, perpetually in movement" (Massie, 1980).

If there is a genetic component to TS-OCD, it is likely something very broad and polygenetically determined such as energy level. This component can be compared to another inherited component—intelligence. There *is* a relationship between the I.Q. of parents and their children, but it is not a straightforward relationship because it results from the merging of billions of possible combinations from the gene pools of both parents. Further, general intelligence—or energy level—is not a single characteristic like eye color, but represents the sum total of many "intelligences." Consequently parents with high levels of intelligence or energy are likely to produce intelligent or energetic offspring but the causal pathways are buried in complexity.

To speak of *excessive* energy is a little misleading. It might be more appropriate to think of the TS-OCD person as having large pockets of unfocused energy, nonsoothable anxiety, or, as being overly motoric because the energy has not been developmentally integrated with other aspects of functioning. The energy referred to here is energy that someone (in the family, school, or in society) finds obnoxious or intrusive and is trying to "contain," but which is too intense and pervasive to be confined. From the perspective of other observers, the energy seems "wasted" and annoying—like static electricity in the air, or background noise on the radio; however, from the perspective of the person with the energy, the energy expended usually has a dynamic purpose such as soothing, testing limits, or attempting to fulfill other basic needs. What appears as senseless circularity to others is core behavioral architecture for the person generating the tics or obsessions.

Examples

Peter the Great is one of the best examples of raw energy—striding into the far flung frontiers of his day with out-of-breath countrymen struggling to keep pace. In Samuel Johnson there was more subtle manifestation of energy, seen in his foot racing, rolling down hills, and imitating kangaroos. This same energy also drove his higher-level behaviors such as conversation and writing:

> He had always, for example, been able to write rapidly. But now, as John Nichols said, "Three columns of the Magazine, in an hour, was no uncommon effort, which was faster than most persons could have transcribed that quantity." Since a column there contains a little more than six hundred words, this would mean an average rate of at least eighteen hundred words an hour, or thirty a minute. On one day—and that was not a long one, beginning perhaps at noon, and ending early in the evening—he wrote twenty columns (about twelve thousand words). (Bate, pp. 205–206)

Johnson's reputation as a talker was no less astounding, and during two decades of his greatest fame, he largely abandoned writing for talking; much of which took place either at the Club (formed by Johnson and some intimate friends for the purpose of "talking") or at taverns:

> The formation of the Club was a great landmark in Johnson's life. It ushered in that period in which he built a second reputation, as a great talker, on the basis of his first one as a writer and scholar. (Wain, pp. 239–240)

High energy is one of those necessary-but-not-sufficient risk factors. Indeed, energy can hardly be considered a liability unless (as often occurs in cases of TS-OCD) attempts to contain it become too strenuous, shaming, paradoxical, or otherwise "Touretteogenic." This is the only risk factor that one doesn't try to reduce. Instead, attention should be given as to how high-energy infants and toddlers can be accommodated in nonconstricting, non-shaming ways without tiring others or allowing the behaviors to become obnoxious. Experienced and sensitive teachers in day care centers, nursery schools, kindergartens, and the early grades are the resident "experts" in this area, because a child entering such structured settings usually requires "containment" and highly active children present unique challenges.

Others have also been impressed with the energy of children with tics. Mahler and her associates (1945, 1946) characterized 63% of the children in their sample as "motor minded," with muscular restlessness and hypermotility. Shapiro et al. (1978, p. 47) reported a high percentage of patients with hypermotility. When this high energy comes up against parental constrictiveness the risk for developing TS-OCD increases dramatically.

Mahler and her coworkers described parents of the children they studied as perfectionistic, exacting, and overprotective; either subtly or directly restricting free motor development. They suggested that such children were prohibited from shouting, crying, running, hammering, or playing with abandon. Motor freedom was also restricted through overstimulating infantilization or possessive overprotectiveness.

Somatic Focus or Constriction

Adults with TS-OCD often reveal a childhood permeated with physical concerns. For example, Samuel Johnson was nearly blind and partially deaf as the result of an infection he had a few weeks after birth. Somatic problems increase the risk of TS-OCD because specific body parts or movements become associated with pain, constriction, or some other form of special focus. Consequently, significant portions of the personality become fused with such concerns and significant portions of the *self* become entwined with somatic concerns. Additionally, physical illness tends to delay development, slowing the shift from motoric to mental behavior and resulting in somatically overemphasized development.

Two catalysts that increase the importance of physical focus as a risk factor are *chronicity* and *constriction*. In Johnson's case, for example, a surgeon made an incision in his arm to drain the infection from his system, as was common practice then. The incision was kept open (with a horse hair or other irritant) until Sam was nearly six years old! That kind of *chronic* physical focus places a child at risk for TS because specific body parts or movements become associated with pain or special attention, and the developing psyche forms *part-selves* around such loci of attention. Additionally, significant portions of the developing personality become infused with such concerns, tending to delay development and resulting in an overly somatic personality.

Any kind of physical *constriction* increases risk. Passive constriction (such as being in a lower-body cast, or being forced to wear tight-fitting collars) is probably not as damaging as active constriction. Recall the case of Robb, the electrician who had to touch bare wires whose grandmother tied his arms behind his back with bicycle inner tubes. Remember also that Sarah, the woman who bit legs, had her leg in a cast during some of her earliest developmental days—beginning at 18 months. It's my clinical impression that such early constrictive experiences occur far more regularly in children who later develop TS than in others. Ultimately these are questions for research, and it would be of clinical interest and theoretical significance if children being discharged from a pediatric orthopedic unit were followed for several years to assess whether their incidence of tics was greater than in the general population. Until such research can be carried out, it seems to make sense to view children with early constrictive experiences as being more at risk than others for developing tics.

Bifurcated Personality Development

It's been shown how sometime near the middle of the second year of life normally developing infants make an important shift away from their musculature. Words, symbols, and conversation begin to provide a bridge away from the intensely somatic world of the body to the spacious world of the mind. Ideas and imagination begin to substitute for *real* behavior, and the toddler begins to experience an expansive sense of freedom and movement. Pretend games become an integral part of the repertoire.

However, when shame, constriction, or other risk factors are excessively intense, the comfortable shift from body to mind is arrested or delayed and bifurcation begins. The child maintains a strongly somatic "body self" while another part of the psyche moves haltingly ahead to develop a "psychological self." Somehow these never become well integrated, developing instead side by side. One of Samuel Johnson's biographers wrote:

> Johnson had grown up under the influence of two conflicting but equally dominant sensations—the pride he felt in himself as king among men, and a conviction of weakness and wickedness that would remain with him until his death. (Quennell, 1973, p. 27)

We've seen how in the case of children with tics or other "funny" behaviors, the teasing and ridicule they endure produces personal shame, immensely increasing the bifurcation of personality. They develop an angry, helpless, out-of-control "Tourette" self which is primarily experienced in the body, while in their minds, another compensatory "nice" self develops. But their handicap-necessitated "niceness" develops an undertow of resentment and anger which further energizes the angry part of the bifurcated personality.

Finally, it was noted earlier how the somatic self becomes organized as a system of part-selves, organized around specific tics, body zones, obsessions, and the like. The developing personality is thus deeply bifurcated, but also poorly integrated on either side of the bifurcation. The somatic self lacks a *cohesive* self system, being comprised instead of an unintegrated system of part-selves. The psychological self is delayed in development, and develops around themes of compensatory "niceness."

We will now consider a case in which early physical constriction was a crucial factor. The subsequent development of tics and bifurcation becomes clear as the interview proceeds.

CASE STUDY: BLINKING BILLY

He has a master's degree in psychology and is the president of his own company, providing consultation for developing human services. A tanned, athletic, professional-looking man, he blinks and squints his eyes continuously, punctuating it with head shakes. Why would a successful professional man constantly blink his eyes and shake his head? Was he born that way? No, but somewhere during those important years of infancy, toddlerhood, and early childhood something went amiss. Here's how it happened.

> There's something wrong with baby Billy! I just know it, he should be walking—I talked to Norma just yesterday, and Mike started walking on his own last week. He's two months younger than Billy!
> Honey, you worry too much. That's what always happens with the first baby. I see it all the time at the office. These mothers bring their "precious ones" in and worry so much that the kids can't help being afraid of the dentist! You know, worry *is* contagious. Billy is going to be just fine.

Early Constriction

But Billy *wasn't* just fine, and it *didn't* turn out OK. As he matured into the toddler years, it became obvious that something was wrong with his legs—Legg-Calve-Perthes disease it's called. It is a hip disorder that causes one leg to grow longer. By the time he was four, instead of happily jumping and running about, Billy was limping badly. So at four and half he was put in full leg casts. For the next *12 months Billy had to lie flat on his back or stomach*. That's a long time to be helplessly immobilized when you're only five years old.

At about this time—not surprisingly—he started ticquing. He recalls

"My parents tried to interrupt them (my tics), but I was very active, so when I was confined, I started doing other things."

"Other things?"

"Yeah, like blinking and head movements."

Interesting here is the fact that his parents couldn't "confine" him to stop ticquing, and although the casts confined his leg movements, he responded with hyperkinesis of other body parts.

After the casts were taken off, he had to wear braces for the next year. Consequently Billy started school wearing leg braces (certain to elicit the stares of his peers). His memory of those early grades is almost nonexistent. It was likely a very difficult time for a little boy in braces who blinked his eyes and shook his head.

"I don't remember much about my tics until junior high. It was during that time that my Dad and I battled about tics. I'd make noises and sniff and he'd tell me to 'Stop it!' "

"I'd suppress it for a while, but when I'd do it again, he'd say 'Stop it! You're doing that to get to me!' "

"I went to a psychiatrist for one year but I had no tics during sessions. Finally, my Dad, who's a dentist, seemed to realize that I couldn't stop it—that it must be organic—and he quit hassling me.

College, Marriage, and Graduate School

"I went away to college, but I had problems; like how to handle the library. I spent a lot of energy trying not to make noises. I'd get a music study carrel, or go into the record listening room. Tics are worse at night, so I did my library studying in the morning."

"When I got out of college, I married and went to the University of Nebraska to study Clinical Psychology. I was one of the better students for the first two years. Then I went to Philadelphia for internship and I had some conflicts with my supervisors. They used my tics against me. It was a psychoanalytic child internship, and they said my tics would be detrimental in therapy. I ended up leaving the internship. The following year, I went to Omaha for internship and there I tried some behavior techniques such as satiation, counterconditioning with aversive shock. It didn't help much."

"Then one of the psychiatric residents started me on Haldol. My tics got a lot better, but I started getting depressed. I decided that I wouldn't complete my doctorate—even though I had most of the coursework finished. So I left the University of Nebraska."

Bill never completed his doctorate, working instead for the Ohio Department of Mental Health for several years. He currently heads up his own research and consulting firm.

Bifurcated Personality

"So how do your tics affect your life today?"

"I'm *not* my tics or symptoms. I'm Bill   . the person they affect."

"You're saying there's a 'Me'—Bill the person, and a 'Not Me'—tics?"

"Exactly! The *Me* is bright, competent, highly trained, creative, funny, athletic, caring, and sensitive. The *Not Me* is tics, blinking, sniffing, snorting. I'm pretty well coordinated in volleyball, but when a tic keeps me from getting to the ball, it's a tic, not *Me*! I like reading, but in the evening I can't hold my head still—it's not enjoyable. So when I avoid reading because of tics, that's *Not Me*. I deal with the tics, but they're not part of my self concept."

Commentary

Bill was a *high energy* toddler who experienced early *physical focus*. This was intensified by the *constrictive* and *chronic* qualities of the focus. Early in his development he had to spend an entire year lying either on his back or his stomach. Imagine what it must be like for an energetic five-year-old to be "paralyzed" in plaster for a year! Then replace the immobilizing casts with leg braces ("What-are-those-weird-things?") for entering school, and you have a notion of why Bill can't remember much about his childhood. The compensatory nature of his tics also becomes more clear. Recall his words: "I was very active, so when I was confined I started doing other things."

In addition to physical constriction there were also the familiar parental *paradoxical instructions*. Bill's father practices dentistry—a profession that affords its practitioners a comfortable amount of control over immediate circumstances. The patient is confined to lying on his or her back, with mouth open but not talking. An assistant places instruments within easy reach or directly in the hand of the dentist, and receptionists make appointments and handle complaints. All in all, it's a pretty controlled, concrete, no-nonsense environment. And the patients, though not crazy about coming, usually leave satisfied because they know their teeth have been taken care of.

Rearing children, however, is quite another matter. *Nothing* is precise or in control; *everything* is untidy and disorderly. And that's under "normal" circumstances. Imagine how upsetting a child's ticquing must be to a parent used to a controlled environment. Little wonder that when Billy would sniff or make (tic) noises his father would respond: "Stop it!"

Recall that after suppressing his tics for a short time (it seemed like forever to Billy) he would again sniff or make noise and his father would again—this time more angrily—say: "Stop it! You're just doing that to aggravate me!" This kind of escalating interaction cycled and recycled many times during junior high years.

"Finally," Bill recalls "He seemed to realize that I couldn't stop it— that it must be organic—and he quit hassling me." But by the time one is through junior high, much developmental molding is completed and the psychological elasticity of the earlier years is replaced by the ever-hardening behavioral patterns of late adolescence and adulthood. Had Dad concluded "He can't help it" when Billy was four instead of 14 the ameliorative effect might have been much greater.

As a consequence of these early experiences, Bill has a deeply *bifurcated* personality. He articulately describes his experience in this regard: "The *Me* is bright, competent, highly trained, creative, funny, athletic, caring, and sensitive. The *Not Me* is tics, blinking, sniffing, snorting."

One of the problems of "neurologizing" about TS is that it perpetuates bifurcation. TS is seen as a "disease" or "condition" a person *has* rather than a way of *functioning*. Interesting in this regard are the business cards Bill carries with him. On the front is his name, degree, phone number, the name of his company, and a sentence stating that he gives "special presentations on Tourette Syndrome." On the back of the card appears the following statement:

What is Tourette Syndrome?

Tourette Syndrome (TS) is a neurological disorder characterized by involuntary movements (TICS) and vocalizations. TS begins between the ages of 2 and 16, it is lifelong and there is no cure.

This aptly illustrates two major problems of the biological paradigm. It provides a strong basis for bifurcation (me vs. my disease) and it increases despair by suggesting that the condition is lifelong and incurable.

Primary Process Prohibition: Emotional Constriction

"Primary process" refers to those gutsy impulses—such as sex or aggression—that society tries to contain or redirect. Little boys must learn to "talk about it" instead of "socking him in the nose" or "kicking her." The toddler somehow knows he mustn't show off his "wiener" to company and his sister realizes her "private places" must only be seen by rubber ducky in the bathtub. It is necessary, of course, to teach children culturally appropriate manners; but such learning is best acquired in an atmosphere of alternatives rather than *prohibitions*. When parents repress normal impulses instead of teaching alternatives, the result can be reactionary overconcern in the child.

ANGER PROSCRIPTION AMONG THE MENNONITES

Any family or subculture that multiplies prohibitions increases the risk of TS-OCD because it interferes with the development of a full range of verbal expression of the emotions from "That bothered me just a little" and "I was a bit irritated" to "That really got on my nerves!" and "I was so enraged I wanted to kill him!" Instead of building a verbal "anger repertoire" which includes many subtle nuances, individuals who over-inhibit their anger tend to be "bimodal" in their expressions, lacking a middle range. Not only is the likelihood of bifurcated expression increased, it is also more likely that such individuals will express anger using motoric instead of verbal channels.

This may be why, in the far northern town of La Crete, in Alberta, Canada, a disproportionately high incidence of TS-OCD can be found. In this small village of devout Mennonites, with its five churches and population of 700, prohibitions are an accepted part of the subculture. Sacks described the community well:

> Mennonites believe in a return to primitive communal Christianity, in closeness to the soil and closeness to family, in *nonviolence*, plainness and a partial withdrawal from the great world outside. . . . There is a church

in LaCrete for each of the five Mennonite sects . . . the simplicity and down-to-earthness about the place, along with the *tranquillity* and gravity of expressions on people's faces gave us the sense of a biblical town, a place where, *very quietly*, the religious held sway. (1988, p. 97, italics mine)

Researchers estimate that nearly 40% of the extended Janzen family in this area suffers to some degree from TS. Forty-two-year-old David Janzen started manifesting a variety of tics when he was eight years old. This is the typical age of onset; also typical is his adolescent onset of coprolalia. He started shouting "Fuck!" when he was 15. As Sacks put it "Such uttering of obscenities and profanities, called coprolalia, is not an uncommon feature of the syndrome, but it was *not* common in La-Crete" (1988, p. 97).

Imagine the impact of such profanity in a quiet (constricted) community where many people wear dark clothes and grave expressions. Such cultural constrictiveness likely increases the probability of transient tics becoming permanent routines. A subculture can exert emotional constrictiveness which, although not as tangible as the physical constrictiveness of a plaster cast, is nonetheless just as real.

Clinicians have long contended that when repression is too severe the defense of *reaction formation* is likely to be used. To protect one's awareness against feelings of hatred—especially in a family or culture where love is highly valued—the opposite reaction of oversolicitousness is employed. I believe something like this occurs in most cases of TS-OCD. A tic or coprolalic utterance is a *somatically based* oppositional, yet compensatory mechanism. This is consistent with our discussions of brinkmanship and with the epidemiological finding that high-incidence "pockets" of TS-OCD are sometimes found in isolated or closely knit communities like LaCrete where repression of impulses is still highly valued.

Sacks noticed the contrast TS brings to the idyllic village:

> This tranquillity was broken when we reached David Janzen's house. . . . David ran out to greet us, yelping and ticcing. The noises—ear shattering, shocking—seemed to disturb his whole being (he is a well-knit, agile man otherwise) and indeed to disturb the whole placid face of LaCrete. His cheery Tourettisisms set off Lowell. They hugged each other, ticced, yelped—it was both affecting and absurd, reminding me of the excitement of two dogs meeting. (1988, p. 97)

Although favorite biological paradigm explanations of such a large percentage of TS would usually suggest inbreeding and a consequent concentration of recessive genes, such explanations are by no means the only logical way of understanding these occurrences. The genetic biologists hope to bolster their theories of TS by studying inbreeding patterns among the Mennonites of La Crete, but I think future answers will be found by studying *repression* rather than chromosomes. In a multifactorial paradigm however these various lines of research are all enlightening and bear a complementary relationship to one another.

We will continue our consideration of constriction by looking at the Shakers, a small group of religiously devout people whose sexuality and other primary impulses are severely repressed by their teachings and lifestyle. Then we will conclude by considering a contemporary athlete.

THE SHAKERS: SEXUAL REPRESSION AND THE QUEST FOR PERFECTION

Ann Lee was an emotional English girl who was frequently up all night crying "because of the sin she saw everywhere" (Faber, 1974, p. 16). At 22 she was sinking into despair when she met a tailor and his wife who had been searching for a religious answer to the terrible suffering surrounding them in Manchester during the middle of the eighteenth century. This couple had at first become Quakers, but were soon attracted to a small religious group exiled from France (because of radical religious ideas) who had arrived in England in 1706. In France these people were sarcastically called *Les Trembleurs* (The Shakers), a name inspired by their frenzied worship services when their arms and legs moved with peculiar abandon and they shouted strange sounds, as if in a trance.

Twenty-two-year-old Ann, later called "Mother Ann" by her followers, founded a sect called the Shakers. Possibly because she had seen or witnessed scenes of sexual violence as a child, she believed marriage to be a sinful state and strongly advocated celibacy. In this new church, the main focus of meetings was sin. And, doubtless owing to the tailor and his wife's Quaker past, meetings would start with silent meditation. Soon, however, the whole group would be seized with a "mighty shaking" as they described it, in which they could express their indignation against sin.

It is of interest to note how a small group of worshipers, extremely constricted in their outlook and desperately trying to be perfect and eliminate sin (especially "fleshy lusts"), carried on their worship services. A Baptist minister who visited a service described it in the following words:

> When they meet together for their worship, they fall a-groaning and trembling, and everyone acts alone for himself; one will fall prostrate on the floor, another on his knees and his head in his hands. . . . Some will be singing, each one his own tune; some without words, in an Indian tune, some sing jig tunes, some tunes of their own making, in an unknown mutter, which they call new tongues; some will be dancing, and others stand laughing, heartily and loudly; others will be drumming on the floor with their feet, as though a pair of drum-sticks were beating a riff on a drumhead; others will be agonizing as though they were in great pain; others jumping up and down; others fluttering over somebody, and talking to them; others will be shooing and hissing evil spirits out of the house, till the different tunes, groaning, jumping, dancing, drumming, laughing, talking and fluttering, shooing and hissing, makes a perfect bedlam; this they call the worship of God. (Faber, 1974, p. 47)

Some years later in America, this same kind of spiritual "frenzy" gripped the small group. Originating first among the girls in the children's division, this sort of religious "dancing" and trembling became widespread. During this period many new songs were added to the Shaker collections which, despite their supposedly heavenly origin, were quick tempo jigs. (Along with the tunes black slaves were singing, these jigs helped lay the foundation for twentieth-century jazz in this country.)

One need not be a classical Freudian to see sublimated sexuality in this "religious jitterbugging." Here was a group of celibate believers, controlled by an emotional woman who was extremely conflicted about her own sexuality. It was only after marrying—with misgivings—and bearing four babies of her own, that she decided sex was sinful and imposed this "inspiration" on her followers.

Shakerism provided channels of "expression" along the entire TS-OCD continuum—religious jitterbugging at the somatic, primitive pole, and the *obsessional pursuit of perfection* at higher cognitive levels. Either could serve to sublimate primary process urgings. There were numerous Shaker rule books which were available to channel believers' obsessiveness:

> "Not a single action of life," it said, lacked "a rule for its perfect and strict performance," and among the examples given were the rules for stepping first with the right foot in ascending a flight of stairs, folding the hands with the right-hand thumb above the left, and kneeling, then rising again with the right leg first. (Faber, p. 153)

It's noteworthy in the present context that whenever primary emotions are severely repressed, expression tends to become extreme when it does occur. The utter silence of Shakers at work, for example, was counterbalanced by their frenzy in worship. And this phenomenon was not restricted to Shakers.

Around the beginning of the twentieth century, as the American West was opening up, an epidemic of religious agitation seemed to occur among many religiously devout—and likely sexually repressed—believers. Many would gather on the edge of the prairie and encamp for several days and nights, conducting impassioned services. The descriptions we have of these gatherings seem remarkably like "group ticquing." These devotees lived very serious (primal impulse-repressing) lives most of the time, but when they "let go" it was with gusto.

Their bodily gyrations or exercises were numerous and called by various names such as the "dancing exercise," the "falling exercise," the "jerks," the "barking exercise," the "laughing and singing exercise," and so forth. What is remarkable is the extent to which these various "exercises" resemble symptoms of TS-OCD. In the "falling exercise," for example, the persons would, *with a piercing scream*, fall like a log on the earth or floor and appear as dead for a short time.

The "barking exercise" seems to have originated with an old Presbyterian preacher from eastern Tennessee, who probably suffered from TS-OCD, and others simply attributed religious significance to his symptoms. He had apparently gone into the woods for his private devotions when a passerby noted that he was "seized by the jerks." He caught hold of a small sapling to steady himself, and as his head jerked back and his face pointed upward he grunted and "barked." The observer—apparently a bit of a comedian—reported to others that he had found the pastor "barking up a tree." The "barking exercise," the "jerks," even the "dancing exercises" seem remarkably like a typical repertoire of TS-OCD symptoms:

> *The barking exercise* (as opponents contemptuously called it) *was nothing but the jerks. A person affected with the jerks, especially in the head, would often make a grunt, or bark, if you please, from the suddenness of the jerk.*
>
> *The jerks cannot be so easily described. Sometimes the subject of the jerks would be affected in some one member of the body and sometimes in the whole system. When the head alone was affected it would be jerked backward and forward, or from side to side, so quickly that the features of the face could not be distinguished.* When the whole system was affected, I have seen the person stand in one place, and jerk backward and forward in a quick succession, their heads nearly touching the floor behind and before. . . .
>
> Though so awful to behold, I do not remember that any one of the

thousands I have seen ever sustained an injury in body. This was as strange as the exercise itself.

The dancing exercise. This generally begins with the jerks . . . Such dancing was indeed heavenly to the spectators; there was nothing in it like levity . . . Sometimes the motion was quick, and sometimes slow. Thus they continued to move forward and backward in the same track or alley till nature seemed exhausted, and they would fall prostrate on the floor or earth, unless caught by those standing by. (Faber, pp. 90–91, italics mine)

CASE STUDY: "TIGER" WITH TOURETTE

Before ending our examination of emotional constriction in the development of TS-OCD, we will study—via the sports pages—a contemporary athlete. Far removed in time and life-style from the Shakers, he nonetheless has much in common with those quiet, obedient, sometimes frenzied folk. He appears quiet, calm, almost shy; but there's a "tiger" inside.

When you think "tiger" what comes to mind? You might picture a large, powerfully built, athletically hinged animal stalking slowly through tall grass, tail twitching, eyes intently scrutinizing a skittish herd of gazelles. One of the sentry bucks stops grazing, quickly scans the nearby bush, anxiously sniffing the air for a scent of danger. But today there's no breeze, not even a rustle-the-dry-grass zephyr. While the buck's nostrils search for danger, the tiger crouches—coiled. Although leg and shoulder muscles are like springs of steel about to snap, the tiger is motionless—except for the twitching, the relentless, flowing twitching of the lithe tail, and the jerky, ticquing of the facial whiskers. Suddenly—the mighty, twitching animal explodes and with a fifty-mile-an-hour burst of velocity overtakes the nearest gazelle dispensing it a fierce finish.

Different jungle, different Tigers—it's Saturday night at the Louisiana Superdome. The 54,321 fans make this the largest crowed ever to see a regular-season college basketball game. These Tigers aren't simply trying to surprise and run down gazelles. Their enemy is the powerful Georgetown University basketball team with standout freshman, 6'10" Alonzo Mourning leading the assault. But Louisiana State has its answer to Alonzo in the form of their twitching Tiger Chris Jackson. CJ scored 48 points in his third varsity game and a freshman record setting

53 points in his fifth college game. And just the previous week he pummeled Tennessee with 50 points in a crucial South Eastern Conference (SEC) game that put the Tigers ahead in the conference.

It's a back-and-forth, now-we're-ahead-now-we're-behind sort of game—the kind that happens when evenly matched teams take to the boards. Well, *almost* evenly matched. There's one Tiger Georgetown just can't contain. With the game deadlocked 80–80, and 20 seconds remaining, Chris has the ball. Three players surround him, but somehow, remarkably, he wriggles free, passes the ball, and when the game ends the score stands Tigers 82, Georgetown 80. An elated team mate declared: "I knew he'd get out of that trap, though. They locked up Houdini, and he got out, didn't he? Chris dances. He skates. Gee he evaporates. It's like *Shazam!*"

> "I never knew which way Chris was going," said a baffled Alonzo after the game. "He puts you in a triple-threat position. You don't know whether he's pulling up to shoot or to pass, or whether he'll keep driving inside or what. Then, which side? Where? He's everywhere. Give him one step and it's over. I think he's the best shooter in the country." (C. Kirkpatrick, pp. 48–49)

Like his jungle counterpart, this Tiger moves restlessly about, twitching then exploding. Curry Kirkpatrick, staff writer for *Sports Illustrated*, observes: "Depending on the intensity of the game, CJ's face and eyes will twitch and blink with such ferocity it's a wonder he can concentrate on the basket (1989, p. 51).

With characteristic good humor, CJ remarks: "I can put on some awesome head fakes." He sees himself as having a mission to encourage others with TS:

> I want to face this in a positive way and help others who have it. To convince them not to worry about the looks and the jokes and just deal with it the way I have to. (Kirkpatrick, 1989, p. 51)

Before Basketball

CJ grew up a stone's throw from the beach in Gulfport, Mississippi. Chris remembers the ridicule:

> Kids are gonna tease you. People will say things about why you keep tapping on things or why you keep moving or blinking your eyes. But it didn't really bother me. Sometimes I couldn't just relax. When I got excited or nervous the tics increased. And there were a lot of times, especially before a game, when it took me a long time to get dressed and tie

my shoes. I'd always be the last one getting dressed and it was very frustrating and I'd be wondering if it [tics] would ever stop. And there were times that I'd sit up at night and there was so much that I'd be doing that I'd just cry. It's like, why? That was in junior high or high school. I'd try to stop and it just wouldn't. It was very frustrating. But I got to the point that I could concentrate and suppress the tics during games. (Levitt, 1989, p. 6)

Middle Son of an Overcontrolling Mom

CJ experienced more than his share of stressful relationships during childhood and adolescence. In addition to the usual ridicule from peers during elementary and junior high years, he grew up with a mother who was overcontrolling. When Chris was a senior in high school, recognized by coaches as an adult athlete—capable of choosing where he wanted to attend school—his mother thought it *her* right to decide where he lived and for which college he played basketball.

The second of Jacqueline's Jacksons three sons—each by a different father—Chris never knew his Dad. That, of course, amplified the importance of relating satisfactorily to his mother. Children of single parents are always at risk of becoming overly "pleasing" because when the one parent is moody, irritable, or otherwise displeased, there is usually no balancing by another significant adult to lessen the intensity of the dyadic interaction. Such seems to have been the case with CJ:

> Jackson's huge numbers [scores] are nearly as impressive as his humility and the eagerness with which he strives for perfection. He answers his elders with "yes sir," and "no sir." He is also deeply religious. "When I even think something wrong or bad," says Jackson, "I'll say a prayer for forgiveness right away." (Kirkpatrick, 1989, p. 50)

As impressive as such "humility" and striving for "perfection" might seem to sportswriters, it belies an overconcern with his mother's opinion. But C.J.'s mother is not an easy person to please. During his senior year of high school, Chris became close friends with Lousiana State University (LSU) assistant coach Craig Carse and announced that he intended to go to LSU. "My mom said, 'No, Chris, you only think you want to go to LSU," says Jackson. "That's when I knew somebody else had gotten to her."

> Letters with Jackson's forged signature announcing that he was not set on LSU appeared at other schools, including Georgetown and UNLV. Someone claiming to be Jackson also called North Carolina to discuss his recruitment. Rumors spread in the press about Mrs. Jackson's wanting to "sell" her son to the highest bidder. After Jacqueline refused to sign Jack-

son's national letter of intent—she was pushing him to attend Alcorn State—she had an angry meeting with Brown (basketball coach Dale Brown at LSU) at which they basically agreed to disagree. It wasn't until August, when CJ arrived on campus, that Brown realized he had won the fight.

"It got so bad last summer I had to leave home," says Jackson. "I came up to LSU and it hurt, but I had to prove to her this was the right place for me." Not long afterward Jackson was listening to a tape by the group 4 By Four, when he heard a sad ballad entitled *Mommy-Daddy*. He broke down and cried. "Right then I wrote her a long letter," says Jackson. "I never sent it, but I went back to Gulfport to tell her how much she meant to me." (Kirkpatrick, pp. 50–51)

This Tiger Might Slap You

Blanton, who uses the locker adjacent to CJ's, reports that he has often been slapped by Jackson's hand and that CJ's knuckles take a beating from pounding his hand into the dormitory wall. Jackson expends a great deal of effort trying to keep from flailing his arms or crying out suddenly. Chris relates:

> I try to look on it as just another habit. . . . I try not to think about it, but it's hard. . . . When I first came here, I knew guys were looking at me like, wow, this boy is crazy," says Jackson. "But, hey, this is just me." (Kirkpatrick, p. 51).

Sometimes his TS gets him into trouble on the court. "During a game the Tigers lost to Mississippi, a referee mistook one of CJ's involuntary screams—'dom, dom' is the approximate sound—as a complaint about a call" (Kirkpatrick, p. 51) After that game, LSU notified the SEC about CJ's condition and now his TS isn't a major factor on the court.

Better Late Than Never

Although he had symptoms throughout childhood, he wasn't diagnosed until college.

> "The tics were the same," observes Chris, "no matter if they had a name or not. But it was better that I found out—to know there was help, medicine and things like that. To tell you the truth, I didn't really think anyone else had it but me. And when I started finding out that other people had it, it kind eased me a little bit." (Levitt, 1989, p. 6)

CJ's coping strategy is straightforward:

"Don't worry about other people," he advises. "People are going to talk
and do what they want to do. And just don't worry about what people
say. I mean you're you, and if they don't like you for you, you can't worry
about that. You've got to live your life."

"Parents," he suggests, ought to "learn all they can about TS and be patient and understanding about the condition. Because a lot of times the
kid gets depressed. I know I used to get depressed and uneasy about
things and just wanted to tell people how I felt. So it helps to have someone to talk to." (Levitt, 1989, p. 6)

Commentary

Chris was exposed to a number of the risk factors during his development. His controlling and constrictive mother, reminds one of Mother
Ann who ruled her Shaker followers with absolute authority. What
emerges as important here is not only that Chris's mother was trying to
force him to attend the college of *her* choice, but that during 18 years of
living with such a "manager" mother, hundreds of other "I'll-tell-you-
how-it's-gonna-be" incidents must have occurred.

Such parents find it impossible to be "laid back" about a child who
twitches, blinks, or makes noises. It's probably safe to assume that Mrs.
Jackson gave Chris abundant orders to "Quit it!" which he internalized
as his own conflict. This is reflected in his remark: "I try not to think
about it but it's hard."

His deeply bifurcated personality development is most obvious in the
split between the ferocious, explosive Tiger and the humble man who
says "yes sir," "no sir," and *immediately* prays for forgiveness of even a
wrong *thought*. Such moral scrupulosity reminds one of the Shakers'
quest for perfection. This is not to arrogantly judge CJ's spiritual experience, but simply to note that such intensity of concern with *immediately*
righting wrong *thoughts* seems excessive.

We again observe the ubiquitous *brinkmanship* which persons with TS
so carefully calibrate. For CJ it happens most dramatically in the locker
room where he frequently—"accidentally," I'm sure—slaps his team-
mate. A less socially-aversive but more physically painful form of brinkmanship occurs when he smashes his fists into dormitory walls. Like
the lady who smashed mirrors, CJ apparently miscalculates at times and
hurts his knuckles.

Finally, it's worth noting that he integrates the natural *explosiveness* of
TS with his sport. Much like "Witty Ticcy Ray" the drummer who "ex-
ploded" into his drums and produced intense and wild music, Chris explodes on the basketball court:

"What explosion!" muttered Georgetown's Dwayne Bryant after the game. "Jackson lulls you to sleep by drifting around with the ball. Then he explodes."

Overattentive Parent(s)

Rearing children is one of the most rewarding, frustrating, creative challenges any of us ever faces. Most parents try to do what seems best for their children. Sometimes, however, parents unwittingly play a role in creating the very problems they most want to avoid in their children. The father who was teased as a child for stuttering is not going to find it easy to *ignore* the stuttering that often occurs in normal children as their active minds race ahead of less-coordinated tongues. Ironically, such overattention, often accompanied with instructions ("Slow down when you try to talk—*think* about your words!"), facilitates the very stuttering it was intended to prevent. Speech, which should flow spontaneously, now becomes an anxiety-laden focus for parents and child alike.

Likewise, a father who is teased about bed-wetting during childhood (recall the boy who had been nicknamed "Peabody" by his "friends") finds it difficult to be relaxed about toilet training his children. Similarly, the parent who as a child experienced tics or other obsessive problems—and approximately 30 percent of children do—will have enormous difficulty *ignoring* ticquing in his or her own child. This is likely the reason that stuttering, tics, bedwetting, and a host of other problems "run in families." I think it has little to do with genetics and much to do with attention.

"Showing Off" One's Children

Showing off one's children is another kind of parental overattention that increases the risk of developing TS-OCD even though it's not discipline based or anxiety laden. Nonetheless, whenever parents are overconcerned about their children whether for disciplinary or narcissistic reasons, it enlarges the child's self-consciousness which, if other risk factors are present, increases the risk of TS-OCD. Undue attention may create a generalized "performance anxiety" toward life. This kind of "stage consciousness" can become recursively turned on self and promote the circular somatic rituals we see as tics.

If you've ever carefully observed speakers immediately before an address, you've undoubtedly seen them engaging in some transitory ticquing. This usually takes the form of repetitive throat clearing; but

I've seen speakers twist their necks several times, as if to break free from the constraints of their "tight" collars, or repetitively drum their fingers or toes while waiting to approach the microphone. This heightened self consciousness usually abates once they begin speaking, but sometimes persists during the first part of their address in the form of repeated throat clearing.

CASE EXAMPLES: SAMUEL JOHNSON AND JEAN-PAUL SARTRE

Samuel Johnson's mother began to teach him to read when he was three or, at most, four years of age. The young prodigy learned quickly and soon became the pride of his father, who lost no opportunities for parading his precocious son's talents before company. Thus, at a very early age, Johnson's self-consciousness was overdeveloped. Many years later, he would complain of how he "loathed" his father's caresses because he knew they were sure to precede some embarrassing display of his early abilities. This became so aversive to him that when neighbors came to visit, he would run off and hide by climbing in trees in order that he wouldn't be found and "exhibited." He confided to his friend Mrs. Thrale:

> That is the great misery of late marriages, the unhappy produce of them becomes the plaything of dotage: an old man's child (continued he) leads much such a life, I think, as a little boy's dog, teased with awkward fondness, and forced, perhaps to sit up and beg . . . to divert a company, who at last go away complaining of their disagreeable entertainment. (Bate, p. 19)

Just how aversive this practice was to Johnson is illustrated by an incident which took place much later in his life. Apparently a friend wanted his two sons to recite Gray's *Elegy*, one after the other, for Johnson so he could judge which boy did it better. Samuel Johnson suggested: "Let the dears both speak at once; more noise will by that means be made, and the noise will be sooner over" (Piozzi, 1897, pp. 153–154).

Jean-Paul Sartre

We briefly refer to Sartre's development because it provides an example of a child who experienced some of the risk factors yet did *not* develop

TS-OCD so far as can be ascertained. He experienced some neonatal traumas that resemble Johnson's. Sartre's father became very ill and died shortly after Jean-Paul's birth, and like Samuel Johnson before him, Sartre was put out to be nursed by another woman.

> The sleepless nights and the worry exhausted Anne Marie; her milk dried; I was put out to nurse not far away and I too applied myself to dying, of enteritis and perhaps of resentment. . . . Upon the death of my father, Anne Marie and I awoke from a common nightmare. I got better. But we were victims of a misunderstanding: she returned lovingly to a child she had never really left; I regained consciousness in the lap of a stranger. (Sartre, 1981, pp. 16–17)

Unpleasant Childhood Memories

Like Johnson, Sartre remembers his childhood as unpleasant. "I loathe my childhood," he wrote, "and whatever has survived of it." Sartre seems not to have spent much time mourning the death of his father, describing it rather as "the big event in my life." He saw in it, freedom for himself and bondage for his mother, who went back to live with her parents: ". . . it sent my mother back to her chains and gave me freedom. . . . It did not take long for the young widow to become a minor again" (1981, p. 18).

Her parents "forgot" to give her any pocket money, and only reluctantly allowed her to go out alone. When she was invited to dinner by former friends, most of whom were married, she had to ask her parents for permission and they would only "allow" such outings if her hosts promised to bring her home by 10 o'clock.

Jean Paul's grandfather, Charles Schweitzer, became his psychological surrogate. However he was more narcissistically concerned about the impression he made in society than about the psychological well being of his family. Sartre describes a typical scene in which he and his mother would play their roles in the obligatory ritual of meeting his grandfather returning from work. This tall man in a Panama hat, cream-colored flannel suit, and watch chain strung across his breast was an arresting figure, and he knew it. His height, his "dancing-master's" walk, and his regal pretense accomplished what he most desired—being noticed. Five-year-old Jean-Paul had a part to play as well:

> As soon as he saw us, however far away, he would "take his stance" in obedience to the behests of an invisible photographer: beard flowing in the wind, body erect, feet at right angles, chest out, arms wide open. At this signal, I would stop moving, I would lean forward, I was the runner

getting set, the little birdy about to spring from the camera. . . . I would go hurtling against his knees, pretending to be out of breath. He would lift me from the ground, raise me to the skies, at arm's length, bring me down upon his heart, murmuring: "My precious!". . . We would put on a full act with a hundred varied sketches: He would display the sublime, artless vanity that befits grandfathers . . . (Sartre, 1981 p. 26)

Here we see some of the same exhibitionistic, doting behaviors that Sam Johnson so "loathed" in his father, amplified by the narcissism of Schweitzer's own personality. It was important to Schweitzer that *both* he and young Jean-Paul be postured correctly.

Ambivalence

Of special interest is Sartre's account of his early struggles with ambivalent thoughts which occurred—where else?—in church. He relates that although neither his mother nor grandmother were practicing Catholics, "the faith of others inclines them to musical ecstasy."

They believe in God long enough to enjoy a toccata. Those moments of high spirituality delight me: everyone looks as if he were sleeping, now is the time to show what I can do. Kneeling on the prayer-stool, I change into a statue; I must not even move a toe; I look straight ahead, without blinking, until tears roll down my cheeks.

But such proper behavior is not without its ambivalent conflict: ". . . *what if I stood up and yelled 'Boom!'? What if I climbed up the column to make peepee in the holy-water basin?"* (Sartre, 1981, p. 27, Italics mine).

But for young Sartre, such ambivalence wasn't expressed in ambitendent behaviors. Instead it was resolved in the direction of compliance: "Not for a moment were the temptations giddying; I am far too afraid of creating a scandal. If I want to astound people, it's by my virtues" (Sartre, 1981, pp. 27–28).

Here we begin to see why Sartre, though showered with attention by a widowed mother and two doting grandparents, did not develop resentment. His grandfather was doting, but not intrusive or controlling. His mother was passive—more of a playmate than a parent—and hence there was probably little tendency to overcontrol on her part either. Young Jean-Paul's natural narcissism was stroked by these adults, and since his physical defects (he was small in size, and nearly blind in one eye—which turned outward in a "wall-eyed" fashion) did not become apparent till later in childhood they did not cast the long shadow over development that Johnson's chronically aggravating incision and visual and auditory deficits did. In short, Johnson grew up amid chronic conflict, Sartre did not.

A Gentle Blond Boy

As is typical, however, even his doting mother couldn't totally smooth the road for him. For example, she wanted him to be gentle, as Sartre put it, "feminine around the edges." Consequently she let his hair grow long which got on Grandfather Schweitzer's nerves. "He's a boy," he would say. "You're going to make a girl of him. I don't want my grandson to become a sissy!" A short time later Grandfather succeeded in sneaking Jean-Paul off to the barber shop where he was promptly shorn of his long blond locks. Upon returning home his mother locked herself in her room to cry. Her little boy with the lovely blonde ringlets was no more. Grandfather had been entrusted with her little wonder and he'd brought back a toad (Sartre, 1981, p. 104).

Shamed by His Peers

Things weren't much better in the arena of peer relationships:

> I had met my true judges, my contemporaries, my peers, and their indifference condemned me. I could not get over discovering myself through them: neither a wonder nor a jelly-fish. Just a little shrimp in whom no one was interested. . . . In any case things weren't going right. (Sartre, 1981, pp. 134–135).

Notice, however, that although Jean-Paul wasn't accepted by his peers, he was *ignored* not ridiculed. His was rejection by omission, not the more damaging rejection by humiliation experienced by children with tics.

Comparing Johnson and Sartre, we've noted that although Sartre experienced physical problems, it was later in development. Although he was exposed to overattentive parenting, it was not in a chronically conflictual situation. And although he experienced ambitendency, he was able to resolve it in the direction of compliance and pleasing others because he did not grow up immersed in conflict.

It seems clear, that the configuration, number, and intensity of risk factors determine finally which children will pee in the holy water and which will not—which youngsters will develop lifelong patterns of "peeing" (coprolalia, tics, and other "testy" TS-OCD behaviors) and which, like Sartre, will resolve their conflicts without tics or obsessive rituals.

Before leaving the discussion of Sartre, it's worth noting that his mother, Anne Marie Schweitzer, had a first cousin named Albert. That Sartre became a pessimistic existentialist while his cousin became an altruistic missionary seems more consistent with the developmental paradigm than with chromosomal determinism.

Paradoxical Instructions

This is related to overattention, but goes beyond the parent's unspoken worries or concerns about the child's behavior. Here the parent actively tells the child to "Stop it." Paradoxically, this *increases* the occurrence because it continues to focus on a behavior that the child has repeatedly tried—unsuccessfully—to contain. This is similar to what is ordinarily called a "catch-22" or "double bind." But the term "paradoxical" suggests an additional consideration. We are here referring to instructions that are entangling because of their *recursive, self-reflexive* nature.

An example is the request "Be spontaneous." To *demand* a behavior that is spontaneous which can only happen if it occurs freely is an entrapping paradox—difficult to even think about, and impossible to fulfill. Experienced clinicians know that telling an insomniac "Just relax and go to sleep!", reassuring a paranoid person "You can trust me!", or asking a sexually inhibited person to "Just let go!" is a waste of time. Much of the art of psychotherapy involves *indirectly* recruiting the clients' motivational capacities without paradoxically locking them into defensive patterns.

As anyone who has photographed young children knows, it's futile to tell children "Just go on playing (naturally, as if I weren't here). Because once they become aware you're trying to photograph them, the wonderful spontaneity of play and expression which naturally occurs in children disappears and no amount of cajoling can bring it back.

Likewise, the photographer who instructs his subject to "Smile!" is asking for the paradoxically impossible, because a genuine smile is a spontaneous reflex which cannot be forced. People may *appear* to smile by curling the corners of their mouths upward, or by saying "cheese" but mouth-curling is not smiling because it lacks the spontaneity that is the essence of genuine smiling. More will be said about this in the chapter on treatment, but for the present it suffices to note that most *direct* instructions are therapeutically unsuccessful, because they fail to deal with the underlying need that gave rise to the symptom in the first place. Worse, they typically increase the persons *focus* on the behavior and sense of *futility* about controlling it. Like the instruction "Be spontaneous"—which is existentially and logically impossible to obey—telling children with TS or OCD to "Stop it" only increases their sense of frustration and futility. Parents who continue to do so increase the risk of entrenching the very behaviors they so desperately want to eliminate.

The "Red Monkey" of Self-Consciousness

The story is told of an alchemist who used to travel from village to village, promising to show people how to change pebbles into gold. After instructing the people to fill a pail with pebbles, he would engage in much dramatic ceremony, designed to distract their attention, while he covertly slipped a small gold nugget into the pail. Then, to the profound astonishment of the simple villagers, he would "produce" the gold nugget from the pailful of pebbles. For a handsome fee, he promised to reveal the secret formula to whomever paid the price.

After the gullible had paid their money, the "formula" would be explained with much verbosity, circumlocution, and ritual. During each step of this multiphase process he would interject: "While you're doing this it's *very* important that you don't think about the red monkey!" "If you think about the red monkey," he warned, "it won't work." Of course, they did, and it didn't work. Afterwards they blamed themselves, not the alchemist. "If only we hadn't thought about the red monkey," they thought, "it would have worked."

Telling someone with TS-OCD to "Just Relax" or "If you think about it, you can control it" is creating a "red monkey." The harder one tries *not* to think about it, the more intrusive the obsessions or tics become, as aptly illustrated by Gary Larson's cartoon (Figure 8.1). This is why *all* attempts at direct intervention with tics or obsessions should be avoided. It is *always* iatrogenic—always increasing the risk of lifelong circularity. In the next chapter paradox theory will be discussed more fully.

RIDICULE OFTEN STARTS AT HOME

Parental, Peer, or Sibling Ridicule

Last but *not* least is the problem of ridicule. As has already been shown in the various case illustrations, ridicule and shame are omnipresent for children with tics. Ideally all ridicule that has anything to do with TS-OCD ought to be eradicated. This is probably the *single most important*

THE FAR SIDE By GARY LARSON

FIGURE 8.1 Tics, like itching, only become more compelling as one focuses on them. Thus, focusing on tics always intensifies them.

consideration in prevention. It's often very difficult to accomplish, however, because such teasing is often carried out by peers. Just as Sartre's mother was powerless to make the other children play with her "precious" Jean-Paul, it becomes impossible to remove all teasing from the life of a child with TS-OCD. It's probably impossible to completely remove teasing from the life of *any* child.

This is especially true when the teasing is done subtly. No one can eliminate the stare of strangers while shopping at a mall or riding public transportation. In the classroom the teacher ought to make every effort to eliminate ridicule; but there are limits to what can be done about whispering in the hallways. It's virtually impossible to eliminate the more subtle forms of peer rejection—such as not being chosen on a team, or being chosen last. Such experiences are nonetheless intense for the child. Even in the classroom, the teacher cannot—without creating paradox—insist that other children *not* look at the ticquing child. However, although such efforts may not be totally successful, parents and teachers should actively educate children about others who are "different." Such efforts will enhance childrens' sensitivity to the problems experienced by others and might ultimately have an ameliorative effect on the school milieu.

It is in the home that much can be done to prevent transitory tics from becoming TS. When parents are understanding, but not intrusive, they can *totally* eliminate any parental ridicule—which sometimes occurs as a misguided attempted at "treatment." Sometimes even professionals will make statements (e.g., "He's just doing it for attention") that implicitly give parents and siblings permission to mimic.

Bad Trip

One of the more painful memories from my childhood involves a trip to our family physicians office. He was a small-town doctor, trained in surgery. The incident happened many years before the establishment of the Tourette Syndrome Association or public education regarding TS-OCD; but I remember it as clearly as if it had happened yesterday. My mother, puzzled by my eye blinking and facial tics, had taken me into town to see the doctor. She was called into his office while I sat in the waiting room wondering what they were talking about. After what seemed like hours, I heard my mother's laughter in the short hallway between his consulting office and the waiting room. "Strange," I thought, "Why is she laughing?" Suddenly, I knew. For Dr. Sanders appeared, blinking his eyes and twitching his face; and my mother was laughing, uncomfortably—much like people sometimes laugh uncomfortably at an off-color joke told at a party. But this was no joke, it was my family doctor standing in front of a packed waiting room mimicking me. "See," he said, "I can do it too! It's just a habit." This was apparently his idea of how to cure tics. He should have stuck to surgery.

Most persons with tics have similar "horror stories." Recall the electrician's school experience with ridicule. After slapping proved unsuccessful, Robb's teacher placed him in front of the school in order to embarrass him into quitting. As he told me during our interview:

They sat me in front of the class facing the other kids—knowing the other kids would imitate and ridicule me. Of course you know what happens—it just makes it worse. It wasn't a fun time!

Few professionals really comprehend how much strain protracted shame places on personality development. Anger, explosively expressed in tics, is an attempt to restore self-esteem. It is a protest against the overwhelming feeling of powerlessness, the excruciating self-consciousness, and the peer group's implication that one is not a worthwhile human being. Tics are an opposite and violent flip side to the typical behavioral manifestations of shame described by Kaufman: "The head is hung. Spontaneous movement is interrupted. And speech is silenced" (1985, p. 8). In TS-OCD the head is jerked—not hung. Spontaneous movement is exaggerated—not interrupted. Speech is amplified as vocalizations—not silenced. The entrapping thing about ticquing, however, is that the attempt to restore self-esteem generates more shame, escalating the intensity of the cycle.

To summarize, it isn't possible to entirely eliminate ridicule and the subsequent shame from children's lives. But it *is* possible for parents, teachers, and other professionals to *never* initiate or model such tactics. In the past some uninformed persons have, tragically enough, attempted "cure" through ridicule. Parents ought to exert every effort to keep children from even noticing—much less ridiculing—siblings or playmates with TS-OCD. This *is* possible in a family. It is less possible, but nonetheless important in the classroom, and teachers should do whatever seems prudent to reduce or eliminate ridicule in general. This includes but should not be limited to educational strategies. It may be necessary to use disciplinary procedures in order to emphasize how serious one is about such rules. However, this always runs the risk of backfiring when the children aren't being directly observed, so discipline should be used very judiciously.

I believe that if ridicule could be largely eliminated early in the lives of children with TS-OCD, the number of new cases could be substantially reduced.

Commentary

The pathway from birth to TS-OCD adults is unique for each person, involving a distinctive configuration of risk factors. While it is not possible to predict with precision which children's tics or obsessions will develop into lifelong TS-OCD, the greater the number of risk factors present the higher the likelihood of permanent circular rituals. Other elements also influence outcome. The age and personality of the child make a difference. The duration, intensity, chronicity, and pervasiveness of the risk factors must also be taken into account. Although this may seems perplexingly complicated, the implications for prevention are straightforward.

PREVENTION

Reduce the Intensity and Pervasiveness of Risk Factors Whenever and Wherever Possible

Never try to directly reduce the intensity and pervasiveness of the tics or obsessions, either by constriction or more subtle forms of attention. Endeavor to assess and attenuate the risk factors—not the symptoms. Try to discover the needs that give rise to the TS-OCD rituals, and creatively devise means to gratify those needs so that ticquing or obsessing don't need to be resorted to.

Early Intervention

Early intervention is recommended—provided it isn't intrusive, doesn't focus directly on the TS-OCD, and doesn't increase the child's self-consciousness. Since TS-OCD usually begins with a single tic—typically of the eye, head, or face—and then gradually becomes more intense or more pervasive, all tics should be taken seriously, but interventions should be *subtle* and *indirect*. The usual round of medical workups, multiple neurological consults, numerous electroencephalograms and computer-assisted tomography scans, might well be bypassed, since they typically raise anxieties, find nothing organically wrong, and tend to result in the prescription of drugs. A single trip to the ophthalmologist—if the child has an eye tic—will suffice. There is little reason to take a child with a facial grimace or head shaking to anyone for medical assessment.

Maintain a Developmental and Family-Systems Perspective

Implicit in the discussion of prevention is the notion that TS-OCD is not an organic medical problem; rather it's a developmentally based disorder emerging from the dynamics of family and peer interactions. Consequently, at the first indication of tics or obsessions in a child, parents should seek consultation with a child clinical psychologist, child psychiatrist, or family therapist for help in assessing the ambience existing in the child's experiential world. Such consultations are *much* less expensive than CT scans, and more likely to yield information helpful for relating to the child in a therapeutic way.

Don't Expect Children to Turn Around on a Dime

It takes time for children to become comfortable without the use of tics or ritualization, but if the stressors are lessened this becomes much more likely. Habits—and tics are habits—once established are difficult to reverse. That's why "an ounce of prevention *is* worth a pound of cure." It's easier to modify tics when risk factors are reduced early in the developmental process. When, however, this has not been the case, the steady attenuation of risk factors may still pay dividends, though much later. Persistence pays off.

In the next chapter treatment issues will be discussed in more detail, but it will become clear that the distinction between prevention and treatment is rather arbitrary. The very best treatment is prevention. It's much wiser to educate teenagers not to begin smoking than to persuade them to join smoking cessation clinics when they're adults. However, in cases of TS-OCD, individuals often come to the attention of professionals after their rituals are deeply ingrained. This presents additional challenges requiring even more creativity.

Chapter 9

PSYCHOLOGICAL TREATMENT OF TS-OCD

Throughout this book we've followed an expansive developmental paradigm, emphasizing object relations. Our theory of causality has been multifactorial, taking into account numerous situational risk factors as well as internal personality dynamics. Catastrophe Theory (CT) provides a sort of "Grand Central Station" where various "trains" of theoretical thought, arriving from diverse directions, are "housed." We've suggested that TS-OCD is a *functional* disorder, established early in life and influenced by numerous factors along the way. Now, as we consider treatment techniques, additional concepts will be drawn from a variety of theoretical frameworks. However, they will be complementary to what has gone before, and "housed" within the broad parameters of CT.

ETIOLOGY, PREVENTION, AND TREATMENT: THE EVOLVING NATURE OF BEHAVIOR

A complex relationship exists among etiology, prevention, and treatment. Understanding etiology seems basic to prevention, because prevention deals with behaviors in their embryonic forms. The relationship between origins and early behaviors seems a close one. Treatment, on the other hand, typically focuses on well-established behaviors that are sometimes far removed in time from their origins. Treatment is complicated by the fact that current behaviors usually appear quite different from their precursors. Much like an oak tree, which changes extensively as it evolves from acorn to full grown tree, behaviors lose many of their original characteristics as they develop. Consequently, appropriate treatment must take into account current behaviors *and* etiologic origins. This requires a balancing of past and present issues in such a way that neither excludes the other, while both sharpen the focus of treatment.

The challenge of sawing down a large oak tree in such a way that it doesn't land on the roof or break telephone wires requires more than a careful study of acorns. Oaks lose their "acornish" characteristics early in development. Similarly, although adolescent or adult tics and obsessions resemble their early precursors more than oak trees resemble acorns, there are still important differences. Etiologic understanding alone is not sufficient. Competent treatment requires careful examination of *current* behaviors as well as thoughtful investigation of origins.

Intertwined Behaviors

Preventing adolescents from beginning to smoke, for example, is a different challenge from conducting cessation clinics for adults who have been smoking many years. Once established, smoking is extremely resistant to change because it is intertwined with such emotions as anger, joy, and boredom, and becomes enmeshed with virtually all other behaviors in the person's repertoire, including driving a car, drinking coffee, and making love. Exceptions might include showering or scuba diving, but there are few for two-pack-a-day smokers.

Similarly, eliminating tics or obsessions is difficult because they are so enmeshed with current behaviors. Though arising from the basic needs of the early years, they soon acquire many self-reinforcing qualities—they begin to have a "life of their own." To use Allport's term, they become *functionally autonomous* (1961, p. 229). Furthermore, tics and obsessions—like smoking or drinking—generate additional problems that circularly feed back into the very problems they attempt to soothe. Like the alcoholic who drinks to soothe his or her worries but whose drinking produces additional problems, persons with tics or obsessions get some relief from ticquing or obsessing but this temporary comfort is more than offset by the additional problems resulting from these compulsive behaviors.

Relationship Between Persons and Situations

Consistent developmental experiences become internalized within an individual as consistent expectancies. If a little child consistently experiences being presented with a cake with lighted candles on her birthday, she will come to *expect* such an event on each birthday. Children who consistently see green trees with lights during the month of December develop an internalized expectancy about Christmas trees. Analogously infants tend to "internalize" and "re-present" daily experiences to themselves, until such experiences become part of the self-system—until they are "owned." Their own responses then begin to follow a more predictable pattern. Referred to as *cross situational consistency*, this means that a person behaves similarly across a wide variety of situations. Friendly people tend to be friendly at home, work, and in social situations, while whiners tend to complain in a wide variety of situations. Although we know that much of the consistency we observe in behavior comes from within the person, it is apparent that *situations* also influence consistency. It isn't considered in good taste, for example, to tell your funniest jokes at a funeral. Screaming and shouting is considered appropriate in a football stadium, but not in a cathedral. Thus, the external situation and the internal personality are always in dynamic interaction.

When implementing treatment techniques we need to be aware of the individual's personal history *and* also of current situational parameters. Behavior is the end product of person-by-situation interaction, and is best understood from this dual perspective. Shapiro captures this well in the following illustration:

> Suppose we observe an Indian, whose culture is unfamiliar, performing a strange dance with great intensity. As we watch, puzzled, we may notice that there is a drought and that this is an agricultural community; we consider the possibility that this is a prayerful dance designed to bring rain and that possibly it is an expression of apprehension as well. By careful observation, we may be able to decipher certain regular gestures that confirm our guess. There is no doubt that, at this point, we have achieved a significant measure of understanding. But the limitations of that understanding become apparent if we only consider that nearby, watching, is a non-Indian farmer who also suffers from the drought but does not join in the dancing. It does not occur to him to perform these gestures; instead, he goes home and worries. *The Indian dances not only because there is a drought, but also because he is an Indian.* (1965, p. 16)

A similar phenomenon occurs with TS-OCD. When confronted with stress, most adults don't increase the frequency and intensity of ticquing in a futile attempt to comfort themselves. Instead, like the farmer, they worry, sometimes developing migraine headaches or ulcers. Ticquers, like Indians, ritualistically "jump around," not to placate gods, but in an attempt to relieve their own anxieties. To paraphrase Shapiro's words, they tic, not only because there is stress, but also because they are ticquers. Situations and persons coalesce to form the phenomenon known as TS-OCD. To understand and change this dynamic person–situation interface is the major goal of treatment.

Summary

We've seen that etiologic understanding contributes importantly to prevention and treatment. However when TS-OCD is well established, it is not enough to know how tics or obsessions came into existence. It becomes necessary to analyze current issues as well. Consequently in developing treatment strategies we will utilize concepts from the fields of communications, cybernetics, and philosophy to sharpen our understanding of ritualistic behaviors and thoughts. Terms such as *black box, feedback loop, paradox,* and others will be carefully examined and then utilized to understand more clearly TS-OCD. This doesn't negate what has been said about developmental needs, shame, brinkmanship, and other such issues; it rather expands on it with a pragmatic treatment focus.

In the ensuing discussion there will be (to the chagrin of my high school English teachers) mixed metaphors. Although this may not seem conceptually "pure," it is necessary, because TS-OCD is a complex phenomenon, requiring multiple levels of analysis. Since each discipline has its own special language, utilizing favorite metaphors, a comprehensive understanding of TS-OCD will include a number of "second generation" hybrid metaphors. This does no damage to our understanding of TS-OCD, however, because all metaphors—indeed all words—only approximate true reality. And viewing the phenomenon of TS-OCD from diverse vantage points, using concepts drawn from a variety of disciplines, will sharpen our understanding.

INFORMATION, COMMUNICATION, AND CYBERNETICS

In this discussion, I intend to show that TS-OCD is an information-rich phenomenon. Here I'm not referring to a particular theory of communication or information exchange, but rather emphasizing that TS-OCD always communicates meaning. Sometimes bizarre, typically puzzling—to others and self—the various manifestations always carry information.

Information versus Energy

Many contemporary theorists have cogently argued that Freud and other nineteenth-century scientists tried to establish a bridge between behavioral data and the fundamentals of physics and chemistry, and they erred in choosing *energy* as the bridge. "If mass and length are inappropriate for the describing of behavior, then energy is unlikely to be more appropriate. After all, energy *is* mass × velocity^2, and no behavioral scientist really insists that psychic energy is of these dimensions" (Bateson, 1972, xxii).

For example, the differences in saluting, waving, or flipping someone off are best understood as *information* exchanges, not *energy* transformations. In a military situation, one is required to salute superior officers by briskly raising one's right arm with all four fingers extended and momentarily touching one's forehead. To wave to a friend, one raises the arm less briskly without touching the forehead. The very same motor movements (briskly raising the arm) with only the middle finger extended (flipping someone off) is not acceptable to military personnel or friends. Far from showing respect or friendliness, it suggests defiance, a willingness to fight, and so on.

Surely these profound differences emerge not from biochemical or energy differences between extending one finger or four fingers while waving. The differences are informational and are amplified by the social contexts in which they occur. It is more serious to flip off a policeman than a fellow motorist. If you're in boot camp you salute your drill sergeant (at least to his face) and flip him off when he's not looking. Attempting to understand TS-OCD neurologically—in terms of energy transformations—is like trying to understand obscene gestures physiologically or holy water biochemically. The theoretical machinery is inappropriate.

Cybernetics: The Study of Steermanship

We will now consider a few concepts from cybernetics that will be helpful in treating TS-OCD. Although cybernetics began in close association with physics, it currently deals with issues of behavioral regularities, bypassing issues of materiality, lawfulness, or energy as defined in the "hard" sciences. Ashby (1961) suggests that cybernetics is best understood as "the art of *steermanship*":

> Cybernetics started by being closely associated in many ways with physics, but it depends in no essential way on the laws of physics or on the properties of matter. Cybernetics deals with all forms of behaviour in so far as they are regular, or determinate, or reproducible. The materiality is irrelevant. . . . It does not ask "what *is* this thing?" but *"what does it do?"* Thus it is very interested in such a statement as "this variable is undergoing a simple harmonic oscillation," and is much less concerned with whether the variable is the position of a point on a wheel, or a potential in

an electric circuit. It is thus essentially functional and behaviouristic. (Ashby, 1961, p. 1)

"Steermanship" may seem limited in TS-OCD, because both the person and others experience it as a loss of control. However, as we've already noted, there is always present—even in the most violently expressed tic behaviors—a degree of control. Ticquers are able to eat, drink, drive automobiles, and engage in various finely tuned behaviors, which illustrates that steermanship is not totally absent. However, for the person with TS-OCD it's a little like driving an 18-wheeler down a mountain road with brakes in marginal working condition. A degree of steermanship exists, but control is severely compromised.

Tics as Black Boxes

Engineers use the term *black box* for a device that contains unknown components. It accepts signals and transforms them. By varying the input and observing the output, one can conclude something about the nature of the box's components. Our knowledge of the human brain is still fragmentary. Although recent advances in technology have introduced a new era of noninvasive brain study, utilizing such techniques as computer-assisted tomography (CT scans), our knowledge of how the brain chooses among billions of neuronal connection possibilities remains mysterious.

Most body systems are only understood in black-box kinds of ways. Blood, for example, contains components that represent various states of the biological servo-system attempting to maintain homeostasis. Numerous organs of the body react to and influence the composition of blood by differentially distributing its components. By sampling the blood and measuring the various components we are examining the system's output. If we engage in stress testing or dietary manipulations before sampling we are also varying input. Thus, our study of blood is really (in cybernetic terms) the study of a black box.

From a cybernetic perspective brain functions can be studied and much can be learned about informational patterns, feedback loops, and the like without waiting for neurology or biochemistry to precisely define the components of the complex black box we call the brain. This proves useful in our understanding of TS-OCD because we can deal with functional relationships between psychological inputs and subsequent symptomatic outputs without necessarily knowing anatomical or neurological details.

Black boxes are much more pervasive than most realize. Ashby writes:

> We do in fact work, in our daily lives, much more with Black Boxes than we are apt to think. At first we are apt to think, for instance that a bicycle is not a Black Box, for we can see every connecting link. We delude ourselves, however. The ultimate links between pedal and wheel are those interatomic forces that hold the particles of metal together; of these we see nothing, and the child who learns to ride can become competent merely with the knowledge that pressure on the pedals makes the wheels go round. (1961, p. 110)

When tics are seen as black boxes, it becomes possible to study how their output changes (intensity, frequency, modality) as a function of input and personality factors. This can be done with surprising precision, knowing almost nothing about the biochemical substrates of such behaviors.

Feedback

Feedback is defined as *the return to input of part of the output* of a machine, system, or process. The importance of feedback to the regulation of systems—simple or complex—will become more clear with illustration. Ashby uses the example of a child's train—the kind that runs along the floor, not on tracks—to illustrate. If the cars are slightly out of line, trying to back them up only worsens the problem, but *pulling* them with the engine in front straightens the cars. This, of course, is why semi-trailers are pulled not pushed down the highway by their drivers.

Negative Feedback—Complementary Loops

Negative feedback is technically defined in the following way:

> A simple test for stability (from a state of equilibrium assumed) is to consider the sequence of changes that follow a small displacement, as it travels round the loop. If the displacement ultimately arrives back at its place of origin with size and sign so that, when added algebraically to the initial displacement, the initial displacement is diminished, i.e., brought nearer the state of equilibrium, then the system around that state of equilibrium, is (commonly) stable. The feedback, in this case, is said to be 'negative' (for it causes an eventual *subtraction* from initial displacement. (Ashby, 1961, p. 80)

Bateson has applied the notion of feedback loops to human relationships, suggesting that two broad classes of relationships derive from the two kinds of feedback. A *complementary* loop, utilizes negative feedback and involves individuals in relationships which include dominance-submission, exhibitionism–spectatorship, nurturance–dependence, or other similarly interlocking, complementary dyads. Examples include parent–child, boss–employee, alcoholic–nagging spouse, teacher–student, movie star–fan, and so on. Such complementary loops are usually *degenerative*, which means they tend towards homeostasis instead of escalation. Engineering examples of such self-correcting loops include a house thermostat or the governor on an engine.

Positive Feedback—Symmetrical Loops

Whether the relationship is between two individuals or two groups of individuals, *symmetrical* loops always involve competition and tend to escalate. Examples include two boxers, rival street gangs taunting each other, two children boasting to be the strongest fighter, or two men at a bar matching each other drink for drink. As we shall see, it is possible to think of symmetrical loops between two systems within the body. Scratching itchy skin often makes it itch more; and hyperventilating makes one feel even more out of breath. These kinds of symmetrical relationships between components of the body are relevant to understanding TS-OCD.

Symmetrical loops are *regenerative*, tending to escalate. Known in ordinary conversation as a "vicious circle," such loops include a chain of variables such that an increase in A, causes an increase in B, causes an increase in C . . . until the loop returns causing a further increase in A. Such systems will generally operate at *escalating* rates or intensities. An example in a bus route that begins with busses equally spaced along the route. If a bus is delayed, extra passengers collect at the stopping points, so that it has to pick up more passengers than usual. The bus that follows, being closer than usual, has fewer passengers to handle and thus takes a shorter than average time between stops. Such a system, as frustrated route managers know, is self-aggravating—escalating, rather than self-correcting. This kind of loop bears a strong resemblance to TS-OCD. Ticquing is like scratching an itch; it only helps temporarily and usually worsens the very situation it was generated to ameliorate.

DEVELOPMENTAL CYBERNETICS

In the ensuing discussion cybernetic concepts will be mingled with developmental theory. Concepts from the study of "steermanship" will be utilized to understand development. Although engineering terms like "feedback," "black boxes," and "coupling" are not typically found in developmental psychology textbooks, they provide analytic tools that allow one to balance intricate psychological analyses with more global perspectives.

Varieties of Feedback

Recall that during the first eight months of life normal infants engage in repetitive acts, which Piaget designated as circular reactions. The most basic of these are simple repetitive acts that center on the infant's own body, such as thumb sucking, hand clasping, or foot grabbing. They are highly somatic, intrinsically preverbal, and usually soothing in their effect on the impressionable infant.

Endogenous Complementary Proprioceptive Feedback

Primary circular reactions provide endogenous complementary feedback to the neonate. The complementarity takes place *within* the infant's body among opposing systems (extensor–flexor or excitation–inhibition). Because of its utter dependency on others for survival, the infant is locked into a *complementary interpersonal* system with the mothering one. Whenever parents are not adequately soothing or in other ways responsive, circular reactions exist as backup "parents," providing self soothing through repetitious, proprioceptive "bursts" of comfort. (See Chapter 2.)

These circular reactions are intrinsically complementary. The oscillatory acts of inserting a thumb into the mouth—removing it—inserting it—removing it, and so on is in keeping with the infant's more general "circularity" seen in the neonate's cyclic build up and discharge sequences of movement, attention, pleasure, and distress. In optimal development such sequences are *degenerative*, tending toward quiescence rather than escalation. This is especially true when parental soothing is readily available; because under such circumstances the "significant other" is able to "contain" mounting anxieties with soothing patterns, which are then "taken over" (internalized) by the infant as self-soothing behaviors. Such self-soothing patterns are not likely to become ritualistically repetitive or somatically symmetrical (tics), because they are closely coupled with a larger "damping" system (the soothing mother) that interpersonalizes the loop, moving it towards homeostasis instead of escalation.

DYNAMICS OF TICQUING

It has already been suggested that tics are not symptoms of neurological malfunction, they are *normal but exaggerated* movements. Muscles normally operate in a context of balanced tension between antagonistic groups—such as flexors and extensors—with movement resulting from tipping the balance in either direction. Extending or flexing one's arm, occurs as a result of tensing one group of muscles while simultaneously relaxing opposing ones. The usual balance is such that a small increase of innervation on the extensor side causes your arm to move away from your body, while a small shift in innervation causes it to flex back toward your body. "Curling" barbells requires noticeably more flexor activation but is similar in dynamics.

Internal Tug-of-War

In the development of tics, the usual antagonistic tension existing among selected muscle groups is exaggerated—only slightly at first, but with increasing intensity as the tic develops. The explosive nature of fully developed tics occurs when the rapidly increasing symmetrical tension between opposing muscle groups suddenly gives way to one group "pushing through" and *briefly* restoring a complementary relationship. Grunting, for example, results from rapidly forcing sound through a tensed diaphragmatic musculature.

Explosively "breaking through" feels good to the ticquer because it provides a rapid shift from symmetry to complementarity. There is an almost symmetrical escalation of activity in antagonistic muscle groups with tension continuing to mount until punctuated by a satisfying "explosion" (tic). This occurs when the extensor muscles succeed in suddenly dominating the now subservient flexor opponents. This tug-of-war between muscle groups is an internal proprioceptive version of what one sees at picnics when members of two teams line up at opposite ends of a rope and begin trying to pull the persons on the opposing team over a line. Typically the pulling seems at first "balanced" with much grunting and groaning, but little movement of the rope. Suddenly, however, the rope moves rapidly in one direction, and it's "all over" in a few seconds. This rapid shift—from tense muscle symmetry to quiescent complementarity—though lasting only a few seconds, is highly pleasurable.

Sex

Most pleasurable phenomena also show a rapid change from symmetry to complementarity. Sexual arousal, for example, can be seen as beginning with a pre-orgasmic symmetrical buildup of tension between various antagonistic muscle groups in the body. The rapid switch to pulsating complementarity during the orgasmic phase is experienced as highly pleasurable.

Golf

Even golf can be seen as an explosive change from symmetry to complementarity. The golfer stands up in front of the ball preparing to tee off. Muscles tense even prior to the backswing. With the initiation of the backswing, the tension mounts, building to a zenith at the top of the back swing. Then, rapidly, the momentum changes: shifting from tense, coiled-like-a-spring symmetry to explosive complementarity as the clubhead approaches the ball and the golfer snaps his wrists. Only then does the player relax as the ball begins its trajectory down the fairway.

Drugs

Something akin to the above examples occurs when a person uses a rapid acting drug to increase tension (symmetry) or relaxation (complementarity) of muscles or other body systems. In the current discussion the drugs that escalate tension or *symmetry* can be categorized as "uppers" and those that induce quiescence or *complementarity* as "downers." Interestingly, there is a direct relationship between the addictiveness of a drug and its speed of action—the more rapid the onset, the more addictive the drug. The addictive potential of secobarbital (Seconal®), a short acting barbiturate, is well known and significantly greater than that of the much slower onset phenobarbital.

Doubtless one of the reasons quitting cigarettes is so difficult for smokers is that nicotine acts so rapidly on the nervous system. The time that elapses between the moment a smoker inhales until the brain picks up the "pleasure" punch is about *seven seconds*! Much more could be said, discussing various drugs, but the principal is similar. Rapid changes of state—especially in the direction of complementarity—are very pleasurable. Oscillating between two states can heighten pleasure, especially when the effect "decays" rapidly. Here the resemblance between puffing a cigarette and ticquing becomes more apparent. Just as a smoker puffs several times a minute receiving a "buzz" after only a seven-second interval, the ticquer gets "buzzed" several times a minute as well, with an even shorter delay. In a certain sense, a ticquer is "addicted" to immediate proprioceptive feedback, much as the smoker is addicted to short-delay nicotine feedback.

Incessant Oscillation Between Proprioceptive Complementarity and Symmetry

A number of influential learning theorists (e.g., Hull, 1943; Miller & Dollard, 1941) have defined reinforcement in terms of *tension reduction*. Other theorists have emphasized the importance of *immediacy* of reinforcement; experimentally demonstrating that a small but immediate reinforcement has greater power to shape behavior than a large but delayed (even for a few seconds) reward. A more complete discussion of the nature of reinforcement is unnecessary in the present context, except to note that tics *reduce tension* and they do it *immediately*. Consequently, they are extremely reinforcing.

From a cybernetics viewpoint, breathing is complementary, sniffing is symmetrical. In the slow, heavy, alternating rhythms of inhalation and expiration, the sleeping person provides a pristine picture of *complementarity*. Such rhythms, uncontaminated by consciousness, are primal to life itself, and even persons with TS-OCD return to this peaceful complementarity when sleeping.

Upon awakening, normal persons interrupt the smoothness of such complementarity *subconsciously,* by engaging in various activities requiring differing amounts of oxygen. Consequently throughout the day, breathing quickens, slows, and changes frequency. However, the *antagonistic balance* remains relatively constant and the process of breathing subconscious. Whether breathing is shallow or deep, rapid or slow, the antagonistic balance changes little—there is no tendency away from complementarity.

Not so with TS-OCD. Tics always involve a *conscious* amplification of one side of a physiological process. However, in order to get satisfaction there must be a corresponding increase in the antagonistic side as well. Consequently, the process becomes more intense, more conscious, and more *symmetrical*. Thus, it matters little whether the nasal tic consists of sniffing in, or blowing out; the malfunction occurs when consciousness intrudes into the unconscious, disturbing the optimally balanced breathing observed when a person is asleep. Hypertrophy of consciousness and conscious activation in either direction creates ticquing.

In Summary

Tics occur when the normal complementary balance between muscle groups carrying out movements is "symmetricized" by amplification of either side of the balance. Once this occurs, movements become explosive as they oscillate between symmetry and complementarity. This style of functioning increasingly replaces the primal complementarity of muscular rhythms present in optimally developing neonates. The immediacy of explosive reinforcement that occurs with rapid shifts from symmetry to brief complementarity makes tics highly resistent to extinction. In the broadest sense, however, they remain incessantly disruptive because, like all symmetrical loops, they escalate. Only sleep returns the TS-OCD individual to stable complementarity.

Defining Tics

Cybernetically speaking, tics are oscillations between *proprioceptive symmetry and complementarity*. They are *endogenous, symmetrical muscular loops* that rapidly reach a breaking point and *suddenly, explosively* switch to *complementarity* resulting in *brief* quiescence before recycling.

Constriction

Constriction increases risk by providing additional strength on the "containing" side of the antagonistic balance, which necessitates greater intensity of extensor activity, further escalating the process. When such constriction is consistently provided by external sources (plaster casts, bicycle inner tubes, or parents), or by internal cognitive mediators, it tends to stabilize the symmetry over long periods of development—thereby "normalizing" this heightened extensor state in the experience of the individual.

Consciousness

A word needs to be said about consciousness. When tics *originally* develop, there is likely some consciousness in their initiation. The first grader who starts blinking his eyes or engaging in facial grimacing does so with a moderate degree of conscious steermanship. Soon, however, like the motions associated with driving a car, or riding a bicycle, the actual movements (putting in the clutch, shifting, or pressing the accelerator—blinking one's eyes or twisting the neck against the collar) become semiautomatic. Nonetheless they always remain potentially conscious; easily brought into awareness. Even if you've driven for 30 years, you can still teach someone to operate an automobile on a step-by-step basis. In Freudian terminology such behaviors remain "preconscious," not directly in awareness, yet easily focused upon.

In the case of tics or obsessions that have settled into the "semiautomatic" phase, there is a level of awareness somewhere in between the unconscious breathing of a sleeping person and the automatic driving of an automobile. This is because *self consciousness* is an important amplifying variable. As we noted in our discussion of shame, tics incessantly generate attention, consequently the ticquer's awareness is continually drawn to them by the ridicule and attention of others. This is especially true during childhood, though it remains lifelong. It's like driving a car with a policeman in the front passenger seat, or as if you were taking a driving test. Under such circumstances the driving is *not* semiautomatic. Tics and obsessions are like that—hovering somewhere between preconscious and embarrassingly conscious.

Checking and Balancing

Ticquing children perform "security checks" on particular systems (e.g., the muscles innervating the eyelids or neck) reassuring themselves that they are free to forcibly shut their eyes or jerk their heads. Adults who obsessively "check" locks several times before going to work are engaging in a higher order version of the same thing. Unfortunately both kinds of behaviors have symmetrical (escalating) qualities about their compulsiveness, and diminishing returns in terms of satisfaction.

Interesting in this regard is the *symmetry* seen in the higher order obsessions of TS-OCD. The constant attempt to perfectly balance all sides of an issue—resulting in the inability to make decisions—is a classic characteristic of OCD. Through the years, clinicians have reported cases where the ability to decide has been crippled by overconcern with balance. Persons regularly just about reach the point of taking the *risk* of deciding but then think of an alternative course of action directly in conflict with the path about to be entered. Although this seems like an intellectual process of weighing and evaluation, in reality it has more to do with feeling safe and avoiding the risk inherent in any true decision; and the adult's attempt to feel secure is not psychologically far removed from the child's attempts to do the same.

Ticquing More, Enjoying It Less

A pervasive characteristic of *all* tics or obsessions is their unsatisfying escalating quality. Whether this is the endogenous somatic escalation of checking one's own musculature by ticquing, the cognitive escalation of performing obsessive rituals, or social escalation expressed as interpersonal brinkmanship, there is present in all cases a compulsive, escalating, symmetrical quality. Like the Rolling Stones who sang: "I Can't Get No Satisfaction," persons with TS-OCD tic with increasing intensity but decreasing satisfaction. The same phenomenon is well known in addictions as "tolerance."

Tics as Sedatives

We've often referred to the soothing qualities of tics and their function as transition objects—proprioceptive "Mammas." It is of interest to note that in a widely differing context, Tomkins (1987) refers to *sedative scripts* and suggests that, when self sedation proves effective, the sedative act is terminated and its frequency reduced. However, in cases where the sedative act proves *ineffective* it will be repeated and frequency will increase. Paradoxically, the use of sedative acts increases, says Tomkins "as a conjoint function of the density of source affect and of the *ineffectiveness* of the sedative affect" (1987, p. 188).

In Tomkin's analysis sedation refers not to overcoming the source of the negative affect but to attenuating or reducing negative feelings that result from the source. Further, he notes that while addiction sedates intense negative affects, it also reproduces shame, thereby energizing the cycle to repeat. In the current discussion, this is clearly the case with tics. They inevitably induce the curiosity and stares of others and generate shame incessantly. Consequently although there is a momentary sense of relief immediately following the tic, it is short lived, while the shame generated reverberates endlessly.

From Somatic to Symbolic/Social Symmetry

As development proceeds, primary circular reactions expand into *secondary circular reactions* during the fourth to eighth months of life. Such behaviors begin the shift away from the infant's body to the external world. The infant *reaches out* to shake a rattle, reaches for a toy, or otherwise manipulates objects discovered in the environment. With this movement away from the body, development begins to move toward *symbolic (cognitive and linguistic) development and social interaction.*

For the TS-OCD-prone child these cognitive and social loops may be symmetrical from the earliest beginnings. For example, in repetitive banging of toys against the side of the crib, the environment may play the role of (symmetrical) "resistor," instead of (complementary) "soother." As development proceeds into the "terrible twos" the relationship between mother and infant tends to become *more symmetrical,* even under the best of conditions. Many mothers experience this as a tumultuous tug-of-war with toddler asserting autonomy and mother struggling to teach obedience. Unwittingly, many toddlers and parents engage in symmetrical oscillation around issues of autonomy. It should not be surprising that children engaged in tics ("endogenous" somatic rituals) would also be at risk for symmetrical social rituals. The conflictual, escalating, symmetrical style which is originally proprioceptive can generalize to the social orbit. What we've previously called "brinkman-ship" is, in cybernetic terms, an exquisitely balanced symmetrical inter-personal loop.

THEORY OF TREATMENT

Understanding how and why TS-OCD patterns develop, and what can be done to reverse them is crucial for any successful treatment program. We've delineated the intricate "anatomy" of such behaviors, spent significant time clarifying the developmental roots, and now we will focus on treatment with special attention to understanding the circular, entrapping nature of tics and obsessions.

Treating the Bifurcated Personality

Two "orbits" will be designated where feedback loops exist. These orbits correspond to the two sides of the bifurcated personality. The rules governing behavior differ in each of these orbits, and the mechanisms of feedback and cybernetic control are dissimilar.

Somatic Orbit

We've already discussed how during the first months of life infants engage in simple repetitive behaviors such as thumb sucking, hand clasping, or foot grabbing. These center on the neonate's own body, are necessarily preverbal, and are usually soothing to the impressionable infant. In optimal development, these primary circular reactions are *complementary* in nature. The oscillatory acts of inserting a thumb into the mouth, removing a thumb from the mouth, re-inserting the thumb, show a pattern of buildup and discharge.

Cognitive/Social Orbit

As the infant begins to differentiate himself or herself, this is carried on in the context of significant others—the parenting ones. The parent-infant dyad *begins* complementarily with the earliest interpersonal exchanges involving feeding, bathing, diapering, and—we noted earlier—facial and psychological interaction. There is rhythmic complementarity to the urgent, yet highly dependent needs of the neonate for nutrition, nurturance, and "dryness" and the capacities of the parenting one to accommodate such needs.

Toddlerhood: The Shift from Complementarity to Symmetry

However, as the neonate develops into toddlerhood, the balance changes and the parental orbit begins to become more *symmetrical*. In the children at risk for TS-OCD, the ambitendency of the toddler typically engages parents in *symmetrical* (escalating) oscillation around issues of autonomy and control. For some, these issues are never satisfactorily resolved. We've previously referred to the pervasive phenomenon of "brinkmanship." Now we can see such behaviors as symmetrical loops in the social orbit.

Persons with TS-OCD continue symmetrical relationships of the toddler years into their adolescent and adult lives. Additionally, symmetrical cognitive rituals may develop as well. Even for such persons, however, society presents opportunities to become involved in satisfying complementary relationships. It is such complementarity of relationships in social interactions that gives stability to families, communities, and society at large. Each person "knows his or her place" in the order of things.

For persons with TS-OCD social complementary occurs just outside the actual "brinkmanship" interaction. In society at large, most adults—unlike six-year-olds—do not directly stare at ticquing persons, don't usually ask embarrassing questions, and for the most part relate with benign tolerance. Except for the immediate brinkmanship interaction, the persons with TS-OCD achieve with other adults a sort of social homeostasis which could be illustrated by the following generalized conversation:

TS-OCD PERSON: I can't help it! I've tried to quit, but I really can't. There must be something wrong with me.

SOCIETY: We understand—there is something wrong—you have an organic disease. Something like alcoholism. It's O.K., just take your medications, and we'll work along with you.

Even if the interaction is negative or cruelly humiliating, it still remains *complementary*. Recall that when "Twitchy" Robb couldn't be contained by his grandmother's bicycle inner tubes or by his Navy chief's instructions to quit "winking" (i.e., he remained ambitendantly *symmet-*

rical), he ended up being confined and contained (*negative complementarity*) in mental hospitals.

TS-OCD: A Stable "Sandwich"

Symmetrical social relationships tend to be short-lived. They are unstable and easily escalate to the breaking point. By contrast, TS-OCD shows remarkable stability. Although ticquing or social brinkmanship occurs as a symmetrical loop—tending toward escalation and subsequent instability—it is sandwiched between *complementary* loops (circular rhythms of the body and social mores of society) that tend toward quiescent stability. This configuration of a regenerative, escalating loop—contained on both sides by stable degenerative, homeostatically biased loops—accounts for the tremendous resistance to change seen in TS-OCD. The neighboring loops support the status quo by accommodating the symmetrical TS-OCD loop and insulating it from disturbance. Consequently, the therapist faces the difficult problem not only of how to change the tics, but how to achieve this without destabilizing the surrounding social systems.

Numerous examples could be given to illustrate how this intricate system of feedback loops resists destabilization. For example, the lady who shattered mirrors with her fist was *symmetrically* testing: hitting and pushing toward the outer parameters of the ambitendence-permeated TS-OCD loop. However she crossed some kind of invisible boundary when the mirror shattered, cutting her hand, and was immediately in a social orbit where others *complementarily* take care of helpless victims.

Coupling

Before discussing treatment techniques, it will be useful to introduce the notion of *coupling*. As we've seen, TS-OCD can be understood as a series of interlocking feedback loops. Each orbit has its own parallel series. In the somatic orbit, for example, thumb sucking, toe sucking, single-finger sucking, and multiple-finger sucking might exist as *parallel* primary circular reactions. At a slightly higher level—closer to the cognitive/social orbit—are the secondary circular reactions such as banging or sucking a rattle, or sucking a pacifier. These kinds of loops interface or *couple* with loops from the cognitive/social orbit such as sucking on Mommy's finger, nipple, or clothing. From a cybernetics viewpoint, simple behaviors (like sucking) become more complex as they interface with orbits from the larger world. Through coordination or *coupling*, lower level functions are brought into a more collaborative relationship with higher level functions. Thus, sucking (a simple, rhythmic, somatic loop) becomes coupled with feeding at the Mother's breast.

It is helpful to view coupling as relatively *loose*, or *tight*. Information theorists suggest that when lower level functions are incorporated into higher level functions or evolve into more complex behaviors, the levels of the hierarchy are "tightly coupled." (Pattee, 1973). In the previous example, if sucking became part of a larger feeding repertoire, we would say it was *tightly coupled*. If, however, sucking assumed a lot of functional autonomy—developed a life of its own—we would see sucking and feeding as more *loosely coupled*.

Hierarchical levels that function independently of each other (e.g., a University's board of trustees and its students) are loosely coupled. It has been observed that

> . . . emergent properties often appear when a higher level is only loosely coupled with those below it, as when molecular properties emerge from atomic interactions or linguistic behavior from hominid intelligence. Living systems are loosely coupled with their physical environments, though tightly coupled with themselves. (Palombo, 1985, p. 124)

Persons with TS-OCD experience two kinds of coupling problems. Individuals with tics are too tightly coupled to the soma, anchored in the "motoric" realm of life, never transcending the body ego. Persons with obsessions are too tightly coupled to mental life, obsessively intellectualizing away the conflicts of the body in compartmentalized rituals. This is what is meant by *bifurcated* personality development. Dual selves exist side by side, each tightly coupled either to the body or the mind, but only loosely coupled with each other.

The challenge of treatment is to loosen the ticquer's coupling with somatic processes, the obsessive's coupling with cognitive processes, and to tighten the coupling between them; so that the ticquer's repetitive movements become accessible via cognitions and the obsessive's cognitive rituals become modulated by emotional input. This is similar to what clinicians do when they "integrate" the alternate selves of MPD patients.

This is not easy, because treatment techniques have multiple effects, rippling out into a labyrinth of feedback loops, thus making it difficult to know outcomes beforehand. As we've seen, no stimulus has a single, predictable effect. However if treatment is undertaken with an awareness of the interfacing complexity of the various reverberating loops, techniques can be refined and focused specifically on one subpart of the system. Just as a piano is tuned string by string—even while all strings vibrate in resonance to the one being manipulated—it may be possible to "tune" a person's TS-OCD bit by bit at a time; eventually achieving a balance in the personality that enables the person to function more comfortably and effectively.

PARADOX THEORY

Because the study of paradox has fascinated mathematicians and philosophers for centuries, a complete discussion is beyond the scope of this chapter. However, our understanding of TS-OCD will be enriched by a brief consideration of paradox. A classic paradoxical statement was made by Epimenides of Crete when he said, "All Cretans are liars." Because Epimenides was himself a Cretan, such a statement is paradoxical because it is true only if it is not true—that is, Epimenides is lying only if he is telling the truth and he is telling the truth only if he is lying. Paradox arises from the *self-reflexiveness* of the statement.

Logical Types and Levels of Language

Epimenides violates the central axiom of the Theory of Logical Types (Whitehead & Russell, 1910–1913, p. 37) which asserts that whatever involves all of a collection (class) cannot be one of the collection (member). In other words, a collection or class is a *higher order* than its members. The paradox can only be resolved by distinguishing two levels of language—the first-order language in which the problem itself is framed, and a second-order higher level using a *metalanguage* to talk *about* the problem. This enables one to break out of the self-reflexive oscillation characteristic of paradox.

Bateson (1972, p. 283) illustrates this by noting that the simplest form of change is motion—a change of position. However motion itself can change (by acceleration or deceleration) and this *change of change*, or *metachange*, must be studied at the next higher level of analysis. Proceeding even higher, one can speak of a change of acceleration—*change of change of change*, or *metametachange*. Following Bateson's line of reasoning, it can be seen that change always involves the next higher level of analysis and requires a new language. This holds true for the study of most phenomena—not just motion. Language, for example can be used to express many things (first level), but when linguists or semanticists want to speak *about* language itself, they have to move up to a higher level, and utilize a language *about* language (*metalanguage*).

Shifting to the Next Level

Watzlawick, Weakland, and Fisch (1974) utilize the analogy of driving a car to illustrate different levels of operation.

> The performance of the engine can be changed in two very different ways: either through the gas pedal (by increasing or decreasing the supply of fuel to the cylinders), or by shifting gears. Let us strain the analogy just a little and say that in each gear the car has a certain range of "behaviors" (i.e., of power output and consequently of speed, acceleration, climbing capacity, etc.) *Within* that range (i.e., that class of behaviors), appropriate use of the gas pedal will produce the desired change in performance. But if the required performance falls *outside* this range, the driver must shift gears to obtain the desired change. Gear-shifting is thus a phenomenon of a higher logical type than giving gas, and it would be patently nonsensical to talk about the mechanics of complex gears in the language of the thermodynamics of fuel supply. (p. 9)

Paradoxical Injunctions in the Development and Maintenance of TS-OCD

In daily life we encounter many injunctions that are structurally and logically similar to the classic paradoxes, and for that reason impossible to fulfill. The request to "Be spontaneous" is a case in point. To *demand* that a behavior be spontaneous—which can be so only if it occurs freely—creates an entrapping paradox. Likewise, instructing an insomniac to "relax and you'll soon be asleep," or a stutterer to "Forget that you stutter and stay calm while you speak," is paradoxical. As we've mentioned earlier, even the photographer who asks you to "Smile!" is paradoxically asking for the impossible, because a *genuine* smile is a spontaneous reflex that cannot be forced without being destroyed in the process.

In virtually all cases of TS-OCD there is a developmental history that includes numerous paradoxical injunctions of the "Be spontaneous" or "Don't think about the red monkey" variety. Ticquing children invariably arouse the interest and ire of parents, siblings, and teachers who instruct them in paradoxical ways as illustrated by the following conversation:

ADULT: Relax, why are you so tense?

CHILD: I'm O.K., I'm not tense.

ADULT: Then why do you keep fidgeting? If you would just relax and not fidget you'd be a lot happier, dear.

CHILD: I've tried, but I can't stop.

ADULT: Honey, you could if you tried harder!

CHILD: I've tried; I can't.

ADULT: I've asked you to relax—please do so. And quit arguing with me!

Such interactions attempt to solve the problem of ticquing at a *first-order* level. This is similar to what we've referred to as *symmetrical* interaction. Parent and child are locked into a head-to-head confrontation with neither being able to "shift up" to a higher level of analysis. Such interactions always tend to escalate.

Paradoxical Self Talk

Children *internalize* the injunctions they hear from parenting adults and later reverberate them as their own inner dialogues. This dialogue typically occurs between the two selves of the bifurcated personality. Typically the *somatic* self houses the powerful "Terry Tourette" while the weaker, underdeveloped self of the *mind* contains the impotent "Willy Willpower." These two selves argue, but the outcome is a forgone conclusion:

WILLY: Quit jerking.

TERRY: It feels *good* to jerk.

WILLY: But it gets on people's nerves—quit it!

TERRY: Try and make me!

WILLY: *Please* quit it.

TERRY: I won't and you can't make me. You've tried lots of times, and you know it doesn't work!

WILLY: Stop it . . . now!

TERRY: I won't.

Such internal arguments are always "won" by the somatic "Terry" whose dominance is a lived-with reality. The child might as well have instructed himself to "quit breathing!" In this mind–body dialogue, the body always wins. It's an upsetting reversal: "matter over mind."

Games Without End

Such conversations, whether with actual persons, or within one's mind, are always doomed to non-resolution, because they attempt first-order change. They stay within the domain of the automobile accelerator, never "shifting" up to the next level. The incessant recycling of such first-order loops has been referred to by Watzlawick, Beavin, and Jackson (1967, pp. 232–236) as a "Game Without End." Indeed all the repetitive manifestations of TS-OCD could be viewed as games without end, if one is clear that "game" doesn't necessarily mean "fun."

TREATMENT TECHNIQUES

Having developed a variety of theoretical perspectives to assist in clarifying the nature of TS-OCD, we will now suggest specific techniques for treating tics and obsessions once they are established. Specific interventions will be suggested for reversing compulsive patterns in both the somatic and social orbits. At the outset it needs to be understood that *any* technique that attempts to *directly* contain or stop ticquing is sure to fail. Worse, it is likely to *iatrogenically* intensify the behaviors. This occurs for two reasons.

First, tics are deeply entrenched in the *somatic orbit*. They are primal, comforting, proprioceptive loops only loosely coupled to the mental processes of the social orbit. They "do their own thing" in the somatic world of the neonate, with little connection to outside influences. Second, focusing on stopping tics *replicates* the early ambitendent struggles with parents, and for persons with TS-OCD this must always be resolved in the direction of autonomy. No matter how carefully presented or subtly framed, the request to control ticquing is primitively experienced as "Quit it!" and the obligatory answer is "No! I won't!" Such techniques reverberate symmetrical loops in the *social orbit* and escalate internal conflict. Finally, increased focus on tics by parents, peers, or professionals simultaneously increases the ticquer's focus, which is always iatrogenic.

As we've seen, the original conflict with parents is internalized as conflictual self-talk. Consequently attempts to intimidate, castigate, or cajole children into containing their tics is seldom successful. Unfortunately, the simplistic formulation: "I'm sure you could stop if only you tried harder!" has been the one most commonly tried for eliminating tics or obsessions. Ironically, the interventions meant to lessen problems have instead exacerbated them because conflict—even when it originates socially or cognitively—increases tension which accumulates in the somatic orbit and discharges through ticquing.

The treatment dilemma is how to gain access to the *somatic* orbit without increasing the tension pouring into it or reverberating the autonomy conflicts of the cognitive/social orbit. This is why a variety of techniques specifically targeted to either the somatic or cognitive/social orbits will be utilized.

TREATMENT TECHNIQUES IN THE COGNITIVE/SOCIAL ORBIT

Channel Switching Techniques

These techniques (which use TV as a metaphor) follow from our preceding discussion of paradox and involve *second-order* change. As we've already seen, attempting to amplify a person's "willpower" never succeeds because it's a *first-order* attempt at change, which iatrogenically increases the very problem that needs to be eliminated—excessive self-consciousness.

By the time somatic tics become apparent, the dyadic struggle between parents and toddler is usually internalized and "preconscious" (this means probably uncoupled from most mental processes, and certainly uncoupled from the somatic orbit). There simply is no *cognitive* access to the somatic orbit that does not simultaneously increase conflict, self-consciousness, shame, rage, and other negative emotions that have been paired with ticquing throughout previous development. Consequently *all* cognitive attempts to directly control ticquing are destined to fail.

To implement *channel switching* the therapist (or parent, teacher, etc.) suggests to the person that whenever they begin to think about ticqing, controlling ticquing, other people noticing their ticquing and so on, they immediately *switch* attention to something totally outside the realm of ticquing. What's being suggested is a *second-order* "shift" of gears to another realm of consciousness. Instead of paradoxical injunctions—"Relax!" or "Try not to think about your tics"—the therapist facilitates transcending such paradoxically entrapping directions and uses a variety of techniques to cognitively refocus the person.

Relaxation Imagery

This offers the person a way of switching from the tense, ticquing somatic orbit with its accompanying "Stop that!" self-talk—to the incompatible relaxation response. The therapist instructs the person:

Imagine yourself lying on a warm, sandy beach listening to the waves roll in. The sand is clean and white and a slight breeze keeps the warm day from being uncomfortably hot. As you lie there looking up at the blue sky a few puffy white clouds slowly drift across your vision. The squawk of sea gulls riding the air currents is faint in the distance and pleasant. Your arms and legs feel totally relaxed and heavy as you lie there with the blue sky above you and warm sand cradling your body. The waves gently rolling in have an almost hypnotic relaxing quality about them.

Imagery is individualized to create scenes that a person can quickly and naturally become immersed in. Developing an "imagery repertoire" of at least a half dozen scenes is desirable. Then when the person is confronted with tic-amplifying self consciousness, he or she can switch channels. Like systematic desensitization, or biofeedback training, these scenes are not magic; they are substitute cognitions which need to be practiced numerous times during sessions so they become relatively easy for the person to implement when needed.

Such refocusing bypasses recursive self-talk which otherwise becomes a "game without end." This technique facilitates "shifting gears" and transcending the "Yes you can!-No I can't!" loops which otherwise oscillate endlessly. This kind of *patient-initiated*, therapist-facilitated thinking significantly differs from previous futile efforts at "self-control." Here there is no effort to control or contain tics. This is a reeducating, reconditioning technique, designed to distract the person from becoming mired down in recursive self focus. It is *not* an attempt to increase self control. The therapist assists the person in letting go of direct confrontation with tics and refocusing on unrelated matters.

Intense Focus

Guided imagery is but one method of switching channels. Almost *anything* that effectively distracts the person by shifting cognitions away from the body or ticquing is worth trying. However, one must assiduously avoid becoming paradoxical in the efforts to refocus. Thus, substituting "Refocus!" for "Quit that!" is hardly therapeutic. The effort to therapeutically assist the person should be carried out in a laid-back, hang-loose manner by presenting all ideas tentatively and allowing the person to "own" them. Otherwise it will become just one more externally-imposed, ego-alien paradoxical injunction.

Traveling by public transportation is difficult for most ticquers. Here, surrounded by potential starers, persons with TS-OCD naturally focus on themselves. It may be helpful to practice intensely focusing on a specific element of the situation. For example, the ticquer riding a subway who becomes aware of people staring (which in turn increases self consciousness, which in turn increases ticquing, which in turn . . .) may find it useful to intensely focus on the advertisements along the side panels; carefully reading them one by one. Like the insomniac who counts sheep instead of trying to "make" himself fall asleep at night, this will shift the focus away from the futile effort of trying to "make" oneself not tic.

Stare-for-Stare

This consists of looking directly at the person staring (instead of lowering one's gaze, or looking away) and focusing on some aspect of their physiogamy that is interesting. One could, with an overweight person, stare at the abdominal region as if assessing precisely the shape and extent of fat distributed throughout the body. Or one could focus cognitive effort in estimating their weight (in ounces!). Such efforts might cathartically release some of the pent up anger that results from being the object of stares. The counter hostile calculating of weight of the staring obese person may be helpful to some ticquers.

It may not be necessary in all cases, to return a curious stare with an angry counter stare. The person with TS-OCD may be more comfortable with a nonhostile focus on something or someone else. One could, for example, estimate the number of freckles on the starer's face or nose, or calculate the length of their nose or the circumference (in centimeters) of their nostrils. If one is single, or has no moral compunctions against sexual encounters with strangers, various sexual fantasies could be utilized. Instead of estimating nose length, one could estimate breast characteristics, buttocks size and firmness, or how well someone were "hung." *Anything* that allows one to focus on *someone or something else instead of the self* will be of value for the person with TS-OCD.

Shame Activation Imagery

Similar to systematic desensitization, this technique avoids any attempt to "control" tics through will power. The therapist assists the person in recalling shame scenes. When such a scene is vividly in mind, the therapist coaches the person in talking soothingly to the "hurt child" within. Such self-talk brings the adult's competence and nurturance to bear on the child's shame and pain; effectively releasing some of the painful emotions that have been frozen in time. The following shows how the therapist might guide the patient through this.

> Therapist: Close your eyes and imagine the scene as vividly as you can. You're in kindergarten and it's only the first week of school. Several children are gathered near the merry-go-round laughing. You hadn't noticed

before but as you approach them the horrible truth suddenly hits you—
They're laughing at you! One of them—vigorously shaking her head—
shouts: Hey! Jello-Head! Jello-Head! Look at Jello-Head shaking! The
other kids—laughing and imitating you—take up the chant: "Jello-Head,
Jello-Head, Terry is a Jello-Head!" You wish you could die! No you wish
you could kill them. It's confusing. You'd like to withdraw into a hole and
hide, but you'd also like to choke them . . . choke them so they couldn't
talk and so their heads would quit shaking, quit making fun of you.

When the shame scene is graphically focused in the client's mind, accompanied by the appropriate emotions, the therapist allows the person
to remain "immersed" in the rage and shame for three to five minutes.
Then, soothing self talk is introduced:

> Now I want you to imagine that you pick up that angry, embarrassed
> little boy [girl] and rock him gently while you say: "I *know* it hurts honey.
> It hurts a *lot!* Here, let me hold you and rock you a little bit. I'm sorry
> those kids are so mean. They don't know any better. They don't have *any*
> idea how *much* it hurts to be teased! Don't worry about beating them up
> or hurting them. It's not necessary. Big Terry [client's name] is here to take
> care of you. Big Terry will run those kids off the playground. You won't
> have to do a thing. Just relax and forget about them.

This basic format—activating the shame, then soothing it—can be utilized with a variety of individualized scripts covering a number of different shame scenes.

Shame Desensitization Imagery

Another use of imagery is analogous to traditional systematic desensitization. The therapist begins by training the person in Jacobsonian relaxation, and assists in constructing a "shame hierarchy." Beginning
with the least-shaming scene and working up the hierarchy, therapist
and client work as a team to desensitize the impact of the shame in both
past and contemporary settings using the incompatible response of
muscle relaxation. This is analogous to the widely used technique for
desensitizing phobias. The intense experience of shame carries with it
the built-in phobia that it could happen again. Once having been humiliated on the basis of a personal characteristic (such as the shape of one's
nose), a person never feels totally safe again. There is a chronic—albeit
unconscious—phobia that the experience will occur again. Consequently techniques proven successful in treating phobias may be especially appropriate for dealing with shame-generating tics.

Imagery techniques are therapeutic because they assist in shifting
blocked out, painful scenes out of the nonverbal, somatic orbit into the

realm of actively-conscious cognitions. This is both cathartic and educational. It redirects repressed rage, and embarrassment—which otherwise increase muscle tension in the somatic orbit—into the more competent cognitive/social orbit. Raising these intense negative emotions to the level of conscious awareness provides a corrective emotional experience. Shame otherwise pulls awareness painfully inward, with a subsequent increase of negative self-consciousness. Reexperiencing and remastering shame scenes breaks up automatic, ritualized response chains *indirectly*, allowing the person *nonparadoxical* access to thoughts or feelings that might function to trigger tics or obsessions. Whether such scenes occurred amidst the vulnerabilities of childhood or took place more recently, imagery offers the opportunity to get on with life in the present, less angry and less handicapped by the shame-based baggage of the past.

There is intrinsic mastery built into reexperiencing childhood events with the psychological assets of an adult. This is why parenting can be such an enriching experience. As we reexperience with our children many of our own childhood conflicts, as adults, we experience a sense of competence and mastery that was never available to us as infants or children. It reminds me of remakes in the music industry. Old favorites are reworked with state-of-the-art electronics; the "cleaned-up" compact disk retains many of the desirable characteristics of the original recording, but with a lot of background static, and distracting distortion removed.

TREATMENT TECHNIQUES IN THE SOMATIC ORBIT

The general treatment principle in this orbit is to provide alternate activities that use the same muscle groups ordinarily employed in ticquing. The effect is both distracting and releasing. The inner tension is released in a nonticquing manner and the person's consciousness is distracted away from the self to an outside activity. A number of games will be suggested that parents can use with their children.

It is important to emphasize, however, the activity need not be in the form of a game. Any alternative movement that serves to release a particular child in nonticquing ways ought to be considered; and parents should feel free to creatively (but nonintrusively) try various alternatives with their children. For example, if a child compulsively chews his tongue or the side of his mouth, a natural alternative is to provide the child with unlimited supplies of sugarless gum—see if your dentist or grocer can get it for you by the case—and encourage him or her to chew it a pack at a time. This provides the child a "mouthful of alternatives," lessening the necessity of chewing one's tongue or the inside lining of one's mouth.

About Ovaries, Appendixes, and Tics

When health considerations necessitate removal of the ovaries, surgery is only part of the treatment. Hormones normally secreted by the ovaries must be medicinally replaced in what is known as ERT (estrogen replacement therapy). Such is not the case when an infected appendix is removed. After recovery from surgery, life goes on as usual. Removing tics is more like removing ovaries than appendixes; they function importantly for the person with TS-OCD. In planning treatment, the individual's needs should be carefully considered and alternative experiences planned to provide adequate "replacement gratification" for the lost tic.

Because tics are self-soothing for persons with TS-OCD they should be handled with care. The therapeutic way is to gently crowd out the tics with other comforting activities, not to suddenly snatch away the behavior—as some insensitive parents have been known to snatch a child's favorite blanket or teddy bear on the fifth birthday (or some other arbitrary date) announcing: "You're a big girl now, you don't need to carry that around any longer." The nurturing nipple—whether part of mother's breast or the warm bottle she provides—isn't removed from the infant without replacement. The pacifier—either commercially produced from soft rubber or graciously provided by Mother Nature in the form of an everpresent thumb—eases the infant's loss. Similarly tic removal shouldn't be attempted without "replacement therapy." Parents and therapists should think creatively and carefully about the kinds of substitute behaviors that will enable the person to endure the loss while simultaneously moving a rung higher on the soma-to-psyche ladder of development.

"Let's Pretend" Games for Kids and Their Parents

Channel-switching and imagery techniques prove most useful when working with motivated adolescents or adults. A number of additional considerations are necessary when working with children. It is essential to avoid alerting young children to their tics. *Anything* that increases the child's awareness of his or her "problems" is iatrogenic and should not be used. Furthermore, since switching and imagery techniques are pri-

marily cognitive, young children, functioning mostly in the somatic orbit, may find it difficult to perform these cognitive tasks. The "let's-pre-
tend" approach allows the child to function somatically but
non-repetitively. These games also reduce parental anxiety by providing
something to *do* when a child begins ticquing.

Parents (with the help of a therapist) can create a repertoire of "pretend games" to play whenever they notice their child ticquing and experience their anxiety increasing. The following are provided as proto-
types which can be easily expanded. With a bit of creativity the
possibilities are nearly limitless, and therapists should encourage parents to devise their own versions.

Airplane

Four-year-old Terry begins making grunting noises at the supper table,
his mother's face becomes noticeably tense, but she knows she
shouldn't say anything. Father lowers the tension in the following way:

> FATHER: Hey Terry, let's take a break from supper and play our airplane
> game.
>
> TERRY: Yeah!

Father then puts Terry on his shoulders, instructs him to "Put your
arms out like an airplane!" and they begin swooping around the house,
possibly outside, making smooth, engine-like purring noises. After a
pleasant airplane "ride" Terry is brought back to the table. Unbeknownst to him, his mind has been defocused from grunting, Mother
has had time to "get a grip" on her own worries during the interlude,
and it is likely that the grunting will be reduced in frequency and intensity during the remainder of the meal.

Choo Choo Train

Another variation might be to play choo choo train and engage the child
in making train-whistle sounds and choo-choo noises, while riding
around on Father's back.

Helicopter

Suppose that instead of grunting noises, Terry's tics included hitting his
elbows against his body or against the table. Then helicopter game,
which would require "flying" with both arms whirling above the head,
might be a good way to discharge tension in a nonspasmodic fashion.

Examples could be multiplied, but we will conclude by noting the general principle: whenever a child is ticquing parents may *casually* distract him or her with a game that gives the child opportunity for tension release utilizing similar muscle groups as those involved with the tic, but involving smooth—instead of explosive—movements. Such movements may be totally incompatible with the ticquing, or they may be "smooth-release" tic analogues. Thus instead of the eye-blinking tic, one could ask the child to slowly (and smoothly) close her eyes tighter and tighter, then to slowly relax and let them open. This kind of activity could be presented as part of a game, thus substituting the smooth discharge of tension instead of abrupt ticquing. Games should be carried out casually with *no mention* of the tics and only with the child's complete and enthusiastic cooperation.

Big Foot Stomp

Children tic more intensely when angry or stressed. We noted in our discussion of prevention that proscription of anger increases the risk of tics. When a child's ticquing seems related to pent-up anger an alternative way of letting off steam can sometimes be devised. One can pretend to be Big Foot stomping through the "forests" of the kitchen, dining room, and recreation room. Or Big Foot may want to stomp up a "mountain" (stairs) looking for enemies. Parents can play this pretend game either by becoming members of Big Foot's family or by playing the role of frightened enemy. In any event, there should be a lot of anger-releasing foot stamping.

Appropriately modulated expression of anger is an important coping technique at any age, and assisting the young child in developing a repertoire of socially acceptable anger-releasing behaviors is essential. This is important at all ages, but with adults therapy usually has a less somatic emphasis; assertiveness training may take the place of foot-stomping exercises. However both children and adults with TS-OCD benefit from vigorous exercise if it's not explosive in nature.

Swimming

It can be stated unequivocally: *Swimming lessons should be a part of every therapy program designed to reduce tics.* Water is a therapeutic medium both physically and psychologically. When submersed in water individuals are less likely to jerk. They may try to jerk, but water smoothes the movements—changing jerking into more fluid motion. And this motion occurs *without paradox*; there is no constraint and no external voice demanding that one "Quit it" or "Relax." Instead, the person is implicitly given permission to "Go ahead and thrash around—jerk, be spasmodic—if you like!" There is no subtle message proscribing "violent" activity, but water naturally softens the intensity of sudden movements. Consequently the swimming pool or lake functions as a "good mother"—*holding* the person without constraint, requiring movement to stay afloat.

Swimming lessons are essential for children with tics; they facilitate the development of basic strokes that enable them to swim laps as a "jerkless" way to relieve tension. Daily swimming of laps provides a person with tics a rare opportunity to be fully awake, fully conscious yet not jerking. Other "smooth" aerobic activities such as dancing, ice skating, bicycling, rowing, might be preferred by some and provide similar nonexplosive discharge opportunities. I personally prefer swimming because the medium is so "immersing" and the "holding" so complete, but any intense athletic activity provides a ticquer an alternate somatic channel and psychologically focuses awareness away from self-as-ticquer.

Massage and Related Somatic Techniques

The use of massage as an adjunct to psychotherapy has not received wide acceptance among mainstream psychologists. Massage "therapists" are often seen to exist on the fringes of acceptable practice—indeed sometimes on the edges of society, where in certain "health spas" the boundaries between massage and sexuality are purposefully liquidated. Sleaze rather than science is what comes to mind when most people think of massage.

Nevertheless, massage and other "body work" techniqes deserve careful study as a way of treating TS-OCD. They may provide another viable way of smoothing the sudden jump that takes place when a person tics. Such techniques resonate with the earliest needs for tactile contact, and replicate the good-enough mother's soothing of an angry or frightened infant via caressing. It seems logically sound to provide significant proprioceptive feedback of a nonspasmatic nature to children who have developed an "addiction" in this domain. It might be possible to "fade" from tics to massage, even instructing the child in how to carry out self-massage as a substitute for the self-soothing tics.

Singing or Other Music Lessons

It is interesting to note how many persons with TS naturally seem to gravitate toward sports and music. Darren plays saxophone, the DJ in

Iowa City plays sax, and Orrin Palmer plays guitar. Many of these persons find solace and relief in their instruments. As has already been discussed, singing—by providing resistance—is a smooth yet somewhat satisfying way of releasing tension in the somatic orbit.

Summary

It is crucial that therapists and parents explore nonmedicinal ways of reducing tics by offering their children satisfying alternative behaviors. Asking children to contain their tics is always iatrogenic, increasing self-consciousness and ultimately ending in defeat of willpower. The permission-giving, nonconstrictive quality of the activities discussed provide outlets for somatic tension and opportunities for cognitive learning.

Intuitively it seems that explosive sports such as boxing, racquetball, or karate would exacerbate symptoms while smooth sports such as swimming or biking would reduce them. However it is probably not so simple, as the following case illustrates.

KARATE KID

A story entitled "Brenner Kicks Back at Tourette Syndrome," appeared in the Morton Grove (Illinois) Champion newspaper, July 9, 1987:

> Darren Brenner bounds up the stairs after turning off the movie on the video cassette recorder and plops himself into a kitchen chair, where hours earlier he sat to devour his favorite food—pizza.
>
> The freckle-faced bundle of energy chats with a visitor and flashes a toothy grin, typical of any 11 year old.
>
> But Brenner is far from typical.
>
> Despite suffering a nightmarish neurological disorder for the past five years, Brenner won a USA Karate Federation (USAKF) regional title and has qualified for the national championships to be held Aug. 15–17 in Columbus Ohio.
>
> He suffers from Tourette syndrome, an incurable condition that afflicts between 50,000 and 1.2 million people, according to various experts.
>
> People with Tourette syndrome suffer from tics and muscle contractions they can neither predict nor control. Grunting, snorting, and shouting obscenities often overtake them with no warning or explanation. The humiliation can be devastating.

Yet in the nine months Brenner has been studying karate at the North Shore Martial Arts Academy (NSMAA) in Morton Grove, he has pushed aside the Tourette terror long enough to forge his own success story.

His crowning moment came last month at the USAKF Atlantic regional, where he won eight straight fights to capture the 11-year-old beginner Kumite (sparring) division title.

"It was a great, uplifting experience," says Jeff Kohn, chief instructor at the NSMAA. "This is the one story that stands out in all of my 15 years of teaching."

An orange belt, Brenner beat four purple belts (two classifications higher) on his way to the title.

I recently spent some time with Darren's father, Jenard ("Jerry"), who informed me that his son received the Karate black belt at the age of 14 (it's unusual for persons under 16 to even be allowed to take the test) and now is a national champion in Karate. He further described Darren:

> He's always been full of energy. Karate has allowed him to redirect a lot of this energy. He also plays the saxophone and piano. He still has head tics and some vocalizations, but he just goes from dawn to dusk. With Karate, jazz band, and other activities he keeps really busy—he *likes* it that way. No one forces him.

Jerry was insightful regarding his own expanding acceptance of Darren's behaviors:

> When he used to start coughing in a movie, I would say "Stop it!" Now I don't bug him anymore. I figure if you're in a room with him and it's bothering you, it's OK to get up and leave . . . but just remember the child has *no* escape. Also I think it's OK to feel resentment sometimes.

Diagnosed when he was six, Darren has never been on medications. Jerry is glad:

> We were very fortunate. We had the prescription and everything. But we were going on vacation the next day, so we decided to wait and see. He improved on vacation, so we never started him on his meds. At home he was always free to do it (tic). Sometimes it was very bad at home.

In a letter to me, Jerry elaborated his view:

> As I mentioned to you, enrolling Darren in Karate was not intended to replace drug treatment as a "cure" for the disorder. It just happened that through Karate, Darren has attained a better working control over his mind and body and this in some part may be responsible for the fact that

he has never had to be medicated. This is purely an observation, not based on any scientifically controlled study. I am only glad that it has had the effect on him that it has. I cannot predict if it would have the same effect on other children with Tourette Syndrome iven their own individual set of genetic and environmental influences.

I certainly would recommend it to anyone as long as it was taught by a competent instructor who had the ability to motivate with a balance of discipline and praise. Darren was lucky to have found such an instructor; an individual who really has his students' best interests at heart and truly loves kids and what he is doing.

As if to underscore his admiration for coach Jeff Kohn, he included a newspaper article about an eleven-year-old boy with cerebral palsy that Kohn had coached successfully to the level of yellow belt (the second rung on the karate ladder). The winning combination here seems to be kindness mixed with karate. The personal caring is likely as important as the exercise.

Commentary

Darren's story illustrates a number of points. Discussions of TS by "experts" as reflected in the media typically couch the condition in organic hopelessness. Discussions are permeated with phrases like "nightmarish neurological condition," "incurable condition," and "nothing to do with the mind." Parents, on the other hand, live some distance from the rarefied world of biochemical research and genetic theories of transmission. Much closer to the dirt and turf of the playground, they often modify the expert wisdom with parental practicality. Darren's case illustrates this. His parents decided to "wait and see" until after vacation, and fortunately for Darren his symptoms improved and he was never exposed to the mind-dulling effects of Haldol® . I seriously doubt he would currently be a national champion had he been treated with the "drug of choice."

More important than what they did *not* do, is what his parents *did* for Darren. Their provision of alternate channels for expressing his tensions is consistent with what is being suggested in the present context. Although these alternate channels have not totally eliminated his tics, they seem to have permitted him to achieve high levels of physical and social attainment. This was not done single-handedly by his parents. They fortuitously found a karate coach who functions like a psychologically trained "activities therapist." His work with other children who have special needs illustrates the depth and sensitivity of his understanding of children.

My guess is that all of this could have been accomplished by a sensitive swimming coach as well—possibly with even greater reduction in tics. Although my own belief is that "smooth" rather than "explosive" sports are most therapeutic, it would be easy to settle this issue with research. Children with tics could exercise "smoothly" or "explosively" on alternate days, and have a "blind" rater record their tic frequency for 15 minutes following exercise to see which kinds of activities reduced tics most. Until this research is carried out, however, parents should informally conduct their own research by noting which activities seem most therapeutic for their child.

In this chapter we've offered a number of suggestions for dealing with the "nitty gritty" problems encountered in the everyday lives of persons with TS-OCD. In the following chapter we will expand our focus to include a number of related problems such as stuttering, eating disorders, and spouse abuse.

Chapter 10

ADVANCED TREATMENT CONSIDERATIONS: CATASTROPHE THEORY IMPLICATIONS FOR TREATING EATING DISORDERS, TS-OCD, SPOUSE ASSAULT, AND STUTTERING

Imagery techniques, modulated expression of anger, music lessons, swimming, and other soothing exercises are relevant treatment methods. The current chapter will serve to broaden our discussion to include treatment of eating disorders, stuttering, and spouse abuse and, at the same time, continue to refine our thinking about TS-OCD.

MORE COMPLEX CATASTROPHE MODELS—THE BUTTERFLY

The *cusp* model we've been discussing is a three-dimensional figure with two control parameters and one behavior surface. Using comparable mathematics, it is possible to construct a catastrophe model with four control dimensions and two behavior surfaces. The result is a five-dimensional catastrophe with a "pocket" formed by the interpenetration of several surfaces. (See Figure 10.1.) This has been referred to as a *butterfly* catastrophe because of the shape of this pocket.

The reader may recall that seven catastrophe models have been math-

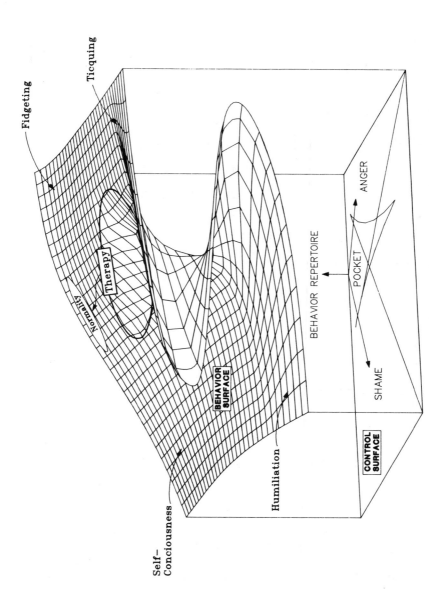

FIGURE 10.1 In the butterfly catastrophe, trimodality replaces bimodality, making possible compromise solutions. This is represented as a pocket between three cusps on the control surface. This translates into alternate behavior modes, eliminating the hysteresis of the cusp model. Psychotherapy can be seen as a way of building up the middle sheet of alternative behaviors, which allow movement between the top and bottom sheets without a sudden jump.

ematically derived—some even more complex than the butterfly. By expanding the dimensions of the control and behavior spaces, an infinite number of catastrophe models could be constructed. V. I. Arnold, a Russian mathematician, has classified them up to 25 dimensions. However, it defeats the purpose of modeling when the models become unwieldy due to complexity. Zeeman recognizes this and doesn't advocate utilization of extremely complex models:

> For models of phenomena in the real world, however, the seven described above are probably the most important because they are the only ones with a control space having no more than four dimensions. One particularly common class of processes, those determined by position in space and by time, cannot require a control space with more than four dimensions, since our world has only three spatial dimensions and one time dimension. (Zeeman, 1976, p. 79)

Of these seven models, we agree with Zeeman in utilizing the *cusp* and the *butterfly*: "Finally we come to the butterfly, which deserves more attention, because after the cusp, it is the most important catastrophe for the behavioural sciences" (Zeeman, 1977, p. 29).

The butterfly can be understood by first remembering that *bifurcated* behaviors evolve from *unimodal* behavior. (How bifurcation occurs as a developmental process is described in extensive detail earlier in the text; see Chapter 2.) Analogously *trimodality* emerges from *bimodality*. Zeeman writes: "Since trimodality often emerges out of bimodality, the natural way to analyse the butterfly is to regard it as an extension of the cusp" (1977, p. 29).

The Butterfly of Psychotherapy

This extension of the cusp represents the emergence of *compromise* solutions to conflicts. It is for this reason that the butterfly is a "natural" for modeling psychotherapy. As experienced clinicians know, much of the art of psychotherapy involves enabling the client to experience new alternatives—different ways of construing reality that get beyond the black-or-white, all-or-none alternatives we label "rigid" thinking. In a word, it is a movement from bimodal to trimodal thinking—from conflict to dialectic transcendence. And, if I may indulge in a bit of poetic license, the cusp—like the caterpillar—evolves into a butterfly, transcending the confines of the cocoon to fly freely in space.

Let us look more closely at how bimodality can be transformed into compromise. With the butterfly model, the bifurcation set lies in a four-dimensional control space and the behavior on a five-dimensional "surface." Since it is impossible to draw five-dimensional pictures, Zeeman illustrates the mathematical intricacies of the model using two- and three-dimensional cross sections (Zeeman, 1977, p. 31). However, even that is more complex than is necessary for the general reader, and we will rely on Figure 10.1 to summarize the ideas. Notice that on the behavior surface there are essentially three cusps that form a triangular "pocket." Above this pocket is a new triangular sheet connecting the top and bottom sheets, replacing the "unaccessible" hysteresis zone of the cusp model. This new sheet—representing a third behavior mode—allows for a compromise to emerge, bridging the bifurcation and making movement possible between the sheets without "sudden jumps."

ANOREXIA NERVOSA AND BULIMIA

Zeeman proposes that the bimodal fasting and gorging of severe anorexics is a cusp catastrophe. "The anorexic," he suggests "is caught in a hysteresis cycle, jumping catastrophically between two extremes, and she is denied access to the normal behavior in between" (1976, p. 80). Working closely with a British psychotherapist, J. Hevesi, who uses trance therapy in the treatment of anorexia, Zeeman concludes that the trance represents a "third state" of the limbic system, occurring in the inaccessible zone between gorging and purging. He believes that when the patient is fasting she views the world with anxiety and when she is gorging she feels overwhelmed by that world. During trance, however, her mind is free of food and planning how to avoid food, so reassurance is possible:

> Reassurance becomes the butterfly factor in the model. It creates the new sheet of the behavior surface, which lies between the other two sheets and which eventually gives access to the stable, normal region behind the cusp.
>   . . . the personality is fused into a complete whole again. When the patient awakens from this trance, she may speak of it as a "moment of rebirth," and she finds that she can eat again without fear of gorging. The trance has seemingly opened a pathway in the brain back to the more balanced limbic states, so that the patient regains access to normal behavior. Subsequent trance sessions reinforce that experience. (1976, pp. 80–82)

THE BUTTERFLY MODEL IN THE TREATMENT OF TS-OCD

By now the resemblance of anorexia to TS-OCD is no doubt obvious to the reader. As noted previously, the emotion of shame and the "jump" to explosively letting go and ticquing closely parallel the experience of the anorexic. Zeeman describes advanced cases of anorexia as follows:

> Now the anorexic is no longer trapped in a cycle of constant fasting but is caught in a hysteresis cycle, jumping from the bottom sheet to the top one and back again. In the words of a typical anorexic, the catastrophic jump from fasting to gorging takes place when she "lets go" and watches helplessly as the "monster within her" devours food for several hours, sometimes vomiting as well. The catastrophic return to fasting comes when exhaustion, disgust, and humiliation sweep over her, an experience that many anorexics call the "knockout." (1976, p. 81)

This cycle is precisely the cycle of ticquing but in slow motion. The ticquer is concerned with "not doing it" or going on a "diet" with respect to tics, and spends a fair amount of waking hours trying to inhibit or control tics. However, this resolve continually breaks down (usually in a matter of seconds for the typical ticquer as compared to minutes or hours for the anorexic), the person "lets go" and tics anyway. Ticquing is, of course, followed by shame, and the cycle is refueled. As we've shown before, the same kind of control–shame cycle occurs with obsessions. Consequently "butterfly" therapy seems relevant for TS-OCD.

There may be a number of ways of building up the "butterfly factor" or the middle sheet. Whatever mediates between extremes of humiliation and rage, repression and ticquing is worth trying. Many of the therapeutic suggestions of earlier chapters are designed to provide transcendent alternatives. Soothing exercise, soothing music lessons or performances, relaxation imagery, are ways in which the middle sheet can be somatically built up; and the cognitive technique of "switching channels" whenever one begins to become entrapped by paradoxical thoughts is a cognitive middle sheet.

Hypnosis

An overview of the work to date using hypnosis in the treatment of tics and other TS-OCD symptoms is provided by various clinicians (e.g., Turpin, 1983; Young, 1991; and Zahm, 1987). Results have been mixed, ranging from complete remission to temporary relief, to worsening of symptoms. It is hoped that when hypnosis is utilized in a way that is consistent with the paradigm developed in this book, more consistently positive results will be obtained. In the following discussion, the limitations of the current treatments will be considered and suggestions will be made to improve the efficiency of hypnotherapy.

Organic Paradigm Limits Expectations

Working within the traditional organic disease paradigm, most clinicians have been satisfied with lessening the intensity of tics or reducing the medication dosages. Typical statements read:

> In a consideration of treatment outcome, it is important to keep in mind that Tourette syndrome is a chronic neurological disorder . . . It may be unreasonable to anticipate total symptom cessation. The patient and his parents are best aided by frank discussion of the chronicity of T.S. and the limits of hypnotherapy outcome to avoid excessive expectations or unrealistic expectations of cure. (Zahm, 1987, p. 326)

Obviously one shouldn't unrealistically raise expectations for cure, but *in the clinician's own thinking*, it is important to be free of organically based limitations, otherwise creativity and enthusiasm may be attenuated for both the therapist and the client.

Direct Focus on Tics is Iatrogenic

As has been stated previously, direct attention to tics is *always* counterproductive. Hypnosis is useful because it allows a clinician indirect access to the patient's tics. Unfortunately this very feature of treatment is sometimes compromised when direct behavioral methods are utilized. For example, some studies have reported *increases* in ticquing as a result of massed practice, a behavioral technique designed to reduce tics by instructing patients to tic until exhausted. Treatments utilizing self-control techniques have typically resulted in short-lived improvements. Nonetheless, most clinicians still utilize such direct techniques, because they believe TS-OCD to be a straightforward neurological disorder, and tics to be neurological spasms. For example, Young discusses what he terms "a promising behavioral intervention" known as habit-reversal training, in which he attempts to teach a person to replace the tic with a competing muscle response. Young writes "The technique is based on the premise that tic behaviors are maintained by response chaining, *lack of awareness* of their occurrence, and excessive practice and social tolerance of the tics" (1991, p. 99, italics mine).

Not surprisingly this leads to a treatment approach that Young calls "hypnobehavioral treatment," in which discrimination and skills training are core components. He writes:

> A commonly described characteristic of people who have tics is that they tend to be *unaware of the type, frequency, and intensity of their tic behaviors.* The first step in phase 1 is to *increase the patient's awareness of ticquing and to help them to discriminate the tic from other motor behaviors.* This is accomplished in the following manner. . . (1991, p. 103, italics mine)

Such direct approaches, aimed at raising awareness of ticquing misses most of the important dynamic aspects of TS-OCD we have discussed in this book. Better treatment might include (a) hypnotherapy designed to heal the bifurcation of personality, (b) *indirect* (i.e., nonparadoxical) suggestions for how to relax, how to become less obsessed by thoughts or tics, or how to express intense emotions, or engage in self-soothing in ways other than ticquing.

Healing the Bifurcation

There exists quite a field of literature using hypnosis in the treatment of multiple personality disorder (MPD)—especially as it relates to "integrating" the multiples into a single personality. Such technique will likely prove useful in treating TS-OCD, inasmuch as this typically involves a "multiple" personality (of two). Although the sense of "two different persons" is perhaps not as great in TS-OCD as in MPD, the bifurcation does exist, and TS-OCD patients often refer to their experience in dual-personality terms. Saul Lubaroff, the DJ with coprolalia is typical:

> I call my Tourette's "Tony." I don't like Tony at all.

Michael Brooks, the man who received a leucotomy to control his TS-OCD, describes his bifurcated personality in the following words:

> It's a Jekyll and Hyde situation . . . which sometimes one half of the person wins and the other doesn't. (1990, p. 13)

"Blinking Billy" also experienced his personality as comprised of two components—Me and Not Me:

> The *Me* is bright, competent, highly trained, creative, funny, athletic, caring, and sensitive. The *Not Me* is tics, blinking, sniffing, snorting. I'm not well coordinated in volleyball, but when a tic keeps me from getting to

the ball, it's a tic, not *Me!* I like reading, but in the evening I can't hold my head still—it's not enjoyable. So when I avoid reading because of tics, that's *Not Me.* I deal with the tics, but they're not part of my self-concept.

The extensive experience of many clinicians using hypnosis to treat Multiple Personality Disorder (MPD) provides a fertile source of ideas that should be utilized in treating the dissociative aspects of TS-OCD.

Indirect Suggestion

As has been noted in numerous instances, attempts to directly contain, control, or direct tics are iatrogenic. Here is where modern hypnotic techniques, influenced by Milton Erickson's theories emphasizing *indirect* suggestion, seem especially well suited to working with TS-OCD.

Recall the story about the "red monkey," illustrating the paradoxical entrapment of trying "not to think" about something. Torem (1991) uses a "purple elephant" technique to make a similar point when working with eating disorders:

> This hypnotic session is followed by a discussion with the patient in which he or she learns to avoid self-entrapment using the principle of "don't think about the purple elephant." The patient is asked to engage in a thought exercise where he or she is asked not to think about a purple elephant. Most patients smile and report immediately that they pictured a nice, big, purple elephant. The patient is then told, "You see, people don't like to be told 'don't.' Your subconscious mind does not incorporate the word 'don't, and only hears, 'think about a purple elephant,' and then complies appropriately. The same thing happens when you say to yourself, 'don't binge,' or 'don't purge.' You are, in fact, giving yourself the suggestion to binge and to purge, and thus entrapping yourself in doing exactly what you're wishing to avoid. In this new approach, anytime you get the impulse to binge, purge, or use self-starvation, this is your signal to engage in a state of self-hypnosis, and to reaffirm your commitment and your vow to respect and protect your body for the rest of your life. (1991, p. 245)

HYPNOSIS FACILITATES TRANSITIONAL PHENOMENA

Recall that we earlier discussed how tics, like teddy bears and blankets, can function as transitional phenomena. Sanders (1987) sees hypnosis as a transitional phenomena occurring in an intermediate area of experience:

> In this arena of experience, one has the capacity to experience both external and internal reality in a blended manner. . . Winnicott clearly indicates that any object, thought or concept can become a transitional object—it need only be experienced in the intermediate area of experience. By this definition, an infant's babbling or humming can become a soothing intermediate area of experience as a transitional phenomena. Even adults can experience this intermediate mode of experience since the task of reality acceptance never ends and one needs to escape the strain of relating inner and outer reality. . . The transitional object and the transitional phenomena provide something very valuable: time out, a quiet, soothing place.
>
> In one sense, the concept of transitional object functions as a bridge between the inner and the outer, the imagined and the real, the soothing comfort of security and the fantasy of safety. The bridge is partially constructed from the primary tools of sensory motor channels, continuously providing stimulation from sensory organs: olfactory, kinesthetic, tactile, visual, thermal and body memories. (pp. 115–116)

Sanders then concludes by stating that "A hypnotic environment would facilitate the development of a transitional object experience" (p. 116).

From this discussion it can be seen why tics (transitional phenomena) are so resistant to extinction. Tics soothingly blend inner and external experience, and they are heavily anchored in kinesthetic, tactile, and other body memories. From a treatment perspective, it seems apparent that since hypnosis also operates in this transitional space, it is well suited to access tics whereas strictly cognitive or insight-oriented approaches might not "connect."

An Example

The following hypnotic narrative was developed for use with a man who sought treatment because of an intense head-jerking tic. It takes into account the dynamic aspects of ticquing by attending to the bifurcated personality, developing alternate modes of tic discharge (foot bending instead of head jerking), yet accomplishes this *indirectly*:

After an appropriate induction, using whatever method the clinician finds comfortable and the patient finds acceptable, the following narrative is used.

> Just feel the relaxation beginning in your head, and gradually expanding in a warm diffuse manner down into your neck, and then flowing into

your arms and shoulders. It's a nice warm comfortable feeling, just flowing down through your body. Think of it flowing right on down past your elbows into your forearms and right out the tips of your fingers. It's like a warm shower—a relaxation shower, but in addition to flowing over the outside of your body, this flows throughout your insides as well. Feel the relaxation moving down into your chest, your abdomen, and your pelvis. Now let the relaxation flow down through your legs, past your knees, into your ankles, and out your toes. Your entire body is relaxed, heavy, and comfortable. You can feel the relaxation move into all of your inner organs, right into each cell of each organ—totally, deeply relaxed.

Now that you're completely relaxed, your body feels heavy, your breathing is steady, and your muscles feel loose. I want you to imagine your favorite place. Where might that be? (e.g., "At the beach.") OK, you're at the beach. I want you to continue relaxing and noticing how good it feels to let your muscles go limp and your arms and legs to simply plop comfortably onto the warm sand. I want you to feel the sand as it is softly supporting your body. Feel the slight breeze as it comfortably sweeps across your face and body, keeping you comfortable in the warm sun. I want you to notice the sounds around you. The waves are gently lapping up onto the shore near you, and in the distance you can hear some sea gulls screeching, but it's so far away it doesn't startle you or bother you.

Now I want you to think of how good it feels lying on the sand totally relaxed with both parts of your personality in harmony. Notice how relaxed your neck and head feel and how you don't feel much like jerking. Unlike sometimes when the jerking part of you seems to fight with the other part of you that wants to keep control, or stop the jerking, you now find both sides of your personality in quiet, comfortable, relaxed harmony. Now there is no need for one part to fight or control another part, and there is no need for one part to prove it can tic if it wants to, rather both parts are in relaxed harmony, just enjoying "hanging out" together.

Now I want you to think about your head, and how relaxed it is and how as you are lying there, you don't feel a need to jerk your head or neck or to prove that you can move them. It's possible to just let your head and neck be totally relaxed. Sometimes, though, you may need to drain off a little tension, and instead of doing it with your head, we're going to open a "tension pipeline" to your right foot. This pipeline will pass from your head, down your neck over to the right side of your body, down your body past the right side of your stomach, farther down your right pelvis area, down your right leg, past your knee, down into your lower leg, past your ankle, and finally pooling the tension in your right foot. Now that the pipeline is complete, think of a little tension building in your head and neck area. Now instead of releasing by jerking your head or neck, let it flow down the pipeline. Let it flow down your right side, down your right leg, past your ankle into your right foot. Now when you feel the tension accumulating there, I want you to flex your toe upward—that's it, point it up at your face—hard—hold it tight—feel the tension. Now let it go. Let it completely relax. Notice how good it feels relaxed. Notice the contrast between tension and relaxation.

In this narrative, mending the bifurcation, transferring the tic, and general relaxation have been combined for illustrative purposes, and indeed can be combined in treatment. However, it is also possible to develop narratives that focus on just one of these aspects at a time. Clinical flexibility is of prime importance, and there is no absolute "right" or "wrong" way to go about this.

Summary

In the previous chapter we recognized that tics and obsessions have much in common—are "topological equivalents." In the current chapter we've examined in detail the many subtle nuances that occur within this broad range of similarity. We've also seen parallels between MPD and TS-OCD. Catastrophe Theory has refined our understanding and made possible a more precise focus. The *cusp* model has been relatively easy to comprehend and is similar to the more complex *butterfly* model, which proves helpful in devising treatment strategies.

All treatments—the "commonsense" variety as well as hypnotic trance inductions—seek to develop alternative behaviors that bridge the "jump" between the lower and upper sheets of the behavior surface. Any ethical technique that shows promise of "bridging" the "jump," by providing access to intermediate behaviors ought to be seriously considered. Various techniques that seek to build up this "middle sheet" could be employed in complementary fashion.

One could reasonably treat a single child by

1. showing films in the classroom to increase understanding of tics and reduce ridicule.
2. enrolling him or her in swimming lessons.
3. enrolling him or her in singing, saxophone, or other music lessons.
4. facilitating the open and appropriate expression of anger through discussion and "stomping" games if necessary.
5. practicing relaxation imagery (self-hypnosis. during a "quiet time" each day.
6. utilizing the skills of a reputable hypnotherapist trained in working with MPD or familiar with the applications of hypnosis to TS-OCD.

7. etc.! All of this and more, could be carried out *without any specific focus on tics, or mention of self-control*.

SPOUSE ASSAULT—WHEN THE SHAME-RAGE CYCLE STRIKES AT HOME

Spouse assault is an excellent candidate for analysis using Catastrophe Theory (CT) because of the "sudden jump" quality of abuse. (See Figure 10.2.) Clinicians working with assaulters typically hear: "We'd been arguing for awhile and then *something snapped*! or, "I saw her talking to this guy at the party and *I lost it.*" Such narratives are consistent with the CT cycle of gradual buildup, sudden jump, and brief return to equilibrium. Additionally, the actual abusive behavior occurs in the *inaccessible zone*, where no middle sheet exists prior to therapy:

> The incident that led to his being in the [wife assaulter's] group occurred at his wife's office party: about 30 people were drinking and chatting when, according to Robert, his wife disappeared (i.e., he could not find her in a large, unfamiliar house). After 10 to 15 minutes he did see her and insisted that they leave the party. He recalled feeling nothing at this point. They drove home, she went to bed, and he began to watch television. His next memory was of seeing her lying in a pool of blood and realizing that he had severely beaten her. He called relatives and the police. (Dutton, 1988, p. 34)

Unless one dismisses such narratives as "rationalization" or "defensive forgetting" they seem puzzling to the ordinary person. Why would a man severely beat his wife and not even be aware he was doing it? While this defies ordinary logic, it is remarkably consistent with the Catastrophe Theory's hysteresis cycle. Intense anger leads to severe battering, with more complete "inaccessibility" (forgetting) compensatorily taking place. The shame following such episodes would be of immense proportions.

In this discussion we employ the generic term *spouse assault*, rather than *wife abuse*, because of the surprising finding from the U.S. national survey (Straus, Gelles, & Steinmetz, 1980; Straus, 1980) that among those responsible for violence within marriage, approximately half are males and half females. The annual incidence of violence by husbands was only negligibly higher: 12.1 per 100 husbands compared to 11.6 per 100 wives. Straus summarized the findings as follows:

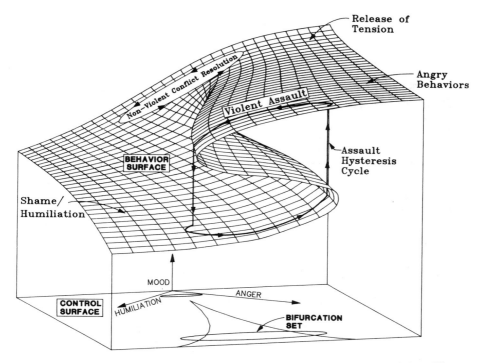

FIGURE 10.2 Spouse assault is shown as a cusp catastrophe in which humiliation and anger are conflicting moods on the control surface resulting in assault on the behavior surface. Likelihood of assault increases when shame or anger intensify. As the control point crosses the cusp, the mood regularly—but catastrophically—changes from shame to anger, suddenly reversing the emotional states as well as the power relationships in the dyad. When one spouse violently assaults the other he/she feels powerful and in control; but soon after the assault this mood reverts to shame and humiliation. With the passage of time, the cycle moves toward the front edge of the behavior surface, making nonviolent resolution of conflict less probable and the repetition of the abuse cycle more likely.

Contrary to our original expectations, the wives in this sample maintain their rough equality with respect to violence, irrespective of whether one measures it by incidence rate, mutuality of violence, degree of severity of the violent act, or prevalence of violence at each level of severity. (1980, pp. 685–686)

Numerous formulations and discussions have been proposed to explain domestic violence. Although valuable concepts are contained in the diverse theories, the current discussion will be limited to applying CT to assaultive behavior.

Abandonment or Engulfment—Alterations of the Optimal Zone of Psychological Intimacy

Interpersonal distance during conversation fluctuates dynamically and each person has an *optimal zone* they attempt to maintain (Patterson, 1976). Similarly, psychological intimacy exists in an optimal zone and *invasions* of this zone trigger fears of *engulfment*, while *evasions* arouse *abandonment* anxiety. This constantly shifting intimacy is carefully monitored by most spouses—possibly *too* carefully in the case of assaultive partners. In such assault-prone persons rapid changes in intimacy may trigger violent behavior.

Engulfment Anxieties May Trigger Assault

Pollack and Gilligan (1982, p. 40) utilized Thematic Apperception Test stories and found that fear of intimacy is a predominantly male anxiety, and that males perceiving intimacy in relationships to be dangerously engulfing may respond with violence. Dutton suggests that:

> Affective reactions to engulfment may vary but probably carry an admixture of anxiety and resentment, along with a sense of guilt. When coupled with a lack of verbal assertiveness to extricate oneself from engulfment, the probability of verbal or physical abuse may increase. (1988, p. 41)

This seems similar to the territorial behavior of certain tropical fishes that nest on coral reefs. Zeeman suggests that"

> The parameters controlling aggression might in this case be the size of an invading fish and proximity to the nest. The behavior is once again described by a cusp catastrophe. A fish foraging far from the nest would flee on meeting a larger adversary; once it reached the "defense" perimeter of its own territory, however, its attitude would suddenly change and it would turn to defend its nest. Conversely, if the fish were threatened in its nest, it would chase the invader, but only until it reached the "attack" perimeter of its own territory, where it would abandon the chase and return to its nest. (1976, p. 69)

The distance from the nest at which such behavior changes suddenly occur is determined by the bifurcation set. Because of the characteristics of the cusp, the CT model predicts that the "defense" perimeter is smaller than the "attack" perimeter. Furthermore, the dimensions of both perimeters depend on the size of the adversary, with a larger assailant allowed to approach more closely before defenders would be provoked to fight. This model is consistent with field observations, where, in the case of mated pairs of territorial fish, the partner nearest the nest offers the most forceful resistance. This is also consistent with the concept that if a spouse feels personal "territory" is being invaded, engulfment fears might—as a desperate last resort—erupt into violence against the "invading" spouse.

Abandonment Anxieties May Trigger Assault

The neonate's earliest negative emotions are likely centered around issues of abandonment—not shame. The "fixed-face" experiments (Beebe & Stern, 1977) suggest that even six-week-old neonates become drastically distressed when mother's face remains expressionless—a kind of intimacy-distancing maneuver. When parents of toddlers fail to respond to them emotionally, these toddlers will angrily *demand* attention by hitting, pulling, tugging, or otherwise engaging the mother in what Mahler et al. (1975) term "coercive refueling."

This is not unlike what seems to drive some assaultive spouses to their actions. Ironically the abandonment panic is exacerbated by their own assaultive behavior. Such persons often lack verbal skills in conflict resolution and the futility of trying to coerce love from a frightened or angry mate increases the abandonment panic and the probability of violence. Jealously is often mentioned by victims as the issue that incited the assault. Thus, a sense of helplessness or futility in managing psychological intimacy with one's spouse increases the likelihood of violent behaviors.

CASE EXAMPLE: ANGER CATASTROPHES AT HOME

Dan came into treatment on a court order, having been convicted of assault. He was articulate and intelligent, if a little disorganized. The incident that led to his being in the group occurred when Dan was phoning a movie theater to find out when a film started. His wife called to him from another room and he somewhat curtly told her to be quiet because he couldn't hear the telephone announcement. His wife became enraged and began screaming, smashing furniture, striking Dan, and verbally berating him. The color in her face turned to purple. Dan tried to leave but his wife threatened to follow him and publicly embarrass him and to kill herself.

After five hours of abuse, Dan "lost it" and struck his wife. She called the police.

Dan's wife had been sexually and physically abused by her stepfather and would fly into rage states when she felt dismissed or neglected. She promised to seek treatment after these episodes were over but subsequently reneged. Dan was strongly attached to her but felt powerless to either change or leave her. (Dutton, 1988, pp. 34–35)

This case dramatically illustrates both engulfment and abandonment anxieties occurring simultaneously in these spouses. Dan's anger suddenly "jumped" to abuse, following his wife's persistent attempts to *intrude* into his "space." For her part, she felt psychologically *abandoned* by his curt manner when he was trying to listen to the phone recording.

Similarities Between CT and Neal Miller's Approach-Avoidance Formulations

The similarities between Miller's classic approach-avoidance formulations and CT are worth noting. In the current discussion, for example, Miller would likely utilize a diagram of approach and avoidance gradients (e.g., 1959, p. 208) to illustrate that with only a weak avoidance tendency, Dan's wife would not experience fear until she approached him quite closely—too closely. This could be understood as a normal part of marital familiarity, exacerbated by the fact that she had gotten "used to" seeing a raging man (her stepfather) as a child. Miller might then suggest that Dan's wife was displacing her conflicted rage/fear attitudes regarding her stepfather onto her husband. In keeping with the theory, she would cease approaching him and abruptly shift to avoidance behavior only when her husband would *increasingly appear much like her stepfather* (which would occur only when he started becoming violent, at which time it was probably too late to withdraw).

This has been thoroughly discussed by Miller (1959, p. 208) and I mention his theory only to show the consistencies between approach-avoidance formulations and CT. Although this is of some historical interest, I find CT more mathematically sophisticated, heuristically rich, and clinically applicable.

Shame—A Neglected Construct

The primary difference between my CT-based formulation and other writings in the field of spouse abuse, involves my emphasis on the centrality of shame.

Like most behavior cycles, assaultive behavior begins gradually—with the first incident often characterized by a relative lack of severity. This is why abused spouses seldom leave the situation immediately. Negative feelings of self-worth develop in response to continued assault (Porter, 1983; Rounsaville, 1978), making it even more difficult for the assaulted spouse to leave the situation for fear they could not make it on their own and would not be attractive to anyone else. I will forego further discussion of the social forces keeping couples enmeshed in abusive relationships, choosing to focus instead on the catastrophe cycle itself.

Treatment Dilemma—Blame Induction or Shame Reduction

Catastrophe theory suggests treatment alternatives quite different from those currently employed in the field. There seems to be a consensus—albeit based on widely differing perspectives—that because male assaulters rationalize their violence they need to be confronted with the seriousness of such vicious behavior and urged to control their brutality. Some come to this perspective via the women's movement and a conviction that males have ravished and violated females for centuries and this must stop. They agree in spirit with John Stuart Mill's observation: "How vast is the number of men, in any great country, who are a little higher than brutes. . ." (1869, p. 62). Others, writing from a more dispassionate social psychological perspective nonetheless come to a similar treatment paradigm. Dutton, for example discusses some of the cognitive mechanisms utilized by assaulters to "dissociate" consequences from the behavior. These include displacing responsibility through such methods as euphemistic labelling, palliative comparisons, and ignoring consequences to the victim. He then suggests: "A major objective of treatment is to confront and alter these forms of neutralization of self-punishment" (1988, p. 60).

Notice that if such treatment is successful the net effect will be to *increase* self-punishment! A curious outcome at best. Treatment manuals (e.g., Ganley, 1981) often provide explicit directions for therapists to confront clients' use of various forms of neutralization of self-punishment. Deriving in large part from the famous social psychological experiments of Milgram (1974) and others showing that aggressors behave less punitively when they see and hear the victim suffering, the attempt is to increase the assaulters's awareness by facilitating self-blame.

Thus, whether writing from a social psychological perspective or from the women's movement viewpoint, there is consensus regarding the necessity of increasing the assaulter's self-blame. This seems flawed in two ways. First if the problem is really one of *spouse* (not only *wife*) abuse, then viewing male assaulters as misogynistic monsters transforms "treatment" into an acting out of feminist or societal anger against males. Second, in 20 years of clinical practice I have never seen self-blame to be ameliorative. "Owning" one's behavior—taking responsibility for consequences that ensue as a result of one's actions is quite a different thing from *blaming* oneself.

Figure 10.2 illustrates that one of the driving forces leading to assaultive catastrophes is *shame*. CT predicts that increasing shame—even when construed as therapeutic "altering of the neutralization of self-blame"—will exacerbate assault by pushing the person forward and to the right on the "shame sheet." When a person with proclivity to violence finds himself or herself in such a location, the probabilities for a violent catastrophe are quite high.

Toch (1969) studied a population of assault-prone individuals and found that men were more likely to respond with violence to humiliating affronts to reputation or manly status than to physical pain. High sensitivity to perceived devaluation (perhaps because of chronically high levels of already existing shame) is characteristic of wife assaulters. The remedy for this is *less*, not more shame.

Treatment consistent with CT would include building up the middle sheet—the butterfly factor, with alternatives to violence. In a manner analogous to working with TS-OCD clients, the therapist could help the person to develop a "talking-out-my-anger" repertoire of responses to replace the existent "acting-out-my-anger" catastrophe. It's possible to help such persons *without increasing their self-blame or shame*.

CT also provides a way of understanding the ubiquitous finding that abusive spouses remain interlocked with each other in spite of the often dire consequences for the assaulted. Walker (1979) interviewed over 120 battered women and described a cyclical pattern occurring in three phases: (1) During the initial phase tension *gradually builds* up, (2) during the second phase an *explosive battering* incident occurs, (3) followed by a period of *calm*, loving respite. Notice how well this coincides with the basic patterns of CT. To extend this analysis to the couple as a unit, we need only to note the complementarity of each spouse's experience. Walker discusses this complementarity, and suggests that a battered woman's psychological reaction in each of the three phases "bind a battered woman to her batterer just as strongly as 'miracle glue' binds inanimate substances" (1979, p. xvi).

Leaving behind such emotionally laden words as "batterer" and "battered," let us briefly analyze these intertwined interactions as complementary CT cycles. The assaulting spouse experiences a gradual buildup of shame-based anger that suddenly erupts into violent attack. The assault releases pent-up anger and briefly produces calm. This calm rapidly turns to shame as the damage is assessed, leaving the assailant penitent and remorseful. The assaulted spouse experiences the steady buildup of the mate's anger with growing concern, but fear-based attempts to placate the anger only exacerbate the imminent attack. When the assault occurs, the spouse on the receiving end of the violence experiences immediate shame, humiliation, and helplessness as compared to the assaulter's "burst" of relief and sense of power.

During the calm that follows the violence the assaultive spouse becomes increasingly ashamed, embarrassed, and powerless—especially if the mate presses charges. The victimized spouse gradually grows to feel more powerful. This is reinforced by the (temporarily) contrite, loving, and affectionate behavior displayed by the now-embarrassed mate. Walker describes this reversal of the power relationship as experienced by assaulted women in the hospital:

> Within a few days they went from being lonely, angry, frightened, and hurt to being happy, confident, and loving. . . . These women were thoroughly convinced of their desire to stop being victims, until the batterer arrived. I always knew when a woman's husband had made contact with her by the profusion of flowers, candy, cards and other gifts in her hospital room. (1979, p. 66)

Dutton elaborates further:

> The batterer throws himself on his victim's mercy, reversing the power relationship between them dramatically. He places his fate in her hands; he will be destroyed—lost—if she doesn't rescue him by returning to the relationship. (1988, p. 111)

Typically this pleading is reinforced with promises to change, and behavior that makes such promises believable.

> When a woman finally leaves an abusive relationship, her immediate fears may begin to subside and her hidden attachment to her abuser will begin to manifest itself. At this particular point in time, the woman is emotionally drained and vulnerable. At these times in the past the husband has been present, contrite, and (temporarily) loving and affectionate. As the fear subsides and the needs fulfilled by her husband increase, an equilibrium point is reached where the woman *suddenly* and *impulsively* decides to return. (Dutton, 1988, p. 111, italics mine)

In summary I've suggested that CT offers an alternative to current formulations of spouse abuse. The watershed difference is in how to relate to shame. Many therapists currently seek to increase self-blame, but if the driving forces in Figure 10.2 are correctly modeled, a major thrust of therapy ought to be the *reduction* of shame. In cases where engulfment or abandonment anxieties trigger violence, such fears must be addressed in treatment. When therapy decreases shame and anxiety while building in verbal techniques of conflict resolution and anger management, conflict will be resolved at the "back edge" of the behavior sheet, significantly reducing the probabilities of violence as a cusp catastrophe.

Although this topic may seem far removed from TS-OCD, it has been my purpose to illustrate the applicability of CT for a variety of "sudden-jump" problems. The explosive nature of spouse assault, combined with verbal reports by assaulters that "something snapped" or "suddenly I lost it," make it an obvious candidate for CT analysis. The more subtle aspects of the dual cycles is sometimes lost when they are not seen in tandem. For example the fact that an assaulted woman *suddenly* decides to return to her violent husband, is just as much a catastrophe as the original assault. Finally, whether shame amplification or reduction is most effective is an empirical question, one which ought to be investigated experimentally. Additionally, other techniques mentioned earlier for building up the middle sheet—the butterfly factor—could be tried with assault-prone persons. Hypnosis, desensitization of abandonment or engulfment anxieties, are all viable treatment possibilities. CT provides heuristic and theoretical impetus for carrying out this important research.

STUTTERING—A TIC-OF-THE-TONGUE CATASTROPHE

By now the reader will likely anticipate our analysis of stuttering. The similarities between ticquing and stuttering are so numerous and so obvious that stuttering can be seen as a tic of the tongue, or more generally, of the vocal apparatus. As a shame generator, it is only slightly less pervasive than ticquing, since the stutterer can take refuge in silence— an option not available to the ticquer. Whenever speaking occurs, however, stuttering—like ticquing—generates enormous amounts of shame and compensatory anger. Over the childhood and adolescent years, stutterers develop deeply bifurcated personalities differing little from ticquers. Like tics, stuttering occurs in bursts of speech—indeed it is these bursts that characterize stuttering as opposed to smooth, fluent speaking. We will utilize CT to enhance our understanding of stuttering, but first a brief survey of some developmental issues.

Developmental Psychodynamic Perspectives

Traditional psychoanalysts overemphasized the importance of biological development, implying that "anatomy is destiny." Combined with their emphasis on psychosexual development, everything seemed to have sexual overtones. While little girls experienced "penis envy," four-year-old boys wanted to "make it" with Mommy, but were held at bay by fear of castration by Daddy. And while worry about losing the "valued organ" was ever on the little boy's mind, his sister was concerned about why she'd never had one in the first place! The average person, unable to understand the abstract and symbolic qualities of many of these conceptions found all the "sex talk," absurd and suggested the "Emperor has no clothes!" More recent analysts has deemphasized biological drive theory and placed more emphasis—I think appropriately—on the development of self and on the functioning of ego (thought) processes. Let us look briefly at developmental issues surrounding stuttering from the analytic perspective.

Stuttering as Oral Gratification

Classical analytic theorizing, marginally convincing when it was first proposed, finds even fewer adherents today. When Coriat (1932), for example, referred to stuttering as "oral masturbation," many found it difficult to consider such formulations seriously. Nonetheless, there is a general notion implicit in the early analytic writings that deserves mention—*gratification*. Stuttering, like ticquing, feels soothing, and in this regard Coriat was not totally off base. He believed that stuttering consists essentially of a persistence into adult life of infantile nursing activities, and developed the concept of the "illusory nipple." In the rhythmic qualities of nursing, he saw the root of rhythmic speech fluctuations, and in classical analytic fashion described stuttering as "oral masturbation."

Stuttering as Developmental Family Dynamics

Glauber suggests that stuttering occurs in a family where the mother communicates mixed messages to the child: "I have been struck by the strength of the tie to a mother who is anxious and ambivalent, who weans even while she nurses" (1982, p. 4).

While we might disagree with the classical analysts' biological-sexual emphases, Glauber, along with most contemporary theorists, correctly sees the parent–child relation and the family milieu as crucial influences in psychological development. Notice how analogous the developmental issues of ticquing and stuttering are. Speech is *obviously* communicational, but as we've pointed out earlier, so are the expressions of TS-OCD. Both originate in the early months of life when needs are primitive and means of fulfilling them archaic.

> The child endows words and thoughts with a magical omnipotence having the power to charm people and even fate itself to do his bidding. Words and thoughts become magical gestures for the attainment of a multiplicity of needs, hostile and libidinal, as well as destructive reactions to frustration. (Glauber, 1982, p. 5)

The reader may transcend the concrete graphics of "anal period" or "anal products" to understand that what is being designated is an early developmental period when autonomy and conflict first begin to emerge—often around issues of toilet training. Then the following observations overlap with previous considerations regarding tics—especially coprolalia:

> A very important meaning of speech stems from a later, anal, period of development. Here, words are equatable with dangerous anal products which . . . must be held back or, like any dangerous tool, handled very cautiously. In this context belong obscene words and oaths . . . When conflicts over such acts or fantasies are projected upon the articulatory apparatus, stuttering may result. (Glauber, 1982, p. 7)
>
> Psychoanalysis of stutterers reveals the anal-sadistic universe of wishes as the basis of the symptom . . . Speaking means, first, the utterance of obscene, especially anal, words and, second, an aggressive act directed against the listener. . . . "Words can kill," and stutterers are persons who unconsciously think it necessary to use so dangerous a weapon with care. (Fenichel, 1945, p. 312)

Soothing, Ambivalence, and Autonomy

In both these passages we see elements that are dynamically similar to the manifestations of TS-OCD. The earliest roots are found in the infant's self-soothing and the toddler's ambivalence and autonomy. The adult "echoes" the infant in attempts to soothe the self through ticquing or stuttering. Similarly the toddler is "echoed" in the ambivalence and autonomous anger of the adult stutterer. For example, a common problem encountered by persons with speech catastrophes is that their stuttering makes others uncomfortable. This is due to the unconscious hostility embedded in the symptom. There is a mixture of both anger and humiliation contained in the symptom. The stutterer keeps the "audience" (of one or more persons) on edge by making them wait during the "tongue ticquing." In the process he or she is both powerful and powerless—powerful in dominating others and making them wait, powerless in compulsively needing to do so.

Freud Treats a Stutterer

Interesting in this regard is Freud's classic case of Frau Emmy von N.; so far as we know, the only case Freud discussed in which stuttering played an important role. Of most interest to the current discussion is the fact that she experienced facial and neck tics as well as a group of speech disturbances that included a tic-like clacking sound, involuntary repeating of her own name, and a ritualistic repetition of "Keep still! Don't say anything! Don't touch me!" Freud paid considerable attention to the stutter and the clacking, describing the latter as a curious sound that defied imitation, but which, colleagues "with sporting experience" informed him, sounded like the call of a woodcock—a ticking sound ending with a pop and a hiss.

At times Freud referred only to the clacking as a tic, and at other times to both speech symptoms—the stuttering and clacking—as tics. In the course of treatment of all patients, Freud repeatedly inquired into the onset of symptoms. When patients couldn't recall a fact, Freud sometimes utilized hypnosis to facilitate memory. In the case of Frau Emmy, she remembered—with great agitation:

> How the horses bolted once with the children in the carriage; and how another time I was driving through the forest with the children in a thunderstorm and a tree just in front of the horses was struck by lightning and the horses shied, and I thought: "You must keep quite still now, or your screaming will frighten the horses even more and the coachman won't be able to hold them in at all." It came from that moment. (Breuer & Freud, p. 58)

Apparently her stutter began immediately after the first such occasion, disappeared shortly afterward, and then recurred following the second similar occasion.

Freud stated that the patient's clacking sound went back, like the stutter, to similar precipitating causes, beginning ". . . at a time when she was sitting by the bedside of her younger daughter who was very ill, and had wanted to keep absolutely quiet" (Breuer & Freud, p. 54).

The precipitating cause of both the stutter and the clacking were Frau Emmy's fear of uttering a sound or making a noise. In one instance the sound might have caused horses to run wild, in another the wakening of a sick child. In both instances the common element was that a child might be harmed or killed by sound or noises. This then became the central conflict—with the making of noise taking on unnaturally dangerous connotations. More importantly, this became the basis for the *paradoxical* loop which continued to drive the cycle long after the actual danger was past—that is, trying to "keep quite still," failing to keep still, worrying more about keeping still, and still failing, formed the core loop that kept the stuttering and clacking catastrophe fueled.

Automatic Speech Is Best

Glauber (1982, p. 149) described stuttering and tics as *dysautomatization* of preconscious ego functioning, a view consistent with our previous discussions. Viewing mental functioning in the Freudian tripartite fashion of unconscious, preconscious, and conscious, Glauber writes: "In the presence of dysautomatization, however, the balance between the three is disturbed." He continues by analyzing the developmental roots of the disorder:

> This viewpoint emphasizes a unique fact that stuttering emerges while speech in its advanced form—the automatic form—is still in the process of being mastered. Speech, like other ego functions in their developments, commences as narcissistic play, then progresses by playful conscious imitation and unconscious identification toward utilitarian aims beyond play (meaningful verbalization) involving objects and object relations . . . Finally, the process operates as an automatism, that is to say, the transformation from thoughts to words and the supervisory tasks of monitoring and feedback of sound and fluency take place preconsciously. . . .
>
> The normal developmental pattern of the automatism, then, is: first, simple, smooth automatic expression of lalling and echolalia (unconscious, or id); then, less fluent, halting imitation (conscious, or conscious ego); finally effortless, fluent, most efficient expression (preconscious, preconscious ego). The essence of the pathologic formation is the repetitive intrusion of some attempts at conscious monitoring in a process that has already developed to the more efficient phase of automatic functioning. . . (Glauber, pp. 150–151, 155)

Stuttering Becomes Functionally Autonomous and Overdetermined

Like ticquing, stuttering soon becomes functionally autonomous—separated from the etiologic roots, it continues to generate shame, anger, and soothing. It often becomes what psychoanalysts term a *monosymptomatic* disorder—a way of coping where one central symptom subsumes a variety of conflict areas. The stuttering becomes "overdetermined,"—a kind of central clearing house for nearly all the stresses experienced by the person. Whereas originally stuttering was tied closely to speech and anxieties about conversation, in the adult it is triggered by many different stimuli, most having no relationship to the speech mechanism whatsoever. Conversely, although patients suffer speech problems because of hyperconsciousness, such over-emphasis on conscious control is often seen in a wide variety of other areas.

Stutterers Have Bifurcated Personalities

After considering the maladaptive aspects of their functioning, Glauber discusses what we have termed bifurcated personality development:

> The addresser, the self, is split into two self-representations. The one representation, that of a stutterer, is regarded as damaged, not merely partially but in a total sense . . . the other, the compensatory self, more deeply repressed, is that of a great Demosthenes-like orator. It is as if the pluses and minuses of the function, and now the total personality identified with it, *have been split asunder, defused, and polarized.* (1982, p. 156, italics mine)

Psychoanalysis and catastrophe theory share much in common. Without burdening the reader with detailed psychoanalytic case studies we can summarily state that there exists significant congruence in these formulations derived from such differing perspectives. Stuttering, tics, and other problems of *hyperconsciousness* begin when traumatic events early in development interfere with smooth automatic functioning. A particular pattern of speech, muscle movement, or thought sequence becomes overdetermined (overloaded) with excessive meaning for the individual and begins to have a life of its own: functioning to sooth, shame, or assert the self, while simultaneously coercing, testing, or soliciting the sympathy of others. The self, meanwhile oscillates between two very different identities—the angry, testy self versus the compliant, pleasing self—leaving the personality deeply bifurcated (see Figure 10.3).

Treatment from the psychoanalytic perspective is difficult. Glauber writes:

> A peak time is the fifth or sixth year—corresponding to the more advanced stages of the speech development also corresponding with the time of beginning of school as well as the height of the oedipal phase. At this time the stutter constitutes one of the most spontaneously resolvable

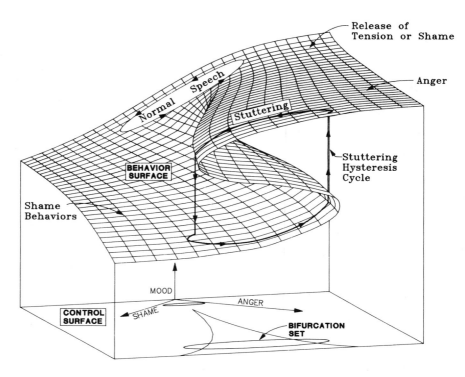

FIGURE 10.3 Stuttering is a cusp catastrophe in which shame and anger are conflicting moods on the control surface resulting in stuttering on the behavior surface. The likelihood of stuttering increases when shame and anger become more intense. As the control point crosses the cusp, the mood chronically—but catastrophically—changes from shame to anger/testiness which results in stuttering and *briefly* gives access to calmer emotional states. There is a reversal of power as the stutterer now "tortures" his listeners as he has been tortured by their ridicule. After momentary calm, the cycle is refueled by the shame resulting from stuttering. With passage of time, the cycle moves further toward the front edge, and fluent speech is less likely.

of all symptoms. However, when it is not resolved at this time, spontaneously or therapeutically, it continues to develop, and becomes rooted with characterologic concomitants. . . .

Classical psychoanalysis may lessen the severity of the stuttering symptom, but seldom, if ever, effects a complete resolution. . . .

It becomes ego-syntonic. The tenacity of the symptom and its use or adaptation also stem from the fixed idea of the damaged self-image, and hatred of it, both of which are projected outward. (1982, pp. 164–165).

Summary

The reader by now comprehends, and may indeed be weary of further consideration of, the fact that the tics and obsessions of TS-OCD share much in common with such diverse phenomena as eating disorders, spouse abuse, and stuttering. All can be understood as "sudden-jump" catastrophes prompted by the lack of middle sheet alternatives allowing smooth transitions between the extremes of moods and behaviors. As Figure 10.3 illustrates, stuttering, like ticquing, is really a rapid-fire sequence of hundreds of mini-catastrophes. In terms of the timetable of occurrence, tics and stuttering are more similar to each other than either of them is to spouse assault or eating binges. Although the latter two exhibit the sudden "bursting" common to catastrophes, they do so more in slow motion and on a less frequent basis.

Finally, it can be suggested that most of the considerations previously discussed in the context of TS-OCD, eating disorders, and spouse abuse are applicable to the treatment of stuttering. All of those basic middle-sheet-enhancing therapeutic strategies are worth exploring with the stuttering client. Helping the individual to express anger in appropriate, modulated ways will relieve tension. Likewise, "switching channels" of focus—away from self to other arenas—seems highly relevant for the stutterer. Indeed it could be argued that the reason speech therapy works is that the focus represents a diverting of attention away from self and the accompanying shame and anger, to aspects of word production. This is much like the student taking voice lessons who thinks more about tone production, quality, and so on than about how nervous he or she will be when attempting to sing before a live audience. Helping the person cope with the shame resulting from the speech disorder must be high on the agenda. And, rejoining the deeply bifurcated selves of the personality—indirectly, through the foregoing techniques, and more directly through the use of hypnosis, systematic relaxation, and reassurance—is a necessary part of treatment.

SOME FINAL THOUGHTS ABOUT BASINS, WHITECAPS, RODEOS, AND OUR TRIPLE BRAIN

Scientists search for unity in diversity, and in this chapter we've discussed a variety of heterogeneous notions, at times seeming to lead the reader far afield, on what might have appeared to be a scientist's version of a wild-goose chase. Hopefully, by now it has become increasingly apparent that although TS-OCD, eating disorders, spouse assault, stuttering, and numerous other clinical phenomena appear diverse they share a core of similar processes that can be understood in terms of developmental processes and catastrophe theory.

Overdeterminism, Basins, and Attractors

The psychoanalytic notion of overdeterminism—the idea that a symptom such as ticquing or stuttering is really a funnel or a final common pathway for many stimuli—has much in common with what cybernetic theorists refer to as "basins," and what catastrophe theorists call "attractors." Before concluding this chapter we will briefly consider these apparently diverse constructs and show that they all refer to the fact that during development multiple behaviors tend to become interwoven with or clustered around major symptoms.

Basins

Dynamic systems (both living and nonliving) can be studied by initially setting the system, allowing it to go on without interference, and observing all the changes that take place. An example of studying a dynamic living system would be placing a hamburger near an ants' colony and observing all the changes that ensue. One could also observe, as an example from a nonliving system, all the changes that take place in an automatic telephone system following the dialing of a number. Eventually such a system comes to a state at which it stops or a cycle around which it circulates. Such systems can be plotted to form what in cybernetics is known as a kinematic graph. Ashby (1961, p. 23) describes such a graph as ". . . like a map of a country's water drainage, showing, if a drop of water starts at any place, to what region it will come eventually. These separate regions are the graph's *basins*."

The concept of the "behavioral basin" proves useful in understanding tics which, like water, flow in diverse patterns through multiple modalities. There are a number of different kinds of basins for TS-OCD symptoms. Sleep provides a tranquil oceanic basin at the end of each day, receiving input from lakes, rivers, waterfalls, and even rain. Behaviorally, it is the "granddaddy" of all basins. There are also the "Great Lakes" basins—of lesser but still significant magnitude. These would include soothing and encompassing pastimes such as singing, swimming, sex, or biking. Other behavioral basins resemble whirlpools such as racquetball, running, or karate where there is intense activity, but focus remains outside the self and thus "drains off" symptoms temporarily. The metaphor of basins can be meaningfully extended to cover virtually all TS-OCD symptoms.

Tics utilizing assorted modalities are comparable to different kinds of water. The musculature-based jerking movements of various body parts seem as different from vocalizations as Niagara Falls is from the Mississippi River; yet both sources of water drain into ocean basins, much as muscle movements and vocalizations drain into the "basin" of sleep at the end of a day. Rain is to geologic rivers, lakes, and basins as stress is to TS-OCD symptoms. Rivers and symptoms alike swell their respective basins when intense rains, or stress, cause excessive drainage.

Attractors

The "attractor" is to CT what the "basin" is to cybernetics. It is a single stable state which like a magnet "attracts" other nearby states toward it. When CT is applied to such complex processes as thinking or behavior (which are the end products of some ten billion brain cells interwoven with as many as a hundred thousand connections with one another) we should think of the points on the thought or behavior surface not as fixed psychological states but as "attractors," that is centers around which the brain behavior cycles. These cycles, however, are not static, indeed they incessantly shift. Loss of stability of equilibrium is known to generate *auto-oscillations*; tics could be defined as "auto-oscillations," resulting from a loss of equilibrium. The reader will recall that we earlier related this to the part-selves that exist as unintegrated "pieces" in the somatic side of the bifurcated personality.

The Loss of Equilibrium through Auto-Oscillations

Arnold (1984, pp. 21–26) differentiates between *soft* loss of equilibrium— where the steady state becomes a periodic oscillatory state—and *hard* loss of equilibrium where the system leaves its steady state with a jump to a different state of motion. It may not be possible at this time to precisely decide whether tics or stuttering are soft or hard changes of equilibrium, however viewing them as *hard* losses of equilibrium seems most consistent with their sudden-jump qualities. Further, there exist *strange attractors* that are neither equilibrium states nor periodic oscillations. What *is* clear however, is that degeneration of equilibrium states into oscillatory states, sudden jumps, or even chaotic states of turbulence occur with regularity throughout the macrouniverse. Utilizing cybernetics, CT, and other mathematical models such as bifurcation theory to study such discontinuous phenomena has proven extremely fruitful in the macro-universe studied by physicists. Utilizing such analyses in the microuniverse of tics, stuttering, and other TS-OCD manifestations, may help us understand more clearly how muscle balance (equilibrium) changes to auto-oscillation (e.g., ticquing or stuttering).

Ripples and Whitecaps

The reader may recall the earlier discussion about the *interactional* quality of behavior. I'm convinced the interactional perspective offers the most balanced way of analyzing behavior, and I'd like to offer an analogy. The surface of a lake could be compared with the behavior surface of the CT model (see Figure 6.2). With little or no wind blowing, the surface remains placid with perhaps a few gentle ripples from time to time. Such ripples appear almost continuous with the surface, and no "sudden-jump" phenomena are present. However, with an increase in wind velocity, larger waves begin to form—smooth to a point, but suddenly "breaking" into whitecaps. The seething surface is now transformed into a multitude of catastrophes (whitecaps). Whether ripples or whitecaps occur is determined primarily, not by the characteristics of the water comprising them, but rather as a function of the wind's velocity *interacting* with the water. (The size of the lake modifies the interaction slightly.) Similarly, the difference between the "ripples" of ordinary movement and the "whitecaps" of intense ticquing seen in TS-OCD is not a difference of organic constitution. Rather, it is a matter of how intensely the "winds" of stress have shaped the developing child's life, and how forcefully they continue to blow. Just as most lakes can be churned into whitecaps by high winds, almost any child can develop TS-OCD, eating disorders, assaultive behavior, or stuttering, if through accident or design a pathogenic combination of stressors occurs, and remains in force during crucial developmental eras.

A Final Bit of Psychoanalytic Theory

Freud's model of mind proposed three different spheres of functioning—id, ego, and super-ego. Even with his tendency toward biological determinism, Freud did not regard these as literal regions of the brain, rather he used them as theoretical constructs, describing them using analogies and personifications.

The *id* (meaning "it" in Latin) contains the impulses and seeks immediate gratification. Developmentally speaking, babies are "all id." We could substitute the word "baby" for "id" and not do very much violence to Freud's description of the id; and conversely, the description would aptly characterize the newborn just prior to feeding:

> We approach the id with analogies: we call it a chaos, a cauldron full of seething excitations. . . . It is filled with energy reaching it from the instincts, but it has no organization, produces no collective will, but only a striving to bring about the satisfaction of the instinctual needs. . . . The logical laws of thought do not apply in the id, and this is true above all of the law of contradiction. Contrary impulses exist side by side, without cancelling each other out or diminishing each other. . . . It even seems that the energy of these instinctual impulses is in a state different from that in other regions of the mind, far more mobile and capable of discharge. (1933, pp. 73–74)

The *ego* (meaning "I" in Latin) grows out of the id, and functioned to delay immediate gratification, interposing *thinking* between the felt need and attempts to gratify the need. As Freud put it:

> The ego controls the approaches to motility under the id's orders; but between a need and an action it has interposed a postponement in the form of the activity of thought, during which it makes use of the mnemic residues of experience. In that way it has dethroned the pleasure principle which dominates the course of events in the id without any restriction and has replaced it by the reality principle, which promises more certainty and greater success. (1933, pp. 75–76)

In Freudian theory, the id is present at birth, the ego begins to emerge at about six months of age, and the *superego* (the moral arm of the psyche) emerges between the ages of three and six as a result of what Freud called the Oedipal struggle. Further discussion of these various relationships is beyond the scope of the current discussion, but a word of caution—given by Freud near the end of one of his lectures—is still apt:

> In thinking of this division of the personality into an ego, a super-ego, and an id, you will not, of course, have pictured sharp frontiers like the artificial ones drawn in political geography. We cannot do justice to the characteristics of the mind by linear outlines like those in a drawing or in primitive painting, but rather by areas of colour melting into one another as they are presented by modern artists. After making the separation we must allow what we have separated to merge together once more. You must not judge too harshly a first attempt at giving a pictorial representation of something so intangible as psychical processes. It is highly probable that the development of these divisions is subject to great variations in

different individuals; it is possible that in the course of actual functioning they may change. . . . (1933, p. 79)

Freud's foresight in naming the impulsive member of this tripartite ruling coalition "it" and the thinking member "I" is succinctly analyzed by Hampden-Turner:

> The id and ego come directly from Latin and mean literally, the 'it' and the 'I.' We normally speak as if we were ego controlled, e.g., 'I cook a meal', but when beset by impulses we often refer to id forces 'It makes me mad' . . . The id consists of instinctual energies and drives which are without rationale or inhibition, but clamour to be satiated, e.g., hunger, thirst, assertion, the general category of aggressive instincts, and the sexual instincts. The ego usually functions intelligently to serve the id. Hence the ego would know that a tin can contained food and how to open it. The id would know only the hunger that demanded satisfaction. (1981, p. 40)

According to Freud, the thinking member of the ruling coalition does not have an easy time:

> We are warned by a proverb against serving two masters at the same time. The poor ego has things even worse: it serves three severe masters and does what it can to bring their claims and demands into harmony with one another. These claims are always divergent and often seem incompatible. No wonder the ego so often fails in its task. Its three tyrannical masters are the external world, the super-ego and the id. (1933, p. 77)

TS-OCD and the "Rodeo Effect"

With this summary of Freud's basic model, we are ready to discuss the *rodeo effect*. In one of his most famous similes Freud stated:

> *The ego's relation to the id might be compared with that of a rider to his horse.* The horse supplies the locomotive energy, while the rider has the privilege of deciding on the goal and of guiding the powerful animal's movements. *But only too often there arises between the ego and the id the not precisely ideal situation of the rider being obliged to guide the horse along the path by which it itself wants to go.* (1933, p. 77, italics mine)

Like a rider desperately trying to stay atop a bucking bronco the ticquer always feels barely in control. For the person with TS-OCD it's not a matter of "being obliged to guide the horse along the path," it's rather a desperate attempt to remain in the saddle! In the case of the ticquer "the ego's relation to the id might be compared with that of a rider to his horse"—but what a horse! The jerking, bucking, twisting, contorted mass of horse muscle and sinew, provide a challenge that only the nimblest of riders survives.

Our Brain—In Triplicate

While on the topic of horses—Hampden-Turner in a chapter entitled "Lying down with a Horse and a Crocodile" quotes Paul MacLean as saying: "We might imagine that when a psychiatrist bids the patient to lie on the couch, he is asking him to stretch out alongside a horse and a crocodile" (1981, p. 80).

MacLean believes there are three distinct "brains" within the human brain. The "reptilian" brain seen in reptiles, turtles, alligators, and lizards is found near the *top of the brain stem*. Encircling this is the "old" mammalian brain—known as the *limbic system*—found in rabbits, kangaroos, horses, and so on. Finally the "new" mammalian brain—also known as the *neocortex*—is highly developed in primates and humans. These function in the manner of brains-within-the-brain; interrelated, but distinct.

Each of the three "computers" is discernibly distinct in structure and chemistry, as shown by differential staining using the Golgi method of staining brain tissue. Although the functions they perform overlap, they differ in *style*. Looking specifically at the relationship between the horse (limbic) and its rider (neocortex), we find that the limbic cortex registers basic emotions, hunger, thirst, pain, shock, and general stimuli that are not tied closely to specific stimuli but serve rather to motivate behavior. Research has shown that if the limbic system is irritated by infection, epilepsy, or experimental stimulation, sudden gusts of panic, pleasure, rage, and the like can sweep over the organism, which may snarl, attack, salivate, or become addicted to self-stimulation. Thus hunger—a limbic system drive—is more unspecified, yet more urgent, than a "yen for fresh strawberries"—a neocortical notion.

MacLean suggests there is a "design flaw" in the system because although the human brain is well integrated *laterally* the same cannot be said for its *vertical* integration. MacLean has shown that vertical connections between the limbic systems and the neocortex are relatively few, indirect, and slow to react. Seizures induced by stimulating the *limbic* cortex of monkeys remain contained within that system—in much the same way that epileptic seizures in humans do not cross from one hemisphere to another if the corpus callosum has been severed.

Interesting also is the fact that when a "homunculus" is mapped on the neocortex showing where sensory or motor stimuli from various body parts are processed, there is a general correspondence to gross anatomy, with the head, face, tongue, and mouth being a "respectful" distance from the genitals and "lower" functions. In the case of the limbic system this is not the case; instead the genital, anal, oral, and olfactory come full circle into close proximity with each other. It's probably not coincidence that many "earthy" tics exist alongside "higher" social testiness. Recall, the lady who stuffed rabbit droppings up her nose (an anal-olfactory combination) and also carried out socially sophisticated coprolalia, often rhyming in the process ("I have AIDS, I really do; gonorrhea and syphilis too!).

Limbic Brain—The Home of "Terry Tourette"

So where does this lead us? A return to the organic model? Hardly. We are recognizing that the limbic system *functions* to mediate messages between the environment and the neocortex of the brain. It is the limbic system that infuses stimuli with emotions, and there is general agreement that the limbic system functions importantly in the homeostatic and equilibrating (cybernetic) functions of the brain. Not surprisingly, there is also evidence that the limbic system can *oscillate* or *run away*.

We also know that the limbic brain receives both *cerebral* inputs from the neocortex and *somatic* imputs from the body. TS-OCD could be understood neurologically as a disequilibrium in which the limbic brain is dominated either by *cerebral* inputs (OCD) or *somatic* imputs (TS). None of this presupposes organic lesions or necessitates organic causality. What is being suggested, rather, is that during crucial "windows" of developmental an *overreliance* or *hypertrophy* of functions occur—in *either* direction—mediated by the limbic system. This view is congruent with findings in such diverse areas as developmental psychology and biology, cybernetics, and catastrophe theory.

Zeeman, for example discusses the role of the limbic system in anorexia:

> The origin of anorexia may occur in early childhood, when, perhaps for want of love or due to the inability to obtain the attention that it needs, the child retires into its shell; in other words the personality sets up an immunity against disappointment by turning inward, and leaving the shell to act out the game of life . . .
>
> One of the most interesting points made by Paul MacLean is that the limbic brain is nonverbal, being phylogenetically equivalent to the brain of a lower mammal. Therefore the problem of describing its activity in ordinary language is like trying to describe the conversation of a horse; no wonder anorexics have difficulty in explaining their symptoms. The patient can perceive that certain subsets of states are connected, and have boundaries, and so for her the most logical approach is to identify those

subsets as "dissociated subpersonalities," and give them names. In the model these subsets are represented by the different sheets, and the structural relation between them is defined by the unique geometry of the catastrophe surfaces. Therefore we may identify those sheets with the patient's descriptions of her subpersonalities. For example the upper sheet is often called the "monster within," and the lower sheet the "thin beautiful self." When she goes into trance the reduction of sensory input causes a shift in focus, from the close-up to the long-distance, from the immediacy of mood and behaviour to the long-term perspective of personality and insight. . . . Therefore the "monster" and "thin self" recede in importance. . . .

It is doubtful if this type of cure could be achieved while administering drugs that disrupt cerebral activity, because the recapturing of the whole delicate network of normal attitudes must depend not only upon reassurance, but also upon harnessing the full power of the cerebral faculties rather than suppressing them. (Zeeman, 1977, pp. 44–45, 48, 50–51)

Final Conclusion

Surely anything "final" in science is an oxymoron, and "conclusions" are only temporary resting places. By now, both the diversity and commonalities of TS-OCD, and other behaviors such as eating disorders, impulsive assault, and stuttering, must be apparent to the reader, and further examples of how CT could be applied to other clinical problems would likely be wearisome. Continued attention to our *vertical* brains and their interrelationships should facilitate the treatment of TS-OCD and the related problems we've discussed. Learning how to gain better functional access to the limbic system through hypnosis, relaxation, and other "indirect" methodologies seems a logical direction for future work. Since attempts to "reason" the "limbic horse" into a quiet trot haven't met with much success, a few sugar lumps and a bit of stroking may prove more effective.

Chapter 11

FREEDOM, DETERMINISM, AND THE ATTRIBUTION OF BLAME

Introduction

The freedom versus determinism issue has loitered around the edges of philosophical discussion for centuries. Among theologians and moralists it's been debated as original sin versus tabula rasa; jurists, struggling to assign culpability, have related more responsibility to premeditated actions suggesting more choice or freedom exists with premeditated behavior than with impulsive actions. Educators have wrangled about the role of nature versus nurture in learning, and a similar debate has recently been resuscitated in the mental health field as a conflict between biological and psychodynamic psychiatry, or between behavior therapy and traditional psychotherapy. This is more than philosophical self-stimulation, because one's view on such issues may have far reaching consequences. In legal decisions it can mean the difference between prison or a mental hospital. School curriculums can vary profoundly, reflecting prevailing views on the topic, and in mental health clinics the therapists' theoretical preferences shape treatment in subtle but profound ways.

TS-OCD raises these issues with new urgency. If we accord psychological development new respect, does this mean Mom is to be blamed for Jennifer's compulsions? If tics aren't the result of organic lesions or biochemical imbalances why doesn't the child "just quit"? A persistently perplexing problem for parents is deciding if their child is being "naughty" and deserving of discipline or experiencing symptoms that are beyond his/her control. These and many related issues in understanding and treating TS-OCD are importantly influenced by how much choice we assume the person to have. Such issues will be discussed in more detail later in the chapter. We begin with an overview.

Varieties of Freedom

In common usage, the word "freedom" is used in widely differing ways. In sociopolitical terms freedom refers to various personal entitlements such as speaking freely and openly about one's political preferences, sitting in the front of a bus if one so chooses, or seeking an executive position whatever one's sex. Here freedom designates the liberty to *do* something: to exercise chosen initiatives without fear of reprisal, and usually with the anticipation of success. Freedom can also mean the liberty to *not do* certain onerous tasks. Persons who become suddenly wealthy by winning a lottery typically quit their jobs. Free from the burdens of earning a living by daily toil, they typically buy a motor home, take up golf, and dabble in watercolors.

Freedom may also mean release *from* externally imposed negative forces felt to be confining, constraining, coercing, encumbering, hindering, inhibiting, imprisoning, and the like. Putting the prefix *un* before such words produces synonyms for freedom—unconstrained, uncoerced, unencumbered, uninhibited, and so on. In our society freedom from unwanted external constraint is usually deemed desirable so long as external control is taken over by the self. Indeed, the goal of socialization is to produce persons who are self-controlled, self-contained, or self-disciplined. Thus to be self-controlled is desirable, but to be uncontrolled, uncontained, or undisciplined is not. Here freedom amounts to replacing *external* control with *internal* (self) control, a process psychoanalysts refer to as internalization.

When freedom *from* means avoiding societally valued responsibility, consistency, or predictability it will not be valued by others. Persons seen as irresponsible, inconsistent, unreliable, or emotionally unstable, are not sought as perspective employees or spouses. Likewise avoiding culturally approved social involvements is not seen positively. The unattached, uncommitted, unmarried, or unsociable have varying degrees of stigma associated with them. However, freedom *from* socially or medically designated problems is always positive. Freedom from epilepsy, stuttering, tics, obsessions, bigotry, or criminal behavior is highly valued.

We've seen that freedom often designates escape from unwanted domination, but in a more expansive sense it may include the notion of creative fulfillment of potential, as suggested in free-lance writer, free-ranging, freethinking, or freewheeling. Additionally it may include a transcendent quality. Free as a bird, footloose, free spirit, illustrate more than freedom *from* specific constraints, there is a surpassing quality suggesting freedom to *be*—to maximize potential.

FREEDOM AND DETERMINISM IN MORAL, ETHICAL, AND PSYCHOLOGICAL THOUGHT

It has often been the case that freedom and determinism have been pitted against each other as opposite "things." We readily overlook the crucial distinction between words and the things they denote: that is, seldom do we ask how the "things" we describe differ from the words used. We easily fall into the trap of reifying (objectifying) abstractions as if they were concrete. Hampden-Turner has stated it well:

> Our habitual way of speaking is structured in a straight line, a one-way purposive motion in which a subject employs a verb to affect some object. But herein lies a danger since the words passing our lips are in no way identical to the subjects they refer to. . . . Hence, when A says "As an Individualist I fight collectivism," and B replies, "As a Cooperatist I fight selfishness," each tries to make an object of the other, and each pretends that his words are that object. (1981, p. 140)

This concretization of abstractions also gains force from the Cartesian dualism so pervasive in our language. The mind being a place where free will resides and the body a machine that runs according to deterministic rules. In fact, however, freedom and determinism are both abstractions, neither possessing substance in any concrete form and neither having the power to propel behavior in a billiard-like sequential fashion.

Freedom versus Determinism in Moral and Ethical Thought

Freedom has been emphasized by theologians wanting to provide a strong basis for ethical or moral behavior. This is because responsibility, culpability, and guilt are *directly proportional* to the amount of freedom available to an individual. Freedom to choose behavioral alternatives is foundational to all discussions of ethics. If a person's behavior is determined by forces outside himself ethicists cannot hold him responsible. This is why theologians and others have so vehemently opposed behavioristic psychologists who suggest that since behavior is determined by the environment, there are no "good" or "bad" people, just "good" or "bad" environments.

If accepted, such a behavioristic assertion would, in a single coup de grace, wipe out centuries of moral structures so painstakingly erected by philosophers and theologians. Clergymen understand well that confession, forgiveness, pardon, penance, and a host of related religious concepts may be utilized to expunge the believer's moral remorse, but first guilt must be firmly anchored, and free will is the bedrock on which this anchoring takes place. Defenders of morality and the church must first be defenders of free will because without free will there can be no guilt, and the church with its formulae for absolution becomes unnecessary. Ecclesiastics understand this well.

Freedom versus Determinism in Psychological Thought

Among psychologists the standoff has usually occurred between personologists arguing freedom of choice against behaviorists maintaining a billiard-ball causality for the environment. This debate—really an extension of the person versus situation battle—has proved fruitless. *Interactional* theory (e.g., Magnusson & Endler, 1977) resolves this unnecessary polarity with a higher level synthesis. It becomes apparent that—like persons and situations—freedom and determinism *coexist* as two ends of the same continuum. To place freedom, choice, and creativity in an opposing relationship to lawfulness, predictability, and orderliness is to seriously misunderstand behavior. Let us look briefly at how such polarizing rhetoric distorts reality.

Behavioristic psychologists have, through careful planning and observation, been able to effect systematic and predictable changes in many laboratory animals. With humans, the predictability has not been as precise, but even here there have been impressive findings. Conditioning technologies have been widely and effectively utilized in training animals, teaching autistic or learning impaired children, and more. Unfortunately the rhetoric accompanying the behaviorists' articulation and utilization of the *orderly* universe has been inflammatory to theologians and others because it suggests that behavioristic technology displaces earlier notions of freedom and renders values obsolete. B.F. Skinner in such books as Beyond Freedom and Dignity further inflamed the discussion, by insisting that "choice," "freedom," and "dignity" are anachronistic shibboleths—comforting but outmoded catchwords from earlier times.

Personologists have responded with equally polarizing rhetoric insisting that man is *more* than a naked ape; insisting that although behavioral techniques might work in the laboratory with rats and pigeons, they are inappropriately simplistic when applied to the complex organisms known as people. Chomsky (1959) convincingly reasons from a linguistic perspective that most questions that behaviorists attempt to address are hopelessly premature. For example behaviorists glibly speak of "reinforcement" in reference to language *acquisition*, but Chomsky contends it still remains to be known precisely *what* is acquired.

Freedom versus Determinism—A Higher Level Synthesis

When battle lines are drawn with behaviorists insisting on an orderly, systematically programmable universe, and personologists arguing for the transcendent values of choice and freedom, the *complementarity* of these positions is usually lost. The truth lies in understanding that *both* freedom and determinism are necessary. Recall as we noted earlier (see p. 00) that persons *and* situations *coexist* with behavior *emerging* as a function of both. Similarly, freedom and determinism *coexist* and our behavior emerges as a function of *both*. Wheelis puts it aptly:

> Being the product of conditioning and being free to change do not war with each other. Both are true. They coexist. . . . What makes a battleground of these two points of view is to conceive of either as an absolute which excludes the other. For when the truth of either view is extended to the point of excluding the truth of the other it becomes not only false but incoherent. We must affirm freedom and responsibility without denying that we are the product of circumstance, and we must affirm that we are the product of circumstance without denying that we have the freedom to transcend that causality to become something which could not have been previsioned from the circumstances which shaped us. (1973, pp. 87–88)

Degrees of Freedom and Determinism

In statistical theory, the number of possible outcomes is taken into account when assessing whether an experimental result is considered significant. This concept, known as *degrees of freedom*, will help us in solving the dilemma of how to balance choice with determinism. A coin toss (heads or tails being the only possibilities) is an event with fewer degrees of freedom than the event of tossing a six-sided die. As we've noted earlier, freedom and determinism are two ends of a unitary dimension of "agency" or "steering" of our behavior.

In a "going-out-to-dinner" event, it is likely that choosing a restaurant in a large city will have many more degrees of freedom associated with it than choosing items from the menu once seated at a the restaurant. Choosing which bathroom to use while at the restaurant (like the coin toss) will have even fewer degrees of freedom—that is, it will be more highly determined. In all situations, for all behaviors, one can theoretically scale the behavior somewhere along the degrees of freedom/determinism dimension. Freedom and determinism vary *inversely*—the more degrees of freedom, the less the determinism and vice versa. Although they inversely covary, both are always present. Like up or down, hot or cold, wet or dry, one moves by degrees toward one while simultaneously moving away from the other.

In this context it can be seen that both are complementary aspects of reality. In order to make genuine choices—to choose among alternatives—there must be deterministic stability and predictability in the environment. Without such determined orderliness and fixed parameters there could be no genuine choices. You could not, for example, toss a coin to decide which of two football teams kicked off if, while airborne, the coin suddenly became a four-sided tetrahedron. Stable parameters are the foundation for freedom. Even young children soon learn that one doesn't change rules midgame—you don't change the bases while a player is running. Understood in this way freedom is seen to be possible only where determined, predictable parameters are maintained.

Summary

We've shown the necessity of investigating *both* the situational and personologic poles of behavior. By more clearly understanding the environment—especially the proximal environment of early life—we can better estimate the degrees of freedom available later for steering behavior. By sharpening our understanding of subjective experience—that is, the inner life of an individual—we may be more sensitive in estimating the degrees of freedom present to transcend circumstances.

THE ATTRIBUTION OF BLAME

With this background we now turn to a consideration of blame with special emphasis on how this impinges on clinical understanding. Although our focus will be on TS-OCD, stuttering, and other compulsions the principles are applicable more broadly because, whenever something goes awry, it seems natural to "assign responsibility" (a euphemism for blaming).

Clean Tools for Clinicians

Since clinicians spend much of their professional time working with behaviors that have gone awry, there is always the temptation to reduce ambiguity by assigning blame. All too often this is done without reflective thought regarding the complexities of the process. What follows are not simple answers, but rather a call for examined reason. As Austin puts it: ". . . words are tools, and, as a minimum, we should use clean tools: we should know what we mean and what we do not. . ." (1961, p. 181)

To Blame or Not to Blame

Much of what follows is inspired by Shaver's (1985) closely reasoned analysis of the attribution of blame. He begins by pointing out the obvious—we never "blame" others for doing good:

> The events of interest to a psychological analysis of blame therefore will be those social occurrences or changes in physical states that lead to negative consequences . . .
> An assignment of blame is, therefore, a particular sort of social explanation. It is the outcome of a process that begins with an event having negative consequences, involves judgments about causality, personal responsibility, and possible mitigation . . . But the process is by no means as simple as it would seem. . .(pp. 3–4)."

Was it Done Voluntarily?

An important related issue—especially in the case of tics, stuttering, or other compulsive behaviors—deals with how much choice was involved in the behavior. Again, Shaver reminds us that it becomes important to know if a behavior was voluntarily carried out only if the outcome is bad. If, for example, you perform a difficult piano concerto with ease and brilliance, no ordinary person would think to ask you if you had done it on purpose. "Only if you have taken a hammer to the piano's keys would we want to know whether you had done so voluntarily" (1985, p. 79).

Attribution Theory in Everyday Life

As previously noted, blaming someone for a negative event is a complex social judgment, but the *process* of *attribution*, directed toward identifying stable features of persons and environments is even more complex, involving a wide array of factors in the environment and in the individual forming the attributions. Heider (1958) systematically examined everyday language in order to understand the ways in which ordinary persons might interpret the actions of another. Although most people don't have access to such scientific analyses, *everyone attributes responsibility* for behavior, giving varying weights to the relative contributions of luck, motivation, or skill. According to Heider's (1958) theory, the ordinary person—the so-called "naive psychologist"—distinguishes *personal force* (ability, power, and intention) from *environmental force* (task difficulty, opportunity, and luck).

In a more recent formulation of attribution theory, Kelley (1973) distinguishes between casual inferences based on a single event (such as an airplane crash) and those in which repeated observations are possible. Of these, the latter is most relevant to an analysis of TS-OCD where *repeated* observations are intrinsic.

The Nature of Causality

The question "What *caused* that to happen?" turns out to be much more complex than first appears. Philosophers have debated causality for centuries and more recently scientists have shown a greater interest in such issues as well. However, consensus has not been forthcoming, because as Shaver (1985) reminds us, scientific analyses "like the philosophers' prescriptions, carry theoretical baggage that cannot be left behind on the platform" (p. 5). A comprehensive discussion of the many theories of causality would take us far beyond our original intent.

Cause Precedes Effect

With few exceptions, philosophers and scientists include in their definitions of cause and effect the idea that a presumed cause must *precede* the presumed effect in time. In technical terms the cause is a process "the *last* instant of which is also the *first* instant of the segment of the time series occupied by the process which is in effect" (Ducasse, 1969, p. 48, emphasis in original).

However in real life such sequences seldom involve a *single* antecedent and a *single* consequence. Instead, one is typically looking at a behavior that is a "final common pathway" for multiple antecedents, and attempting to discover which of these is the most causally primal. If your car engine stalls, for example, Ducasse suggests that the question of why? the engine has ceased to run is really a search for ". . . the single *difference* between the circumstances of the engine at the moment when it was running, and at the moment when it was not" (1969, p. 19).

Correlation versus Causation

Here we could easily get into deep philosophical waters, but it is only necessary to remind the reader, as we do all science students, that just because A temporally preceded B or co-occurred with B does *not* unambiguously lead to the conclusion that A *caused* B. For example, although we observe a co-occurrence (correlation) of vocabulary words and height in young children, but we do not conclude that words cause growth, or vice versa. Based on other information, we are quite certain that words and height are causally linked to other factors such as growth and maturation, and thereby *incidentally* linked with each other. Thus, we conclude that a cause must be considered *generative* of the effect, not a mere correlate.

This is related to another important distinction—the one between description and explanation. Explanation, like causation, requires clear articulation of the interrelation between variables. Description, like correlation, is a statement of "what is," but doesn't necessarily give us a clear picture of causal pathways.

Human Agency

In addition to the temporal characteristics of cause–effect sequences, another important consideration in the psychological analysis of blame attribution is the fundamental idea of a *human agent*. Our understanding of causality comes from our own experiences of volitional behavior. Because we ourselves have been successful *agents* of change—that is, we can move our bodies across rooms, drive automobiles, build buildings, and *cause* things to happen, we also perceive ourselves to be efficient causes of action.

CASE EXAMPLE: THE CRASH OF AIR FLORIDA FLIGHT 90

In the late afternoon of January 13, 1982, during a blinding snowstorm, Air Florida Flight 90 from Washington, D.C. to Tampa and Fort Lauderdale crashed into the Fourteenth Street Bridge just seconds after taking off from National Airport. The airplane had undergone de-icing procedures 45 minutes before takeoff, but lumbered down the airport's 6,870 foot runway, failed to gain altitude, struck the bridge crowded with rush-hour traffic, and plunged into the iced-over waters of the Potomac River. Upon impact the tail section of the plane separated from the main portion of the fuselage, and this forward part of the aircraft quickly sank into the river. Only five of the 79 people aboard the plane were rescued; an additional four people were killed who had been travelling across the bridge at the time of impact. (Shaver, 1985, p. 11)

"Cause" is a Subset of Antecedents

Many questions were raised by this tragic event. "Was de-icing adequately carried out?" "Was the delay between de-icing procedures and takeoff too long?" "Were the pilots unaccustomed to winter flying conditions, or were they more concerned with regaining time lost on the schedule?" "Should airport officials have closed the runways and cancelled flights scheduled for later in the day?" "Should the personnel in the tower have noticed ice buildup on the plane's wings during the time spent waiting for permission to take off?" "Is the runway at National Airport just too short?" "Were all the flight systems on the plane working properly?" These and many other similar questions were investigated by the National Transportation Safety Board during extensive hearings on the crash. Nearly a year after the accident, the Board issued its report on the crash, concluding that *the* cause was pilot error, both in the original decision to take off and in the subsequent decision not to abort the takeoff. Other potential antecedents, such as de-icing procedures, severity of the storm, and delayed departure, were relegated to the role of "necessary but not sufficient" conditions.

Summary

Let us summarize briefly before proceeding. We've shown that for blame to be attributed, a "bad" event must have occurred. Although most events are not as tragic as a plane crash, nonetheless blame always occurs in the context of establishing who is responsible for the "trouble." We've also seen that *voluntary, human agency* is central to discussions of blame, and that establishing "cause" is a complex process of searching among *multiple* antecedents for *the* cause.

CAUSE, RESPONSIBILITY, AND BLAME IN CLINICAL CASES

Causality in Common Events

Although relationships among cause and blame were complex in the case of the plane crash, it becomes even more perplexing when we study clinical conditions such as TS-OCD, stuttering, or spouse abuse. Here there are no flight recorders to be retrieved from the bottom of the icy Potomac, no tape recordings of conversations between the pilots and the control tower, no wreckage, few reliable eyewitnesses. Instead clinical problems are permeated with fluctuating motives, vague memories, and—if one takes developmental psychology seriously—myriad antecedents. But the "wreckage" is obvious—everpresent in the form of shame-generating behaviors which tragically strew debris over a lifetime.

Shaver (1985) illustrates the complexity of even "simple" daily happenings by considering what happens if he burns a pile of leaves that he has collected in his yard on a windy autumn afternoon:

> What is "the event?" It is certainly true that I am (a) "burning leaves," but I may also be (b) "preparing my yard for winter." My neighbors downwind would notice also that I am (c) "filling the house up with smoke," and they might believe I am also (d) "recklessly endangering the dry woods" behind both of our houses. If there is a county ordinance against open fires before 4:00 P.M., then I am also (e) "breaking the law." The action is (f) "contributing particulate matter to the air" and quite possibly (g) "increasing the discomfort of sufferers from emphysema." Finally, if it is a weekday afternoon, I am also (h) "being unavailable to students." Even simple actions can have multiple, often simultaneous, effects, and any combination of these can be used to define "the event." (1985, p. 40)

Such diverse descriptions lead to a variety of causal attributions and differing responses from others:

> Someone who considered me merely to be burning leaves would not be likely to take any action. By contrast, a perceiver who considered me to be breaking the law, endangering the woods, or polluting the air might very well call the authorities. But even in this case, *which* authorities were notified—police, firefighters, or the clean air agency—would depend on the particular description of the event. (1985, p. 40)

This is consistent with the work of Vallacher and Wegner (in press) who suggest that the question "What are you doing?" can be answered on any of a number of hierarchical levels. Looking for a paper clip, they contend can be described in terms of the discrete muscle movements of the fingers, arms, and limbs; or in terms of more globally recognizable behaviors such as opening and closing drawers; or finally, in terms of the action as a whole. They describe a "fluid system" much like changing patterns in a fountain. The answer to "What are you doing?" can be answered at any of the forementioned levels, but will tend to be identified at a higher level, reflecting our desire to feel in control of our behaviors in the most general way possible.

Levels of Analysis—Searching for the "Real" Event

It can be seen that the description of any event is really a *choice* of which *level* of analysis and communicational language we choose to employ, and that subsequent discussions of *the* event become so permeated with the constructs of a particular perspective that "events" at different levels of description are not strictly comparable. Thus, when each of the 10 blind men of fabled fame touched the elephant, their experiences were uniquely noncomparable. The man who seized the trunk and reported "snake!" had an experience genuinely differing from the one who touched a leg and reported "tree," or the one who grasped the tail and concluded he was holding a "rope." The *real* elephant did indeed exist, but the *real* experience for each observer was at a lower level of abstraction. A clinician could only hope that if any of the 10 were "snake phobic" it was not the gentleman who happened to touch the trunk!

A Linear Analysis

Just as "events" can be scrutinized in terms of vertical levels of abstraction, they must also be carefully dissected in terms of a horizontal line, with attention to the temporal relationships of antecedents–effect sequences. Such linear time analyses ought to be especially sensitive to those repetitive sequences that have become "residualized" in development. It's my belief that development never becomes totally fixated or arrested—these are too immobile and static—but instead particularly comforting age-specific rituals tend to be repeated. Such out-of-phase behaviors are maladaptive later in life. The nine-year-old who sucks his thumb or wets his pants will be in deep trouble with family and peers, whereas the toddler exhibiting the same topographic behaviors would be considered "cute."

Such multidirectional complexity may seem overwhelming, but we can extricate ourselves by realizing that it is much like a spiral stairway with many landings. We can choose to stop, catch our breath, and contemplate, at any level we desire. It isn't necessary—or possible—to climb all the stairs simultaneously, only to appreciate the complexity of the superstructure. We are all like blind persons groping for the "elephant" of understanding. And although there are real "elephants" out there, none of us will ever grasp the entire beast; consequently we must study "snakes" and "trees" and "ropes" and attempt to discover what ropes have to do with snakes.

Dimensions of Responsibility

Although responsibility depends on causality the two are *not* identical. Causality is only one aspect of determining responsibility and not always the most important. The term "responsibility" is used in many different ways. Hart (1968) discusses four different senses of the term. In *role-responsibility* a person is considered "responsible" to perform various duties such as when teachers are supposed to facilitate learning, parents are expected to care for their children, and sea captains are required to operate their vessels with the safety of their passengers in mind. *Causal responsibility*. is the kind in which phrases like "caused it to happen" or "was responsible for" occur. *Capacity responsibility* refers to the situation in which we feel another is responsible for their actions by reason of understanding, reasoning, and planning. *Liability-responsibility* refers to responsibility in the moral realm and assumes that the person possesses capacity responsibility and some knowledge of the wrongfulness of the behavior.

Evil Intent

There is overlap in Hart's categories and we refer to them only to illustrate some of the various meanings that can be attached to responsibility. What is important for our discussion is to note that *blameworthiness* is a special case of responsibility that must also include an *evil intent* on the part of the person being blamed.

BEING PART OF A PROBLEM WITHOUT BEING BLAMEWORTHY

We are now in a position to make a crucial statement: *It is possible to be partially responsible for conditions in other persons' lives—indeed to have contributed to the aggregate of causal antecedents—without being blameworthy.*

This is the pivotal point of this chapter's discussion. We can examine the complex causal networks that shape the lives of developing children *without blaming* heredity, parents, peers, or the child.

Responsibility Must Be Disentangled from Blame

If this distinction isn't maintained, we are likely to settle for simplistic explanations that reduce blame but that are not in keeping with reality. If, for example, we decide that tics are a result of organic lesions, we remove blame from parents and from the individual, but at the price of tremendously oversimplifying the nature of TS-OCD. Similarly, if we maintain that tics are inherited, we will blame parents only indirectly—for passing on their genes—hardly a matter of choice. Clearly, we ought to follow wherever the data lead, but the biological "paradigm bias" has been so pervasive that it has influenced virtually all research and theory to date. As I've pointed out previously, this has synergistically interacted with blame-phobic attitudes of parents and professionals and has led to an unfortunate skew of theory and research in the direction of reductionistic neurobiology.

Establishing blameworthiness—like establishing causality—is a highly complex process; one that would take us far beyond the scope of the present discussion. The interested reader is referred to Shaver's excellent discussion (1985, pp. 155–176) for a thorough examination of the complex process of blaming. For our purposes we will simply note that blaming usually occurs when several of the following conditions are present: (1) personal association with or causality of the problem in question, (2) foreknowledge regarding the possible consequences of the negative actions, and (3) intentionality—perhaps the question of "Did she intend to do it?" is most central in a multidimensional analyses of causality and blame. Further precision is obtained by assessing whether the person "causing" the damage was coerced or did so "freely."

Clinical Blaming

Professionals offering services in what is generically known as "the mental field" are not free from the temptation to blame. Shaver (1985) suggests that blame, denial, counterblame, and so on are "normal" interactional processes, encountered daily, which cannot be totally expunged from human affairs. However, even though blaming cannot be completely avoided, it can be more carefully examined and greatly lessened. This is especially urgent in a field whose members are part of the "helping" professions. Ironically, more blaming is carried out by mental health professionals than by plumbers, engineers, or computer specialists. This is because problems are *the* central concern in the mental health field, and when troubled persons seek the assistance of professionals to help them with their problems or to ease their misery, blame easily emerges—sometimes "short-circuiting" more careful clinical analyses. There is the temptation to feel that once a "cause" (often a precursor for "blame") is established, the presenting problem will be more easily solved.

As has been noted already, the accurate assignment of causality is a complex process, and deciding how to weight the multiple antecedents triggering any behavior is intricately complex. This is further complicated with clinical problems, because, in addition to being caused by multiple antecedents, such problems typically unfold as complex amalgams of *multiple effects*. We've also observed that because of the direct relationship between freedom and responsibility one must have information about the "degrees of freedom" available to the target individual, as well as their foreknowledge regarding possible consequences, before blame can be accurately assigned. Additionally, an understanding of the "about-to-be-blamed" person's *intent* ought to inform the process of locating blame.

How Therapists Blame

Professional training—unless it includes personal therapy as part of the curriculum—doesn't necessarily insure that the student will become less blaming. Advanced training may even provide new language systems that disguise blame in professional terms, beguiling "blamers" and "blamed" alike. A "softened" but nonetheless blaming vocabulary often includes terms like "minimal brain damage," "borderline personality," "learning disabled," "dyslexic," and a host of words—often with nebulous ties to "hard data"—but nonetheless damaging to the target person. Commonly utilized strategies include gene blaming—"It's inherited," parent blaming—"Mom and Dad messed up," "chemoblaming"—"It's due to a chemical imbalance," "alcoholblaming"—"I'm an adult child of an alcoholic," and more. Probably the worst kind of blaming is victim-blaming. "You should be ashamed of yourself," too readily becomes internalized as "I *am* ashamed of myself."

Disentangling Responsibility and Blame

We've seen something of the complexity surrounding the vital questions of: Are behaviors determined or chosen? How many degrees of freedom exist for choosing a particular behavior instead of another? What is the cause of a specific behavior? Who is responsible? and—especially if it turns out negatively—Who is to blame? Yet in spite of the importance of the issues and the pervasiveness of blame, few thorough analyses have been adequately carried out even in experimental settings, much less in the real world. Plane crashes or other mass-transit tragedies being notable exceptions.

Examining these issues more extensively, should facilitate a more blame-free study of TS-OCD, stuttering, assault, and other clinical catastrophes. Instead of subtly seeking to determine which "significant other" ought to be assigned the major portion of blame, clinicians could concentrate their energies on prevention and treatment without offending parents, siblings, teachers or others. Shaver reminds us that

> Many causes can exist independent of intervention by human beings— tornadoes cause extensive damage, bacteria cause disease in animals, lengthening spring days cause new leaves to appear on trees—so the actions of persons constitute *only a fraction of the antecedents of effects*. (1985, p. 87, italics mine)

Don't Blame Mom and Dad for TS-OCD, Stuttering, or Related Clinical Problems

Surely, the enigmatic nature of TS-OCD and other clinical problems, the complex interplay of multiple antecedents and consequences, the difficulties in assessing degrees of freedom, and the usual *intent* of most parents to do well by their children ought to inculcate in clinicians extreme caution in assigning blame—whatever the chosen vocabulary. If parental responsibility and participation in family problems (such as TS-OCD) could be disentangled from *blame*, parents and professionals could carefully study such problems without feeling compelled to "assign causal responsibility." Possibly they could become partners in a mutual quest for wisdom, nondefensively and nonblamingly seeking to better understand the multiple antecedents of TS-OCD. Such a pursuit could lead to clearer understanding and better prevention of TS-OCD and related problems; and to a drastic reduction of blame and shame— neither of which fosters psychological growth.

Don't Blame the Child with the Problem

Blame is the developmental precursor to shame. If a child were never blamed for anything, it is unlikely that shame would ever become a significant part of his or her emotional life. Succinctly stated, *shame is the internalized residual of externally generated blame*. Victim-blaming never results in growth, and any person who thinks that blaming a child will help produce a "responsible" adult, is profoundly—if sincerely—mistaken.

THE BLAME CHAIN—THE "ADAM-'N-EVE EFFECT"

In the earliest social psychology on record, we find *blame* and *shame*. The scene is the unsullied beauty of primeval Eden. Man meets woman and declares:

> This is now bone of my bones
>   and flesh of my flesh;
> she shall be called woman,
>   for she was taken out of man.
>
> For this reason a man will leave his father and his mother and be united to his wife, and they will become one flesh.
> The man and his wife were both naked, and *they felt no shame* (Genesis 2:22-25, The New International Version Study Bible [NIV], Italics mine)

All seemed to be going rather well: no blame, no shame, no clothes. It wasn't the contrived "naturalness" of a contemporary nudist camp, it was genuine comfort with one another in a transparently intimate relationship. Shortly however, a "bad" event occurred, God asked: "Have you eaten from the tree that I commanded you not to eat from?"

When questioned about it, Adam began the first blame chain:

> The man said, "*The woman you put here* with me—she gave me some fruit from the tree, and I ate it."
> Then the Lord God said to the woman, "What is this you have done?"
> The woman said, "*The serpent* deceived me, and I ate." (Genesis 3:11-13, NIV, italics mine)

He blamed the dazzling creature he'd just celebrated, and with a thinly veiled reference, the Creator as well. Eve, for her part, blamed the snake, and the snake having no one to blame was cursed and reduced to crawling on his belly instead of flying. In the blame chain—as in the food chain—organisms feed on the one just below them in power.

In all social systems, people seek to *transfer* blame—the "Adam-'n-Eve Effect." Close on the heels of blame comes shame. What was true in the garden is still true today. Consequently the less we blame the less others will feel compelled to transfer that blame; then shame will be reduced both personally and systematically. Surely a worthy goal.

EPILOGUE: A PERSONAL NOTE

My father wasn't a bad man. He wasn't mean or vicious. He wasn't cruel or abusive. He wasn't an alcoholic—never showed up late or missed a day of work in over 50 years with the railroad. He was simply embarrassing.

He came from the "old country," and just never acclimated to the New World. Arriving on Ellis Island when this century was still in its teens, he was not quite 20. After being processed through immigration, he moved to Chicago, where he soon took a fancy to an attractive young woman who had recently arrived in this country with her mother and was living in the same Hungarian ghetto on the west side of Chicago. Mamma was "nearly 16" when they married.

When, during our teens, Mamma advised Bobby and me "Do you homevork and don't vorry about girls!" we loved to laughingly remind her of the "advanced age" at which she had married. She would respond with a sigh saying "Yoi Yoi eleg buta voltam!" (Oh My! I was stupid enough!) and we would all burst into laughter. I was never quite certain how much of this was theatrics and how much was truth, likely there were elements of both in her response.

It wasn't only my father's behavior that was humiliating to me, it was more primal than that. European immigrants at the turn of the century were not awash in today's Madison-Avenue-created concerns with precise coordination of one's soap, mouthwash, deodorant, and cologne. The essentials of my father's life included providing for his family by working hard, animated talk with whomever would listen, and plenty of good food—generously seasoned with onions and garlic. The results of this value system surrounded my father and engulfed his listeners.

If you were out of range of his breath—some significant distance away—you might have noticed his baggy trousers, or a suit jacket that

295

hung nearly to his knees. His dress-up clothes were hand-me-downs from wealthy Chicago families like the Marshall Fields for whom Mamma worked. She often arrived home with gifts of assorted clothing that were no longer the very latest fashion, through which we would all rummage finding new treasures for our wardrobes. When we later moved to Wisconsin, Bobby and I were the only students in our country school who wore Marshall Field vintage ties with flannel shirts and bib overalls.

Unfortunately, my father was shorter and more slender than Marshall Field, so the gift clothing "fit" him only loosely. And, as luck would have it, tailoring clothes was not one of the old country traditions my parents brought with them. Although Mamma was capable of exquisite needlepoint and of mending the family clothing, somehow those once-elegant three-piece suits did not benefit from tailor's needle or thread. It wasn't that our family couldn't afford to buy new clothing, it was rather a serendipitous merger of Mrs. Field's affection for my mother, our family's old country resourcefulness, post-depression "waste-not-want-not" philosophy, and the fact that Pa was perfectly comfortable with his over-size suits that led to this GQ nightmare. Although others viewed this little Hungarian man with amusement, for me it spelled shame.

To make matters worse my father was an extravert. He seemed to have no sense of social restraint and actively sought social situations in which he could mix with people of higher social standing—"big people" as he referred to them. I often felt as if cast in one of those old movies where Abbot and Costello or the Three Stooges find themselves tuning pianos or moving furniture in the midst of an elegant dinner party, which they botch with their mere presence. My father could turn ordinary social situations into circumstances of excruciating shame. This happened in myriad ways when I was a child and continued into my adult years. I recall one of his visits early in my academic career.

"John," he stated with a gleam in his eyes, "I go see President!"

(Hungarian has no prepositions, so in addition to his heavy accent, Pa never bothered with such unnecessary nuances and spoke in English/Hungarian "telegraphese" his entire 84 years.)

I knew what he had in mind: he wanted to meet the president of the small university where I taught. He always liked to meet with the top people. This is why when "bartering" to buy carpet at Sears—he was proud that he never paid "full price" for anything—he would insist to the salesperson "I vant speak manager!" Thereafter he would direct his bartering efforts to the top brass of the store. It had been unnerving enough when I was a young boy, but now as an aspiring assistant professor trying to make a good impression, I didn't want my father making an appearance at the president's office.

"Dad, *don't* go to his office," I entreated, "he's busy. Besides you don't have an appointment!"

But even while I spoke, I could feel the embarrassment beginning to build, because I knew my words were futile. I knew that although I would take elaborate "precautions" to prevent his encounter with the president, it would take place in spite of my best efforts. I would have plenty of "jobs" to keep Pa busy—mowing the lawn, working in the garden, painting the basement—but it would be of no avail. Pa would—utilizing the same energetic resourcefulness that saw all six of his children through higher education—end up in the president's office.

Pa and I never spoke about it again, but some weeks later, after a faculty meeting, the president called me aside and smilingly said: "I met your father, he's a very interesting man." "I know," I mumbled, as my face began to warm, "he's always wanted to meet you."

Mamma was everything Pa wasn't when it came to social awareness. She had a grace and dignity that allowed her to be equally at ease among the Marshal Fields of Chicago or the Holsteins and Guernseys of Wisconsin. She had dignity and charm that milking cows couldn't tarnish. Her ever-ready laughter was infectious. How we used to laugh, back on the farm.

Pa kept his job with the railroad, coming home on week ends, and Mamma, Bob, and I ran the farm.

Mamma had two remedies for my tics: rest and sympathy. She must have noticed that my outbursts were more intense and frequent at night, and assumed that rest was a reasonable remedy. She would gently say "John, go bed, you tired." The tics must have seemed to her a symptom of weakness or an indication that I was overworked. I recall with fondness her hugging me to her side and murmuring in her gentle Hungarian: "Szegeny fiam, olyan nehezen dolgozik" (My poor son, how hard he works.)

I suppose analysts could suggest I was getting a lot of "secondary gain" for my "symptoms," but it felt rather that she was empathically resonating with my own inner pain. I recall even when she visited me as an adult, during times when I was working long hours at two jobs she would take me aside and let me know that she thought her "Szegeny fiam" (poor son) was working far too much.

I don't think Mamma contributed to my TS-OCD except indirectly (which I'll discuss shortly). For his part, Pa was constantly trying to impose various "remedies," some of which—had they not come from him—actually made sense. For example he would say to me "John, ven you vant jerk, just breath deep—like diss!" whereupon he would demonstrate by taking several deep breaths in succession—like an elephant in oxygen debt. This "incompatible response" as behaviorists would

likely label it, made logical sense, but was impossible for me to utilize
since it came from him. In all likelihood such paradoxical instructions
coming from my intrusive father, only served to harden my autonomy.

Typically Pa's "efforts" on my behalf geometrically increased my
shame. Whenever I saw him talking intently to a professional—of almost any profession—I began to inwardly cringe, because I knew there
was at least a fifty-fifty probability that he was "sharing" my problem
with this stranger. Of course numerous recommendations were offered,
each person "knowing" exactly what would cure me. Suggested remedies ran the gamut from herbal concoctions to chiropractics, and Pa received all with sycophantish respect—especially if they came from "big"
doctors. Because he himself utilized various old country remedies
(leeches, blood letting, garlic, etc.) and was in apparently good health,
he was a theoretical eclectic. I remember at my high school graduation
being pulled aside by Pa to "consult" with a chiropractor—the father of
one of my classmates. In less time than it takes to play "Pomp and Circumstance," I was on a makeshift bed in one of the unused rooms of
the gym enduring a back-crackling chiropractic "cure" for my tics.
When it was over, the embarassment and shame of that experience lin-
gered long after my manipulated spine had recovered.

But these memories get ahead of the story. The roots of my tics reach
back to the earliest days of neonatal life. Mamma developed phlebitis
and was confined to her bed. Because Bobby was only a year and a half
old at the time, it was simply too much for Mamma to care for both of
us, so when Mrs. Bolin—a lady from the church my parents attended—
volunteered to help out by "taking Johnny home," my parents readily
agreed. Mrs. Bolin had no children of her own, and according to all reports she and I hit it off fabulously. She loved her new baby, and (it later
turned out) secretly dreamed that my mother would let her keep "Baby
Johnny." However, about seven months later, when Mamma had recovered sufficiently to care for me, she came to take me home. Mamma
would recount the story with feeling:

> She vass crying and begging, "Oh, *please* let me keep Johnny! You hev fife
> more children—I haff none but Johnny, *please* let me keep him!"

> But I tolt her, "No! you ken't hev my Johnny. I may hev fife utters but I
> ken never give up Johnny!"

Thus, sometime during those critical early months, the interpersonal
rhythms that flowed so smoothly between Mrs. Bolin and me were pre-
cipitously disrupted when I changed mothers. I'm not certain exactly

when this occurred, but sometime during the seventh month of my early life the intense bond that had been established with my first "mother" suddenly disintegrated.

Because this occurred during the time circular reactions (Piaget) are dominant, it is very likely that I utilized some form of rhythmic self-soothing to cope with the traumatic switch of mothers. Recall that such "mother switching" also occurred with Samuel Johnson. I'm convinced that if we could obtain more accurate histories, we would find very early trauma in the cases of most children with tics.

The second trauma occurred when I was in the first grade. During those days children's tonsils and adenoids were routinely removed. Experiencing a "T and A," as they were called, was about as routine as having six candles on your birthday cake, and occurred at about the same time. Unfortunately for me, the typical routine for children did not include adequate pre-operation medication, and I was rolled into the operating room wide awake, and very frightened.

Terrified, I struggled to get off the operating table. Like a cornered animal fighting for its life, I thrashed about wildly but to no avail. I felt strong hands press my ankles tightly against the table, and in a few seconds I couldn't move my legs at all. Later, I surmised they must have strapped me to the table. My panic reached gargantuan proportions when I next felt my arms being pinned and strapped. Now I was totally immobilized. I began screaming more desperately, but shrieks were smothered by a large rubber mask that was pushed tightly over my nose and mouth. I was being suffocated!—or so I thought. The memory of that event is still so vivid that to simply *imagine* being immobilized causes my chest to tighten. My claustrophobia is extremely intense. It doesn't bother me to be in a crowded elevator or a large group of people, as long as I can move my arms and legs, but to be pinned so that I can't move immediately drains me of all reason, and I become like a drowning person who desperately clings to a would-be rescuer with a lethal bear hug.

It was about this time that I first remember having tics, and it seems more than coincidence that one of my tics has always been shoulder shrugging—a kind of twisting motion with my right shoulder, as if I'm still trying to get free of the operating table where I was spread-eagled and smothered. I experience an almost constant need to reassure myself that I'm "free," that no one is constricting me or smothering me. Twisting my shoulder assures me that I'm freely mobile, and sniffing assures me that I can breathe.

As I sit here in my study typing these words onto my monitor screen, I cognitively "know" that I'm free, and that no one is tying me down, yet, it's not enough. There is some deeply-rooted need, which feels as basic as my need for oxygen, that requires me to "jump around" a bit. There are numerous additional social and interpersonal layers that have become "templated" onto those original traumas, but I think the most rudimentary elements can be traced to those two early traumas.

"But," you might reason, "other children experienced traumatic surgeries, and other youngsters were separated from mothers and then reunited some while later and they didn't all end up with compulsive symptoms."

True—but as we pointed out earlier, it probably takes a certain threshold combination of factors to tilt the balance to where ticquing becomes semipermanent. It is of interest to notice the similarity between the early weeks of my life and that of Samuel Johnson's mother-juggling early existence. Later as well, my parents' marriage could have been described with the same words Johnson used to portray his parents' relationship: "They had not much happiness from each other."

Additionally my father's embarrassing intrusive ways became focused on my tics and his efforts to "help" were excruciatingly iatrogenic. It probably took some combination of *chronic* trauma (e.g., changing mothers, my father's embarrassing intrusions, etc.) and *acute* harm (e.g., presurgical "smothering") to reach the TS-OCD threshold in my life. I suspect that is often the case, with single-event traumas providing a basis for symptom formation, but more chronic factors being necessary to keep the "heat on."

It's important to note that although my parents played a significant role in the development of my tics—my mother by adopting me out and taking me back, and my father by being intrusively embarrassing—neither had the slightest intention of hurting me or of increasing the likelihood that my childhood tics would become more persistent. Consequently, as we observed in the previous chapter, they are not blameworthy. Nonetheless, their experience can be helpful in preventing the replication of such patterns in other families.

I'd like to close with a final anecdote. It occurred one November day as I was driving into town with my son to take care of some business. In totally unanticipated ways children provide you with moments that last a lifetime.

We passed a cemetery, where the falling snow had magically transformed the rough granite monuments and neglected headstones into delicate art forms, but I hardly noticed as I carefully titrated the distance between my car and the taillights in front of me on the slickening highway.

"Dad?" a voice called from the rear seat.

"Yeah?"

"When Satan dies will God put flowers on his grave?"

"Uh . . . yeah, I think so . . . uh, yes, He will, I'm sure He will," I stammered after what seemed like forever.

It's not the kind of question you find answered in the "how-to-parent" books. Nor is it the sort of thing most of us spend a lot of time thinking about. Michael had never been a loquacious child, preferring observation to verbalization; but when he did ask questions, they were often thought-provoking. But this was more than I'd bargained for when I asked him if he wanted to ride to town with me. "Whatever possesses kids to ask such questions?" I wondered.

Then I knew. A month or so earlier tragedy had struck at the core of our family. Nina, our Great Dane, had died. It had happened suddenly, without warning. I was returning home from work when she ran to the edge of the driveway and began barking her usual excited greeting. Suddenly—midbark—Nina collapsed. I jumped from the car and rushed to her side. The boys were stunned and watched silently, palefaced. I looked for signs of life, but there was no rhythmic movement of her rib cage. Desperately, I put my ear to her chest—no sound of life.

"She's dead boys."

I announced it with as much contrived casualness as I could muster.

"No use calling the vet, there's nothing he can do."

But this cruel reality required some sort of cushion—something to soften the harsh edges.

"I'll run into town and get some flowers and then we'll bury her. You guys pick some wildflowers. I'll be back in 15 minutes."

We had only a short graveside ceremony, but the memory of three little boys bravely huddled around a big clump of freshly turned earth, clutching long-stem roses while tears ran down their cheeks, still has a painful edge some 15 years later.

Perhaps, as we drove along the snowy highway a few weeks later, the snow-enhanced headstones and crosses reminded Michael of his dog's grave and of the cross and flowers we'd used to embellish that fresh mound of earth. Whatever stimulated it, he had asked the ultimate question; reared in the Judeo-Christian teaching that God is love, and Satan is the epitome of evil, Michael apparently concluded that good (God) will overcome or outlast evil (Satan). But the more important question was *how*? Will it be with compassion? that is, "Will God put flowers on Satan's grave?"

Not a bad question to ponder and one that has relevance to TS-OCD.

I believe that good (tranquillity, control) can ultimately overcome bad (compulsions, tics, etc.). But the more important question is "How?" Can this be carried out with sensitivity and compassion? Can it be done in a way that doesn't compromise the person's mental acuity? Powerful drugs may dampen the intensity of tics or lessen the obligatory nature of obsessions but at what cost to the patient?

In this book, I've tried to create a new paradigm for understanding TS-OCD—one which is sensitive to the complex interpersonal nature of these manifestations and fosters alternatives to drug treatment. I hope these will be seen like the flowers from the story. Not only is it important that we overcome TS-OCD, it is important that we do so sensitively and compassionately.

REFERENCES

Allport, G. W. (1961). *Pattern and growth in personality*. New York: Holt, Rinehart, & Winston.

Arnold, V. I. (1984). *Catastrophe theory*. Berlin Heidelberg: Springer-Verlag.

Ashby, W. R. (1961). *An introduction to cybernetics*. London: Chapman & Hall Ltd.

Austin, J. L. (1961). *Philosophical papers*. Oxford: Clarendon.

Bate, W. J. (1975). *Samuel Johnson*. New York & London: Harcourt Brace Jovanovich.

Bate, W. J., & Strauss, A. B. (Eds.). (1969). *Samuel Johnson, The rambler*. New Haven: Yale.

Bateson, G. (1972). *Steps to an ecology of mind*. New York: Ballantine Books.

Beebe, B., & Stern, D. (1977). Engagement–disengagement and early object experiences. In M. Freedman & S. Grand (Eds.), *Communicative structures and psychic structures* (pp. 35–55). New York: Plenum Press.

Blanck, G., & Blanck, R. (1979). *Ego psychology II*. New York: Columbia University Press.

Braun, B. G. (Ed.). (1986). *Treatment of multiple personality disorder*. Washington, DC: American Psychiatric Press.

Brazelton, T. B. (1980, May). *New knowledge about the infant from current research: Implications for psychoanalysis*. Presented at a meeting of American Psychoanalytic Association, San Francisco.

Brazelton, T. B., & Als, H. (1979). Four early stages in the development of mother–infant interaction. *The psychoanalytic study of the child* (Vol. 34, pp. 349–371). New Haven: Yale University Press.

Breuer, J., and Freud, S. (1893–1895). In J. Strachey (Ed.), *Standard Edition, Vol. 2* (p. 58).

Brown, M. S., & Goldstein, J. L. (1984). How LDL receptors influence cholesterol and atherosclerosis. *Scientific American, 251* (5), 58–66.

Call, J. (1980). Some prelinguistic aspects of language development. *Journal of the American Psychoanalytic Association, 28,* 259–290.

Carpenter, G. (1974). Mother's face and the newborn. *New Scientist, 61,* 742.

Catrou, J. (1890). Étude sur la maladie des tics convulsifs (jumping, latah, myriachit). Faculté de Medecine de Paris, These pour le Doctorat en Medecine, Henri Jouve, Paris. Quoted in Shapiro, Shapiro, Bruun, & Swee (1978, p. 26).

Chomsky, N. (1959). [Review of *Verbal behavior*. By B. F. Skinner]. *Language, 35,* 26–58.

Comings, D. E. (1990). *Tourette syndrome and human behavior.* Duarte, CA: Hope Press.

Condon, W. S., & Sander, L. (1974). Neonate movement is synchronized with adult speech. *Science, 183,* 99–101.

Coriat, I. H. (1932). *Stammering: A psychoanalytic interpretation.* New York/Washington, DC: Nervous and Mental Disease Monograph Publishing Company.

de Jonge, A. (1980). *Fire and water.* New York: Coward, McCann, & Geoghegan.

Deutsch, A. (1949). *The mentally ill in America.* New York: Columbia University Press.

Ducasse, C. J. (1969). *Causation and the types of necessity.* New York: Dover.

Dutton, D. G. (1988). *The domestic assault of women: psychological and criminal justice perspectives.* Boston: Allyn and Bacon.

Erikson, E. H. (1950). *Childhood and society.* New York: Norton.

Erikson, E. H. (1968). *Identity, youth, and crisis.* New York: Norton.

Faber, D. (1974). *The perfect life, the Shakers in America* New York: Farrar, Straus, and Giroux.

Fenichel, O. (1945). *The psychoanalytic theory of neurosis,* pp. 152–153. New York: Norton.

Freud, S. (1895). Project for a scientific psychology. In J. Strachey (Ed.), *Standard Edition, Vol. 1,* pp. 281–397. New York: Norton.

Freud, S. (1920). Beyond the pleasure principle. In J. Strachey (Ed.), *Standard Edition, Vol. 18* (pp.3–64). New York: Norton.

Freud, S. (1933). Translated by Strachey, J. (1965, 1964). *New introductory lectures on psychoanalysis.* New York: Norton.

Furer, M. (1964). The development of a preschool symbiotic psychotic boy. *The psychoanalytic study of the child, 19,* 448–469.

Ganley, A. (1981). *Participant's manual: Court mandated therapy for men who batter: A three day workshop for professionals.* Washington, DC: Center for Women Policy Studies.

Gedo, J. E., & Goldberg, A. (1973). *Models of the mind.* Chicago: University of Chicago Press.

Glauber, P. I. (1982). *Stuttering: A psychoanalytic understanding.* New York: Human Services Press, Inc.

Glover, E. (1932). A psycho-analytic approach to the classification of mental disorders. In *On the early development of the mind* (pp. 181–186). New York: International University Press.

Glover, E. (1943). The concept of dissociation. In *On the early development of the mind* (pp. 307–323). New York: International Universities Press.

Greenacre, P. (1957). The childhood of the artist: Libidinal phase development and giftedness. *The psychoanalytic study of the child, 12*, 27–72.

Hampden-Turner, C. (1981). *Maps of the mind*. New York: Macmillan.

Hart, H. L. A. (1968). *Punishment and responsibility*. New York: Oxford University Press.

Heider, F. (1958). *The psychology of interpersonal relations*. New York: Wiley.

Hibbert, C. (1971). *The personal history of Samuel Johnson*. New York: Harper & Row.

Hill, G. B. (Ed. 2 Volumes). (1897). *Johnsonian miscellanies*. New York: Harper.

Hill, G. B. (Ed.). (1934). *Boswell's life of Johnson*. New York: Harper.

Hochman, G. (1980, Sept/Oct). The disease that makes you curse. *Science Digest*, 88–91, 116.

Holt, R. R. (1967). The development of the primary process. In R. R. Holt (Ed.) *Motives and thought (Psychological Issues, Monograph. 18/19)*. New York: International Universities Press.

Horowitz, M. J. (1977). *Hysterical personality*. New York: Aronson.

Hull, C. L. (1943). *Principles of behavior*. New York: Appleton-Century-Crofts.

Kelley, H. H. (1973). The process of causal attribution. *American Psychologist, 28*, 107–128.

Kaufman, G. (1985). *Shame*. Rochester, Vermont: Schenkman Books.

Kaufman, G. (1989). *The psychology of shame*. New York: Springer Publishing Co.

Kirkpatrick, C. (1989, February 20). Can't hold this tiger. *Sports Illustrated*, 48–51.

Kluft, R. P. (Ed.). (1985). *Childhood antecedents of multiple personality*. Washington, DC: American Psychiatric Press.

Kohut, H. (1977). *The restoration of the self*. New York: International Universities Press.

Kuhn, T. S. (1962). *The structure of scientific revolutions*. Chicago: University of Chicago Press.

Levitt, A. (1989, Fall). Interview with Chris Jackson. *Tourette Syndrome Association, Inc., Newsletter, 17*(3), 6.

Lichtenberg, J. D. (1983). *Psychoanalysis and infant research*. Hillsdale, N.J.: Lawrence Erlbaum.

Lichtenberg, J. D., & Slap, J. (1972). On the defense mechanism: A survey and synthesis. *Journal of the American Psychoanalytic Association. 20*: 776–792.

Lichtenberg, J. D., & Slap, J. (1973). Notes on the concept of splitting and the defense mechanism of splitting of representations. *Journal of the American Psychoanalytic Association. 21*: 772–787.

McAdam, E. L., & Hyde, M. (Eds.). (1958). *Yale edition of the works of Samuel Johnson, Volume 1*. New Haven: Yale University Press.

MacFarlane, J. (1975). In *Parent–infant interaction* (Ciba Foundation Symposium 33). New York: Elsevier, pp. 103–118.

Magnusson, D., & Endler, N. S. (Eds.). (1977). *Personality at the crossroads: Current issues in interactional psychology*. Hillsdale, N.J.: Lawrence Erlbaum Associates, Publishers.

Mahler, M. S., & Gross, I. H. (1945). Psychotherapeutic study of a typical case with tic syndrome. *Nervous Child, 4,* 359–373.

Mahler, M. S., & Luke, J. A. (1946). Outcome of the tic syndrome. *Journal of Nervous and Mental Diseases, 103,* 433–445.

Mahler, M. S., Pine, F., & Bergman, A. (1975). *The psychological birth of the human infant.* New York: Basic Books.

Martin, G., & Pear, J. (1988). *Behavior modification what it is and how to do it.* Englewood Cliffs, N.J.: Prentice Hall.

Massie, R. K. (1980). *Peter the Great: His life and world.* New York: Knopf..

Milgram, S. (1974). *Obedience to authority.* New York: Harper & Row.

Mill, J. S. (1869). *The subjection of women.* London: Longmans, Green & Co.

Miller, N. E. (1959). Liberalization of basic S-R concepts: Extensions to conflict behavior, motivation, and social learning. In S. Koch (Ed.), *Psychology: A study of a science* (Vol. 2). New York: McGraw Hill.

Miller, N. E., & Dollard, J. C. (1941). *Social learning and imitation.* New Haven: Yale University Press.

Moss, H., & Robson, K. (1968). The role of protest behavior in the development of mother–infant attachment. Presented at the meeting of the American Psychological Association, San Francisco.

The New International Version Study Bible. (1985). Grand Rapids, MI: The Zondervan Corporation.

Nicolich, L. (1977). Beyond sensorimotor intelligence: Assessment of symbolic maturity through analysis of pretend play. *Merrill-Palmer Quarterly. 28,* 89–99.

Norman, C. (1951). *Mr. oddity, Samuel Johnson, LL.D.* Drexel Hill, PA: Bell Publishing Company.

Noy, P. (1979). The psychoanalytic theory of cognitive development. *The Psychoanalytic Study of the Child, 34:* 169–216. New Haven: Yale University Press.

Palombo, S. R. (1985). Emanuel Peterfreund: The information revolution. In J. Reppen (Ed.), *Beyond Freud, a study of modern psychoanalytic theorists.* Hillsdale, New Jersey: The Analytic Press.

Parens, H. (1979). Developmental considerations of ambivalence: An exploration of the relations of instinctual drives and the symbiosis–separation–individuation process. *The Psychoanalytic Study of the Child* (Vol. 34, pp. 385–420). New Haven: Yale University Press.

Pattee, H. H. (Ed.). (1973). *Hierarchy theory: The challenge of complex systems.* New York: George Braziller.

Patterson, G. R. (1976). The aggressive child: Victim and architect of a coercive system. In E. Mash, L. Hamerlynck, & L. Handy (Eds.), *Behavior modification and families: I. Theory and research.* New York: Brunner/Mazel.

Peterfreund, E. (1971). Information, systems, and psychoanalysis. *Psychological Issues, 7* (1/2, Monograph, 25/26). New York: International Universities Press.

Piaget, J. (1952). *The origins of intelligence in children.* (M. Cook, Trans.). New York: International Universities Press.

Piozzi, H. L. (1897). *Anecdotes of the late Samuel Johnson, LL.D.*, in G. B. Hill (Ed.), *Johnsonian Miscellanies*, Vol. I, New York: Harper.

Pollack, S., & Gilligan, C. (1982). Images of violence in thematic apperception test stories. *Journal of Personality and Social Psychology*, 42, 1, 159–167.

Porter, C. A. (1983). *Blame, depression and coping in battered women.* Unpublished doctoral dissertation, University of British Columbia.

Poston, T., & Steward, I. (1978). *Catastrophe Theory and its applications.* London: Pitman.

Pottle, F. A., & Bennett, C. H. (Eds.). (1936). *Boswell's journal of a tour to the Hebrides.* New York: Viking Press.

Quennell, P. (1972). *Samuel Johnson, his friends and Enemies.* New York: American Heritage Press.

Rapoport, J. L. (1989). *The boy who couldn't stop washing.* New York: Dutton.

Rounsaville, B. (1978). Theories in marital violence: Evidence from a study of battered women. *Victimology: An International Journal*, 3 (1–2), 11–31.

Sacks, O. (1985). *The man who mistook his wife for a hat.* New York: Summit Books (A Division of Simon and Schuster).

Sacks, O. (1988, September). The divine curse. *Life Magazine.* pp. 94–102.

Sanders, S. (1987). The interface between biofeedback and hypnosis: The biotic band™. In W. C. Wester & D. J. O'Grady (Eds.), *Clinical hypnosis with children.* New York: Brunner Mazel.

Sartre, J. (1981). *The words, the autobiography of Jean-Paul Sartre.* New York: Vintage Books.

Shapiro, A. K., Shapiro, E. S., & Wayne, H. (1973). Treatment of Tourette's syndrome. *Archives of General Psychiatry*, 28, 92–97.

Shapiro, A. K., Shapiro, E. S., Bruun, R. D., & Sweet, R. D. (1978). *Gilles de la Tourette Syndrome.* New York: Raven.

Shapiro, A. K., & Shapiro, E. S. (1980). Tic, Tourette, or movement disorder? A guide to early diagnosis. *Diagnosis*, 77–84.

Shapiro, D. (1965). *Neurotic Styles.* New York: Basic Books.

Shaver, K. G. (1985). *The attribution of blame: causality, responsibility, and blameworthiness.* New York: Springer-Verlag.

Stern, D. (1977). *The first relationship.* Cambridge, Mass: Harvard University Press.

Straus, M. A. (1980). Victims and aggressors in marital violence. *American Behavioral Scientist*, 23 (5), 681–704.

Straus, M. A., Gelles, R. J., & Steinmetz, S. (1980). *Behind closed doors: Violence in the American family.* Doubleday, NY: Anchor Press.

Toch, H. (1969). *Violent men: An inquiry into the psychology of violence.* Chicago: Aldine.

Tompkins, S. S. (1963). *Affect imagery consciousness.* New York: Springer Publishing Co.

Tompkins, S. S. (1987). Script theory. In J. Aronoff, A. I. Rabin, and R. A. Zucker (Eds.), *The emergence of personality.* New York: Springer Publishing Co.

Torem, M. S. (1991). Eating disorders. In W. C. Wester & D. J. O'Grady (Eds.), *Clinical hyponsis with children*. New York: Brunner Mazel.

Turpin, G. (1983). The behavioral management of tic disorders. A critical review. *Advances in Behavioral Research and Therapy, 5,* 203–345.

Vallacher, R. R., & Wegner, D. M. (in press). *A theory of action identification*. Hillsdale, NJ: Erlbaum.

Wachtel, P. (1977). *Psychoanalysis and behavior therapy*. New York: Basic Books.

Wain, J. (1974). *Samuel Johnson*. New York: Viking.

Walker, L. E. (1979). *The battered woman*. New York: Harper & Row.

Watzlawick, P., Beavin, J. H., & Jackson, D. D. (1967). Pragmatics of human communication: A study of interactional patterns, pathologies, and paradoxes. New York: Norton.

Watzlawick, P., Weakland, J. H., & Fisch, R. (1974). *Change, principles of problem formation and problem resolution*. New York: Norton.

Werner, I. (1976, August). *A Tourette autobiography*. (Available from Tourette Syndrome Association, Inc. 40–08, Cpl. Kennedy St., Bayside, NY, 11361.)

Wheelis, A. (1973). *How people change*. New York: Harper and Row.

Whitehead, A. N., & Russell, B. (1910–1913). *Principia mathematica*. 2nd ed. 3 Vol. Cambridge: Cambridge University Press.

Whitney, H. (1955). Mappings of the plane into the plane, *Annals of Mathmatics, 62,* 374–410.

Wilbur, C. B. (1985). The effect of child abuse on the psyche. In R. P. Kluft (Ed.), *Childhood antecedents of multiple personality*. Washington, DC: American Psychiatric Press.

Winnicott, D. W. (1975). *Through paediatrics to psychoanalysis*. New York: Basic Books.

Woodcock, A., & Davis, M. (1978). *Catastrophe theory* New York: Dutton.

Young, M. H. (1991). Tics. In W. C. Wester and D. J. O'Grady (Eds.), *Clinical hypnosis with children*. New York: Brunner Mazel.

Zahm, D. N. (1987). Hypnosis in the treatment of Tourette syndrome. In W. C. Wester (Ed.), *Clinical hypnosis a case management approach*. Cincinnati, OH: Behavioral Science Center, Inc. Publications.

Zeeman, E. C. (1976, April). Catastrophe theory. *Scientific American*.

Zeeman, E. C. (1977). *Catastrophe theory, selected papers, 1972–1977*. Reading, MA: Addison-Wesley.

INDEX

INDEX